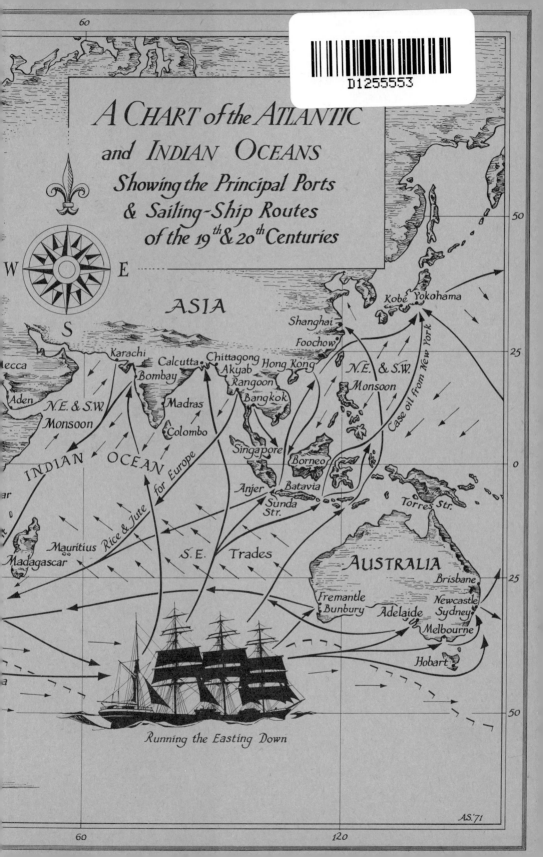

A CHART of the ATLANTIC and INDIAN OCEANS Showing the Principal Ports & Sailing-Ship Routes of the 19th & 20th Centuries

Running the Easting Down

THE WAR
WITH
CAPE HORN

BOOKS BY ALAN VILLIERS

The War with Cape Horn
The Way of a Ship
Sons of Sinbad
Captain Cook
Give Me a Ship to Sail
Posted Missing
Sailing Eagle
The Quest of the Schooner Argus
The Set of the Sails
Cruise of the Conrad
By Way of Cape Horn
Falmouth for Orders

BOOKS FOR YOUNGER READERS

And Not to Yield
Joey Goes to Sea
Stormalong .

THE WAR WITH CAPE HORN

by ALAN VILLIERS

Drawings and Maps by Adrian Small

CHARLES SCRIBNER'S SONS   NEW YORK

CONTENTS

LIST OF ILLUSTRATIONS

THE WAR WITH CAPE HORN

LIST OF ILLUSTRATIONS

MAPS

Preface

I HAVE BEEN doing my best to learn about deep-sea sailing-ships since I was capable of learning anything. Especially during these past four years or so, when the project to rebuild Captain James Cook's bark *Endeavour* as a worthwhile memorial for his bicentenary came to nothing, I have concentrated on the big Cape Horners, the quintessence of man's development in that field, aware that generations to come can have no practical knowledge of them. So I have talked with the last of the British and the German captains, gone to Chile to spend a while with that fine old man Captain Don Roberto Miethe, at ninety-three doyen of the real sailing-ship masters left in the world, and to Germany to talk again with Captains Robert Clauss and Adolf Hauth, survivors of the Laeisz record-breakers. I have browsed through files of the Puget Sound Maritime Historical Society, the records of the San Francisco Maritime Museum (thanks to Director Karl Kortum there), the bound volumes of the old *British Shipping Gazette* and *Lloyd's List Weekly Summary*, and *Lloyd's Weekly Shipping Index* from the 1880's to 1916. I have attended the occasional convention of the Amicale Internationale des Capitaines au Long-Cours Cap-Horniers, mainly Frenchmen, Germans, and Finns. (But their conventions are not really ideal occasions to talk seriously with these lively old boys, for they like to spend their time then singing together lusty old sea chanteys, and wining, dining, yarning, talking, visiting.)

One day two or three years ago I learned at a Council meeting of the Society for Nautical Research held at the National Maritime Museum, of a considerable collection of what were called "Crew Lists," which were about to be discarded and were then stored temporarily in a large hangar at Hayes, Middlesex. What were crew lists? I had not heard of any such things at sea, other than the interminable lists demanded by immigration officers in later days. Perhaps they provided some documentation on Cape Horn ships, so I found that hangar and looked. It was a gold mine rather than hanger, for those crew lists were the original contracts, the "Articles of Agreement," between ship and crew which seamen knew as the "Articles" that they signed on joining

xi

(having failed to hear a garbled reading) and off when leaving, if they had not deserted or been lost. The document listed the "limits" of the voyage—just about from anywhere on earth to anywhere the ship would float, in any order, between 75° N. and 60° or 65° S., for three years, leave if any to be at master's option—the scale of provisions to be supplied (usually eight items and fresh water), disciplinary clauses, the number of the crew to be able seamen, and so forth. The Articles were produced to consuls (if any) at ports of call who were supposed to supervise the master's acts, particularly those in his capacity as a sort of acting magistrate of the ship interpreting the disciplinary clauses of the Merchant Shipping Act. The Articles were at least some statistical and voyage records and were excellent sources for details on crews whose signatures (or marks), last ships, ages, nationality, rate of wages, where they signed on or off (or deserted) were all there, together with such brief entries as the consul felt called upon to make.

With these Articles I found that a considerable number of official logs had also been kept—of hundreds of sailing ships, thousands of steamers. To me these were quite different, for they were not just documentation of proceedings aboard British deepwater sailing ships but, since they were kept by the masters, they could be most interesting and revealing about them, too, and the way in which they ran ships and controlled crews, or failed to control them. There were some eight miles of these articles and logs, filed in boxes: most were from steamships. I went to work at once, with the full cooperation of all concerned from the Registrar General of Shipping and Seamen and the Keeper of the Public Records to Mr. Ron Martin and his staff looking after the shipping documents at Hayes. I felt a sense of urgency, because pressure on storage space held the threat of imminent destruction over 90 percent of these documents. During the better part of two years, whenever I could get to the Public Records Repository at the foot of Bourne Avenue in Hayes (close by London's Heathrow Airport), I dug into those boxes searching for sailing ships' logs and then deciphering them. I found, in all, between five and six hundred, mainly from between 1902 and 1908 (these were the years when they were handed in), for I wished to concentrate on a picture of what really was going on around the Horn in the bad year 1905, *in* the ships, not just to them.

According to some old seamen, the winter of that year was particularly difficult for ships bound to the west'ard on Chilean or Californian voyages. At any one time then, there were four hundred square-rigged ships making or trying to make such voyages, of the four or five thousand sizable sailers still keeping the seas. At least six and often twelve just disappeared (no logs for them). Many more were wrecked, bashed up on Staten Island or other islands near the Horn, or so badly dismasted and damaged that they became "constructive total losses," which means that the estimated cost of repairs in the ports of refuge they reached exceeded their value when repaired: it was better to realize on them then and cut them down as hulks or towing barges. In the winter of 1905, between forty and fifty had to turn away from the Horn and run in distress for the Falkland Islands or Montevideo, or even as far as Rio, to lick their wounds and return to the fight again. At least a dozen more turned away altogether, choosing to run right around the world with (they hoped) the gales behind them, to come eventually to their destinations from the other side.

This was the bare bones of my study, though the winters of 1906 and 1907 were little if any better than that of 1905. I studied every log I found. These logs are not to be confused with deck logs, the ordinary passage records of wind and weather, courses, distances, etc., kept by the watch-keeping officers day by day as the voyage is made. To get a *fully* documented picture of any British voyage is now practically impossible: all voyage logs, company records, masters' correspondence, and other valuable source material have long gone, much of it in the "salvage" drives of the two World Wars. All the British masters are dead. But, with the official logs, port records, and the messages and general intelligence published in the specialized shipping press—particularly *Lloyd's Weekly Shipping Index*—it is possible to get at least a reasonably full picture of things in many ships and voyages. The official logs gave barest passage details, list crews with appraisal for conduct and ability, kept vital statistics, described major accidents, recorded disciplinary matters major and often minor. They could give a good idea (to the discerning reader) not just of what went on aboard the ship but of the character of her master, officers, and crew which could be revealing.

Every official log kept had some sort of vital statistics in it, and that was why it was kept so long. Usually these were of deaths, but there was the occasional birth (to the master's wife, poor woman) and I found one marriage. It was quite usual for whole New England families to be raised together in the spacious and comfortable quarters of a big, well-found down-Easter's poop, but in the British ships the older children generally stayed ashore. Wives and sometimes small children went off with the master. So this marriage was no romance between some beautiful ship master's daughter and Handsome Jim, the senior apprentice. The ship *County of Dumfries* touched at Pitcairn Island in April 1905, on passage from Vancouver towards the Channel for orders. It was a long passage. She was doing poorly and was looking for fresh food— fruit and chickens, perhaps a hog or two. Out came a boat with a gay party including a pretty Island girl named Esther Cotton and one "W. H. Patch, trader, of the Island," asking to be married by the master, as they had been told that this was legal. Captain Inglis demurred, being uncertain of his standing in such matters, but Miss Cotton said she was a sailmaker's daughter, if that were any help. It probably was not, but the master reflected that, after all, there was an empty column ready for marriage entries in his official log. It must be meant for some purpose, so he got on with the job, "Mr. Patch undertaking to have the marriage duly registered in the High Commissioner's Court," if he ever caught up with it. Bride's, bridegroom's, and bride's father's signatures are all in the log.

That was pleasant relief among all the entries in so many logs of near-mutinies, insubordination, refusals of duty, shortages of food (horribly common, and usually—quite wrongly—declared to be the steward's fault), disratings, bald accounts of seamen and apprentices pitched out of the rigging or washed over the side, and ancient mariners signed on as So-and-So, aged fifty-five, declaring on their death-beds that they were in fact somebody else aged anything up to eighty. They left this life quickly, these good old salts, taking their secrets with them. In short, the logs yielded to the painstaking examiner an interesting summary of how life had been aboard all these ships, kept tersely usually (for wise masters tried not to write too much and a great many wrote too little) but adequate enough, in the main, often giving a much clearer idea than the writers probably intended.

To get some picture of the '05 story off the Horn, I had to examine many boxes of logs, for there was no index and the logs were simply put together for the year in which they were returned, in the general order of the ship's official numbers. Voyages could last as long as five years. Logs turned in during 1905 could cover a voyage that began in 1900 or 1901, and logs filed as late as 1909 could begin with a passage which included an '05 winter's Horn rounding. All the logs were of some interest, most of them very interesting.

But it was quickly obvious that the picture emerging had little if anything in common with the Spurling painting and "clipper" book view of the sailing-ship era, useful as these were. This was harsh seafaring. The stuns'l-kited clipper—that worked-to-death word, so often misused—of the Christmas-card industry had no place here. Both the casualty rate and the general state of discipline—particularly in port— were alike appalling, far too often. There was foolish oppression by some masters—very obvious in their logs, though this was not what they thought they were recording. There was endless crew trouble in many ships. *Everybody* "logged"—that is, some offense and punishment entered against them—and deserters by the dozen streamed ashore at every port the vessel touched, some of them off by boat, raft, and even barrel in the open sea. These were not men driven out of some undermanned Yankee hellship by bucko mates. They were seamen of all nationalities streaming away from British tramp sailing ships for the obvious reason that they found life intolerable on board. There was evidence that, in some cases, the intolerable conditions could have been policy to induce the desertions.

It was true that in the middle years of the nineteenth century, the sailing-ship sailor could find himself a grievously exploited man, his life threatened by the perilous overloading too long accepted in older ships, or—more rarely—by seagoing criminals armed with large augurs. But overloading was most carefully guarded against—Plimsoll and others had seen to that—and laden ships' drafts were strictly regulated. The evil of the seagoing wrecker was more difficult to control, for he was a secretive, slimy wretch, working in the hold. Since he intended to escape from the ship he sank, he chose zones of good weather for his enterprise. His activity was often accompanied by overinsurance of falsely manifested cargoes. Exemplary sentences passed on miscreants against whom such crimes could be proved, and more careful and thorough insurance practices, helped to put a stop to this one: so did iron hulls, chiefly because early iron hulls were built of much too thick iron plates.

For an impression of how well established this ship-scuttling could be, reading the transcript of proceedings at the trial in the case of the Queen (Victoria) v. Holdsworth, Berwick, Webb and Dean for the scuttling of the Ship *Severn*,* at the Central Criminal Court in February 1867, is very revealing. Before sending Berwick and Holdsworth to twenty years penal servitude the learned judge, remarking that "a ship cannot be cast away so as to lead the underwriters to suppose it perished by the perils of the sea without exposing the lives of all on board,"

* Published as *The Case of the Severn* by the Association for the Protection of Commercial Interests as Respects Wrecked Damaged Property, Lloyd's, London.

disclosed that Berwick had been concerned with the similar loss of fifteen other ships between 1844 and 1866. No one can say how many more such cases there might have been. Why had it taken so long to bring him to book?

Wrecking in some form or other did not depart from the maritime scene, nor has it yet. The case of the four-masted bark *Gunford,* lost on the coast of Brazil after hitting the place *three times* in 1907, seems very odd. Reading of that, one might reflect that there were ways to lose sailing ships besides scuttling them and wonder, too, how much more evidence was thought to be needed to bring a case against that master. The manner of his appointment to the overinsured ship, his conduct of her last voyage and his choice of crew were curious, to say the least. He lost more than enough lives, too.

But why were there so many casualties in British ships, and among the ships themselves? Just the few hundred logs I was able to study recorded some six hundred deaths aboard, offset by ten births. Of these deaths, thirty-three were masters and seventy-two apprentices, which seems too many of both. This takes no account of the several hundred lost by the shipful. In the first decade of this century, there were far more casualties in Britain's Merchant Service than in her Royal Navy. Apart from the Boer War, these were years of peace, but the private war of the merchant sailing ship with the sea and the ocean winds went on while she survived. Between 1900 and 1910, at least ten thousand seamen lost their lives in British sailing ships alone, without any overloading and little deliberate wrecking.

Such loss of life seems appalling now, but it was taken for granted then. Only those few who read the officially issued statistics on the subject*—in 1905, 4.75 percent of all British ships lost, 501 vessels in all: steamships then and their crews were lost almost as profligately as sailing ships—bothered with the subject at all, and most of these required such statistics to work out insurance risks and rates. Seamen did not bother with such matters as being of no direct concern, unless personal. After all, at any one time in 1905, it was reckoned that at least four hundred square-rigged ships (of the five thousand such ships of all nationalities in world trade) were making Cape Horn voyages. What was the loss of ten or twelve ships gone missing in a year among so many? What was a five percent or even higher loss rate among crews? For these were homeless men, apart from officers and apprentices—

---

* In such publications as *Abstracts of Shipping Casualties, Etc.* from June 1, 1900 to June 30, 1901: London, H.M.S.O., 1902.

world wanderers adrift on their own. Each knew of others only from the quota of his personal knowledge. If such in time covered his own loss, well, that was final. Never having been worried, he was not bothered at all.

At sea, casualties had always been taken as a matter of course. Missing ships were rarely looked for. What was the use? They were not posted as missing until so long unseen and hopelessly overdue that they had no chance of surviving. (Though a very few were found again by routine checks around Southern Ocean islands, such as the *Dundonald* which sailed into Disappointment Island in the Auckland group in 1907. The survivors lived there for over seven months before the New Zealand government's small steamer *Hinemoa* found them. The ship had long been a complete write-off.)

At sea, we all knew something about the casualties, but such knowledge went to the back of one's mind and bothered nobody. Even in the few years I was around the Tasman Sea, I had young former shipmates lost in two ships, the *Amelia J.* and the barkentine *Lindstol.* The rate of the ordinary day-by-day voyage casualties—the swept overboard, the flung out of the rigging, the fallen from aloft, the victims of fevers, and the hard-worked old lads who just fell dead on the job still lashed in their Cape Horn oilskins—we did not know about them. I did not know, until I studied those logs, on how large a scale these casualties had happened—five percent of all crews, or more. It was a shock. The ordinary man and lad at sea in the ships never gave a thought to such things. Any who thought that the sailing ship offered a dangerous life was not there.

Reasons for the bad morale in too many ships had to be sought elsewhere. Gradually it dawned on me where a large part of the answer lay, as week after week I struggled through those logs. It became obvious that some ships were run by—well, masters who were at least past their prime. Thirty-three of those five hundred masters had died on the job just in the logs I saw. Many of them were elderly men, compelled to stay in sailing ships because they knew no other kind of life, and they had no homes of their own. A high proportion had gone to sea in the first place because of economic pressure. They were younger sons from areas of harsh and unproductive land, too greatly subdivided. Older men were of the generation which went to sea very young, in small ships, with six years of plain schooling if they were lucky. I know they were called "natural seamen." No man takes to the sea life naturally. The good seaman would be equally good if not better in other fields:

many became so. The long—or too frequently short—life of deepwater seafaring was forced on them, or it was an escape. Having embarked on it and risen to command, they were caught.

Though there were sailing ships by the thousand right up to the First World War, the life was an anachronism, for *all* those ships were doomed. The sensible, the younger, the farsighted men had gone to steam. Even in 1905, the truth was that apart from a very few real lines (such as the German and French in the Chilean nitrate trade) there was no longer a true economy of deep-sea sail in existence, certainly not in the United Kingdom or the United States. No pool of good British or American masters, tradesmen and sailing-ship seamen existed, either. Ships could continue to exist and operate by the thousand and still be doomed. The few British lines which lasted into the twentieth century stopped replacing fleet losses with new building by 1895, and the last large British Cape Horn ship was built in 1905—the year when a typical listing in Lloyd's of the day's shipping could include up to 4,000 ocean-going square-riggers. The "Index of Shipping" published in *Lloyd's Weekly Shipping Index* for September 7, 1905, for example, lists well over 3,500 large and medium-sized sailing ships, including some large brigs. That day, 800 of them were British, 550 Norwegian, 215 French, 250 German, 350 Italian (this including a number of smaller barks and some brigs, Atlantic traders), 150 American (including a high proportion of large square-rigged ships, and not counting any schooners), and 52 Russian, as well as many Spanish, Portuguese, South American, Austro-Hungarian, Danish, Swedish, and some Belgian vessels. Almost all the British, French, and German were large vessels well over 1,200 tons, many over 2,500.

How could so many, obviously carrying on so considerable a share of the world's carrying trade, all be outmoded and indeed doomed? At the turn of the century, there had been successful auxiliary steamers for seventy-five years and successful steamers for at least sixty. The remarkable thing was that the big sailing ship survived so long. When the last line ordered its last ship, the lot was finished. Survivors would live out their lives: and that was the end of it for nonpowered, square-rigged working sailing ships.

With the ships doomed, so were their masters. Many of them, and some small-scale owners, could not accept the idea that the tramp sailing ship would ever be outmoded, for she was part of their lives. They noted the high loss rate of earlier tramp steamers and chose to ignore their increasing inroads into their trade. They observed the fiascos of the Brunel outsize steamships *Great Britain* (which had soon reverted to sail) and *Great Eastern* (which found useful employment only as a cable layer and then as a side show) and noted the breakdown of the French attempts to cut a sea-level Panama Canal. They noted desired failure with such whole-hearted approval that the seeds of future success blew right past them.

Most masters were far more conservative than owners. After all, an owner could switch the employment of his capital far more quickly and easily than the sailing-ship master could his skill. The younger officer could change easily from sail to power and the great majority did. The older was not so acceptable, even if he wished to change. The skills in steamship handling and passage-making were very different from the ocean lore required in the deepwater square-rigged ship. It was a different way of life. The steamer went along and the master piloted her and navigated her without waste of time or fuel—by the shortest and fastest course, catching favorable tides, turning up when expected. The sailing-ship master did his best under God: the steamship master also had the chief engineer. The deepwater sailing-ship men sometimes grew more than a little hazy on such matters as tide tables and precise coastal navigation. They did their best and they got there somehow, some day: but that was not good enough for the steamer. They hated the smoke, the noise, the apparent contempt for the sea, the soulless mechanized advance of the clanking, throbbing, powered ship. They had found much to love and to live at peace with in their sailing ships. So they stayed with them: but sometimes with a blind feeling of resentment.

Many such masters were older men who had gone to sea in the 1840's and 1850's when standards—and supervision—were slack. Most ships were small then and could be left to their own devices to dodge about the world, avoid wreck, and make a living. Crew lists at the Hayes repository included documents from many such ships back to the 1860's—little things out of Wales, Devon, and Scots ports, with homely names like *Bessie, Maggie, Village Girl,* of 100 tons or so, which sailed the North Atlantic summer and winter, and the *Wandering Chief,* bark, of Banff, 418 tons, which took on the world between 75° N. and 60° S. for years at a time with a crew of eleven including three apprentices, and her companion *Leading Chief* of only 315 tons, which had her handful of hard-bitten mariners sign articles to go to 70° S. when needed (no extra pay, no "nothing") though that was three hundred miles inside the Antarctic Circle where not even Captain Cook had been. So it went. This was the tradition. Sign, and go, and God help them all. Such babes of the wide waters were still making their fantastic voyages into the 1890's and early 1900's, and the standards of their masters were not high, except in the abiding matters of sea skill and courage.

The sea was a hard profession. It was sufficient that they sailed their ships and some day came in from the sea after a moderately profitable long voyage—the Welsh, the Scots, the North Country men, the Kent and Devon men—their way of living was hard, and they were used to high casualties. It wasn't so different in New England.

Who was I then to sit there among the records—few indeed before 1900—and wonder? Yet at the turn of the century a new element had come in. Aware of it then or not, the wind ships small and large were no longer viable. No matter how cheaply capitalized or carefully run, they were finished. Within five years from 1900, none was built in Britain or America and no large sailing ships were built anywhere (except the odd school-ship and three or four fine four-masted barks in Germany). A time of parsimony descended upon too many of the survivors, and it seemed to me that the first sufferers were the masters. Through them, suffering descended to the officers, apprentices, and crews—fast—and stayed with them.

No longer properly paid and without hope of reasonable, honest emolument, these remnants in the condemned ships they were too old to leave were not to be blamed if some became embittered. The fruits of their bitterness were evident in many of these logs. Their good ships once so well and proudly run by owners interested in them became dispersed among the horde of one-ship companies run by those hard-hearted skinflints, the owner-managers. In the true sense, nobody "owned" or "managed" those ships at all. The so-called managers were brokers for groups of shareholders who hoped for a reasonable dividend now and then and often had no other interest. The broker made a little on chartering, storing, insuring—indeed, on everything he could, in every possible way. The shareholders, having—they hoped—bought a good ship cheaply, waited for dividends. The master might have a share or two and this could be of advantage to all concerned, for his ability, perspicacity, and spirit could make a big difference to the success of any voyage. If he had no shares, then the obvious temptation was to make every penny that he could add to his £3 a week, no overtime, no security, and no leave. There were ways to "make"—on a double-billing for food and ship chandlery with kickbacks, on almost every kind of cargo carried and especially on the ballast whenever needed (which was too often), even in wretched, petty ways, out of the slop chest and the crew. A good many masters could have graduated at Harvard Business School in maritime chicanery *cum laude,* without having attended a single seminar.

Who is to blame them? Yet this was a policy of destructive and unforgivably shortsighted foolishness. "Making" on ship-chandlery bills meant short rations for crews already on miserable allowance. Short-changing the ship's maintenance was dangerous and could be fatal. Undoubtedly it led to the deaths of some men, just as "fiddling" the ballast caused the loss of many ships, too many with all hands. The west coast of South America lent itself to the practice of taking foolish chances sailing northward up the coast with insufficient ballast aboard, having paid the owner's money—less kickbacks—for the proper quantity, for the weather was generally good, wind and current favorable, and many ships got away with it. Criminal swindling of ships' ballast was such an obvious racket that sometimes corrupt shore officials operated it even more thoroughly and dangerously than impecunious masters did. The late Captain James S. Learmont* exposed this with a showdown at Callao, whence many ships in ballast had sailed and disappeared.

Masters were still the effective (or ineffective) business managers of their ships in distant ports, as well as autocratic arbiters of seamen's fate at sea. They had perhaps too much power, but there was no answer to that—except, perhaps, a greater discipline over *them* exercised through consuls and senior officers of the Mercantile Marine. Naval courts could be set up to try them, but that was obviously not enough. One would think that such a man as the master of the ship *British Isles* would be held more fully accountable for the loss of four men on his '05 Horn rounding, some of them left to turn gangrenous and die in the foc's'l or in hospital at Pisagua. There the consul seemed concerned only with establishing proof that they had been injured "in the service of the ship," for this made a difference in his responsibilities to the unfortunate men.

The exploitation of the seamen so obvious in many of these logs, it seemed to me, was by his own captain, not his owner. It was the captain who was in control, and as dictator. Men's advances of pay, liberty in port, continuity of fair food rations, and very lives were in his hands. I was aware that these surviving logs being from life-losers could give a biased view. For one ship which lost or maimed men, probably five on the same voyage had no such accidents: there were no logs from

* See his autobiography *Master in Sail,* Percival Marshall and Co. Ltd., London, 1954.

these. Yet there were "death logs" from ships with men known in the profession and to me personally as excellent masters—James Learmont and J. C. B. Jarvis, for example. In a lifetime at sea, Jarvis lost one seaman in the *Lawhill,* who was killed when the handle of a steel brace winch flew off and struck his head. Learmont lost two pitched together from an upper tops'l in a hard gale off the Horn, in the *Brenda.* I wondered when I saw this entry, for it was unusual for two to go together unless something carried away—part of a footrope, perhaps an outer buntline. In this case two young Irish seamen, by name Dunphy and Murphy, had fallen. Dunphy was a fine young seaman, Murphy so useless he had been reduced to ship's boy and told to stay on deck, not to go aloft. But it was night and he went: with an emergency to deal with —getting tops'ls fast was tough, all hands stuff—who could check what the one fool did? Murphy slipped on the footrope, clutched Dunphy off the yard, killed them both.

Any master could lose a life or two: but some ships turned up among those logs again and again, even in a decade—the *Gunford, British Isles, Serena, Kate Thomas, Hougomont, Blythswood, Zinita* among them—losing someone almost every voyage. Some of these ships, probably through minor error in design or perhaps being overlarge for their rigs, were certainly more brutish than others. But a different master could take over a bad ship and her evil ways come to an end at once. Why? Perhaps he took more care of the ship, less of himself.

Captain J. C. B. Jarvis was a man I knew well—the only master I knew whose career in command went back to the sailing passenger-ship days. He had command of the bark *Cicero* in 1883, carrying emigrants to Australia, and earned a handsome bonus by delivering 368 of them sound, happy, and well from Britain to Port Adelaide. As a passenger-ship master he was a man of note in the profession. He had real status. He also had a crew of forty-two, including a surgeon, and a matron to look especially after the single women. There were four mates, his own "captain's cook" and "tiger" (personal steward), and in addition to the agreed bonus there were various perquisites and commissions to be earned by thorough attention to the job. The able seamen were paid £4 a month, which was £1 more than their successors thirty years later. They all made something useful "on the side," as laundrymen, cobblers, hairdressers, and even with books to lend at a penny a day.

Captain Jarvis told me that his sailors and stewards did well and so did he. All these perquisites came to an end when the passengers who brought them, and later general cargo, went to the steamship. Nothing took their place. A very few ships continued to carry a few passengers, such as the composite ship *Torrens* where Joseph Conrad was mate when John Galsworthy took passage aboard in 1893, one of seventeen passengers in that very comfortable and splendid ship that had place for sixty. (What a cruise ship she would make today, among all the blatant part-sailing falsehoods and improbable "replicas"!)

With their hope of reasonable emolument gone, good masters found other employment. Most good owners had preceded them. Masters who stayed too long in sail found themselves unemployable in steam. So they died with their sea boots on off the pitch of the Horn, aged anything up to ninety, and were buried in the sea.

The vast majority had served good ships well. It was no fault of theirs that, in the end, they found themselves thrown ruthlessly on a watery scrap heap where the best they could hope for was to scrape together a sufficiency, somehow or other, to come ashore to die. Some managed. Many did not.

Now and again in his long, confused story, man has after centuries of effort arrived at a straightforward near-perfect creation to help him go about the harsh process of his daily work. In this short list the Cape Horn ship stood pre-eminent, for she was a wind-driven sea vehicle of beauty and, at her best, of astonishing efficiency—the most splendid blend of utility and sea strength and functional beauty ever achieved by European man. I sensed this as a boy, learned it as youth and man, and served the ships when I could. I saw them all discarded.

From the experience, the data I acquired, the memories of men and masters great and not great at all, the five hundred old logs in the hangar at Hayes and other documents, there emerges a picture of several hundred rather wonderful creations slogging it out against the gales of the Horn, taking on the ice, the lee shore, the merciless thrashing of the overwhelming sea and the remorseless howl of the hurricane wind, quietly rescuing one another in their open boats if necessary, smashed on a thousand rocks and islets, with incredible casualties accepted as part of the risk of their workaday world—commanded and manned by men many of them outcasts, some with grievous inadequacies. They died on the job, neglected and forgotten. Many of their ships were driven away, sometimes engulfed in the seas they fought. And some, perhaps, were found a little inadequate, both ships and men.

If the general picture which emerges from close study of these surviving British logs is of the oppressed leading the outcasts in a last hopeless battle off the Horn where tireless courage and endless skill alike could count for nothing, they lived men's lives, under God: and they were aware of that. If many died with their sea boots on this was the price: for these fought the war with Cape Horn.

Their imperfections are obvious. They were habitually tried searchingly and savagely by the life they led and the fight they fought in a manner unknown in other fields, save active war. They fought with their beautiful ships against all odds and they generally won. It was a magnificent achievement of ships and men. Here is a fragmentary picture of some of it as it was, warts and all.

ALAN VILLIERS

Oxford
June, 1970

THE WAR
WITH
CAPE HORN

Chapter one

OFF THE PITCH OF THE HORN

THE BIG BARK lurched like a lopsided bell buoy as the seas flung her to leeward, her bare spars clanging with every violent roll, her boats gone, a few rags of canvas flapping in noisy protest from her topgallant yards, as if sick to death of the wind's scream and the sea's roar, the hail's sting and the driving snow. No one was at the wheel. No one walked the staggering poop or crouched behind the weather cloth in the mizzen rigging. She had no headway, but seemed to come up to the sea as if desperately trying to shoulder the bullying mountains of water aside, only to give up and fall off again, rolling almost on her beam ends, pitching until her jibboom end struck the tops of the great, breaking seas, and they lashed back smashing at her bows. No one was aloft, though there was much to do there. No one appeared to be aboard at all.

Abandoned, by God! Crewless off the pitch of the Horn!

"Captain Stone! Captain, sir!" shouted Second Mate Large in his master's lee ear, "I believe that ship's in serious trouble. May I run her off a little to see?" Mr. Large was a very new second mate.

Captain Barney Stone, rugged, dour, a man of Irish origin, immense endurance, wide experience of the tough business of handling Cape Horn ships, turned a bleary eye.

"In trouble?" he shouted. "Aren't we all? Every damned ship within five hundred miles? What's so special about her?"

"I believe she is the *Deudraeth Castle*," roared the second mate when the next roll to leeward made voice usable for a sec-

1

ond or two. "She was with us at Montevideo. I recognize the old White Star look.

"If she's abandoned, she's salvage. Put me aboard with six men. I could get her to the Falkland Islands."

Barney could see the Harland and Wolff look about the bark for himself. He knew the *Deudraeth Castle,* too, resented his whippersnapper of a second mate, aged nineteen, telling him anything. The fellow had barely finished his apprenticeship, was perhaps on his sixth Horn rounding: and Barney on his thirty-sixth.

But he opened his ancient telescope, steadied it on a ratline and himself with an arm looped in the running rigging. Spume flew everywhere aboard his *Scottish Isles,* staggering sullenly into the violent head sea on her second attempt to get to wind'ard past the Horn that terrible voyage, with a bellyful of English cement bound for Valparaiso. She'd had to turn and run earlier, when the endless strains upon her shapely hull caused by the sea's onslaught and the force of effort of the heavy masts and gale-stiffened sails to fight the ship to wind'ard had caused her to leak, after a month. First, she'd a few weeping rivets down below, but the pumps coped and the water, though seeping endlessly inboard, was below the dunnage. The cement in its sacks was therefore not affected, so that was all right. There'd be no "spoiled cargo" claims, no loss of freight—he hoped.

Barney'd held on with all the veteran skill of fifty years of such experience. (How old was he, exactly? He'd been sixty-three on the Articles so long now he'd forgotten which year he'd first admitted to that age.) The gales would blow out, even in midwinter. He'd get a slant, or fight a way around somehow. He always had. . . . But this dreadful winter of 1905 was quite exceptional. He'd stood on to the south down to well past 60°, then 65° (for he knew in winter that the Antarctic ice, frozen solid to the land, pack and berg, would not be found drifting in ship's tracks: this he reckoned as a summer hazard). There was no slant, no letup in that violent, screaming, senses-consuming wind! He'd gone around, put her on the other tack—rolling her rails under, filling the main deck, washing out the quarters, almost destroying the galley, within a second of losing all the apprentices overboard—and stood to the north again. No change! No hope! He began to think he'd have to hang on down there not weeks but months, until the spring came and the foul gales quietened at last.

Then the leak increased. Soon the watches were at the primitive pumps half their time. The water rose in the hold above the dunnage and, penetrating the cement sacks, caused the bottom tier to harden.

They tried repairs from inboard but this was hopeless.

The sea rose. The gale continued. The crew weakened, wet through, sodden, cold.

And so at last, Barney had to do what he hated doing, turn away from the Horn, run back for a shelter port to dry-dock the ship properly and mend her leaks. The Falklands were nearest but had no dock. It must be Montevideo or Rio, both expensive time-wasters.

What made his temper worse was his awareness that those leaking rivets in the *Scottish Isles* were his own fault. Outward bound from Rochester at the beginning of the voyage, a tug was hired to give the ship a pluck around England's shoal-ridden southeastern corner, clear of the Goodwin Sands, as far as off Dungeness. A Thames pilot was aboard. But, leaving the deck to newly appointed Second Mate Large on his first morning in his first executive job, Barney and the pilot had repaired below for a noggin or two, to pass the time, while the mate snatched an early dinner. It was a beautiful day. Time passed, and the tugmaster also enjoyed the day without sufficient care where he was going, and no regard at all for the deep draft of his tow.

Where there was water enough for the tug, he went: and the new second mate couldn't check him. It wasn't for such juveniles to query anything the master did, ever: in any case, Mr. Large was not familiar with those waters, and no chart was provided, if one was aboard. Charts were the master's property in those days: he provided them from his own pocket, and he guarded them. Such as he had were in unwieldy, dusty rolls, locked away in his cabin for hoarding there, not for ready use.

And so suddenly, with a fearful jar, a twanging of stays and a mighty vibration of masts which threatened to bring the royal yards down, the deep-loaded ship came to a stop.

Up rushed pilot and master, rather late, pilot flustered, master blustering. But the rigging stayed where it was, the ship seemed all right and was making no water, the tugmaster, roundly cursed by a couple of stentorian voices experienced in that pastime, ambled out of earshot. He knew the tide was making and would soon refloat the ship. He'd made a slight error of judgment: that was all.

The tide did rise and the ship did float, but the damage showed up off the Horn. There Barney had to do what he most hated—divert from the appointed voyage, turn away from Cape Horn, go back for help from the shore bastards.

He cursed, in a foul temper, for such diversions always cost a lot of money and could be ruinous. Insurance, at the best, by no means covered everything. Making the best of a thoroughly bad job, he chose to make for Montevideo, ran there in a week, only to find other lame ducks from Cape Horn and no hope of dry-docking for a month. Port Stanley in the Falklands was full, too, mainly with the partly dismasted vessels which could be repaired afloat. Rio also had its full quota. Barney didn't know it then, but at least twenty or thirty big ships which had never turned away from the Horn before (as he never had himself until '05) were scattered among the ports of the southern hemisphere, as far away as Cape Town, Tasmania, Melbourne, and Bluff, New Zealand, as well as along the east coast of South America. One had even run to Batavia in Java.

All Captain Stone's savings were in the *Scottish Isles*. She belonged officially to Messrs. G. Windram & Co., of 17 Brunswick St., Liverpool, England, but this firm—as was often the case then—were more managers and brokers than owners. The sixty-fourth parts into which British ships were divided for ownership and other legal purposes might be held by thirty or forty people. What share Barney Stone held is no longer recorded, but it might have been anything up to eight sixty-fourths. At any rate he had a stake in the ship and her earnings were his hope of savings—his *only* hope, for his salary as master (£12 a month) was ludi-

crous, his security of tenure nil, and his (legal) perquisites nil too
—no percentage on the net freight (if any), no honest percentage
on anything. Barney refused dishonest cuts, and kickbacks or
percentages of anything bought for the ship, for he knew 'all too
well that such malpractices—based on robbing the ship, her
cargo, or seamen—were stupid and could be ruinous. It was hard
enough to make an honest penny. Unless she was fixed for a good
nitrate freight straight back to Europe and made a fast, accident-
free run home with it, hope of profit from this voyage was gone
already.

And now here was this whippersnapper of a nineteen-year-
old second mate telling him to give up some hard-won sea miles
off the Horn and run back on a wild-goose chase, to look at a
bashed-up old bark. Abandoned, indeed? Salvage? Who would
do the boat work? Who *could* do such boat work? Was the second
mate brought up in New Bedford whalers? He hadn't even been
fishing, his sole sea experience was four years or so—his essential "time" to qualify for second mate's examination—in one
800-ton bark where, like as not, there was no real boat work at
all. Four years in a small bark, four weeks cramming in a school
ashore—that was it! And £4 the month as second mate, ink scarce
dry on his certificate, no hope of saving more than sufficient to
finance his mate's examination, no security, no pension. Well,
he'd have the sense to go into steam. Dammit yes, that was sense,
though Barney hated to admit it. Go into steam? That was one
thing *he* would never do. He was far too old, anyway, and unemployable in what he regarded as hulking, smoking, sea-scorning,
infernal unnecessary things. But the second mate—that was different. He'd switch to them as soon as he had his master's license. Barney resented that, too.

Meantime Barney was not going to risk his life or his crew
in any boat. He doubted that either of his boats could survive in
such a sea.

"Sir, my young brother is an apprentice in the *Deudraeth
Castle*," the second mate was saying. "Please, I do not want to
leave him."

"We are *not* leaving him, or his ship," Barney shouted. "I tell you, they're all right! If that bark isn't abandoned, she's hove-to, that's all. Besides, I cannot spare my second mate, nor a boat's crew."

He sniffed the wind. It was easing at last and showing signs of working to the south.

"Set the upper tops'ls, Mr. Large. We've got our slant at last and so has your *Deudraeth Castle*. Helmsman, bring her up to west!"

The wind was indeed changing, at least for the moment. As he went about the decks thigh-high with the tumbling sea, Second Mate Large kept an eye also on the *Deudraeth Castle*. If she was all right, as he fervently hoped she was, now she would follow suit, set a bit of sail, stand to the west'ard.

But no canvas swelled out from her yards. No one climbed into her rigging. The last glimpse he had of her showed her still rolling sluggishly like an abandoned vessel, coming up and falling off, alone by herself in the sea.

A snow squall shut her in. The *Scottish Isles* slugged on alone.

Six weeks afterward she was past Cape Horn, come to the latitude of 50° S. in the Pacific (for Cape Horn seamen always reckoned that rounding as from 50° S. in the Atlantic to 50° S. in the Pacific, keeping well clear of the awkward bulge of Patagonian islands down there and the lee shore of the Chilean coast). A fortnight after that, the big full-rigger reached Valparaiso.

Ashore, Captain Stone and his second mate learned variously that the *Deudraeth Castle* had turned away from the Horn again and run back—it was said—both to Montevideo and Port Stanley in the Falkland Islands. It was also rumored that all her people had been taken off, about the time the *Scottish Isles* sighted her, by a Scots bark called the *Pass of Killiecrankie* which had already landed them.

The strange thing was that *all* these things had happened.

This *Deudraeth Castle* was an interesting vessel. She was an iron bark of 1,737 register tons built as the *Stanmore* by Harland and Wolff at Belfast in 1886, for the White Star Line's cargo trade. At the time, she was a big bark—big enough to carry 2,500 tons or more and earn reasonable dividends, yet not too big to demand large, expensive crews. She sailed well, at times very well. The late Basil Lubbock, who carried on research into such data when it was still readily available (in the shape of company records, voyage books, personal survivors whose yarns could be checked, and so on, now in 1970 all gone), credits her with passages of seventy days Lizard (Channel) to Tocopilla and eighty-one days back from Iquique to Falmouth for orders. Her iron construction, her builders, and her White Star specification gave her exceptional strength and a magnificent seaworthiness. Some time before 1905 she was sold, in the increasing discard of liner "windjammers." Her registered managing owners then were Robt. Thomas, Sons and Co. Ltd., of Liverpool, but the real owners were a group of citizens in North Wales.

By putting their savings together, these had managed to raise capital enough to buy a smaller Cape Horn ship or two, then going for a few thousand pounds, and such groups usually included at least one knowledgeable old master mariner who knew a good ship when he saw one. What they did not normally include was a business manager, a person familiar with the intricacies—and complicated know-how—of chartering such ships, that is, finding profitable work for them. This called for experience and personal knowledge of brokers who sought to place cargoes, to have them safely delivered where at least some expert knew or optimist hoped there was good demand for them—coal from Newcastle, New South Wales or South Wales ports to the fuelless ports of the west coast of South America, then Chilean nitrates to Europe, or guano from some Peruvian island where only a sailing ship could afford time to load (this could and often did take three months), or up to Puget Sound or San Francisco for grain homeward, or general cargo—and access to the market place called an Exchange, a knowledgeable clerk or two to send there, and some finesse in the business of striking a good bargain or at least knowing one when it offered. There was nothing to be earned from long ballast voyages, or lying empty at an anchorage waiting for a harvest.

The skill of such agents and brokers was (or should have

been) in arranging *profitable* round voyages with as few passages in ballast as possible. (The real skill of many was in looking after themselves.) Ballast had to be bought and worked in and out. The ideal broker had his ships always conveniently placed for new harvests as they were ready; at nitrate ports just when some war or rumored war sent merchants scurrying for bottoms to ship the stuff to wherever they thought the war might be; or ready for California grain in a good year there which at the same time was a bad grain year in Britain. No broker could always be right: too many unknowns came into the business. The trouble seemed to be that some brokers were never right—not according to share-holders in ships, at any rate.

The firm of Robert Thomas was mainly brokers. They would take some shares in the ship, and work on a commission basis for the rest. They also acted, usually, as insurance brokers for ships and cargoes, and in home ports had arrangements with ship chandlers and others who supplied necessities for the outfit of long-voyage ships, also on a commission basis. They were the ship's legally registered managing owners, and they bought and sold ships too, making a living the best way they could. They often did very well.

So the shareholders sat back in their pretty villages (where life was hard and capital never easy to come by) interested in their dividends and a relative or two actually in the ships, but with little active say in and no experience of management. The "managing owner" did his best for them and himself. A letter-head of Wm. Thomas, Sons and Co.—a different firm but operating in the same way—dated August 1908, seen in an old official log of the ship *Afon Alaw*, lists fifteen such ships by name, as well as a "William Thomas Liverpool S.S. Co." with five tramp steamers, and five other small steamship companies, all under their management. By 1914, the number of steamships under this company had increased to thirteen and the Cape Horners decreased to five, according to the list of owners and managers in *Lloyd's Register of Shipping* for 1914–15. Another Thomas's, also of Liverpool, were then still managing owners for eight square-rigged ships, ranging from the bark *Penrhyn Castle* of 1,367 tons

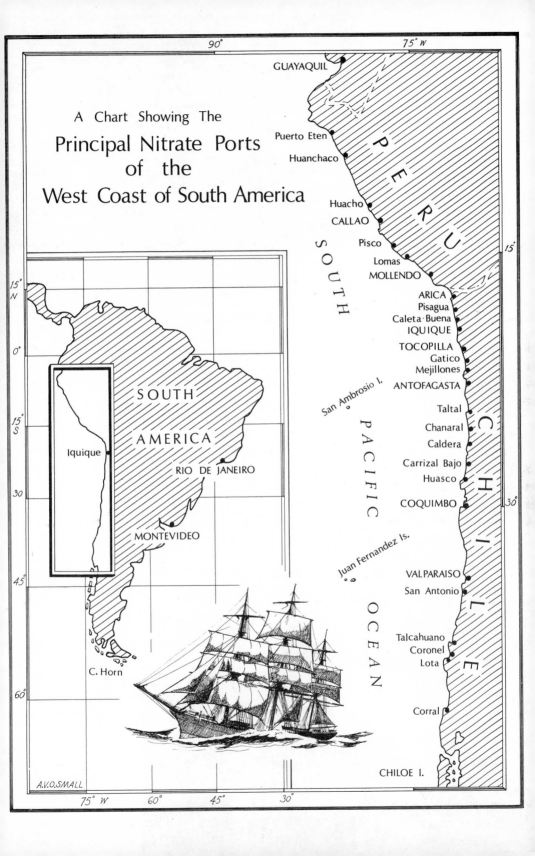

A Chart Showing The
Principal Nitrate Ports
of the
West Coast of South America

90°   75° W

GUAYAQUIL

PERU

Puerto Eten
Huanchaco

Huacho
CALLAO

Pisco
Lomas
MOLLENDO   15°

ARICA
Pisagua
Caleta·Buena
IQUIQUE

TOCOPILLA
Gatico
Mejillones
ANTOFAGASTA

SOUTH

San Ambrosio I.

Taltal

CHILE

Chanaral
Caldera

Carrizal Bajo
Huasco

PACIFIC

COQUIMBO   30°

15°
N

0°

SOUTH

15°
S

Iquique

AMERICA

RIO DE JANEIRO

30°

MONTEVIDEO

Juan Fernandez Is.

VALPARAISO
San Antonio

45°

OCEAN

Talcahuano
Coronel
Lota

C. Horn

60°

Corral

A.V.O.SMALL

CHILOE I.

75° W   60°   45°   30°

The PASS OF KIL- LIECRANKIE *with a gentle land breeze a long way from Cape Horn. Published by permission of the Trustees of the National Maritime Museum.*

The full-rigged ship SCOTTISH ISLES. *Published by permission of the Trustees of the National Maritime Museum.*

Near Cape Horn

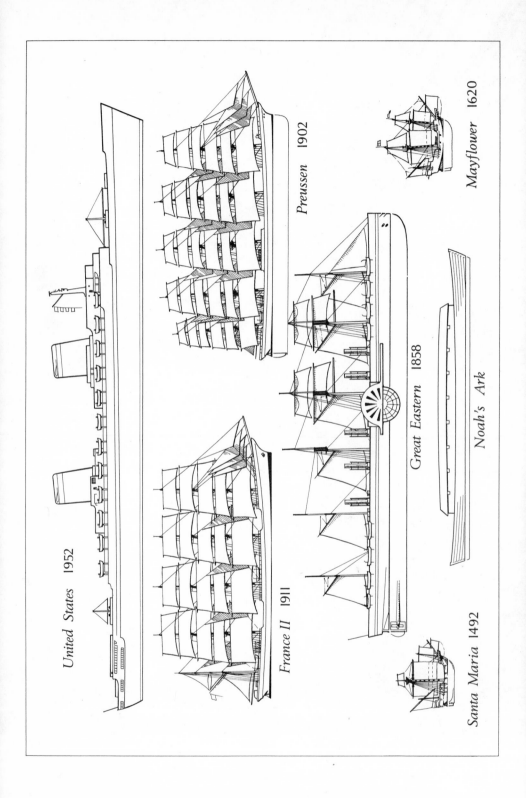

United States 1952

France II 1911

Preussen 1902

Great Eastern 1858

Santa Maria 1492

Noah's Ark

Mayflower 1620

to the ship *Milverton*, 2,215. They must have done pretty well, apart from accidents, though the most cargoes they could usually hope to fix for a deepwater sailer would be three in a two years' voyage—often less. They did their best, but they were essentially commission agents.

Early in 1905, they had fixed the *Deudraeth Castle* to load a full cargo of best coal on the Tyne, in northeast England, for Carrizal, in Chile, with Captain John Jones of the pretty Caernarvonshire village of Nevin, in North Wales, in command of the usual crew—a Welsh afterguard and tradesmen (and none better, for these were Cape Horn die-hards of the best type), the usual very mixed crew of those days (some of vague nationality and unknown ages), and five young British indentured apprentices. There should have been six but one had failed to join.

She sailed on April 8, 1905, which meant taking on the westward passage of the Horn in winter. It was at least a two- or two-and-a-half-month passage from the North Sea to the pitch of the Horn. There she was promptly bashed up, as were at least fifty other ships that fierce down-south winter. It wasn't deck or rigging damage which forced her after some weeks to turn and run for shelter. Her coal had been loaded wet and it was heating. Jones "the Deudraeth"—there were so many Joneses in command of British sailing ships that each had some sort of distinguishing title added, as the thousands of the clan back home also had, and the Hugheses, the Lloyds, the Williamses, the Lewises —wanted no fire aboard, sudden or slow, so he made for Montevideo where the heating coal was discharged, put ashore to cool for a while, then reloaded. Off he sailed for the Horn again, once more in good order.

But the gales still shrieked in his face endlessly. Try as he might, he could not make westing. He could make something but then he could not get north again. He held a press of sail; the wretched wind screamed at him; cold sea filled the decks; the crew suffered from frostbite, lack of warm food (galley washed out), cut hands, cracked fingers, festering torn-out nails —all those common ills of the winter west-bound Cape Horn ship, bearable unless too long continued. Then a violent shift of wind caused rigging damage too great to repair aboard. Again the *Deudraeth Castle* had to turn and flee, this time for the Falkland Islands—not so safe a haven but the nearest offering (no square-rigged ship ever willingly entered the maze of the Cape Horn islands: if she did there was no succor there). Repairs in the Falklands were expensive, for there was a sellers' market.

A cryptic message from Lloyd's agent published early in November 1905 (though sent much earlier) announced that she was safely back at Port Stanley, and the cost of essential repairs was £510. This was grim reading for Messrs. Thomas (who followed the news in *Lloyd's Weekly Shipping Index* with alert interest, sometimes perhaps with some dread) and worse for the little band of shareholders, for indeed this was more than the bark might clear for them from the whole voyage. She had already lost money and time by the visit to Montevideo. The nitrate charter rate was falling, too—so much so that owners were banding together (or attempting to) in an international union to refuse too low freight rates. How was the struggling bark to earn a few pounds from this voyage?

She was far from being alone, for every week's issue of *Lloyd's Index* contained more and more black crosses (marking the casualties) against the names of more and more good ships, driven expensively from their lawful voyages, or wrecked, or—worst of all—gone missing, just not anywhere any more.

That coal had to be delivered to Carrizal (an open bay north of Coquimbo in Chile, between Chañaral and Copiapó) or the full freight would never be paid. Off went the old bark bound for the war with the Horn once more: after all, the worst of the winter months were then over, the crew somewhat refreshed. *Some* time there must be the longed-for break in the gales' dismal constancy. It couldn't just blow from somewhere west forever.

Indeed it did not: for as the now rusted bark pitched and plunged and rolled southward on the starboard tack to get below the zone of westerly direction, the wind hauled to southwest, which was useless on that tack, and blew more savagely than ever. John Jones wore her round to take the wind on the other side, standing toward Tierra del Fuego: the gale changed with him to west and west-northwest, again with fury, spoiling all hope of making any westing at all. In effect, the *Deudraeth Castle* made an effective north on the one tack and south on the other, both plus leeway (which with little canvas set and so high a sea was considerable) and for a ship trying to fight her way past the Horn, both useless.

What the master was trying to do was to make some progress by zigzagging *into* the gales, his ship making good—at best—a course about seven compass points from the wind's direction, at worst drifting bodily to leeward. He could only make the essential turns—tacks—by "wearing ship," which meant turning away from the wind, running before it while hauling the yards right around as far as they would go from one side to the other with minimum sail set, then using great care bringing her up to the wind again, ahead of her other beam. Running off like this and coming up again lost miles and could be dangerous: but to try to tack would be fatal. To "tack ship" meant going around *head* to wind and was a maneuver for use in moderate winds only. A square-rigger's masts were set up and stayed to accept strong wind only from behind the sails. So the Cape Horn shipmaster tried to minimize such maneuvers. Above all, off the Horn he sought to keep his ship on the coming-up tack, trying to foresee changes of wind which would give her a chance to sail somewhere near her course. This could be very difficult. At that time, British sea officers had little or no meteorological training.

A few weeks of this sort of thing could be a very long time, even to hardened veterans from tough North Wales.

The rigging began to go again, the coal to heat again, the older able seamen to show signs of strain, though none had broken down, or did.

Moss began to grow upon the decks where the sea washed constantly.

Visibility was always bad, often impossible. Precisely where the bark might be Captain Jones often did not know, for lacking sights he had no means of telling. He knew only too well, in general terms, where he was. He knew too where he had to get, and the bark would not go that way at all.

It almost seemed that the White Star veteran was remembering her proud origins and did not care if she stayed down there defying all the wind and sea could do to her forever. Sooner or later, return to port would mean at best another flag, at worst sale for a coal hulk somewhere to rot out her days serving steamers.

On the thirty-fifth night, in the three thousandth squall, the two fore-tops'l yards were damaged, their heavy iron fittings distorted so the lower would not swing and the upper would not hoist. At the same time, the truss holding the foreyard—an iron tube of great strength almost ninety feet long—slipped. The yard cock-billed, piercing the wooden deck.

If this had been a first accident, they could have coped. Now it was the last straw. They were fortunate that no one was seriously injured, for several of the yards flailed about murderously with the ship's motion. All hands were about worn out.

Soundings showed some sea inside her.

What now? Back again to the Falklands? Without an effective foremast, she was now unmanageable.

She would not turn away from the wind at all. It was almost as if she had grown too long accustomed to it and had come to like it.

There was no land in sight. One of her two lifeboats was still whole, fortunately that on the lee side. But the chances of getting the boat safely away from the heavily rolling ship were slim, for the boat would smash herself while being lowered against those iron sides, lurching and plunging. And where to go? The bark was somewhere off the pitch of the Horn: to the north was Tierra del Fuego and its inhospitable, storm-lashed islands. To the south was Antarctica. Somewhere roughly northeastward were the Falkland Islands.

They got the boat ready. It might float off safely, in the end. And the force of the gale and the scend of the sea would decide the way to go.

"Aloft to the main royal, Taffy: see if there's any land," Captain Jones ordered the youngest apprentice boy.

"A sail! A sail!" shouted Taffy, pointing astern.

Sliding down the lee royal backstay—a strong iron wire

reaching from top of the mast to the deck—the boy reported that a large bark was coming up on them, through the rain squalls.

"Homeward bound? He'll gallop past, lad, like the others."

They had sighted several such ships, big fellows deep-loaded with nitrates from Chile or grain from California or Australia, haring along under press of canvas, proudly treading the great seas down as if to make way for their graceful beauty. They rushed by at twelve or fourteen knots and were gone in a few moments. One of the master's lesser worries was that one, not seeing them at all—for they no longer showed running lights: there were none left, as the sea had taken them—would run into the *Deudraeth Castle* by night, and that would be the end of her, or both of them. He knew how many big and well-found ships were missing down there—not just unreported, but posted missing after being long overdue, all hope abandoned for them and their people. Down here alone (as far as any man might know) they went at the rate of a dozen a year.

For the wild gales of long winter stacked up the west-bound outward-bounders, pinning them across the tracks of the homeward-bounders running free and proud and fast eastward among them. There were then a thousand Cape Horn ships still in commission, counting Britishers alone, and several thousand others, at any time at least four hundred of them making Cape Horn voyages. Adverse winds could soon pile up a score or more in the vicinity of Diego Ramirez, Staten Island (Isla de los Estados), and south of the Horn.

But this bark was outward bound. She had a slant, and she came up like a thoroughbred.

"The biggest ensign to the gaff, upside down! Look up the Code Book for the distress signals—NC, I think. Haul up the flags!"

The Red Ensign upside down was distress signal enough: all seamen knew *that*.

The stranger shortened down, made straight for them, her own ensign standing out straight in the wind. They saw she was a Britisher, too, with a very long name, hard to read.

She came up warily, observing the distressed vessel's rigging damage and inability to maneuver, signaling with flags. Thank the Lord the senior apprentices in both vessels were well up in that skill, though usually there was little call for it: they had to pass tests to qualify as second mates, after four years of voyaging, and failure in any subject would send them to sea again for six months or a year.

By this time, they could see the long name more clearly: she was the *Pass of Killiecrankie.*

"Send a boat," the stranger signaled.

Putting out his last lamp oil, Captain Jones made a bit of a slick alee. As if trying at last to offer some amends for previous long-continued intractability, the *Deudraeth Castle* stood in her stride a moment, rags of blown-out sails flapping, iron spars grinding against iron masts. Boat falls sang.

"Fend her off! Leggo the painter! Out oars!"

The orders came cheerfully, and the boat, with all hands from the *Castle* crammed aboard, rose on a sea as their old bark, free of all human aid, lurched towards them and then, as if alarmed at the damage she could do just by touching them, suddenly stopped herself and swept upright. It was almost as if she was saying she was sorry to see them go. She had, after all, done her best.

It was the following morning when the *Scottish Isles* came by.

It was a piece of good fortune among so much bad that it was the Scots *Pass of Killiecrankie* which came upon the *Deudraeth Castle* that morning. Her master was Samuel Vint, a Bluenose windship man known even among Cape Horn shipmasters for his iron nerve and his skill at ship-handling: he and his people were good boatmen, too. If the weather then had been really bad, he could have taken off the Welsh crew with his own boats. They were both seaworthy and undamaged, like his ship. She too had fought the full fury of the Horn for many weeks, though she had sailed from Antwerp on the beginning of that voyage only on August 3, bound for Los Angeles—before she sailed, the *Deudraeth Castle* had already been driven once from Cape Horn.

Mrs. Vint was with her husband. It was she who first sighted the lame duck, and she urged her husband to hurry to her assist-ance—not that he needed any urging. Later, the Vints made their home at Penryn in Cornwall, but at that time husband and wife sailed together, for the ship was their only home—a common state in the Cape Horn days. If they hadn't inherited a home they couldn't afford one.

The *Killiecrankie* boys knew very well what boat work was like in heavy seas. This was their second appearance off the Horn in 1905: they had sailed back that way earlier in the year, homeward bound from the guano islands of Lobos de Afuera (off the coast of Peru not far from the Ecuadorean border) at the end of a two-year voyage, bound for Antwerp. That voyage (Mrs. Vint appears on the ship's Articles as stewardess) began with a pas-sage from Liverpool to Victoria, B.C., which involved the usual slogging match to wind'ard past the Horn. A young apprentice named John Adams fell from the mainyard in a gale off the Horn. Captain Vint was on deck, saw the lad go, flung over a buoy which he saw the boy pick up and immediately grab the trailing log line. As he did this, the buoy slipped from his slim shoulders.

Despite the gale, at once the ship was brought to the wind, the lee boat launched with volunteers—the second mate, a couple of A.B.'s, the senior apprentices—but the boy, hurt by his fall, hauled along in the tumult of the sea, weakened and unable to draw breath, slipped off the line and was never found. The boat was recalled, hoisted inboard, and the ship hove to as the gale increased. Young Adams was aloft in his oilskins over warm clothes, and heavy sea boots, like them all. He had no chance, really. But Sam Vint tried.*

To dispose of the case of the *Deudraeth Castle,* His Britannic Majesty's Consul, as was his duty, summoned a Court of Inquiry at Talcahuano to investigate the loss, early in 1906. He had not then read the *Shipping Gazette Weekly Summary* and *Lloyd's List* of January 5 that year, which among the absorbing miscellany of

---

* This is recorded in the official log for the voyage, stored in 1970 in the repository at Hayes. As was the custom, the lad's kit was auctioned during fine weather later. It brought £15–16–11, and included a sextant, a flute, one white shirt with four fronts, and a set of bunk curtains, as well as his uniform and working clothes.

maritime reports—"Brig *Sullivan* of Norwich, Conn., from Fayal, at Rio Dec. 9 with small-pox: expected resume cruise Jan. 9," without smallpox one hopes: bottles with odd messages picked up, wreckage sighted including an upturned vessel 150 feet long, a boat named *Fred,* and a bureau full of ship's papers drifted ashore somewhere in the Baltic—had referred to the "stubborn fight of the *Deudraeth Castle* against the dreadful gales," and casualties of many sorts in the same area. The official log was produced to the Court, but as it contained no vital statistics and therefore did not have to be kept, it has long disappeared. There was probably little in it, for Captain Jones wrote English as if Welsh were his mother tongue, and he was no writing man.

The court found the bark was properly manned and dealt only with the final abandonment. The report says she was off the Horn on October 21, 1905 (over six months after sailing from the Tyne), with thick snow and a heavy southwest gale blowing across a high northwest sea. She lost the two fore-tops'l yards and "in consequence was wrecked." Every effort was made to clear the wreckage but, "owing to the fearful state of the weather, the terrific sea, and the darkness of the night, everybody was fearful of losing their lives, and all efforts . . . were futile . . ." Efforts were continued until October 25, when the weather moderated, to try to run back for the Falkland Islands, "but the ship proved unmanageable, and the temperature of the coals gave reason to fear fire, and the proximity of a lee shore" led to the abandonment "when so good an opportunity offered."

The court expressed the unanimous opinion "that the Master, officers, and crew be exonerated from all blame." This is signed by W. K. Steel, acting vice consul, two British steamship masters recruited in the port, and the clerk of the court.

Far off in Liverpool and the lovely Nevin Peninsula, Messrs. Thomas and the shareholders must have breathed a sigh of relief when they heard the news. At least the bark was written off, and the modest insurance on vessel and freight would tidy up her liabilities—maybe leave capital to buy a larger vessel. Perhaps it was the best ending. From such a voyage they could only have lost money. The one thing the poor shareholders couldn't stand was to lose the hard-earned, hard-saved few pounds they had scraped together for their ship. When adversity put a ship in the red, it was they who had to dip into their pockets to make good any deficiency. Messrs. Thomas could arrange another ship, for larger, more economical sailers were soon on the market, at lower prices. With better luck, they could still make a success of Cape Horn ship-owning with their capital back for reinvestment.

There is no official log from the *Deudraeth Castle* for that voyage. As it contained no vital statistics—nobody died, nobody was killed, or married or born aboard—it did not have to be kept in official files, and was not. The story is documented from Lloyd's reports. But there is an official log of the bark, with the same master, for the preceding voyage. This begins at Hamburg on June 2, 1902, and ends at Hull on February 8, 1905, over two and a half years later, with two long circumnavigations intervening, involving passages to Rio, thence to Newcastle, New South Wales, for coal to Valparaiso, on from Chile to the Delaware Breakwater (with nitrates, probably: the cargo is not mentioned but her draft is deep) and New York: from there to Melbourne (taking 112 days, possibly with cased kerosene), and Newcastle and more coal to Tocopilla (fifty-four days: not at all fast, but she was probably rather foul underwater by that stage). The coal discharged and presumably another nitrate cargo loaded, she sailed from Tocopilla round the Horn to Hull, another 112 days. To judge from the drafts recorded (these are listed entering and leaving all ports) she probably handled six cargoes during these two years and eight months, which if so was better than good. She lost two men—her second mate and an A.B.—fallen from aloft when a violent flap of the fore upper tops'l, caused by the restraining buntlines carrying away, knocked them off the yard together. They fell on deck, the A.B. killed instantly, though the second mate lingered a few days. (His auctioned kit included a pair of "Opera Glasses": the lot brought £11–1–9. The few rags belonging to the dead A.B. brought £1–12–6.)

As was customary in those days, the log is a sad record of desertions, poor discipline, insubordination. Even an apprentice deserts in Australia, leaving his empty sea chest behind him. A warrant is issued for his arrest but he is not found. There are seventy-two names on the list of crew, though these do not include the apprentices: twenty seamen were enough to man the bark. This was not an unusually high turnover of foremast crew in those days. The crimps of Newcastle and New York probably got some of them, and sailors would desert anywhere. Many other logs show a higher wastage.

The *Deudraeth Castle* herself was free of accidents that voyage. She should have paid a fair dividend. During a good deal of that time, many far newer and larger ships spent a year or more in San Francisco, waiting for grain. They did not mind waiting for one harvest but when that failed and world trade was such that it did not pay to crew the ship to go seeking elsewhere, it was a serious matter. In such circumstances, the seamen having long deserted, shipkeepers were reduced to the afterguard (with wives and children, if aboard, as was often the case) and apprentices less a few deserters among them. These sweated it out.

Such long waits paid no dividends either to established companies or the one-ship shareholders under various banners. It was not uncommon for British ships to be idle for two or even four years (as the ship *Cawdor* was, among others) waiting for homeward freights to offer, or to rise above starvation level.

French ships had their "bounty" system, which paid their owners a subsidy on a mileage rate, to help them at least to go seeking. Americans had the protection of their shipping laws to give them preference on intercoastal voyages, which could include the Hawaiian Islands and all trade from any American port to any other. German owners wisely built up shore organizations to foster trade with the west coast of South America particularly, and with Burma, and the Melanesian Pacific islands.

The *Deudraeth Castle* might not have earned so much if she had survived, or lasted under the British flag much longer. The *Pass of Killiecrankie* was herself sold for £3,350 in 1910; then seventeen years old, she was sold to Norway as a going concern, an earning ship. The foreseeable war, due then in four years, gave her plenty of profitable work to do while she lasted. The

Scottish Isles brought a miserable £2,900 when sold to be a coal hulk at Gibraltar in 1909.

How long in fact the *Deudraeth Castle* did survive no one can say. Certainly she was afloat for months after John Jones and his crew abandoned her. She was boarded by the mate of the German ship *Alice* in the late summer of 1905–06, according to a message to Lloyd's. She was then on a position given as 54°S.,57°W.—somewhere south of the Falkland Islands—and the *Alice,* on passage from San Francisco to Antwerp, hove to while the mate went aboard and had a good look at her. He reported that her tough iron hull was quite undamaged but she was partially dismasted. The hatches were open and the hatchcovers gone. The rudder seemed to be damaged, and there was water in the holds sloshing about among the coal. She was nowhere near sinking despite the open hold, and there had been no fire.

Perhaps the stubborn old-timer was trying to make for the Falklands by herself. It might have caused some consternation in Liverpool and parts of North Wales if she had arrived.

NOTE: CAPTAIN JONES HAD QUITE PROPERLY REMOVED THE HATCHCOVERS WHEN PRE-PARING TO ABANDON SHIP. THE WORST THING DRIFTING ABOUT DOWN THERE WAS AN UNLIT DERELICT, WALLOWING IN THE SEA. IF SHE HAD TO BE GIVEN UP, THE SOONER SHE SANK THE BETTER: BUT THE STUBBORN OLD BARK WITH HER GRACEFUL HULL, NO LONGER PRESSED, RODE THE SEAS SO WELL THAT SHE HAD SHIPPED NEXT TO NO HEAVY WATER.

Chapter two

AS RECORDED IN THE LOG

"Now WHAT on earth has got into the Old Man? Spending money on a cable to us in Honolulu? That's not like him! And asking us to 'report damage off Cape Horn.' What damage? We haven't any."

Captain James Learmont, twenty-seven-year-old master of the ship *Brenda,* a big carrier of almost 2,000 register tons, over thirty years old, had just arrived in Honolulu with a heavy cargo direct from Hamburg. The year was 1905: the passage had included a winter rounding of the Horn which the old *Brenda* took in her stride as, indeed, she took the whole passage of 127 days, port to port. The *Brenda* was a strong ship but full-bodied. She had done well, but here was a quite unnecessary cable from the owner, old Captain John Rae, a canny Scot if ever there were one.

No wonder Captain Learmont was surprised. The world of fast communications had not then caught up with British deepwater square-rigged ships, and indeed never did. The average number of cables the Raes sent to ships under their management was three a year, and in company code at that—three words could say everything. Now this wordy flimsy demanded a list of damage that had never happened.

Learmont, a forthright six-footer from the south of Scotland like John Rae and an unusually capable shipmaster in all respects —the business side as well the sailing, the navigating, shipkeeping and all those things—wasted no money on cabling a reply. (Those Cape Horn sailors had an aversion to cablegrams to the end of their days. When the Finns bought a lovely ship

named the *Thomasina McLellan,* they changed her name immediately to plain *Thomasina* just to save one word in cables, if sent.)

There was one reason, perhaps, for his owner's anxiety. The
ship was owned by a family group of shipmaster Raes, known as
J. and J. Rae and Co. and consisting of several brothers Rae, all
sailing-ship masters: as such they were frugal, canny men, and
had accumulated a bit of capital. As such, too, they knew what
Cape Horn could do to westbound ships, and the reports filtering
through from that winter's fight were ominous—half a dozen
ships not heard of at all, twenty or more driven (or gone) back
to the Falklands and elsewhere in distress, the *Bidston Hill*
wrecked on Staten Island (Isla de los Estados), the *British Isles* at
Pisagua, Chile, after a 150-day passage with extensive deck damage and at least four lives lost.

They also were aware that, like the *Scottish Isles,* their *Brenda*
had touched the ground in the North Sea outward bound from
Hamburg toward the Channel and further. She had just brushed
a corner of the Goodwin Sands in fog and calm. It was summer,
the sea like a millpond: Learmont at once carried out a couple of
kedge anchors with his boats, to stop her going on further if a
breeze came. The flood tide soon floated the *Brenda*—not before
the vulture shore boatmen had hurried out as well as the Rams-
gate lifeboat, though no one was in danger. (What they wanted
was alleged salvage, and a laden ship anywhere on those treach-
erous sands was usually a rich prospect for this.) His ship afloat,
a north-northwest breeze coming up nicely, Learmont soon had
her under way, the kedge anchors recovered, and the ship bounding down-Channel. He sent a letter off to the owners through a
boatman so that they would be informed of the grounding by
him, not by rumor.

Months later, the Raes heard of the troubles of the *Scottish
Isles.* It could be that their *Brenda* might have suffered hull damage, too. She was an elderly ship.

Captain Learmont had not to wait too long for a letter from
the Raes, though it had to come from Liverpool to New York by
Cunard (then sixty-five years in regular transatlantic service),
thence by the transcontinental railroad to San Francisco and on

Learmont's BRENDA. *Published by permission of the Trustees of the National Maritime Museum.*

ost off the Horn in 1905, the British BIDSTON HILL—*one of many.*

The PREUSSEN

by steamship to Hawaii. This could take three weeks or more.

When it came, it was almost apologetic. It was not the slight grounding of the *Brenda* that had worried the Raes. It was the misfortunes of another ship, the big full-rigger *British Isles,* which had been off the Horn about the same time and reached Pisagua after months, having lost at least four men, her boats gone, masts seriously strained, many sails lost, so heavily damaged on deck by the constant storms that she would have to be towed to Callao for repairs. Her then owner, Mr. Thomas Shute, sailed her uninsured: his loss would be considerable. It was he who asked John Rae to find out how the *Brenda* had fared.

"Why," said Captain Learmont to his mate, who was a friend, "that's Barker's ship—J. P. Barker, the fellow who says he beat the *Preussen.* He hasn't beaten much this time. Poor fellow, he must have taken a real beating of his own—has his family aboard the big brute, too. And I heard he had trouble with his mate."

Stuck at Honolulu for the moment, Learmont had little chance to find there what had really gone wrong with the *British Isles* that voyage. But those Cape Horning shipmasters knew one another and they knew, in time, what happened on their voyages. Word got around. Most masters shared the same haunts in foreign ports, often at the offices or on the shady verandahs of ship chandlers, brokers, or agents, who had an obvious interest in encouraging them. On his next call at Callao or Pisagua—indeed, at any west coast port—he could find out.

The letter made him curious, for he knew Captain Barker and was among those who were skeptical about his alleged sailing past the five-masted ship *Preussen.* The yarn just didn't make sense to a practical seaman.* The *British Isles,* a brute of a great steel full-rigger 309 feet long by 44 feet beam and 25 feet depth, 2,530 tons register, to his mind was too large for a three-masted ship, and she had a colossal main deck to catch and hold the Cape Horn seas. Her mainyard was 105 feet long, setting a sail close to the maximum size that seamen could stand upon footropes and work. She carried the best part of 4,000 tons in her big warehouse of a hull.

* See note at end of chapter.

Those sailing-ship masters knew more about the sailing qualities of their own and other ships even than the racing yachtsmen of today. One long look at hull and rigging, knowledge of the master, and there was no fooling them. Exaggeration of performance was normal and allowed, but not if overdone. The *British Isles* might run well before a strong fair wind with not too great a sea running—Barker claimed a day's run once of 383 miles in her, without giving chapter and verse—but everyone knew she was a great bitch on the wind. The *Preussen,* new in 1902, had a water line of over 400 feet, registered 5,081 tons, set canvas by the acre on her five masts, was known (like the other German five-master *Potosi*) as a well-handled, consistent performer with an excellent master and crew. She was designed for the nitrate trade, like many of the Hamburg "P" ships of the House of Laeisz, with massive gear yet tractable sail area, and a strong "three-island" hull designed to break the force of the seas on the main deck, not to be their murderous sport.

Learmont was glad the Raes had not bought the *British Isles* when her first owners, the British Shipowners Company of Liverpool, offered her in 1899. Thomas Shute and J. P. Barker could have her. An oversize full-rigger like that could be a heartbreak.

But what had Barker been up to this time? The cable and letter from his owners were a private request to him to find out. This took time, but he found out. Owners had to know the real worth of their masters, for their whole investment was in their hands, particularly when the ship, for reasons of economy, sailed uninsured and, as in this case, with a cargo they had bought for sale, not shipped to earn a freight. Freight rates at the time were very low.

The *British Isles* had sailed from Port Talbot in South Wales on June 10, 1905, bound for the Chilean port of Pisagua with a full cargo of coal, over 3,600 tons of it. She had two excellent mates, the second Barker's brother-in-law, an outstanding officer named Atkinson who later became harbormaster of the port of Liverpool. She had her usual foremast crowd of twenty able seamen, and Barker later said he had chosen them himself from the five hundred clamoring to go when he opened the ship's Articles at the Cardiff shipping office. These Articles are still filed with her official logs—the entries filled more than one. They show the men to have been an odd lot. The first twenty signed at Cardiff on June 9, 1905, and at London before she left for Cardiff were of thirteen nationalities including Italian, West Indian, German, Finnish, and Chilean, among men admitting ages up to fifty-two, which was very old for an able seaman then. Seven of the chosen liked the ship so little they deserted before she had even left Port Talbot. Perhaps they realized she would be off the Horn bound west in winter or, more likely, they heard something about the ship that they did not care for at all.

There were more desertions in Chile and Australia—eight at Pisagua, nine at Sydney—and still more on a subsequent visit to Valparaiso. Indeed, wherever the ship touched there were desertions, so that in the course of that voyage, which lasted from May 10, 1905, to January 21, 1908, the Articles show that it took seventy-eight men to keep up the *British Isles'* crew strength of twenty.

Such promptitude in desertion from long-voyage British sailing ships was then habitual. Men might sign optimistically under the influence of liquor, then realize they had joined a tartar. Ships and masters varied greatly: both quickly earned reputations, good or bad. After signing in a bad ship, the only escape was to melt away before she got to sea. This was an offense, of course: but the deserter could go to another port and ship again. His only evidence of identity and experience then was a certificate of discharge from his previous ship, a flimsy piece of paper more precise about the ship than the man. Mates were supposed to collect these when a man was selected: with a crowd milling around in the shipping office, anything could happen. Like much overregulated procedure conceived by politicians (or anybody else) the drill often broke down on the job. The sailor had learned to look out for himself.

Most of the men were in fact good, experienced seamen, the great majority with prior experience in such ships. The man-power wastage would probably have been even greater had the voyage included calls at a California port or in Puget Sound.

The men had signed, as was usual in foreign-going sailers then, to serve in the ship, accepting indifferent food, ill cooked and strictly rationed, and harsh discipline for a period of three years wherever the ship might go "within the limits of 75° N. and 60° S. latitude, trading in any rotation." For conducting themselves, if they lived, "in an orderly, faithful, honest and sober manner, being at all times diligent in their respective Duties," etc., able seamen were paid £3 a month, if they stayed to collect it. The second mate had £5–5, the mate £8–10, the all-important steward £5–10, and the even more important cook £4, all monthly.

All kinds of petty offenses subject to fines were spelled out in the fine print, and to these Barker added a few of his own as he was empowered to do—crew to work cargo or ballast when and where required, to keep their quarters clean, to be on deck during watch-on-deck or be fined five shillings for each absence. (No going below for a quick smoke, or a warm at the bogey.) The miserable rations are spelled out, too, covering ten items only, one of which is water—three quarts a day, most of it to the galley. Another item is a half pound of rice to be dished out on Saturdays. Salt beef and salt pork on alternate days, a pound and a half of flour and a pound of peas a week, one pound of biscuit, an eighth ounce of tea, half ounce of coffee, and two ounces of sugar daily are the other listed items, "in addition to the lime or lemon juice and sugar, or other antiscorbutics in any case required." The master was empowered to use "substitutes" at his own option entirely.

In fact, the miserable rations as listed were too often made tenfold worse by their appalling quality and the penny-pinching misery with which they were bought, cooked and issued. Much of the bony "beef" never knew an ox or an ancient cow, though hogs must have been found somewhere of quality bad enough to provide the alleged pork. In such conditions, what had a foremast hand to lose? Even small advances of his pay and liberty in port —if any—were "at master's option," too; and the hours of work for the traveling deck-swabbers, sailors, stevedores, assistant riggers, sailmakers, chippers and painters, *et al.,* were twelve a day for a six-day week in port, the same seven-days at sea, with as much more as the master might think necessary. There was neither leave nor hope of pension for anybody: in far too many ships, not much hope of fair treatment either, and an all-too-prevalent sickening meanness about the miserable food.

The ship provided no bedding, no bathing facilities nor even eating utensils. Quarters were in a bare steel house on deck, often not warmed by the crudest stove even in the coldest weather, and vulnerable in a big sea. In this were two rough tables, sometimes with benches to sit at but often not (sea chests were supposed to be used, but at the customary rate of turnover then no foremast hand had a sea chest for long), and a shelflike bunk with a low wooden side to keep the mariner in. These bunks were bare boards: the sailor provided a "donkey's breakfast" (straw mattress) and a blanket or two, if he joined sober and in funds. This was rare.

So it was that voyage aboard the *British Isles* in '05, and the *Deudraeth Castle,* and most of the other British ships besides— most, not all. By the grace of God and the humanity born in them, the Learmonts, the Fearons, the Nelsons of Maryport, the Williamses of St. Dogmaels, the Jarvises of Tayport, and a good many more never sank to such soul-searing stupidity nor tolerated it when inherited. They were in a minority, unfortunately.

In forty-five days from Port Talbot according to Barker (fifty-seven, according to Apprentice Jones who later wrote a book called *The Cape Horn Breed* about the voyage), the *British Isles* had passed the latitude of 50° S. in the Atlantic, and so began the passage of the Horn—1,500 miles of it at least before she could be reckoned safely clear, for she had to get well to the west'ard beyond the Horn too, as well as often beyond 60° S. latitude or almost to the Antarctic Circle, then battle her way somehow to 50° S. in the Pacific, keeping off the sharp-fanged bulwark of the South Chilean islands. Sou'westerly and westerly winds set on these: so did the scend of the surface sea. The sea itself moved eastward: the sets, the currents, the preponderance of gales were all against the west-bound ship. It seemed that the wild west

winds rushing around the watery world down there were mad-
dened by the spine of the Andes thrust suddenly southward into
them and rushed past in fury, tearing up the surface of the sea,
screaming and raging at the obstacle in their world-circling path.
A million years of fury have torn the weather shores of the land
into 10,000 ghastly rocks and islands, each a death trap to any
ship forced near in the sailing-ship era. There were then few if
any navigation marks and no lights. Captain Cook and Captain
Fitzroy of the *Beagle* had done most of the charting. The coastal
shelf of offshore soundings, dipping south toward Antarctica as
far as the rocks of Diego Ramirez, further enrages the rushing
sea: it is a wise master who gives all here the widest berth possible. There is generally plenty of room south of the Diego
Ramirez before serious ice becomes a menace, at least in the
average season, particularly in the winter.

Here Barker and his *British Isles* took up the battle: here, too,
the facts become difficult to get in order. Captain Barker wrote
(by dictation to his son, apparently) his own account in *The Log
of a Limejuicer** more than a quarter of a century afterward, and
at times gets the known facts so wrong that it would almost
appear deliberate. Captain Jones produced his account† at least
twenty years after that: this is loyal to his captain (as a good
apprentice should be) but varies considerably from his yarn and
perhaps at times gives the discerning reader a better picture than
intended. (So does Captain Barker, of himself.) The records entered in the official log differ again, though a master was held
accountable for the fullness and accuracy of its entries.

That official log—never to be confused with the deck log of
weather, courses made good, sails handled, etc.—had to be properly kept. It was the legal record of the voyage, the only record
of vital statistics concerning those aboard, and the record of the
master's administration of the ship's Articles as signed, under
the Merchant Shipping Act—his functioning as medico, disciplinarian, surveyor of damage, criminal investigator, and a sort

* Huntington Press, New York, 1933.
† *The Cape Horn Breed*, as told to P. R. Stephensen. Andrew Melrose, London: later
   reprinted by Jarrolds, 1968.

of magistrate. The requirements, clearly listed, were printed in every copy, and at every port touched, however long the voyage, the master had to produce both the official log and the Articles (often called the crew list, actually "Agreement and Account of Crew") to the British consul or vice-consul ashore there. If there were no such officer, he had to find the nearest port where there was one (if this was practical) before he sailed. These officers looked through his entries critically, often requiring explanations of doubtful points or of unsatisfactory interpretations of the disciplinary clauses of the Merchant Shipping Act under which seamen in British ships worked and were administered. Consular stamps showed that these inspections were passed (or not). At the end of the voyage the whole had to be deposited at the Board of Trade's Office for further inspection (and, perhaps, curt letters sent to slipshod and careless masters who hadn't even entered the names of their casualties correctly). Here they were kept for seven years at least, and indefinitely, if they contained vital statistics.

The 1905–08 official log of the *British Isles* was the death certificate of at least five seamen—the only such certificate. In 1970 it is to be found at the (temporary) repository for such documents, in a large hangar not far from London's Heathrow Airport, at Hayes, Middlesex.

Some shipmasters wrote as little in the official log as possible. James Barker was usually one of these, though there were many far more laconic, who could dispose of a five- or six-months passage, say, from Hamburg past the Horn in winter to San Francisco or Tacoma, Washington, without an entry at all. One wonders why the log was kept until noticing, perhaps, the entry for a birth to the master's wife. For this was a vital statistic indeed, and could well help to keep her husband even more than usually busy. It is difficult to believe that, during so long a passage, there had been need for no entries concerning an "offence for which punishment has been inflicted on board, and the punishment" (in accordance with the master's idea of the appropriate section in the M.S. Act of 1894) or no "illness, or injury that has happened to any member of the Crew . . . and the Medical treatment adopted (if any)," or "Collisions with any other Ship, and the circumstances under which the same occurred"—and so on, through a list of nineteen items. It could be, of course: there were plenty of happy and well-run ships under good masters, even on Board of Trade "pound and pint" allowances, provided these were treated as the minimum intended, not the maximum allowed.

One has a vision of some thoroughly decent, uncomplicated master mariner from Dinah's Cross or Criccieth in Wales or Maryport or a village in Devon or western Scotland (or Ireland, or New South Wales, Boston, Nova Scotia, or some other of the hundred places the extraordinary breed came from) quietly sailing his ship, unhurried, unflurried, just coping with everything that came along, having provisioned, stored, and stowed her completely and properly (with no nonsense "on the side") with the good crews which gravitated to such ships, or gave up other ways when they found one.

Such British masters—there were probably three of them to one indifferent—usually lost no lives: and so there are no longer records at all of many of their voyages. They attracted no attention at the time except among satisfied owners, shareholders, and officials concerned actively with their voyages. So one finds no news "stories," no official inquiries, no logs, in the records at all: and very seldom anything of a book. Far more apprentices wrote books than masters did.

Barker's book recounts five accidents (as well as ten serious cases of frostbite) resulting in four deaths on that passage to Pisagua. The Jones book is more explicit (or mixed-up?). "Of the seamen who had signed on for that tragic outward-bound voyage of the *British Isles,*" he wrote, "three were lost overboard, three more died from injuries, two were permanently disabled, and three partially disabled." The official log lists two A.B.'s—a Chilean named Juan D'Alencon, from Talcahuano, aged twenty-five, and an American named John M'Carthy (or McCarthy), aged thirty-nine, from Boston, Mass.—lost by drowning, and an Englishman named G. J. Harrhy, aged forty-two, died of injuries. At Pisagua a Swedish A. B. named L. Lindquest [*sic*], aged fifty-two,

The BRITISH ISLES *was a large full-rigged ship and heavy. She had a bad name among sailors. Published by permission of the Trustees of the National Maritime Museum.*

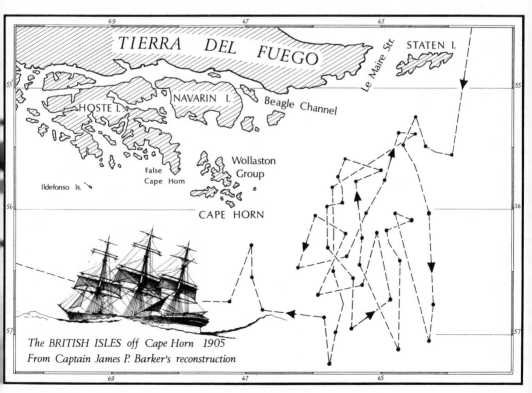

TIERRA DEL FUEGO

Le Maire Str.

STATEN I.

NAVARIN I.

Beagle Channel

HOSTE I.

False Cape Horn

Ildefonso Is.

Wollaston Group

CAPE HORN

The BRITISH ISLES *off Cape Horn 1905*
From Captain James P. Barker's reconstruction

Barker's idea of his BRITISH ISLES *rounding in '05*

A 13645

(O 4)

OFFICIAL LOG BOOK.

NO.

(Consisting of 44 Page
For 87 Men.

FOR EITHER

FOREIGN-GOING OR HOME TRADE SHIP.

For entry
Forth or ...
see page ....

Name of Ship.	Official Number.	Port of Registry.	Registered Tonnage.		Name of Master.	No. of his Certificate if any.
			Gross.	Net.		
"British Isles"	64992	Liverpool	2444	2284	James Barr	Ex. 02760

Port at which and Date when voyage commenced.	Nature of the Voyage or Employment.	Port at which and Date when Voyage terminated.
Port _Pt. Talbot_ Date _16/5/05_	_Foreign_	Port _Dunkirk_ Date _24/1/08_

Delivered to the Superintendent of Mercantile Marine at the Port of _Dunkirk_

on _21_ day of _January_

Countersigned

[signature]

Superintendent.

[signature]

18 Rue de la Cour _Address._

Master.

Note.—The above Entries are to be filled up by the Master, and the Log Book is to be delivered to the Superintendent within forty-eight hours after th[e] Ship's arrival, or upon the discharge of the Crew, whichever first happens, in the case of a Foreign-going Ship. In the case of a Home Trade Ship the Lo[g] B[oo]k for any half-year is to be delivered to a Superintendent within 21 days of the 30th of June or the 31st of December, as the case may be.—*See* Section 2[ ] of the Merchant Shipping Act, 1894.

LONDON: PRINTED FOR HIS MAJESTY'S STATIONERY OFFICE.

Pages from the Official Log Book of the ship BRITISH ISLES *as still in the P.R.O. Repository at Hayes. These include the death entries for the 1905 voyage, the list of ports, etc., various entries more or less dramatic. (What Captain Barker does not mention is that throughout the long period off the Horn these men were left in the ship's for'ard house, one side of which had been badly damage by a sea which killed the Chilean—and their condition steadily deteriorated.)*

LOAD-LINE AND DRAUGHT OF WATER.

Note 5' 8" *Allun'* 6' 6" *POSITION OF DISC.*

* The centre of the disc is placed at 5' feet *Allun'* 6' 6" inches below the deck-line marked under the provisions of the Merchant Shipping Act, 1894.

* POSITION OF LINES USED IN CONNECTION WITH THE DISC.

SAILING SHIP.

Maximum load-line in fresh water, ____ feet ____ inches above the centre of the disc.
Maximum load-line in winter, North Atlantic, ____ feet ____ inches below the centre of the disc.

STEAM SHIP.

Maximum load-line in fresh water ____ feet ____ inches above the centre of the disc.
Maximum load-line in Indian summer ____ feet ____ inches above the centre of the disc.
Maximum load-line in summer the centre of the disc.
Maximum load-line in winter ____ feet ____ inches below the centre of the disc.
Maximum load-line in North Atlantic winter ____ feet ____ inches below the centre of the disc.

* These particulars are to be taken from the certificate of approval of the position, or alteration of the position, of the disc, and the words which are not applicable should be era

DATES OF ARRIVAL AT AND DEPARTURE FROM EACH PORT TOUCHED AT, WITH THE FREE-BOARD AND DRAUGHT OF WATER

Upon every occasion of the Ship proceeding to Sea.

(1)	(2)	(3)			(4)			(5)	(6)
	FROM	Draught of Water in salt water at time of proceeding to sea.			Freeboard amidships corresponding to foregoing draught.				TO
Date and Hour of Departure.	Dock, Wharf, Port or Harbour from which the Ship departs.	Forward.	Aft.		Port.	Starboard.		Date of Arrival.	Dock, Wharf, Port or Harbour
		ft. in.	ft. in.		ft. in.	ft. in.			
16/4/05	Millwall Dock London	12. 4	12. 4.		4' 4	4' 4		24/5/05	Port Talbot
1/6/05	Docks Port Talbot.	21-10	21-10		5-9½	5-9½		27/7/05	Pierpua
1/8/06	Pierpua	12. 6	12. 6		15.06	15.02		24/9/06	Callao

THE SUMMER MONTHS ARE APRIL TO SEPTEMBER INCLUSIVE.
THE WINTER MONTHS ARE OCTOBER TO MARCH INCLUSIVE.

The additional freeboard specified for the North Atlantic trades is to apply to vessels sailing to, or from, the Mediterranean or any British or European Port, whic̶ sail to, or from, or call at, Ports in British North America, or eastern Ports in the United States, north of Cape Hatteras, from October to March inclusive.

The reduced freeboard allowed for voyages in the Fine Season in the Indian Seas only applies to vessels trading between the limits of Suez and Singapore.

The Fine Weather Season in the Indian Seas is defined as prevailing east of Tuticorin from the 15th November to the 25th May, and west of Tuticorin fr̶ 1st September to the 25th May.

BIRT[...]

Columns to be filled in by

Date of Birth.	Name (if any) of Child.	Sex.	Name and Surname of Father.	Rank, Profession, or Occupation of Father.	Name and Surname of Mother.	Maiden Su[...] of Moth[...]
1						
2						
3						
4						
5						

DEATH[...]

Columns to be filled in [...]

Date of Death.	Place of Death (See instruction on previous page).	Name and Surname of Deceased.	Sex.	Age.	Rating, or Rank, Profession, or Occupation.	Nationality (stating Birthpl[...])
						Members of Crew, i[...]
1 3/9/05	59.30 S 67.20 H.	Juan De Alencon	Male.		A.B.	Chillian
2 30/9/05	58.40 S 70.04 H.	G. J. Harrhy.	Male.		A.B.	British
3 13/10/05	45.14 S 79.25 H.	John M'Carthy	Male		A.B.	American
4 10/12/05	Pisagua	L. Lindquest	Male		A.B.	Swede.
5 18/1/08	Iunkergue Hospital	August Bakman.	Male	29	A.B.	Finn.
1						Members of Crew, [...]
2						
3						
4						
1						Persons who w[...]
2						
3						
4						
5						

Officer in Command.

	Father.		Mother.		Signature of Father or Mother.	Signature of Master and Mate or member of Crew.	Columns to be filled in by Official to whom report is made.	
tionality Birthplace)	Last place of Abode.	Nationality (stating Birthplace)	Last place of Abode.				Port and Country at which the report is made.	Signature and Title of Officer to whom reported.

ficer in Command.

place of Abode.	Cause of Death (See instructions on previous page).	Signature of Master or person in charge.	Signature of Mate or other member of the Crew.	Signature of Surgeon or Medical Practitioner, if any.		
on European Agreement.						
Buti Rd Cardiff	Drowning	James P. Barker	Ft. L. Evans		Oningua Chili	F Barker Pr. via Cur
Lothn Rd London	Injuries sustained	James P. Barker	Ft d Evans		do.	F Barker Pr. via Cur
address	Drowning	James P. Barker	Ft d Evans		do.	F Barker Pr. via Cur
andorm St Stockton	Dysentry	James P. Barker	Ft d Evans		do.	F Barker Pr. via Cur
w Castle n. s. w.	Consumption pleurity malaria	James P Barker	Wm. Shael McCum			
rs, on Asiatic Agreement.						
of the Crew.						

22

OFFICIAL LOG of the "British Isles"

from Port Talbot towards Iquique

Date of the Occurrence entered with Hour.	Place of the Occurrence, or situation by Latitude and Longitude at Sea.	Date of Entry.	Entries required by Act of Parliament.	Amount of Fine or Forfeiture inflicted.
			The man saw little convulsions and complained of	
			internal pains he spat up and vomited quantities	
			of cold water and some there grey matter everything	
			quantities of blood was let from his head and mouth	
			everything was done to stop flow of blood &	
			the wounds dressed & bound up. He was	
			put into r' night room and cared for, app'	

Pd Evan Mols
with high seas
18/9/05 During a storm from the West

at about time mentioned mayor

a huge sea overran the whole fore

part of ship carrying clean overboard

the three forward boats which were stationd

on house, also Juan de Alea con AB

who was on look out or house between

boats. A cry was heard immedi-

ately under the quarter but nothing

Lat aud 59. 30' S.
19/05   64. 20 w

(circular stamp) BRITISH VICE CONSULATE FISAGU

23

OFFICIAL LOG of the British Ship

Port Talbot.

from _____ towards Oregon

Date of the Occurrence, entered with Hour.	Place of the Occurrence, or situation by Latitude and Longitude at Sea.	Date of Entry.	Entries required by Act of Parliament.	Amount of Fine or Forfeiture inflicted.
			was seen. A life buoy was thrown	
			overboard but further assistance	
			no human aid could render any owing	
			the violence of the storm The man	
			was drowned.	
			James Barker Master	
			Pat Evans Mate	

24

OFFICIAL LOG of the

"British Isles"

from Port Talbot. towards Iquique

Date of the Occurrence entered with Hour.	Place of the Occurrence, or situation by Latitude and Longitude at Sea.	Date of Entry.	Entries required by Act of Parliament.	Amount of Fine or Forfeiture inflicted.
			# Maitland, AB was washed away from braces down to leeward. He was helped forward and from that date up to present he has been unfit for duties. Complaining of pains in and around lower part of back. Repellox was given him for outward application.	

weable to deal any further with

him.

James H Barker Master

PA Evans Mate

O.Mp. Grüber, Carpenter.

18/10/06 During the whole of this time

from the date of 1st accident every-

thing possible was done to allay pain

and help in the injured men. The

weather has been so temperature

15/10/06.

N.B.—Every entry in this Log Book required by the Act must be signed by the Master and by the Mate or some other of the Crew, and every entry of illness, injury, or death must also be signed by the Surgeon or Medical Practitioner on board (if any) ; and every entry of wages due to, or of the sale of the effects of, any Seaman or Apprentice who has died must be signed by the Master and by the Mate and some other member of the Crew ; and every entry of wages due to any Seaman who enters His Majesty's Service must be signed by the Master and by the Officer authorized to receive the Seaman into such Service.

NOTE.—Reading over Entries of Offences.—The Master's special attention is called to Section 228 (b) (c) and (d) of the Merchant Shipping Act, 1894, which will be found in Notice I. prefixed to this Log.

25

OFFICIAL LOG of the

"British Isles"

Port Talbot towards Pisagua

Date of the occurrence entered with Hour.	Place of the Occurrence, or situation by Latitude and Longitude at Sea.	Date of Entry.	Entries required by Act of Parliament.	Amount of Fine or Forfeiture inflicted.
			as to utterly prevent any entries being made	
			in this Book my whole time has been	
			taken up in navigating ship and looking after	
			injured men.	
			James O'Brien Master	
			Evan Blake 1st mate	
			Chas Grünberg Carpenter	
2/9/08	59° 8′ S. 64′ W. Lat.	18/10/08	On this date found a discharge (CR3)	

discovered the toes of his right foot to be badly diseased with frost bite. He had been off duty since 3/9/06 but had not ever complained about his toes. What he complained about he was stiff all over and could not draw on his boots. The clothing he had been wearing was thrown overboard, new clothing supplied to him and instructions clearly given him to keep his feet and person clean. As each day has come and gone I have

Typical sailing-ship rigs

died from dysentery. No other deaths are reported until the ship is back at Dunkirk early in 1908. Here another A.B., listed as August Bakman, a Finn, aged twenty-nine, died in hospital of "consumption, pleurisy, and malaria." Bakman was not aboard for the outward passage.

In the other official document, the "Agreement and Account of Crew," British Consul Thos. Atkinson at Pisagua certifies "the Master's report to him of the deaths of "d'Alencon [*sic*], McCarthy, Harrhy, and Lindquest." There is confusion about the last name which could be easily be Lindquist or Lindgren: the man's signature signing on is far from clear, and he never signed off.

But the recorded deaths *at sea* are three, not four, the total before reaching port is four that passage, not six. God knows three were enough to lose from any ship even on a Cape Horn winter's rounding, especially going one at a time. It was not at all uncommon for three or four seamen to go at once from a Cape Horn ship, in the same accident—washed over the side by some mighty sea, flung from the rigging by the flap of a wind-mad tops'l blowing out of its gear, pitched to the deck together when a footrope broke, drowned when the driven brute pitched her bows and her whole foc's'l head right under, or mangled in a sudden, violent dismasting. But one at a time, each in a fresh accident—that was harder on the survivors. Who might be next? And when?

Consul Atkinson certifies also "that the following seamen have been discharged and left behind in the port" (with $400 each for expenses and later repatriation) "on the alleged ground of injuries received in the service of the ship and I have inquired into the matter and find the allegation true, and I have accordingly sanctioned their being so left behind . . .

"Henry Haberland 26 A.B.
G. Lazarus 26 A.B."

He lists also W. H. Parker, aged forty-eight, A.B., as "discharged sick, not from injury in the service of the ship." These consuls who dealt with the affairs of ships come from Cape Horn (or anywhere else) with their crews of wild men led by wilder learned to be careful in recording alleged facts about them, even their lists of killed and wounded. The consul was careful to distinguish between illness caused by injury in the ship's service and the more unusual sort. He probably thought that the matter of workmen's compensation came into it, but in this he was wrong. Merchant seamen were excluded from the primitive benefits of any such generosity, perhaps on the score that if included they might use up all the funds. The meager details recorded of them both in the agreement and the official log never list a next of kin. When certified dead, officialdom was notified (on the appropriate form) but relatives if any learned the best way they could. Now and again there is a note that a lost mate or tradesman (such as the sailmaker or carpenter) had left an allotment from his meager pay to his far-off wife, for these were steadier men. For the most part, the foremast hand was on his own.

Perhaps that was one reason why he was a foremast hand.

In due course, the landed men from the *British Isles* recovered, more or less. One wonders what sort of passage home (if they had homes) the balance of their $400 bought them. They were both one-legged men then, with no future in sailing ships: indeed, they were very fortunate to be alive.

Owner Shute had plenty to worry about when his ship came in. Putting right the rigging and deck damage was very expensive. Damage included the for'ard house stove in by the sea, three boats lost and all the skids damaged, even the wheel smashed: the bowsprit and two of the lower masts sprung so badly that she sailed to Pisagua from the Horn with two of them "fished" with splints made from her royal yards: over £1,000 worth of her best sails blown away. The coal venture would have paid, otherwise, for the Pisagua price on it was £4–10 the ton compared with 10/6 at Port Talbot. But discharge was slow: with so many of the crew lost including those who deserted on arrival, shore labor had to be engaged, which was expensive. The ship's full crew including the tradesmen and apprentices was twenty-nine: for such a ship she was not overmanned. The apprentices had to "loblolly" for

Captain Barker, ferrying him ashore and ship-visiting whenever the whim took him (on top of all their other duties) which was often. The apprentices did not desert so easily. They had a stake in the ship, needed their "time" from her and a good reference from the master. They had homes in Britain, too, and close relatives interested in them. But they led a dog's life—a contemporary dog's, not a modern—aboard the *British Isles,* at sea and in port, and they received no wage at all.

It is strange that the ship was so much damaged from her brush with the Horn. She was in the area for ten weeks, which is at least seven longer than enough, but she was strongly built to take that sort of punishment indefinitely. She had the dangerous long open main deck of the typical limejuicer but, apart from helping to mash up two good able seamen, this had killed only one—the Chilean D'Alencon, swept overboard from the top of the for'ard house. In such a ship at such a time, work on the main deck could always be dangerous—far more so than in the rigging. German ships were required to rig life nets above the bulwarks in the waist to help keep the men aboard when the ship knocked them down, but British ships had nothing of this kind. The twenty-one-year-old *British Isles* had high bulwarks, but these were no help when she rolled them under, or drove her bows into a wall of water and filled the decks. The loss of three from a crew of twenty-nine may be acceptable, but the effective loss of the work of another dozen through frostbite is more difficult to understand. The ship had a bogey in each foc's'le and plenty of coal. Temporary frostbite was a common hazard, but to allow it to lead to gangrene and almost total incapacitation was not.

Other masters seemed able to take frostbite in their stride. In the *Marion Josiah,* a 2,400-tonner out of Glasgow, for instance, Captain W. L. Grant had several bad cases aboard off the Horn in midwinter 1906, when bound from South Shields toward San Diego, Cal.—a tough passage which took him 158 days. He lost three men too, but this was coming up to Queenstown in winter at the end of the voyage when a great sea pooped her, smashing the wheel, washing away the mate and the two helmsmen. The mate and one helsman—an American named Frank Root from

Chicago—went overboard. When the sea cleared the decks it was found that the other helmsman had been washed along the deck and smashed almost to pulp against the for'ard house. He was American, too. (The ship had come then from Tacoma.) But the seriously frostbitten were dealt with by rubbing the affected limbs with snow, and then treating them "with packs of wet oakum." This treatment was not recommended by that vague authority, the *Ship Master's Medical Guide*. It took time, but it worked.

The master of a deepwater ship was responsible for the health and well-being of his crew: they should not have been neglected. The ship was hove to—that is, virtually at a standstill under very short sail, no longer trying to make progress as a hopeless effort—for days on end. It was plain humanity and self-interest (if no more) to keep an eye on laid-up men and there was plenty of time—twenty-four hours the day.

"During the whole of this time, from the date of the first accident," Barker writes in the official log under date October 18, 1905, "everything possible was done to allay pain and help on the injured men. The weather has been so tempestuous as to utterly prevent any entries being made in this Book." (He obviously wrote much later.) "My whole time has been taken up in navigating ship and looking after injured men." Was it?

An odd entry. He lists no treatment. He leaves the men in their smashed quarters.

Able Seaman Lazarus's leg became gangrenous, too. Smashed more than broken—there were three fractures, apparently—the carpenter (a competent Swede) made splints for it: but Lazarus sweated it out in his foc's'l bunk, and broke his leg there again trying to look after himself. The original break was on September 3: on October 18, Barker writes, "I would like to amputate but dare not undertake responsibility, although I feel sure that amputation will have to take place to save the man's life." Then he adds, again rather oddly, "I here take opportunity of stating the man has received every attention possible." (Had he? Why the gangrene?)

In his book, he tells of carrying out the amputation with a

butcher's knife, a meat saw, a hot galley poker for cauterizing, and the carpenter as nurse. A master was required to record what he did for his wounded (under such guidance as he could find in the pages of the *Ship Master's Medical Guide,* which in those days wisely omitted serious surgery altogether): but the official log contains no reference to any amputation at all. Lazarus lived to be landed at a hospital at Pisagua where a leg was removed: being obviously a wiry man of immense endurance and courage, he recovered. But it took a long time.

The log records that Edward Emms, the other A.B. who broke a leg off the Horn, "slowly recovered." An early casualty, he was accommodated in "a room in the cabin passage" (a spare cabin aft) where he could be "carefully nursed." His fractures were not so serious: soon he could hobble about, aided by a set of the carpenter's splints. (The *British Isles* had a large poop and several spare cabins aft, but poor Mrs. Barker and her small children also had to live there. Much of the time, they were lashed down together in the large berth in the master's cabin lest they break legs too: James B. cat-napped where and when he could. British Cape Horners had no hospital after the passenger-sailing-ship era. Mrs. Barker, a kindly young woman, could not help in looking after anyone but her own children. Often about all she could manage was to hang grimly on to them. She could never get on the main deck for the sea: and she was seasick whenever the weather was bad. She did what little she could to keep an eye on the young apprentices, and promptly left the ship when at last she reached Pisagua.)

The *British Isles* was seventy-two days on that Cape Horn rounding. Before she had got round, food and stores were short. This was unpardonable, and no part of her owner's intention. Mr. Shute had paid for his ship to be properly stored and provisioned to keep the sea for six months at least. Apprentice Jones speaks of the short rations as the hardest trial of all, for he was a growing boy. Even the fresh-water rations were cut, but this was mainly owing to the foolish habit of placing the only fresh-water tanks amidships, in the wettest part of notoriously wet vessels, where water could be drawn only by rigging a pump (usually kept not rigged) and, in doing this, leaving the tank in use open to contamination by the sea.

Everybody concerned was well aware of this stupidity: an answer had been found years before to so many of these unnecessary open-deck hazards by building large sailers with "three-island" hulls, including a long midships section to house an indestructible galley, dry forecastles, ample sail lockers, ready-use storerooms and everything else, with access to the fresh water under cover. As such a "house" was carried out to the sides of the ship, the seas could not reach it except from above, where there were few openings, heavily protected and easily made secure against the weather. Down here there was room for a dry, warm hospital too.

Big British four-masted barks like the *Reliance* and the *Pegasus* were built like this in 1884, the same year the die-hard *British Isles* was launched, and they were less than a hundred tons larger than she was. Master and officers lived 'midships in these large ships. The ships were sailed and controlled from there, and the three-island hull prevented hundreds of tons of sea filling the main deck. The galley and the quarters were rarely if ever reached by the sea: there were fewer injuries.

The idea was copied in many big-carrying four-masted barks, including the *Lawhill* of Dundee and the *Forteviot* of Liverpool, 3,000-tonners in which I was to sail much later, and note their advantages. Indeed old sailors called this 'midships section a "Liverpool house." But for no reasons other than its unfamiliar and "unclassic" profile, and the alleged inconvenience of the enforced use of a couple of high sets of steps to get along the deck, the safer hull form was never generally adopted in Britain, nor in America for that matter. Its advantages were obvious to the Germans who took it up wholeheartedly, moved everybody 'midships, made better passages and saved many lives. Perhaps the British seamen disliked quarters too close to the afterguard, but many three-islanders still carried the usual poop and its quarters, charthouse, and steering position (if not a whaleback wheelhouse) as well. It was unnecessary for the pigheaded old die-hards to be any closer to their officers than before, and they had accepted the common sense of the move from wet and uncomfortable quarters below the foc's'le head to a house on deck abaft the foremast years earlier. Owners could be pigheads too, and the matter of tonnage measurement could come into it. This affected dues. French ships were built with far more shelter on deck and spacious, safe accommodation for the crew, but a subsidy paid on *gross* tonnage helped with this. The larger the gross tonnage the better: most dues were paid only on net tons.

There was at least the normal proportion both of die-hards and the pigheaded aboard the *British Isles* that passage. That much is horribly obvious from the books, the performance, and the log. Captain Barker would have been well advised to run for shelter to the Falkland Islands—anchoring for shelter cost a ship very little and even the most ill-treated seamen found it hard to desert in Port Stanley—rather than thrash it out so endlessly down there near the Antarctic Circle, bashing up his ship and her men, getting nowhere. He kept hoping, of course, that the conditions would ease. He was hove to once for three weeks on end during which the wind was mostly if not always from north of west, forcing the ship nearer and nearer to the Antarctic Circle —over three hundred miles beyond the southernmost limits by which their articles bound the crew. (This was one reason why many masters then made such an unholy secret of the ship's position: what the men didn't know was unlikely to cause trouble.) It became so cold that at times heavy hoarfrost whitened the masts and yards and all the exposed steel so that it looked like a glorious iced Christmas cake (though not to her people): to touch such steel meant searing pain. No one had dry gloves or dry anything ever for more than about five minutes. Except at the wheel, no one worked in gloves, for fumbling hands aloft could send a man pitching to his death quicker than anything.

In such circumstances, it seems remarkable that there was no serious mutiny. According to *The Log of a Limejuicer,* there could have been. Barker tells of ugly scenes when, instigated (he says) by the mate, all hands lay aft to compel him to make for the

Falklands. Aided by his loaded six-shooter (referred to not for the first time) and the timely intervention of his little daughter who came tripping among the men just at that moment looking for the sailmaker to mend a rag doll he had sewn for her, he coped with this, and quietened the mate and the mutineers. There is some highly improbable stuff about a charge that their captain had buried their shipmate Harrhy *alive,* and this is described by Barker as the immediate cause of the attempted mutiny.

As well as the loaded gun, Barker says he had the "official log book open before me," and required every man present, led by the mate, to sign this, after making an appropriate entry. "They all signed." He did not turn back for the Falklands.

There is only one official log aboard a ship at a time: that which Barker used throughout that passage is still in existence. Its pages are numbered: none has been removed. Like all such, it bears the impress of the official stamps put in it on issue and return. It is *the* log. There is nothing whatever giving the slightest evidence for or bearing the slightest resemblance to this yarn in the log at all.

Jones gives a different version of the "mutiny." A deputation came aft, he says, when the effective foremast crowd was reduced by neglect of frostbite to about twelve, and asked that the ship should run for the Falklands to give them and her a chance to recover. Barker, complete with six-shooter and flanked by his second mate, the carpenter, sailmaker, and four of the apprentices, faced them in the messroom aft, brought in the disaffected mate, and declared his intention of carrying on the passage—no histrionics (beyond the gun-play), no entry of little daughter: and no signing in the log, either.

Perhaps Captain Barker had missed his real vocation.

The *British Isles* was at Pisagua and Callao for over seven costly months, two of them at Callao under repair earning nothing. Unable when ready to find a cargo either of guano or nitrates, and nothing offering from the California coast or Puget Sound, she had to sail to Sydney Heads for orders, in ballast (which had to be bought). Her voyage had lasted well over twelve months when she received a flag signal at Sydney Heads to go on to Newcastle. She was sixty-five days crossing the Pacific—a beautiful, fine-weather passage which Mrs. Barker and the children could have enjoyed, but they had long since returned by steamer to England—and another seven weeks at Newcastle before her second cargo was aboard. This was coal for Valparaiso, which she reached in thirty-five days. After almost three months getting the coal out and sufficient ballast in, she sailed again to Sydney, this time taking fifty-three days. Again ordered up the coast to Newcastle, she was there a month loading yet another coal cargo—the third (and last) that long voyage—this time for Mejillones in Chile, a passage taking forty-five days. It was June 12, 1907, before she reached Mejillones: some six weeks later she was at Iquique (sailing up the coast in four days, lightly ballasted, with wind and current favorable) to load nitrates for Dunkirk. On this passage she rounded the Horn to the eastward with favoring winds: the whole run homeward took 102 days.

It was January 16, 1908, when she arrived at Dunkirk and the Articles (and official log for that voyage) were closed. She had been some two years and eight months away, sailing over 50,000 miles to carry four cargoes, the first to owner's account and none earning a high rate of freight. Considering the delays in port, the costly damage of the first Horn passage, the expensive wastage of crew, she could have earned little or no profit. The log shows almost constant crew trouble in all ports. Desertions are frequent. A supplementary log adds forty-nine names to the eighty-odd of the first. At Iquique, homeward bound at last, Captain Barker records the payment of $30 "blood money" each (for the live bodies of six "seamen") to a "boarding-house keeper"—a crimp. This he writes for the log. The consul adds a reprimand for "not looking after his owner's interests" in having good men desert and paying so much for bad.

Captain Barker left after another voyage, and he does not appear to have been employed again in sail until he had the ship *Tusitala* out of New York in the late 1920's, in the trade thence to Honolulu, using the Panama Canal outward and homeward.

The *British Isles* became a hulk at Buenos Aires after a period under the Italian flag.

In 1934, when Captain Learmont was Superintendent of Pilots at Harwich and was aboard the ship *Joseph Conrad* piloting me from that old English port to the Straits of Dover—I was bound round the world to the west'ard then, and planned a westward rounding of the Horn—I talked with him about all these things. In the intervening years I came to know Captain Barker, too, when he had the *Tusitala.*

"What happened to Barker is plain enough," Learmont said. "The winds off the Horn that year were pretty bad and they were more from north of west than south of it. He put her under short canvas on the starboard tack and hoped for a slant to let her sail her course. But the slant didn't come. She kept on making leeway toward the south; he kept her hove to, in a worse and worse position. The crew got sick. He lost a few. Perhaps the mate didn't cooperate: but he was an experienced man and known as a good seaman. Barker had an odd name.

"He hung about down there for ten weeks and bashed the devil out of the ship. To heave to and wait for a slant is no way to get past the Horn. You have to watch your chance, fight back *all* the time. And you have to demonstrate that you are the leader all the time, too—and not with fool guns.

"But I don't understand all that serious rigging damage he had. Maybe those masts weren't too good when he started, and he knew it. *That* would make it mighty hard to keep fighting; but it does not explain what seems like the deaths of several men unnecessarily.

"At that, he did better than the *Bidston Hill* and a round dozen more which never got past the Horn at all that year, or completed their voyages. The *Bidston Hill* got under the cliffs of Staten Island without even knowing she was there. First thing they knew, the overhanging cliff tops were knocking her t'gallant masts down, and the falling masts and yards killed half the crew before they could get out of the way. Her master said he hadn't had a sight to fix his ship then for twelve days, and he didn't know what the sets were doing. When the clifftops reached down in the fog' on top of him, he was amazed. The court exonerated him, perhaps thinking he'd done his best and not looking too closely into the matter of how he hadn't known where he was.

"Funny thing, we'd come that same way at that time. I was curious, so I looked at my workbook. We'd had good star sights all those twelve days, morning and evening, though it was true the sun never shone. Remember that! Get a stellar fix whenever you can. It often happens even in the worst weather that you'll get a good horizon and sufficient glimpse of the brightest stars either at sunset or dawn. Its a peculiarity off the Horn, and it helped me. But some didn't seem to notice it, or use the data offered if they did. Keep up your star recognition: don't get lazy on the navigation or anything else, my son. You'll grow no hair on your back in this ship or any other that's sailed properly."

I knew the *Brenda* had made the wind'ard rounding of the Horn in twelve of those seventy-two days the *British Isles* was drifting about in misery. Brought up in the South Pacific and Australian grain trade, I had made no west'ard Horn roundings. We ran from west to east with the winds, or sometimes rounded Good Hope. The *Conrad* was a small full-rigged ship of old-fashioned hull form with a rig not much ahead of James Cook's *Endeavour*. I sought the experienced captain's advice. He summed it up:

"You've noted the way the cyclonic movements race across the Southern Ocean—Indian or Pacific, it's much the same. You've learned the signs for shifts of wind—the slight clearing in the southwestern sky, a movement in rising cloud, then the swift, sudden shift. It's the same off the Horn except the wind is madder there, the shifts faster, nights longer, sea higher, ice nearer—you know the odds. Watch the met., look after the crew, be ready to put her round, never be afraid to wear ship the moment it will pay, every time the other tack will give her a better course. Get sail off in time but put it back on, too, every chance you get.

"You'll get no sleep. You'll get so wet so long your skin will come off with your socks, if you get time to take them off. But with luck, you'll get past Cape Horn and, by the grace of God, you won't kill anybody."

NOTE: IN HIS *Log of a Limejuicer,* CAPTAIN JAMES P. BARKER WRITES THAT WHEN THE *British Isles* WAS OUTWARD BOUND FROM THE BRISTOL CHANNEL TO THE WEST COAST OF CHILE AFTER HE HAD ASSUMED COMMAND IN 1903, HE SIGHTED THE *Preussen* AHEAD ONE MORNING (DATE AND POSITION NOT GIVEN) AND *sailed up on her and passed her,* WITH THE *British Isles* MAKING FOURTEEN KNOTS. "BY NOON THE GERMAN WAS ON THE LEE BEAM AND FALLING ASTERN: AT 4 PM SHE WAS HULL-DOWN AND DROPPING AWAY. . . . THERE WAS GREAT ELATION AMONG THE MEMBERS OF THE AFTERGUARD"—AS INDEED THERE MIGHT HAVE BEEN, MINGLED WITH A GREAT DEAL OF ASTONISHMENT, HAD THE INCIDENT ACTUALLY OCCURRED. THE *Preussen* AND HER VOYAGES ARE WELL DOCU-MENTED, AND PORT RECORDS GIVE DATES OF ARRIVALS AND DEPARTURES SUFFICIENT TO ESTABLISH THOSE OF THE *British Isles.* PORT RECORDS AT CARDIFF SHOW THAT THE *British Isles* ARRIVED IN THE BUTE EAST DOCK THERE ON APRIL 13, 1903, AND SAILED WITH HER COAL CARGO FOR CALLAO ON MAY 1. LLOYD'S PICK HER UP WITH A "SPEAK-ING" ON 39°N 14W ON MAY 6 AND AGAIN ON 4°N 26W ON MAY 22: SHE REACHED CALLAO ON JULY 31. THE *Preussen* WAS AT GEESTEMUNDE FROM IQUIQUE FROM HER MAIDEN VOYAGE ON JANUARY 20, 1903. SHE WAS OUTWARD BOUND AGAIN BY FEBRUARY 16, BEAT DOWN-CHANNEL, TOOK HER DEPARTURE OFF THE USHANT ON MARCH 5, CROSSED THE LINE THIRTEEN DAYS FIVE HOURS LATER (FASTEST TIME ON RECORD), BEAT PAST THE HORN IN ELEVEN DAYS, AND REACHED IQUIQUE ON MAY 1, FIFTY-SEVEN DAYS FROM DEPARTURE. SHE SAILED AGAIN A FORTNIGHT LATER AND WAS REPORTED OFF THE LIZARD ON JULY 21. HOW THE *British Isles* COULD EVER HAVE BEEN WITHIN 3,000 MILES OF HER, GOING IN THE SAME DIRECTION ON THAT VOYAGE, NO SAILOR MAY UNDER-STAND. THE ALLEGED INCIDENT COULD NOT HAVE OCCURRED ON A LATER VOYAGE: CAPTAIN W. H. S. JONES (WHOSE *Cape Horn Breed* REPEATS THE MASTER'S STORY WITH-OUT FURTHER DETAILS) STATES THAT THERE WAS NO MEETING AT SEA BETWEEN THE TWO SHIPS WHILE HE WAS ABOARD, FROM 1905 TO 1909, WHEN CAPTAIN BARKER LEFT. PERHAPS BARKER SAW A MIRAGE.

Chapter three

ON THE BEACH

THAT DAY in June, 1905, when the *British Isles* sailed from Port Talbot toward Pisagua, the German ship *Susanna* went to sea on the same tide from the same port, bound for Caleta Buena, Chile. The ports are within a few miles of one another. According to the account in his *Log of a Limejuicer,* Barker challenged Captain Jürgens of the *Susanna* to make a race of it.

"I will beat you by twenty days!" declared J. P. B., and the statement seems in character.

The odd thing is that, despite his own long passage, this was just about what he managed to do, to his and the shipping world's considerable surprise. He attributes the victory to the fact that the German ship "after battling for several weeks off the pitch of the Cape, had despaired of success and decided to square away before those seemingly everlasting westerly gales. The *Susannah* [*sic*] ran her easting down, rounded Australia, sailed over a vast expanse of storm-racked Pacific Ocean, and finally arrived in the port of Iquique after a passage of *two hundred and seven days.*"

So he writes: but he is quite wrong. In fact, the *Susanna* stuck it off the Horn for ninety-nine days, fighting it out all that time. The reason for her very long passage was the oddest of that odd and difficult year—chronometer error, that was all! She had only one of those expensive clocks kept at Greenwich time on which all her observations for the calculation of her longitude depended: as in British ships, in many German this was the personal property of the master. It was little use to have two: if one then went wrong, who knew which was right? They were comparatively large, delicate (though not unduly so), demanding proper care. A battery of three was the useful minimum, really: but a serving master's salary would not run to that kind of investment. In British ships and some others, he had to provide the charts too and, in some, even an aneroid barometer. This was long before the days of radio checks, and the ships made long passages from departure to landfall (which could be accurately fixed by bearings) usually without the chance to check their calculated positions by any other useful land fix at all. This was especially so in the vicinity of the Horn. A glimpse of Staten Island (Isla de los Estados) or the black outline of the sullen Horn seen briefly through snow squalls, perhaps the rock-fanged islets of Diego Ramirez—that was about it, between the Channel and Chile. Masters who saw none of these were not worried by the loss, for the three of them caused wrecks enough and were best avoided.

With no reliable means of finding her longitude and not knowing that, the *Susanna* worked to wind'ard in that most savage winter at least five hundred miles farther than she need have done, losing two months or more in the process. No one had sailed into the ghastly waters she traversed that passage, far to wind'ard of the Horn and all south Chile, since that great seaman Captain James Cook had sailed his little *Endeavour* there in early 1769, looking by order for the mythical Terra Australis. Cook was there in summer, his ship a snug, sea-kindly bark (actually, a small full-rigged ship) in excellent sailing trim—a very different proposition from a deeply laden modern iron square-rigger, gambling on her strength, defiant of the gale as long as she dared to be, manned by a minimal (though often excellent) crew. By comparison, the *Endeavour* had men enough to eat her. Her boats could tow her. Her great anchors had immense holding power and could be quickly ready for use. Cook could dodge into odd little anchorages around Staten Island and the southern coast of Tierra del Fuego, and did. He hadn't a cargo to deliver, money to earn.

So the slowly increasing error in the *Susanna*'s one chronometer went unchecked, though not unsuspected.

In the ship, serving as deck boy on his first deepwater voyage, was a lad named Hermann Piening, later to become an outstanding Cape Horn shipmaster in the last of the big "P" ships of Hamburg, to command the four-masted barks *Peking* and *Padua* on many splendid voyages and to rise to be marine superintendent of the company. I knew Piening well, by reputation at first and then, after 1931 (when I helped to buy the "P" four-master *Parma* from Laeisz in Hamburg) personally. He was a kindly man, lean, very blond, strong-featured with hard sea-blue eyes which could twinkle quickly. He *looked* what he was (as Learmont, Fearon, Hilgendorf, Nelson, and de Cloux all did, though many quite outstanding masters did not, unless roused).

He told me about those ninety-nine days in the *Susanna.*

"Of course, as the 'Moses' (youngest lad) aboard that voyage, I hadn't any idea at the time that this was really quite abnormal. I thought it must be the regular thing, and how sailors could stand it—and cheerfully sign on for it again and again as they did—I couldn't understand," he told me in his home at Bahrenfeld, near Hamburg. "I learned years later that an error in the chronometer had caused Captain Jürgens to make several hundred miles more westing than there was need to do. He and the mates thought there could be something wrong with the navigation, as they knew the ship was making better westing than the positions worked from data in their observations showed. They thought there must be abnormal sets and they took no chances. If the Greenwich time aboard was wrong, it didn't matter what else was right: the result couldn't be.

"The second mate had his navigation books with him and his workbooks from school. So they looked up Lunars—you know, the method Captain Cook worked out so well, of using the moon and certain stars to get a position, regardless of the chronometer—and whenever there was a chance, they worked out some of these. But there were few chances. It isn't easy to get good Lunar data in a constant zone of severe storm (like winter off the north of Scotland or off the Horn). When they did get workable Lunar data, the results showed the ship to be considerably further to the west than the data based on chronometer time ever showed.

"But they weren't sure. They didn't get that many sights. They were rusty on Lunars. Captain Jürgens was a very careful man. So he'd plug on to the west'ard another week: like as not, during that time an absolute rip-snorter would drive us east again. And so it went, on and on and on. It would be quite fatal to make northing if the Lunars *were* wrong. We'd be flung on the rocks of Patagonia and there wouldn't be a piece of mangled iron left recognisable.

"He found the Lunars were right, for certain, only when we'd at last stood up to the nor'ard to make for Caleta Buena, turned east on about its latitude to run in for it, and it wasn't there! Those Andes in Chile, with their splendid grandeur against the clear sky especially at dawn and sunset, were the first land seen by outward-bounders, and I looked forward to a sight of them. I'd heard of Chilean earthquakes, but it must have been a mighty earthquake that shook them down altogether for hundreds of miles! I began to get real worried about them. They just seemed to be gone.

"We sailed 400 miles due east before we saw them, and a hundred more miles after that before we were near our destination. Everyone was astonished. I knew this was unusual. The weather had been so beautiful over the last few weeks of the passage that I didn't care. I was all right again. The ship was all right. We hadn't lost anybody. We'd been a long time—yes. But I figured that, after that voyage, Cape Horn could never do a thing to me again. Except kill me, of course: but that's final. I determined that when I got to navigation school, I'd learn all I could about Lunars!"

The boy Piening had in fact been seriously injured in one of the many extra blows the *Susanna* suffered in the vicinity of the Horn.

"The *Susanna* was a tough ship of the old style," he said. "Everything was still operated according to the approved 'Armstrong patent'; that is, strong arms must take the place of all mechanical aids. The least loved job for me at any rate was to hold the halliard-end when the upper topgallant sails were set by the capstan, as they were in bad weather. There one sat with the thick topgallant halliard runner in his fist, squatting on the deck near the capstan, around which the others were running like circus horses. It was wet and cold and it could be dangerous. If then the sea came over the rail with a real breaker, your watch mates could high-jump out of it. You just had to stay and hang on! Like iron, one clung to the halliard. The entire icy flood washed over one; and I was happy if, half-strangled, I could just stretch my head above the gurgling water in order to spit out the salty stuff from mouth and nose. Meanwhile you didn't just hang on for life to the end, but held on to the whole coil as well to prevent it being washed overboard through the scuppers and whipped away. If it did that, it took the whole watch to get it back. And always the cold! Fingers benumbed, oilskins leaking, both wrists and the skin of the neck rubbed raw by the constant chafing of the hard oilskin, the hands split at the knuckles in deep, bloody cracks. The sea salt ate the wounds deeper. After setting the sails, watch mates seek the job of overhauling the gear aloft. Even if the ice-cold storm bites through to the skin, a man is not washed into the scuppers and drenched every three minutes up there.

"All this work does not go on without injuries and some bone-breaking. One day I had started to take the coffee kettles to the galley, just as the command, 'Weather main brace!' rang out. I had just stepped out of the shelter of our deckhouse when a big sea came over the lee bulwarks. Before I could get hold of the life line, the heaving mass washed me away with both my kettles. I couldn't stand. A violent roll sent me pitching just as the mass of water lifted up one of the heavy spare spars which were lashed by chains along the deck. The water flung me across the deck, still clinging to these precious kettles, with both legs stuck out in front, and rammed me like a wedge under the spar while it was lifted. Then it slipped back a bit, jamming me there. I lay helpless, locked fast with feet of sea above me. I was sure I would drown. I twisted and tugged; then I felt the spar settle back suddenly along its whole length. A frantic pain burned through my legs. The thought flashed through me: now your good bones are done for forever. Then everything went black.

"Fortunately, Captain Jürgens had seen the accident from

the poop. I could have been drowned under the spar. All hands rushed to me, my comrades, and worked themselves through the roaring water to where they knew I must be lying. Ignoring their own danger, they dived into the icy flood, seized me, and tried to pull me out. No use: the spar held me down. They had to work all together as the ship rolled violently to lift the spar with crowbars and capstan bars: then they pulled me out of my heavy leather boots. Whether it was still worthwhile, no one knew. I lay in the arms of my companions without a sign of life as they carried me to my berth. They told me I still held those kettles! They were full of sea by then. They had to prise them out of my hands. I must have absorbed the lesson that ship's gear was precious and irreplaceable at sea.

"I absorbed a few other lessons pinned underneath that spar. The next thing I was conscious of was lying on the deck of the quarters—alone. From the deck outside came the roaring of the wind and the crash and smash of heavy seas. The *Susanna* was rolling madly. She had thrown me out of my berth. My companions were still at the braces. Sea washed over the deck of the quarters, too: but overpowering joy flooded through me. I staggered semi-conscious to my feet. I felt crushed, half-drowned, and every bone in my body hurt; but my legs would still hold me up! I guess it was sailor's luck."

No one else was injured.

Both the *Susanna*'s and the *British Isles*'s passages that '05 winter were lengthy, the big limejuicer's slightly faster (if that is the word to use). But there was no bill for repairs aboard the *Susanna* and nobody landed in the hospital. She sailed again in due course with the same crew, the better team for the experiences they had shared.

The *Susanna* in 1905 was one of some 240 large German square-rigged ships (of 1,000 tons and more: I make the count 238) then in deepwater trades. The count is made from the eighteen closely set, double-columned large pages of such ships listed under "Sailing Vessels" in *Lloyd's Weekly Shipping Index* for September 7, 1905, which deals almost entirely with commissioned ships making voyages or necessarily in port loading or discharging cargoes, waiting for orders, or temporarily in distress. Of the 238 German ships listed, at any one time that year at least two-thirds were on Cape Horn voyages. Of these, the *Susanna*'s is the longest passage, and the *Pitlochry* is the only ship which was driven away. A serious partial dismasting sent that "P" ship back to Montevideo from the Horn battleground, forcing her to break off temporarily a passage from Hamburg toward Talcahuano. She left Hamburg June 25, 1905, was at Montevideo (under such rig as the gales had left to her) on October 6. It was owner's instructions to make for Montevideo and not for the expensive Falkland Islands, if any of his ships were driven from the Horn (which was rare).

The *Pitlochry* waited for new masts and spars sent out by German liner from Hamburg while her people got everything ready to ship them smartly when they came. She was not delayed for long: the second time she took the Horn in her stride, and continued to do so for the rest of her working life, which lasted until 1913 when a steamer knocked her down in the English Channel. Her masters always seemed to like the *Pitlochry,* which was a steel four-masted bark of over 3,000 tons register, 319 feet long by 45.2 feet in beam, built in 1894 by the famous Scots firm of Stephen and Sons of Dundee. She was noted as a particularly responsive ship to sail—"If there was a perfect ship it was she," said Robert Miethe, her most famous master—but a Cape Horn squall of that ship-destroying winter of '05 whipped half the masts out of her, just the same.

At that, the *Pitlochry* was fortunate. She lost no one. Miraculously, the falling upper masts and yards mostly went clear, doing only minor deck damage. When steel ships like that were suddenly dismasted—it was never a slow accident—the very strength of the steel masts and the iron wire stays holding them to the ship's side made them the greater menace. A ship in a Cape Horn sea—or in any other bad conditions—didn't just shed its rigging gently, and stop. All hell broke loose. The wind roared. The sea screamed, and the great rollers rushing at the ship broke over her as if she were a half-tide rock. Thank God for the *Pitlochry's* stout Scots construction! And the great 'midships "island"—that so-called scorned "Liverpool house"—built into the strong hull which broke the sea's vicious onslaught, leaving only the much shorter well decks for'ard and abaft the "house" to be overswept.

The ship rolled, lurched, pitched, flung herself about in the sea, and the twisted torment of the tangled rigging was flung with her, at her, flailing at her sides, clinging to her with mad, inescapable embrace while her crew, led by the mates, worked desperately at heavy rigging screws or with hacksaws on the wire—sledgehammers, chisels, crowbars, anything—to rid her of the destructive tangle before it smashed plates, started rivets, or pulled her over on her beam ends. Out of control, the ship wallowed in the trough of the sea, her motive power reduced to a force for her own destruction. Seamen's sure foothold on deck and aloft was made possible by long familiarity with the rhythm of their ship's motion. Now that was at an end. No one could walk anywhere: they could just hang on.

It took days to clear the *Pitlochry*'s flung-down rigging, saving what could be saved to get her manageable before the wind again to sail back, lame duck as she was, to the roads at Montevideo, avoiding the salvage vultures, the wreck-makers, the horde of "helpful" lip-licking land-bound cads always ready to add harassment to ships in trouble, to make lesser difficulties greater and profit from all.

There is a brief but interesting description of a dismasting (and a rescue) off the Horn that winter in the official log of the ship *Garsdale,* 1,755 tons, of Liverpool, which was abandoned off the Horn after losing her rigging that year. The *Garsdale,* Captain W. J. King (his certificate was Canadian), sailed from Tyne Dock, South Shields, on June 22, 1905, and was still off the Horn when abandoned nearly five months later. She had already had an eighteen-year-old ordinary seaman swept from the jibboom.

"Heard a splash: saw a cap floating, then 2 hands appear," states the log.

It was impossible to launch a boat. The lad's effects (which included "8 neckties, 1 housewife, 6 Xmas cards, 1 dictionary and navigation books"—unusual items for an ordinary seaman, though there were many intelligent lads who refused to accept the exploited life of the indentured apprentice and preferred the forecastle) were left in the ship when she was abandoned "as no one saved anything except what they had on."

As for the dismasting which caused the abandonment, this began with a "strong westerly gale with high sea, vessel under main lower tops'l and rolling very heavily." The main backstays started to go. "Called all hands" (the crew had been twenty-nine) "but the mainmast went by the board while trying to wear ship: also brought down part mizzen and foremasts, breaking the higher yards. Broke the main pump. In a few moments the fore-mast went by the board, smashing the for'ard boats. Started cutting and clearing away the wreckage to keep it from making a hole in the ship's hull. Sounded: found no water in the hold. Covered stumps of masts and secured the mizzen mast to best advantage. Continued to try to save ship. The cargo shifted. One of the after boats" (the ship's two lifeboats were carried on skids aft, one each side) "smashed by sea, leaving one only."

The following day, the wild weather continuing and the ship "rolling and lurching heavily," spoke the Italian ship *Ascensione*— at the time there were at least three hundred Italian square-rigged ships in commission, many of them former Britishers but some built in Italy—and asked him to stand by, as the *Garsdale* would have to be abandoned. Through the rest of that day the *Ascensione* remained in company, a difficult thing to do, waiting for wind and sea to go down. In the morning the weather was as bad as ever, and the Italian had been driven away. Visibility was about two miles. The following day was better: Captain King got a sea anchor rigged, and the lame duck lay to that a little more easily. Two days later, the Dunkirk ship *Berangere* (a giant three-master of 2,850 tons) came along—King calls her *Berengere:* spelling is not his strong point) and stood by.

"We could not launch our last boat on account of the rolling of the ship. A boat from the Frenchman could not get close enough for us to get into it." (And no wonder—in that sea!) "Only thing to do was to jump overboard and trust to being picked up. Decided first to launch our boat." So they swung the boat out with nine in it but it was stove in before it could get away from the ship's side. The French boat picked up fourteen of these and took them to the *Berangere*. The five left were Captain King and four of the crew. The boat came back and saved the lot, hauling the master as the last, in a bowline.

The entry is signed by W. J. King, master, and S. Forrest, mate: the log was turned in at the Mercantile Marine Office in Greenock on November 20, 1905, and is one of those I saw at Hayes.

How the twenty-nine crew shrank to nineteen is not said. Only one death is recorded, though three A.B.'s had failed to join at South Shields. This should have left twenty-five. Captain King's reckoning must be correct somehow, as it is not queried by the Mercantile Marine superintendent at Greenock.

The flight from the wet battlefield of Cape Horn that bitter winter, with its forever snarling storms and never-ending onslaught of the sea, was on a scale almost unprecedented, though even then the great majority of the fighting ships successfully made the wind'ard rounding with only minor wounds. A good many of the best had no casualties and scarcely noticed the fight at all—like Learmont's *Brenda,* the beautiful big French ships with their hardy Breton crews, the great Flying "P" liners *Preussen* and *Potosi* and the rest.

The *Pengwern* and the bark *Penrhyn Castle** (neither had any connection with the Hamburg "P" ships: they were limejuicers) both ran back to Montevideo. The *Pengwern* (Captain Jones), a ship of 1,492 tons, on passage from Rotterdam towards Coquimbo, in Chile, put back to Montevideo in distress from the Horn, according to a telegram to Lloyd's. She probably lost no lives, as no official log is filed for her from that voyage. The *Penrhyn Castle,* a smallish bark of no particular distinction, was bound from Northwest Europe toward Antofagasta, Chile, with a heavy cargo which had been very badly loaded. This caused the main t'gallant mast to come down in the northeast trades, a poor omen for the handicapped bark's performance off the Horn. Despite a new t'gallant mast, she proved so "stiff" and

* See the case history in *The Last of the Cape Horners.*

A bad landfall was final.

Bad landfall—had the Master corrected his charts? Published by permission of the Trustees of the National Maritime Museum.

Beating off the Horn

thoroughly bitchy there as to be unmanageable, and the whole "crowd," after doing their best and getting nowhere for some weeks, marched aft and requested that the *Penrhyn Castle* be turned around and run for Montevideo forthwith. She had heavy damage on deck and aloft.

The crew were right: to keep so handicapped a vessel trying to work to wind'ard down there would very likely have been fatal. Her cargo included railway iron, barrels of cement, mooring chains, anchors, machinery, bags of nuts and bolts, all slung in anyway more or less anywhere, with no proper regard to sailing trim or stability. This was a field in which some masters were somewhat ignorant: they had to be expert at stowing their own ship. If they were not, or took insufficient interest, she suffered and so did everybody aboard.

So back to Montevideo the old bark slunk. The cargo was properly stowed at last, the rigging repaired, and off she sailed from the Plate to Antofagasta in forty-seven days, which was very good going. A previous master had amused himself by catching albatrosses in calms and letting his pet dog worry them to death. This behavior so upset his crew that they lay aft to protest and one of the apprentice lads, who was working aloft, so far forgot himself as to shout down at his captain in forthright English. For this he was kept at the masthead the rest of the watch, in frigid weather, and became so incapable from the cold that he fell overboard in his heavy clothes and was lost soon afterward.

That master was relieved of his command the moment the bark reached a port in Europe. The hardworking bark, after too many misadventures, went missing in 1915 on a passage toward Australia.

The crew who compelled the master of the *Penrhyn Castle* to turn away from Cape Horn, though technically exposing themselves to a charge of mutiny which was never brought, were probably more sensible than their master. Another vessel which turned back because of her crew was the four-masted bark *Gunford,* but this was a different story, made all too clear from too many entries in the official log. Messages to Lloyd's from Punta

Arenas report the *Gunford,* on a passage from Port Talbot toward Iquique which began on June 16, 1905, as putting in at the Falklands in October that year, with steering gear disabled, and "refractory crew."

Like the *Penrhyn Castle,* this *Gunford* seems something of a dog with a bad name. She had then recently completed a round voyage to San Francisco which had brought her to the notice of Lloyd's underwriters when she was thrown on her beam ends in an Atlantic gale. "Everything moveable" (which might not be much but could include her boats, spare spars, chicken coops— if any—and harness casks) was swept overboard. The "main tops'l sheets were let go, but she did not recover until the squall was over." Her cargo shifted, giving her a bad list, and some cargo had to be jettisoned "from the sail-room and the lazarette hatches," as the principal hatches were under water. She had a general cargo (in 1905 it was still a tremendous haul for steamships to make San Francisco from Europe) which included, as usual, a good consignment of Scotch whisky, kept aft to be under better surveillance. Some of this would be "jettisoned," doubtless.

The following voyage was to Iquique, and here we sail on a well-documented passage. The official log, since it records the death of a forty-eight-year-old Welsh steward named Charles Davies in hospital at Iquique (of chronic anemia), is preserved. The voyage began with a coastal passage to Port Talbot from Liverpool on May 4, 1905, to load coal for Iquique. Leaving the South Wales port on June 15, the *Gunford* did not reach Chile until over six months later, having been delayed off the Horn and by diverting to Port Stanley in the Falkland Islands. The *Gunford* was a Scots ship of a little over 2,000 tons, handy enough. She set out commanded by one John Watt, but Arthur Gomm took over at Port Talbot. Before she left her loading port, the usual crew difficulties and desertions, so rife at the time, had caused trouble. Seamen who signed in these Cape Horning limejuicers seem to have included some of the bloodiest-minded mariners on earth, but there is more than a suspicion that some masters, and fewer mates, helped to make them so. Men signed on and "failed to join" so frequently that many ships carried rubber stamps to indicate both "failed-to-joins" and deserters on their overlong crew lists. It is odd that British ships, then among the most government-regulated at sea, were the worst for crew trouble—endless in many ships, destructive, often apparently pointless. The crews included many foreigners but, though often blamed, these do not appear as the principal troublemakers. One wonders what they were doing, signing in British ships: but the sailor was a hopeful type. He had to be.

American big square-riggers had a far worse name (the big schooners were all right) but that was for hazing, a deliberate and well-documented policy of driving seamen out of ships.* Some of the British just seem to have been mean—utterly, intentionally, and sometimes dishonestly mean—with the food above all, for master's profit, not owners' (owners did not want discontented crews). There was a wretched pound and pint allowance, called the "whack," and often not properly issued. Once a deep-sea sailing ship left port, she and her people were on their own, the most thoroughly inward-turning entity on the face of the sea and earth.

The Merchant Shipping Act, meant among other things to protect seamen (who needed the protection), too often sheltered the misdeeds of bad masters who didn't—not against their seamen anyway. More on this subject later, as the evidence unfolds.

Whatever was the state of affairs aboard the *Gunford* that voyage, she had not got very far before Captain Gomm began his lamentations in the log. There are "refusals of duty": four men in the mate's watch are "playing sick," with Cape Horn fever. Down toward the Horn passage, things get worse, much worse. Master and crew are at loggerheads, which is a fool way to be. One would suspect it is also culpable. (Show me a bad crew and I will look first for a bad master.) Refusals of duty under the challenge of a west'ard winter's rounding were unheard of in well-run, well-found ships. The contented seaman could take a lot, and go on taking it.

---

* See the *Red Record,* a file kept by the early seamen's union on proven cases of brutality against seamen.

By the 11th of September, on latitude 55° S., longitude 64° W., Captain Gomm records his masterpiece.

Owing to the dastardly way the crew are behaving, laying up with no complaint but cold feet and hands (sometimes ten men off at a time), I decided to run for the Falklands for *justice:* also I feared that the few men who were loyal to the ship would soon give out.

This is signed by "Arthur W. E. Gomm, Master, James Stewart, 1st Mate, and Geo. M. Stevenson, 2nd Mate."

Back in distress for *justice?* This is astonishing, unique, and inexcusable. Indeed it comes near to being the most amazing entry in any of the official logs I saw at Hayes—hundreds of them.

"That man who sails a Cape Horn ship must be the *leader* of his men, and be seen to be their leader," as that great seaman Robert Miethe said. He will lead no one scribbling feebly in logs. Such stuff is the weak man's excuse to himself for his own inadequacy.

The ship is turned around: but the weather improves and the wind fairs. (There never is any mention of steering difficulty.) Gomm swings her back again, to head for the Horn. By this time it is the end of September. The rascally crew give trouble again. (None of their complaints, which could well have been genuine, are listed or mentioned as dealt with.) A couple of lower tops'ls blow out, while "the men huddled together under the foc's'l-head and would not assist." A day or two later, that ink-drunk pen is at it again. "I have now been one month drifting between the Falklands and 60° S. owing to not being able to make or shorten sail . . . I must put back, hoping to get the four ringleaders punished."

This was on September 30, 1905. Nine days later, the ill-run *Gunford* is at Port Stanley. Here one man was found to have rheumatic fever, and one was sent home D.B.S. (as a distressed British subject), but what other "justice" might have been dispensed the log does not say. Nobody says. According to the log, the four ringleaders were still "playing sick" at Port Stanley a month later. On December 16, the *Gunford* back at sea—it was summer then—the log records more crew difficulties. By January 25, 1906, she is at Iquique, and now the mate (according to Gomm) joins the troublemakers or at any rate starts something on his own account. As a certificated officer, he is brought before the British consul and (according to the log at any rate) reprimanded.

More important, perhaps, some justice seems at last to catch up with the unnecessarily harassed *Gunford*. Captain Gomm is fired. One Captain J. Sinclair takes over. The *Gunford* sails from Iquique on April 5, 1906, in ballast for Sydney for orders, is there seventy-four days later, goes up to Newcastle, loads coal for Valparaiso, runs there in forty-five days, arriving on November 5. The usual range of Chilean ports to discharge coal and load nitrates precedes her sailing from Caleta Buena on April 7, 1907, to reach Plymouth (another orders port like Falmouth and Queenstown where sailing ships touched to find where to deliver their cargoes, probably sold and resold while they were on passage) after ninety days. Ordered to Rotterdam, she was there a few days later and the last remnants of the dastardly crew dispersed.

In fact, there were few if any left by that time. She had been over two years on what should have been a straightforward voyage, and the turnover on her crew list adds up to eighty-four.

The poor *Gunford* is back in the news a year or so later, again somewhat disgracefully. The headline "TERRIBLE TALE OF THE SEA" caught my eye, reading through Lloyd's list summaries quietly one morning in the National Maritime Museum at Greenwich, near London. (They have everything there, and a place to sit down, too.) "Loss of the Barque *GUNFORD*" is the subhead. What, Arthur Gomm on the job again? I wonder. But it is not Gomm this time, though perhaps an equally transparent master.

I read, slowly. The *Gunford*, it appears, has been outward bound for the Horn again on passage from Hamburg toward Santa Rosalia in Mexico, a long passage but straightforward. It meant a fight to wind'ard off the Horn, of course, but the *Gunford* didn't get that far. Instead, she had hit the coast of Brazil not once but three times, and finally stayed there. The "terrible tale" concerned a group of "Brazilian pirates" who had boarded the four-master there and looted her. The Gomm successor, it seemed, had made a job of it this time. Looted her? That would take care very nicely of her log and so forth. I wonder who had cheered those "pirates" on, for the coast around there is inhabited by quiet fishermen who go out from the beach in their frail balsa-wood sailing rafts called *jangadas*.

The news item in Lloyd's reported that the *Gunford* had managed to get herself embayed behind Cape San Roque on the easterly bulge of Brazil—a fool thing to do and quite an achievement for a weatherly, deep-loaded ship which had only the southeast trade winds of the Atlantic to cope with after crossing the line. Lesser luminaries of the sailing-ship masters' profession, through the slovenly sailing of some brutish, left-handed product of an inferior shipyard or their own incompetence, did from time to time manage their passage of the doldrums and the trades so badly as to find themselves near-jammed on that bulge of Brazil, and had to beat off again. Those I heard of were in ballast, bound out to Australia, and they got away all right, their masters sheepishly talking about the strange strength of the currents setting west, long spells in the doldrums, or too much southing in the southeast trades which, taken on the port tack, pushed them from their course. But hit Brazil, and stay there? That really took an effort. They had only to fix the ship's position—and in that zone of good weather the old-fashioned drill of morning-sight-for-longitude and noon-sight-for-latitude would do—keep their eyes open, note the crossing of the 100-fathom line (well offshore thereabouts), or take a few soundings, to know very well they had come too far.

Being deep-loaded, the *Gunford* had the better grip of the water and should have made the better wind'ard course. Any properly handled, well-balanced square-rigged ship should make good a course within six and a half points or so of the wind in the southeast trades (or northeast), and the northeast for the outward-bounder were a fair wind allowing her to cross the doldrums belt more or less where she wished. There was no real danger of hitting Brazil and no need to take the risk of doing any such stupid thing. Of course, there was skill in crossing the doldrums belt. It was sense to cross, usually, about midway between the bulge of West Africa and the coast of Brazil. The currents set toward the west, and it was unwise to stay in the area too long— not only for that reason. By that stage in the sailing-ship era— the first decade of the twentieth century—there was plenty of data on all this, or should have been. There certainly were excellent German directions and American, though the British Hydrographic Office never did bother much about the finer points of sailing-ship long-voyage passage making. It published some very general directions and left it at that. (After all, the steamship developed in Britain, both for peace and war: the British were the first to give up sail-training for naval officers when they tossed out the priceless asset of their squadron of splendid training brigs round 1900. It seems to the unbiased observer that a high price was paid. It wasn't what the smart brigs did for seamen vocationally that mattered: it was the effect of the best of that challenging life on seamen's *minds*.)

Well, there the *Gunford* was, well and truly ashore, wrecked, "pirated," looted, and soon abandoned, for her master (one Sember) had put his crew in one of the lifeboats and sailed along the quiet coastal waters to the little port of Macao in the northeastern province of Rio Grande do Norte. From here they made their way—in time, and hit by yellow fever—to the larger port now called Recife, then Pernambuco. Here, in due course, they took ship back for the U.K. Ten of the crew died of the fever in Brazil.

In due course, an official inquiry was held into the wreck, at Caxton Hall, Westminster, in London, a somewhat unmaritime spot but with the full dignity—and ability—of the law about it. Soon the learned gentleman sitting as judge (aided by two nautical assessors, both sail-qualified old master mariners, the sort who knew their way across the doldrums and round Westminster too) was finding out things. First, the navigation. Captain A. W. Sember was navigating on the usual big chart of the South Atlantic, the so-called "Blue Back" (it had a blue linen back guaranteed to hold it together for a century or so and was therefore economical). This showed the Brazilian coast much as Cabral had known it: no matter, the use of such charts was common practice though regrettable, and the *Gunford* had not been bound for Brazil. There were few marks on this chart, very few positions for astronomical fixes made in the *Gunford*. Perhaps Captain Sember valued his chart so much—it *was* his: he'd had to pay for it many years earlier—that he disliked marking it. (He had others for the South and North Pacific: they would have got him to Santa Rosalia, with luck.) Fixes by bearings? No evidence of these anywhere. Sight of land? Soundings? No log. *No* log? (The assessors looked grave.) Yes, there was the deck log: but the vital pages were torn out. (Useful fellows at times, "pirates.") A slight stir at this: some searching questions. Why only these pages?

They might have been loose and dropped out in the lifeboat.

Only those pages? (One of the assessors showed his disbelief.)

The ship had been looted. The natives were hostile. He had to look after his crew, said the captain.

Reasonable enough, perhaps. But there were many more questions.

Why, for instance, had he hit the coast three times?

She began to make water after the first time, then floated off, her captain explained. She had a heavy cargo. He had to put her aground again to save her. He had to try twice. The crew demanded that he put into a nearby port, after she floated off, because of the leak. He closed the coast to try to make a port. The second time she touched on a bank, well off shore. The third time a sounding showed nine fathoms just before she struck. She was under all sail then, making eight or nine knots. She did not come off. When she was abandoned, the hull was full of water. It was here the pirates came.

But why under all sail, in waters he had learned had a habit of throwing up "banks" to grasp ships?

He was keeping good way on her, he explained, intending to tack-ship quickly if the soundings showed shoaling, but she was hard and fast before they did. The ship was then eight or twelve miles off shore.

Why had he allowed the ship to get so close to the coast in the first place? And why had he crossed the Line on 29° W.?

Captain Sember blamed this on "the extraordinary state of the currents which were difficult for a deepsea sailor to understand," and "some bad steering on the part of the crew." He added that these (all Germans and Danes) "understood English when they liked."

It might have occurred to the court that whatever the master and his sailors might or might not have understood, the master could scarcely have made better use of the currents if his intention had been to lose the ship. As for the Hamburg crew's "bad steering," it would take a great deal of atrocious helmsmanship *and* bad watch-keeping to allow the *Gunford* to get so far off course. There were no better seamen than a crowd of Germans and Scandinavians, signed in the great sailing-ship port of Hamburg. None was present to speak for himself. After all, ten were dead.

Had the captain not lost the bark *Perthshire* in 1885?

He had. At the subsequent inquiry, he was found to blame. His certificate of competency as master was suspended. He had not been to sea in the interval. In the *Gunford* he, the two mates, and one ship's boy were the only Britishers.

Francis Briggs, of Glasgow, the ship's registered manager, said that he did not know that Captain Sember had been so long ashore. He admitted that an underwriter, inquiring about him, expressed dissatisfaction and would write no more insurance on the ship.* It appeared, however, that she was more than amply covered. Mr. Briggs said she had cost £20,750 to build and was still valued at that sum when lost. The insurances on her on the

---

* In the days of sailing ships, Lloyd's kept files on masters as a help in trying to figure risks. A sailing ship was very much in the hands of her master, and a voyage was a highly individual business. Masters who grounded ships, dismasted them and failed to cope, or who showed excess of zeal in seeking distress ports, cost their owners more for subsequent insurance. In those days, too, underwriters knew that masters stayed in ships sometimes for very long periods, for they had no rotation of appointments, no assurance of leave, and very often also no homes. It was possible to build up useful files on them. This was done not only for British masters.

last passage totaled £35,800, including the freights she would earn on the whole voyage (not just the gross on the Santa Rosalia cargo of coke and patent fuel for the smelter there), the necessary disbursements to earn the freights, an additional £6,500 which Briggs said he had advanced personally on the ship to keep the company going, £200 for the master's effects, and so forth. The list was as follows:

Insurance on the hull	£18,500
Insurance on the freight	5,500
Insurance on the disbursements	4,600
Insurance on the master's effects	200
Hull additional, replacing sum previously insured in a mutual society	500
Manager's personal	6,500
Total	£35,800

The ship's actual value when beginning the voyage was £9,000. She had made no profit for the preceding seven years. (Gomm could have helped with this.) Briggs said he had spent £1,615 on her, making good voyage damages, since 1905.

There were some searching questions about all this insurance, which certainly appeared to make the *Gunford* a better proposition on the beach of Brazil than battling down the South Atlantic to take on the Horn.

The court rose.

It did not take long to deliver judgment. The *Gunford*, it found, had been navigated in a grossly negligent manner. She was overinsured. There was no proper explanation for a missing page from the log. The master's certificate was suspended for twelve months, and he was refused a mate's licence for the interval. It seems improbable that the loss bothered him greatly. After all, ten seamen would never be able to deny the miserable charge he had made, that their "bad steering" had helped to put a good ship ashore. A considerable sum of money had been paid over. (That £35,800 would be worth £200,000 today.) Such losses increased the rates which underwriters had to charge other ships, which managed to make their way from the Channel to the Horn without hitting Brazil.

There were "not a few suspicious circumstances about the case," as a leading article in the *Shipping Gazette Weekly Summary and Lloyd's List* pointed out on March 20, 1908. "If the charges meant anything they meant that the ship was deliberately cast away," though the court "did not take quite that view." (On what evidence they could take any other view one doesn't know.) "The navigation of the *Gunford* was deplorable. Three times did she butt into the land because her navigator had brought her too far to the west'ard. She may have been jammed by the South-east Trades, but a prudent navigator would have known that was one of the risks in crossing the Equator on 29° W. She was on a voyage from Hamburg towards Santa Rosalia, but his trouble seemed to be to get down the South Atlantic without bumping into the coast of Brazil."

Trouble?

His success would appear to be in getting away with making so good a job of it.

Poor *Gunford!* Something of her was still there when I sailed down that way on passage from New York toward Rio early in 1935. After Sember, Gomm, Briggs and company, perhaps she deserved a long rest. I had chosen to go that way in the *Joseph Conrad,* and had no difficulty sailing happily along in glorious weather within sight of the beach, among the pretty *jangadas* skimming in from sea, their "pirates" waving cheerfully as we passed.

NOTE: HITTING THE COAST OF BRAZIL WAS NOT SO UNUSUAL AN ACCIDENT AS IT SHOULD PERHAPS HAVE BEEN. THE FOUR-MASTED BARK *Trafalgar* OF GLASGOW GOT ASHORE THERE IN THE SOUTHEAST TRADES WHILE ON PASSAGE FROM SYDNEY TOWARD FAL-MOUTH FOR ORDERS IN 1905, AND BECAME A TOTAL LOSS. THIS SEEMS INEXCUSABLE: THERE WAS AN INQUIRY, OF COURSE, AND THE MASTER'S CERTIFICATE WAS SUSPENDED. THE TROUBLE WITH THE MASTER OF THE *Gunford* WAS THAT HE WOULD NOT LEAVE BRAZIL ALONE. MANY LONG-VOYAGE MASTERS SEEM TO HAVE BEEN PERHAPS EXCES-SIVELY CASUAL IN BOTH THEIR PILOTAGE AND NAVIGATION. WHEN THE SHIP *Clan Robertson* GOT HERSELF AGROUND IN THE GULF OF SAINT VINCENT, SUBSEQUENT IN-QUIRY ESTABLISHED THAT HER COMPASSES HAD NOT BEEN ADJUSTED FOR THE PRECED-ING *nine years.*

THE SHIP WAS THEN DETAINED UNTIL THIS WAS DONE. AS FOR CHART OR LIGHT LIST AMENDMENTS AND CORRECTIONS, NONE HAD EVER BEEN DONE SINCE THE MASTER'S MINIMUM OUTFIT WAS BOUGHT, PERHAPS TWENTY YEARS BEFORE. SOME OF THE OLD BOYS MUST HAVE BEEN WONDERFUL OPTIMISTS. THEY CHEERFULLY (AND CARELESSLY) TOOK ON TRANSPACIFIC VOYAGE AFTER VOYAGE WITH THE SAME OLD UNCORRECTED "BLUE-BACK" CHART, BASED ON THE WORK OF JAMES COOK AND HIS IMMEDIATE SUCCESSORS, THOUGH THERE WERE A THOUSAND REEFS IN THE WAY OF THE WESTBOUND SHIP COMING BACK IN THE TRADE WINDS FROM CHILE AND PERU. AT LEAST WHEN THEY GOT THEIR SHIPS UP ON REEFS, THEY MARKED THEM WELL FOR THEIR SUCCESSORS. THE RUSTY GREAT HULLS OF MANY CAPE HORNERS SAT ON PACIFIC ATOLLS AND REEFS FOR TWENTY OR THIRTY YEARS, LIKE THE *County of Roxburgh* ON TOKARVA IN THE TUAMOTUS (WHERE HALF THE CREW TOOK TO THE BOATS WHEN SHE STRUCK AND WERE DROWNED: THEN SHE CHARGED RIGHT OVER THE REEF AND SAVED THE REST) AND THE BIG *Thistle* OF GREENOCK ON PALMERSTON REEF. THERE WAS THE OCCASIONAL ASS WHO, SEEING ANOTHER SHIP ANYWHERE, CONCLUDED THAT WHERE SHE WAS HE COULD GO, AND SWIFTLY WRECKED HIMSELF: BUT SUCH A DEGREE OF STUPIDITY WAS FORTUNATELY RARE.

Chapter four

MISSING!

In that dour, savage, sea-tossed struggle of the two hundred ships and their five thousand men which went on in the vicinity of the Horn practically without cessation or ever more than some fleeting easement throughout the winter of 1905, there were many casualties both of ships and men. Documented inadequately in brief messages to Lloyd's, in the official logs and the crew lists, sometimes made credible by the surviving stories of a few masters and apprentices but never of the men, the heroic accomplishment of those five thousand outcasts in their outmoded ships seems to new generations quite incredible. Why were they there at all? For they *were* outcasts, odd men opted out —or thrown out—from an odd civilization, men who preferred to stay with the ships they knew and loved despite what the ships did to them. Any of those professional seamen, except the older masters perhaps, could have gone in steam: all the apprentices (there were at least a thousand of them) did so, as essential to their professional advancement. But the tradesmen and the foremast hands were accustomed to move from one big sailing ship to another all the days of their often brief lives. They took what came. They accepted a high casualty rate, for that was the way of their sea and always had been. Drowning was a swift death and clean, they said: and a man had a rapid re-run of his brief career as the sea claimed him. At least, some said so: some who were dragged back to life from overboard almost at the last moment.

During that year of 1905, fifty-five sea-going vessels were posted missing in Britain. They sailed and they were never seen or heard of again: to be posted (announced and advertised) a missing ship was a legal finality. All hands were dead then, the ship written off. Insurance could be paid, estates wound up (if any). The last act was not undertaken lightly. First, an overdue vessel was (and still is) posted "for inquiry." Has any ship sighted her, or spoken her, or seen anyone or anything whatever identifiable of her or from her or her people? Only after long silence, after this, is she declared "missing," for the merchant vessels of the world go about their business quietly, without any blare of publicity. It is only chance or the temporary "news value" of some incident or person aboard which may bring a missing ship occasionally to wide notice—or if she be a passenger ship, or a cadet ship full of boys.

The fifty-five ships of 1905 made no headlines and rated no mention outside the small type of the shipping press. Thirty-two of them were British, four each French and German, several American, one or two Italian. Fourteen were long-voyage sailing ships from the Cape Horn trade—among them the *Eulomene, Alcinous, Glenburn, Principality, Bay of Bengal,* and *Lafayette.* Two were American four-masted schooners. Six were steamships: these could be overwhelmed too, though they rarely if ever went near Cape Horn. Winter North Atlantic was trial enough: so, indeed, was the British coast, and the Dutch and North Sea German. There had been fifty-seven ships up for inquiry at one stage, but the figurehead of the *Loch Vennachar* and some cargo that could have been hers was found washed up on Kangaroo Island in South Australia, and, after many months, the sole survivor of the Tasmanian trader, *Brier Holme,* staggered in torn rags into Hobart to announce that the little bark had been dashed to pieces on the island's west coast. In time there was a clue, too, to the possible fate of the *Bay of Bengal,* which was 210 days out from Cardiff toward Taltal before being "posted." Some wreckage found on the coast of Ireland was very like fittings known to be aboard this ship, and there was a bottle message. It could have been that she had never got going.

The silent, uncommunicative sailing ship could disappear suddenly from the face of the earth in narrow waters as well as wide, or burst her steel hull upon unyielding rocks suddenly gripping her keel to rip her apart, bounce off, and sink forever, leaving no identifiable trace. She was so secure for sea that there was nothing to float away. One of the big fourteen that year was the 2,700-ton four-masted ship *Eulomene,* built in 1891, seventeenth and last of the Fernie Line. She was being towed the short distance across the North Sea from Bremerhaven to the Tyne, to begin another long voyage. The weather was bad, with poor visibility. In a nasty squall her tug, the powerful ocean-going towboat *Polzee,* had to slip the tow line temporarily. She stood by. In due course, the squall cleared, but she could not find the tow line again, or the *Eulomene,* or a boat from her or anything whatever to show that the big sailer had ever been there. The *Eulomene* was gone forever from the face of the sea, though she had been hardly out of sight of land.

It may seem odd that a vessel which could take on Cape Horn, and often had, should be lost because she broke adrift from her tug in the North Sea. The big French four-masted bark *Alexandre* had done exactly the same thing when towing from Dunkirk to Shields a year or so before. The fact was that, on such tows, sailing ships could be much more vulnerable than on regular voyages. It was customary to carry small crews of "runners" —seamen hired at so much the job, a few pounds or so, to steer and so forth—and as the towage bill was accepted to get the ship only to a loading port (after working out that the cost of tug-plus-runners would be a lesser sum than the cost of putting full crew aboard, sailing the ship across in winter, and keeping the crew by at the loading port), it could happen that the minimum ballast was put aboard. This ballast had to be bought, and its handling in and out had to be paid for. As she was not to sail, enough for her to stand up behind her tug should suffice. The runners were good old seamen, often specialists, but they would not know the ship nor have other than a passing interest in her. The ballast (and perhaps the hatches) might not be all that well secured.

And so, in an accident, the undermanned ship could be out of luck. She could capsize: shifting ballast plus insecure hatches quickly adds up to calamity. Sailing-ship masters were not men who normally took chances, but the home base worked out the economy of these short tows and the unfortunate master of the *Eulomene* was not there to spend more of his owner's money than the owner's view of enough. That run, Captain W. L. Thomas had his wife and children aboard. He had faith in his ship, though it was the depth of winter.

There were official inquiries into all cases of British missing ships. What was lacking was evidence. The court could only satisfy itself that the ship had gone to sea properly loaded, equipped, and manned, and in seaworthy condition. There was an astonishing number of such cases. A White Paper prepared for the House of Lords in July, 1909, and presented by Lord Muskerry,* pointed out that between 1904 and 1908, twenty-six of the larger British sailing ships alone—the Cape Horn type—had to be written off with all hands because they "went missing," taking with them fifty-nine young British apprentices as well as 312 able seamen, of whom 167 were British. The total tonnage of the twenty-six was 31,490 register tons.

All things considered, 1905 was not a particularly bad year for missing Cape Horners. It was a dreadful winter off the Horn and it bashed up many ships, but all they had to do was to fight back successfully and avoid the land. On the whole, it was sudden disasters (not dour fights) which wiped ships from the sea, like ice. The year 1905 was not bad for ice. Some years, for reasons not then understood (they still are not wholly comprehended, as far as I know), icebergs adrift from the Antarctic and even some pack ice littered the seas south of Diego Ramirez and Staten Island, off Tierra del Fuego, and were far too commonplace north of that, even as far north as beyond the Falkland Islands. Many bergs were reported as miles long—in 1907, for example, when six large square-rigged ships were among the twenty-nine sizable vessels then posted missing.

Five of these were known to have been trying to get past the Horn at a time when a great deal of ice was reported. Two of these were large French barks of over 2,000 tons, the *Daniel* and

* Referred to in a leading article in *Shipping Gazette Weekly Summary (S.G.W.S.)*, London, July 16, 1909.

the *Hautot.* The first was bound from Bellingham, Washington, toward Delegoa Bay, the second from New Caledonia to the Clyde with nickel ore. The master of the French bark *Chateau d'If,* when he reached port, reported that he had "met a lot of ice, in which a big sailing ship was locked." There were no signs of life aboard. He thought he recognized the vessel as the *Daniel,* which he knew. None of her crew got out of the ice: nothing, indeed, was ever seen of her again. Sailing ships that year reported seeing huge Antarctic bergs which it took hours to sail past. They were lucky enough to see them by day.

Any iceberg is bad news to any ship: but the Antarctic bergs, when they drift into the sea lanes, can be enormous and often come as large ice islands. Fortunately, as Antarctica is a land mass, it acts as a huge anchor holding down infinite areas of pack in which the bergs, large and small, spend much of their time imprisoned. It would have been better for Cape Horn ships if it had been so all their time. Being more or less a water hemisphere capped by frozen land, the southern is warmer than the northern hemisphere, which in far greater part is continental land surrounding a frozen sea. Icebergs melt more rapidly in the south, scientists tell us, but they can be mighty solid menaces to ships while they last. Fortunately, they were not so much a menace in winter as in spring and summer when the weather and visibility were both better, but they had a tendency to bring their own bad visibility with them.

The big *Fingal,* when she arrived at Victoria, B.C., on November 2, 1906, reported so much ice off the Horn and off Staten Island (Isla de los Estados) that "the ship's running gear was frozen up . . . We could see no open water, not even from the mastheads, either to the S.E. or the N.W., and we had to sail 50 miles E. to round the ice-field. We saw a full-rigged ship on the N.W. edge or in the pack. There were more icebergs off Cape Horn."

The same month the British bark *Bankburn,* at Portland, Oregon, from Hamburg, reported "large fields of ice and bergs off the Horn, with SW gales, mountainous seas, and constant snow." The *Crown of India,* at Cape Town from Pisagua, and the *Leyland*

Bros. at San Francisco, reported similar conditions. The German ships *Posen* and *Persimmon* (she counted eighty icebergs one day) and the Britishers *Inverclyde, Cumbermere,* and *Naiad* all had to sail around or through masses of ice the best way they could. Fortunately most were then homeward bound and had at least favorable winds: in the lee of the ice the sea was quieter, too. The *Clan MacPherson* reported unidentifiable wreckage on a berg, and the Norwegian bark *Smerø* was with or in ice from the Horn homeward until she reached latitude 48° 16′ S. north of the Falklands.

Some of the wreckage in the ice, or one of the ships seen stranded in it, could have been the *Ormsary,* which sailed from Caleta Caloso with nitrates for Antwerp early in November, 1906, and was never seen again. She was "probably lost in the ice," said the *Shipping Gazette Weekly Summary* in its editorial comment on May 3, 1907, pointing out that the *Ormsary* "had not been in dry-dock since 1904 and this would make her perhaps difficult to steer, a serious handicap when sailing through ice-infested seas," or any other.

Strong old sailing ships *could* sail into icebergs on occasion, and get away with it—especially iron ships. That ice of '06 seems to have taken several years to clear away. In '08, for instance, the Italian bark *Cognati* limped into Montevideo somewhat crushed about the bows, with her bowsprit at an odd angle and other signs of damage. She was in fact the tough old Britisher *Ben Voirlich:* she had sailed head-on into a large iceberg and damaged the iceberg, before she backed out and sailed away. All square-riggers had a long anticollision "prong" at their clipper bows in the shape of a substantial steel bowsprit, and the very shape of their bows also helped to fend them off. This was just as well, for abaft that the great majority had only one watertight bulkhead, the so-called collision bulkhead quite close to the bows.

The master of the *Cognati* reported that he had seen "a lot of wreckage and a lot of boats adrift in the ice," but he could not get near enough to identify anything. Reporting this, the editor adds ominously that "not far short of twelve sailing ships in the Cape Horn trade are now named in the Overdue List."

These included the big Americans *Arthur Sewall* and *Bangalore,* the Britishers *Falklandbank, Carnedd Llewelyn,* and *Toxteth,* and the German *Adolf Obrig,* none of which was ever heard of again. Rather unusually, a search was organized for possible survivors from these ships, and some search was made around the coasts of Tierra del Fuego and some of the Patagonian islands. Nothing was seen of them, though from time to time odd pieces of wreckage and even whole ships were found and, once at least, some skeletons beside a heap of mussel shells. Living castaways saved themselves, or else no one saved them.

Various ideas for removing the wall of perpetual silence which shut round all these missing vessels were put forward, usually when passengers came into it, as in the case of the 9,340-ton steamer *Waratah.** The *Waratah* vanished in 1909 with ninety-two passengers aboard off the southeast coast of Africa. Many bottle messages allegedly from this vessel came ashore in various parts of the world. A source of torment to relatives, a little investigation was enough to establish that none could be genuine. A correspondent, writing to *Lloyd's List Weekly Summary* in March 1911, from Grimsby, offered a £50 prize for the invention of an unsinkable, unbreakable bottle—a "suitable message carrier," he called it—which would bear unmistakable evidence of the ship it came from and float off when necessary. But float off to where? Nobody seems to have taken this up.

Unfortunately, any sort of ship could go missing almost anywhere. About the time of the unsinkable-bottle idea, five small sailers—the ketch *Beatrice Hannah,* and the schooners *Jessie, Victoria,* and *Lucy Johns,* which sailed from Ballinacurra in County Cork, three for Dublin, one for Southampton, and the schooner *Sappho* from Waterford for the Channel Islands—sailed on December 15, 1910, and all five went missing. There was bad weather after they sailed. It would seem that all foundered. There was a local outcry for better weather forecasts, but it sounds as if the need here was more likely for better schooners.

A better answer at least for communications had come to the notice of Lloyd's by June 1910, when the American Captain E. R.

* See Villiers, *Posted Missing* (Hodder and Stoughton, London, 1956), Ch. 9.

Sterling fitted his six-masted barkentine *Everett G. Griggs* (the former iron four-masted bark *Lord Wolseley* of 1,580 tons, which the captain was reported to have bought for $27,000, and later named for himself) with the newfangled stuff called wireless. It seemed as if this really worked, at times.

"It has often been suggested that sailing-ships should carry wireless telegraphy, but there are only two American schooners so fitted," commented Lloyd's, "the *Pendleton Sisters* and the *Dorothy B. Barrett*. The *Pendleton Sisters* has transmitted messages 250 miles and received from a much greater distance."

The *Everett Griggs,* presumably, was the third. No British sailing ship paid attention. It was another decade or so before a few began to carry battery receivers to pick up time signals to check their chronometer's idea of Greenwich time (and so improve their navigation). Few working sailing ships of any nationality ever took up Captain Sterling's innovation. The square-riggers which did were mainly big school ships. Oddly enough, two of these were among the last sailers ever to be posted missing—the big Dane *København,* a five-masted bark with sixty boys, and the German *Admiral Karpfanger*—long after the First World War. No message bearing on her fate was received from either. They went in silence like the others.

So many ships were wrecked, driven away badly damaged, or missing on Cape Horn passages that twice in the first decade of the twentieth century the proposition was seriously put forward that the route that way should be abandoned, at least for winter westward passages. The first suggestion was that there should be powerful tugs based in the Strait of Magellan to tow the big sailing ships through from the Atlantic and give them an offing at the Pacific end. This proposal was put up seriously at least by Otto Larsen, a Norwegian presumably in the towing (or possibly ocean salvage) business. In 1906, it was reported from Hamburg in the London shipping papers that Mr. Larsen proposed the establishment of a "strong tug fleet at Punta Arenas to tow sailing-ships westwards through the "Straits" of Magellan." Among other advantages—safety, and so on—such a tow should mean, it was said, a saving of "several weeks." Even if it could mean saving several months, neither owners nor masters were interested. The idea was never tried.

It was obviously impractical for many reasons. Many Cape Horn ship masters, especially in the British ships, were old-timers very set in their ancient ways, and some of these ways were bad. Since they owned their own charts, these were usually few and small-scale. Far too many rarely or never bothered to work up star sights, if competent to take them. They feared the land: to make landfall on Cape Virgins at the eastern end of the Strait of Magellan could be a hazard. To be left on a lee shore at the western end off the hungry maze of rocks and islands, toward which the west winds set up a constant drift if not an impetuous shove, could be an even greater hazard. These tugs would have to be powerful, ocean-going vessels, based where coal and other costs were high. What was their proposed scale of charges? Mr. Larsen didn't know. It would depend upon demand.

Once she was at sea, the running costs of the average lime-juice square-rigger were not high. Able seamen cost £3 a month and their primitive keep less than half that. Petty officers and mates cost a few pounds more in wages. Masters had £12. Apprentices cost nothing except their keep. Long after the First World War, it cost between 11d and 1/1 a day each to feed the crew of our four-masted bark *Parma* and they were on the basis of "sufficient without waste"—good food, not salt horse left over from Trafalgar (sailors said), and rubbishy products of the utmost inferiority produced and "whacked out" with wretched parsimony, and labeled "Crew." (Hateful label! For it meant the sweepings of warehouses, the exploitation of lost taste buds, the absence of strain upon incompetent cooks, the saving of galley fuel as there was so little worth the cooking: the practice was to prepare no evening meal.) So the running costs of a four-masted bark of 2,800 tons or so, well-manned with a total crew of thirty-two—master, two mates, bos'n, carpenter, sailmaker, steward, cook, sixteen able seamen, two ordinary seamen, six indentured apprentices, giving her a dozen in a watch (compared with the 3,000-ton *Parma*'s nine)—would not exceed £150 a month, on passage. Say £200, adding something for wear and tear of canvas and cordage, and assuming an absence of serious accident. An expensive tug which had to wait for jobs at a place like Punta Arenas and make a reasonable return on her high building and running costs would have to charge at least £100 a day. Real rip-snorters up to full storm strength can tear through that strait. Time could be lost sheltering from them, for these big square-riggers offered a lot of windage. It would have to be a fast tow to save anything on a month's sea costs.

An even more important point was that, after all, the Horn was only one of many hazards against the ocean-going sailing ship, though probably the best known to landsmen. Seamen had equal respect for what they knew as W.N.A.—Winter North Atlantic—and there was indeed a special mark on their load-line discs (called the Plimsoll line) for this, compulsorily increasing their freeboard for winter passages in the North Atlantic. (There was no special mark for winter Cape Horn.) The sea coasts of Vancouver Island, indeed the whole coasts of Oregon and Washington north of 45° latitude, including the mouth of the Columbia River, were another bad-weather zone, a death trap for many fine ships. So were the approaches to the English Channel, the Scilly Islands, and the coasts of Cornwall. Cape Horn had sea room. It was not a landfall. A master didn't have to see it, but just to get past it and keep on going for a voyage-end thousands of miles away. But if you were bound for Puget Sound, or the Channel, or the Columbia River, you *had* to come to grips with the land with some precision. Were there to be ocean tugs off all these points too? And where else? A friendly haul through the Atlantic doldrums could be a help. (It could have kept the *Gunford,* and a few others, off the coast of Brazil.)

Who knew how many ships were in fact missing in the Cape Horn area? They were all on the *qui vive* down there. God knows they could have gone missing almost anywhere. The *Bay of Bengal* was probably not the only ship, not missed for months, which had never got going on her voyage. Another ship named the *Hartfield,* missing later, gave some indication of her probable fate when a photograph of her in a picture frame cut in the form of a lifebuoy was found by a lighthouse keeper, washed up on Vancouver Island. The poor ship at her last gasp had flung her visiting card ashore.*

As for the Scillies and the coasts of Cornwall, storm-battered, tide-ripped, too often hidden in the murk of driving southwesterly gales, the ships flung themselves up here, and were swiftly ground to pieces. Small-scale charts for the North Atlantic Ocean, neglect of Light Lists, and chancey sun sights were poor prelude to Channel landfall. Inquiry into too many such losses (when there was anybody left to give evidence) showed that the masters had not bothered to keep their charts and light information up to date. The characteristics by which navigation lights should be recognized are never changed without the widest possible circulation of the new data, before the change is made. This went out in the form of "Notices to Mariners," and files of these were kept at all coastal consular offices and shipping offices. It was part of a master's duty to read these carefully and bring his charts up to date, or at least to send the second mate ashore to do the job: but too many did not. Some masters were very old, so old that they belonged to the tradition if not the days of so-called "service certificates," that is, when licenses as masters were granted to those already acting in that capacity without official qualifications at all. Many older masters of the 1890's-1910 era had served at sea with such old men, who were indeed splendid seamen, but their regard for *all* official requirements was not great, and for the bureaucrats who thought them up and tried to enforce them they had no regard at all.

Many masters relaxed ashore at agents' offices, or chandlers', where cronies assembled and the warm days could be idled pleasantly away. Landfall lights? Such things were far away,

---

* The photograph had been made in San Francisco when the *Hartfield* was there at the end of 1905 and for the first six months of 1906. An entry in her official log for this voyage, dated April 20, 1906, begins: "1.30 p.m. cast off moorings from Filbert St. wharf on account of all Frisco on fire and wharfs. Could't get regular tug: took pilot tug boat: he asked $10,000 to tow into the Bay. Refused. My decks full of refegues [*sic*] put aboard by authorities and wharfs crowded with more. Told him authorities should send a boat: tow me out and settle the towage later." This was done. The *Hartfield* had her sails unbent and couldn't sail out. There is no further reference to the $10,000. The following day the carpenter deserted. There was plenty of work for him in San Francisco then.

and so were the drizzly nights of on-shore gales that went so often with their finding. Many inquiries into losses censured masters for their carelessness in this matter, but the habit persisted. The very infrequency of landfalls in the average sailing-ship voyage made it more important that they be approached with, at the very least, all the appropriate information necessary to make them safely and correctly.

The master of the iron ship *Lismore* paid the penalty. Bound from Melbourne for Talcahuano with a wheat cargo in 1906, his Blue-Back chart of the South Pacific had been corrected up to 1904, which was not too bad as these things went. But his principal landfall light—that upon which he had most to rely for identifying his port of arrival if he arrived in the vicinity by night, as he did—had been changed early in 1905. He was off his course a little anyway, so he picked up the wrong light, misidentified it, wrecked his ship and was drowned. Unfortunately, so were twenty-one of his twenty-six-man crew, which included eight young apprentices.

What most sailing ships seemed to need was not more tugs.

If not tugs, why not auxiliary sailing ships? But to put a power plant in big sailing ships to kick them through calm belts and perhaps help them past the Horn was no answer either. It was tried in several ships including one of the two five-masted barks called *France,* but taken out again. Diesels were fitted into two other big sailing ships: the German four-masted bark *Magdalene Vinnen* (built in 1921 for Vinnens of Hamburg) and the Danish five-masted *København*. As a Soviet trading school-ship still sailing in 1970, the *Vinnen* may have need of it: the big Dane took hers to the bottom in 1929. Before the diesel engine was generally accepted, the enterprising German company of R. C. Rickmers had put a 1,000-h.p. steam engine into their five-masted bark of the same name, in 1906, complete with large coal bunkers, steamship funnel with the company's markings (which must have been a curse when it belched smoke into the rigging) and everything but a steamer's bridge. The *R. C. Rickmers* was built in the company's yard at Bremerhaven. She was 5,548 gross and

A sea spills over the rail.

Bashed-up hull, patched sails, Limejuicer Cape Horner CELTIC GLEN *sails slowly in from the missing lists.*

Missing! The bark PENANG *just disappeared.*

High side of the Cape Horn sailing-ship—not much chance to climb back aboard.

A net between life and death—it was horribly easy to go overboard.

The seamen keep near the stretched wire life-line. The net protects them in the ship's waist.

4,696 net register tons, 410.5 feet by 53.6 beam by 30.4 depth. Her deadweight was approximately 8,000 tons. She was rather bigger than the non-powered *Preussen* (5,081 tons gross) of 1902 and the *Potosi* (4,026) of 1895. But because of the *Rickmers* engine, boilers, and bunkers, the *Preussen* carried more, and cost much less to run. More important, both the big "P" ships made just as good as, if not better than, average speeds as the big smoke-maker.

The Rickmers firm, founded in 1834 by one of those solid, competent, enterprising characters who keep coming into the shipping story (like the early Runciman, Brocklebank, Savill, Bates, Laeisz, and a few more), were respected shipowners, and the operation of their giant auxiliary was watched closely by the surviving British and American sailing-ship operators. Already in 1905 these were reported to be "firmly convinced that the days of the windjammer were practically over, never to return."* After two and a half years, examination of the *R. C. Rickmers'* perfor-mance showed that on two and a half voyages of the usual sort that sailing ships then made, she had steamed 100,310 miles in 608 sea-days at an average 165 miles a day—about seven miles (not knots) an hour. Her earnings were £47,000 gross, reckoned at 9/6 a mile sailed. She had carried 42,000 tons of cargo, at the average freights then prevailing, which were low. (There was a shipping slump in 1907.)

It was obvious from these figures that she could not be cov-ering her depreciation and all her other costs, though she had been working hard, with reasonable turn-around in a variety of ports. (Her voyages are listed as Bremen–New York–Saigon–Bankok–Bremen: Hamburg–San Pedro–Sydney–San Francisco–Tacoma–Antwerp: Antwerp–San Francisco.) The Rickmers Com-pany's own publication, *Rickmers 1834–1934,* by W. Rickmer Rickmers, Ph.D., says the engine gave her speeds of eight knots in ballast, seven knots loaded. She sailed well, despite the drag of the propeller, but economically she was a failure.

"Engines and coal took away space," writes Dr. Rickmers.

* *Shipping Gazette Weekly Summary* of April 27, 1906, in a leading article, "Wind and Steam."

"Engine-room hands increased the pay-roll. Days saved were swallowed up by the cost of coal. Steam did not work as well nor as economically as motors do. The greatest disappointment was . . . the fact that she could not manoeuvre in narrow waters without the help of tugs."

Freight markets did not improve—at least, not sufficiently to cover the *R. C. Rickmers'* costs. "Times were as bad as possible, freights brought nothing but losses, and tramping was hopeless because the regular lines had practically captured all the traffic of the seas, profitable or unprofitable," the shipowning doctor laments. Rickmers sold their other sailing ships—they'd had a distinguished line including an outstanding four-masted full-rigged ship, the *Peter Rickmers,* a skysail-yarder lost on Fire Island in 1908, and the *Maria Rickmers,* a Scots-built five-masted bark smaller than the *R.C.,* but also with auxiliary power, which went missing in 1892 homeward-bound with 60,000 bags of rice from Saigon—and would have sold the *R. C. Rickmers* too. But no one would buy her. They decided to use her as a trading school-ship for their steamships. War caught her at Cardiff loading coal in 1914. As a British prize named *Neath,* she was sunk by submarine while on passage from Mauritius to Liverpool with 7,000 tons of sugar.

Rickmers had never been die-hard sailing-ship owners. The line had built and operated big tramp steamers since the late 1880's. Their two steam auxiliaries seem like expensive mistakes. As the leading article in the *Shipping Gazette Weekly Summary* of April 20, 1906, pointed out, one "would have thought that the sailing performances of the *Preussen"* (she had made seven round Chilean voyages with seven west'ard Horn roundings in three and a half years, the longest rounding taking eleven days) "might have had an influence in demonstrating the possibility of smart passages under sail alone." Perhaps Bremen did not care to learn from Hamburg.

No merchant sailing ship intended for Cape Horn westward roundings ever had power put into her. It made no sense. If she had power enough to push all that rigging to windward, she had no need of the rigging.

As for the other idea, this would not stand examination either. It amounted to giving up the attempt to beat past the Horn altogether, and to set out from Europe to make eastward passages around the world no matter where in the Pacific the ship was bound. The Horn route would then be for sailing east only, at least in winter. Ports along the whole of the west coast of the Americas and in Baja California (like Santa Rosalia) would be reached by the sailing route around Good Hope, followed by a run of 12,000 miles or more in the Roaring Forties, south of all Australia and New Zealand, until it was time to turn northward toward Valparaiso, Iquique, Acapulco, San Francisco, Puget Sound, or wherever else the ship might be bound. To make anything approaching a great circle course down there was impractical, for Antarctica got in the way. Those latitudes were far more consistently hazardous for ice than the neighborhood of the Horn. Nor might a ship swing eastward south of Good Hope and just run. The same cyclonic movements of the globe-circling air were to be met down there as near the Horn (though they could be less regular and were more often unpredictable in their behavior, near the Horn). A master had to be on the alert all the time to use them properly. In winter experience showed an occasional preponderance of easterlies, especially in the area between the south of New Zealand and the Horn. (We had plenty there in the ship *Grace Harwar* in 1929 and were almost two months from Australia to the Horn.) Instead of being less hazardous, this tremendous eastward run could be more dangerous than the more or less straightforward fight with Cape Horn. For deepwater square-rigged ships, there were no easy answers to anything.

Ships driven from the Horn by damage did carry on eastward now and again, of course, but generally this was because they first sought refuge ports not as expensive as Port Stanley nor as dilatory as Montevideo or Rio. (For this reason, the four-masted bark *Miltonburn* ran as far as Bluff, New Zealand, in 1906, and other ships made for Cape Town, or even Melbourne.) But for an undamaged ship, still with a good and sufficient crew aboard, to turn away eastward deliberately, without first being at least badly beaten up, as far as I am aware, is unknown. (See note at the end of the chapter.)

"This was defeatist stuff," said Captain James Learmont. "They were both stupid ideas—the tugs and the eastward sailing route. The way was the way of the Horn and that was the way you should go. Charters required ships to sail the shortest route. Anybody could be driven off, of course. But then you come back and take it on again.

"I never heard of a well-found ship, properly handled, that didn't make it—unless she was a loss altogether. Remember, the losses are added up and the successful passages taken for granted.

"As for that, you could lose your ship just as easily running east in the Roaring Forties, for that was a wild zone, too. I very nearly lost the *Bengairn* down there, bound out of Newcastle, N.S.W., towards Valparaiso. A nasty shift of wind knocked her on her beam ends, and the coal shifted with her. I thought I was getting a lesson in what happened to missing ships on that run where many had been lost—so many that underwriters were getting worried about the loss-rate."

As the *Bengairn* had gone to sea from Newcastle loaded with coal, she was followed by a Missions to Seamen launch, as was the pleasant custom of the port. As the lads rushed up the rigging loosing sail and down again to man halyards and sheets and the white canvas clothed her shapely yards, the lovely voices of the Mission choir rang across the water. They sang many hymns, but that which lingered on the breeze and in the memory was "God be with you 'til we meet again." They sang beautifully, for there were many among them in that coal port town who were Welsh: it was long before the last echo died into the sound of the wind across the sea.

It was a pity, perhaps, that the same sentiments did not enter into the minds of the stubborn stalwarts who had trimmed the coal. It was heavy stuff: she was down to her marks well before she was filled. This left room in the hold for the coal to shift and, having shifted, kill her. It would have been much safer if the hold had been trimmed full to deck and sides 'midships and as far aft and for'ard as possible. Then there would be less room for the rest of the coal to move. If it did move, it couldn't throw the ship on her side. Many beautiful ships had sailed from Newcastle and never been seen again. Learmont wondered if this could be the reason: for such a cargo cannot be retrimmed at sea. He had spoken to the boss trimmer, only to be curtly snubbed.

"You do your job and we'll do ours," he said. "We put the coal in." The coal trimmers of Newcastle were not interested in what happened to missing ships. They scurried ashore, and no one dare stop them. Some of the evils of "job control" were early evident in Australian ports.

The *Bengairn,* right over on her side, was making water. Half the main hatch had gone under and the sea had burst it in. A new tops'l was rigged over the broken hatch before the ship foundered. This saved the ship only for the moment. Somehow she had to be brought somewhere near to upright again. To do that, first everything above the tops must go before she could be made to right herself at all.

With the usual heavy wire rigging, this was not easy. Nothing in such ships was easy: but it was done. Speed was vital, for the list was increasing with the weight of the sea that had got down below. It would take too long to saw through the rigging screws or the backstays and shrouds. Learmont cut the wire seizings. (Such stays were secured by being *turned* around a fitting on the upper part of the rigging screw, then doubled back and seized— stoutly lashed—with ligher wire.) The seizings gone, over went the lot—eighty tons of top-hamper into the sea.

There was access to the hold through the sail locker aft. All hands except the carpenter rushed below. It was not possible to shovel coal from the lee side to the weather. This was uphill and it wouldn't go. There had been shifting boards in the tween-decks (supposed to prevent cargo movement) but the coal lay piled against these. It had shifted on *both* sides, onto the bulkhead of the built-up shifting boards on one side, away from it on the other. Tackles had to be rigged to haul the coal in sacks back to wind'ard for the first thirty-six hours, and the crew led by their captain worked in a terrible, dusty, heaving gloom, their ears assaulted by the smash and clump of the great seas tearing at the ship. The *Bengairn* was fitted with a donkey boiler for cargo-working in port: meanwhile the carpenter (who was also donkey-man) worked to get this going. The boiler was now almost on its side, like the ship: it took hours to get fresh water into it, hours to light a fire and have it drawing. But these things *were* done: a messenger (a connecting line) was rigged to the main pumps. In time, as imperceptibly the big *Bengairn* slowly lifted her immersed side a little from the sea, the pumps began to draw properly, the four foot six inches of water below to lessen. Then the coal was more easily shifted back to the high side.

After five days the coal was retrimmed enough for the vessel to be left with a heavy list, but manageable. Most of the foremast still stood. Much of the other steel rigging—masts and yards—still lay attached to the ship, far below the lee side. There was time now to cut this adrift. The weather was better. The wind stood fair for Sydney. (The *Bengairn* had had time only to get well out into the Tasman Sea.) The remaining yards on the foremast were resecured—they had been slung awry by the weight of the sea as the ship lay on her side—a bit of sail bent, and the near derelict put on course for Sydney Heads.

She made it, though the lee rail was still underwater when she came in, and she looked like a broken ship come back from the dead. It was only her masts that were broken: no one aboard had suffered as much as a scratch. After that, one might have hoped, heavy coal was loaded more carefully into ships at Newcastle. (But it was not. Ships continued to go missing.)

"You can lose a ship anywhere," as Captain Learmont said, years afterward. "You can lose a ship in so many ways. And it isn't trying to sail the easy way that will save you, or adding auxiliary power—or hiring unnecessary tugs to tow you through Magellan Strait. Fight the shore bastards and look after the ship *all the time.* That's what you'd better do."

Captain Learmont was praised by Lloyd's for his "commendable resourcefulness" and "splendid audacity and success" not only in saving the *Bengairn* but for the efficient job he did rerigging her afterward. When he got the ship into Sydney his troubles were not over. Bids for repairs to hull and rigging were more than the ship was worth. Always the sworn (and capable) enemy of shore-side incompetents and other exploiters (often no better than racketeers), the captain rejected all tenders.

"Between them and fortune stood the experience of Captain Learmont and his regard for his owner's interests," said Lloyd's. The owners shipped the necessary new masts and spars from England while captain and crew got on with clearing up the decks and hand-sewing new sails. The carpenter turned out over a hundred new blocks. When the spars arrived, the master sail-maker became master rigger. The total cost of the *Bengairn's* extensive refit done in this manner was some £1,000. The captain's rigging gang consisted of his mate, second mate (both former apprentices that voyage), two other young apprentices, and three excellent able seamen. Two of them were Negroes and the third a Japanese. The ship looked "better than new" when she sailed.

Learmont was then twenty-eight and had already been in command of the *Brenda* and *Bengairn* for six years. An exceptional seaman, he was not always popular with brother shipmasters. Unlike some, he treated his crews well and fed them well, having no patience with the common doctrines that to treat seamen decently was to spoil them, and the way of petty economy was the way to owners' hearts. If an owner was worth sailing for, he wanted an efficient ship.

Learmont got after "rackets" wherever he found them. He had the advantage of sailing for intelligent owners, former ship-masters who knew their business as seamen as well as owners. As early as August, 1895, that pioneering reformer, J. Havelock Wilson, M.P., was pointing out the disadvantages of too many of the other kind. Shareholders should take an active interest in the management of their ships, he said, and not leave them to the so-called "managing owner, with no direct interest in the ship, who was also the broker and the chandler." Such persons, he went on, "must be made to understand that they are the servants of their employers, the shareholders."

Well said, of course, but the breed continued to flourish. The poor shareholders were interested in the sight of a dividend, and knew even less about owning and management problems than the pen-pushing percentage-chaser in the office. It was their misfortune that they attracted few Learmonts to their service.

NOTE: THERE IS, HOWEVER, THE CASE OF THE SHIP *Pass of Balmaha*, IN WHICH— ACCORDING TO THE SURVIVING OFFICIAL LOG OF THE SHIP FOR 1905—THE CREW PRESENTED A WRITTEN PETITION TO THE MASTER, OFF THE HORN FOR THE SECOND TIME AFTER A DISTRESS CALL AT MONTEVIDEO ON PASSAGE FROM ANTWERP TOWARD SAN FRANCISCO, ASKING HIM TO TURN AWAY AND SAIL EAST-ABOUT. SAILING FROM BELGIUM ON MAY 19, THE SHIP WAS NINE WEEKS OUT WHEN SHE CAME INTO THE URUGUAYAN PORT, FOR REASONS NOT STATED IN THE LOG. THERE A MONTH, SHE WAS SOON OFF THE HORN AGAIN. HERE SHE LOST AN APPRENTICE, AGED SEVENTEEN, OUT OF THE RIGGING, AND THE THIRTY-THREE-YEAR-OLD MATE DIED. AFTER A COUPLE OF WEEKS BACK OFF THE HORN, ALL HANDS LAID AFT WITH THEIR PETITION, WHICH IS COPIED INTO THE LOG.

IT READS: "WE THE UNDERSIGNED REFUSE TO PROCEED FURTHER TO WESTWARD WITH THE SHIP AS WE CONSIDER THAT OUR LIVES ARE ALL ENDANGERED THROUGH HEAVY LURCHING AND STRAINING OF VESSEL, ALSO DECKS BEING CONSTANTLY FULL OF WATER FORE AND AFT AND ALL OUR CLOTHES AND EFFECTS SOAKED. AS WE ARE UNABLE TO STAND THE EXPOSURE AND HARDSHIP ANY LONGER, WE DEMAND THE MASTER TO PROCEED BY THE EASTWARD ROUTE."

THIS IS SIGNED BY THE SAILMAKER, CARPENTER, BOS'N AND THIRTEEN A.B.'S. WHICH WAS THE SEA LAWYER AT THE BOTTOM OF THIS MOANING IS NOT KNOWN. THE DOCUMENT SIMPLY DESCRIBES THE NORMAL CONDITIONS OF A WINTER WESTWARD ROUNDING: THE *Pass of Balmaha* CERTAINLY WAS NOT STRAINED, FOR SHE WAS STILL A FINE FULL-RIGGED SHIP OVER TEN YEARS LATER, STRONG ENOUGH TO CARRY GUNS AS THE RAIDER *Seeadler* FOR COUNT FELIX VON LUCKNER, WHO RAIDED AND SANK CAPE HORN SHIPS UNDER ALLIED FLAGS WITHOUT KILLING ANYONE. (THE COUNT HAD BEEN A LIMEJUICE SAILOR HIMSELF AND HATED TO SINK THE BEAUTIFUL SHIPS. BUT IT WAS WAR. HE ALWAYS LOOKED AFTER THE MASTERS AND CREWS GENEROUSLY AND WITH UNBLEMISHED HUMANITY.)

IT IS UNCERTAIN WHETHER CAPTAIN GRAHAM PAID ATTENTION TO THE PETITION: HE DOESN'T SAY. BUT HE RECORDS ITS DATE, AND HE TOOK ANOTHER 147 DAYS FROM THAT DAY TO REACH HIS PORT, NEARLY NINE MONTHS FROM ANTWERP. APPARENTLY CHANGED AT MONTEVIDEO, THIS WAS SALINA CRUZ ON THE GULF OF TEHUANTEPEC IN SOUTHERN MEXICO, NOT FAR FROM THE GUATEMALA BORDER. HE COULD EASILY HAVE MADE THE LONG HAUL EASTWARD IN THAT TIME IN A SMART SHIP LIKE THE *Pass of Balmaha.*

AT SALINA CRUZ HE WAS DISMISSED. PERHAPS HE SHOULDN'T HAVE GONE THERE, EITHER.

Chapter five

MASTERS MOST VULNERABLE

FEW CAPE HORN shipmasters were Gomms or Sembers, but even fewer were Learmonts. Learmont had two unusual advantages in the last days of the sailing-ship era—he was a young man who had chosen to make his career in sailing ships, not an old has-been stuck with them: and he had learned his seamanship not by the chance experience that indentures with the average owner might bring him, but in smaller ships *first,* with his tough old father and others who were interested in him. In these he began young and stayed long: when he turned to deep-sea ships, it was not as an exploited apprentice with his eyes, perhaps, on the bridge of a steamship but as an able seaman learning his further business thoroughly in sail.

A boy in Scots or Welsh or Devon short-voyage schooners, brigantines, and the like learned cargo stowage too, especially when his father had an owning interest in his ship, and got plenty of experience. The trim—the seat in the water—of sailing ships was a very important point in both their sailing and earning. A properly trimmed ship loaded more, strained her rigging less, and sailed better. Unlike steamships, the sailing ship was all hull, so to speak: she had no boiler rooms, coal bunkers, engine space, shaft housing. She had finer lines for the sake of her sailing qualities. Stowing her properly with various bulk cargoes, or general, could be a problem. A ship hurt herself less in great seas if she was at her best trim, when she was rolled about and her heavy masts were flung and jerked as she pitched, throwing enormous strains on their whole fabric. It was not enough just to jam

85

stuff into the big hold, especially general cargo, despite the fact that being bound usually to the one port only—not a range of them—the stowage problem was much simplified compared with that of the cargo liner. Seamen learned these things better if they served in smaller ships first.

James Learmont learned how to cope under his father's hard eye and was far better off never having been an apprentice at all. It was a fortunate apprentice who got close to such problems. On the average four years indentures spent almost invariably in one ship, the apprentice might see six cargoes handled, or eight at the most, and perhaps a lot of ballast. If bad freight markets caused his ship to be laid up in San Francisco Bay or elsewhere for a couple of years, that still counted toward his "time," though he became a lesser assistant shipkeeper then and was learning little or nothing. The change from the old idea of apprentice *seamen* to apprentice officers was no service to Cape Horn ships. The old idea was that all seamen should learn their skilled work properly, and from them the leaders would emerge by merit shown consistently among their peers at sea. The notion that premium apprenticeship was for an officer class for whom four years' indentures was service enough no matter how spent, and a sufficiency of examination stuff could be crammed at the end, was in some ways a backward step. The seamen themselves maintained their standards in former days. "Managing owners," bureaucratic regulations and such could be a poor substitute.

Many of the deep-sea sailing-ship masters of the best reputation and of the finer ships were graduates of the older school, and many great seafaring nations—among them Germany and France—did not use the indentured cadet system at all. Masters like James Nelson (of the *Acamas* and others), Dai Williams (of the *Medway*), many other fine Scots, Welsh, and Devon masters, all the clipper men and all the great Germans did not begin as indentured cadets. The indentured apprentice system at its worst was a form of cheap labor and at its best should have been unnecessary. The Scandinavians early introduced a school-ship system, with vessels like Denmark's *Georg Stage* of 1882, Sweden's *Carl Johann* of 1848, and Norway's brig *Stratsraad Ericksen* of 1858.

Germany's *Grossherzogin Elisabeth* of 1901 soon followed, as well as others, including the United States' *St. Mary's* of 1875, Japan's *Meiji Maru* of 1874, and Holland's brig *Venus*. The idea was to give *all* lads choosing the sea career their first training in ships designed for them, run by men interested in them, whose whole job was the care and training of the boys. From among such lads the best would emerge as officers, in due course. Britain had several stationary hulks, of which the Marine Society's *Warspite* was the best. Later, several companies ran big sailers as cadet-manned ships in the Cape Horn trade, including Messrs. Devitt and Moore and the White Star Line. These did excellent work for premium cadets and produced many fine officers.

The fact was that, provided she had the right sort of master, any sort of sea-going square-rigger could provide first-class training. The ordinary indenture system was something of a lottery which, though it killed too many and forced others to prefer desertion, turned out splendid officers and men by the hundred. Many a good lad, perhaps, prospered in spite of it, not necessarily in the merchant service.

Sailing-ship apprentices who could stand the life usually did well. They certainly had survived a long and often severe testing. A presentable lad of twenty or twenty-one with a good certificate had no difficulty in establishing himself as an officer, provided times were reasonably good. Most preferred to qualify as masters before beginning a serious career. The big liner companies —passenger and cargo—recruited only the sail-trained if they could, on the grounds that they had probably been indoctrinated more thoroughly and were the surer converts from the land to the sea. Until recent years—even after the Second World War— Cunard senior masters, for example, were almost all former Cape Horner apprentices, and so were many in Alfred Holt's Blue Funnel Line, despite the fact that the number of young officers taking their certificates only in power had equaled the number qualified in sail by 1914, and then rapidly forged ahead to stay there.

Apprentices in tramps were little better off than those in

deep-sea sailing ships, except that watches below were more regular. Many were treated meanly. The incredible parsimony habitually used toward them in sail is exemplified by the experience of Captain A. G. Course when an apprentice in the John Stewart Line of London. The bark *Lorton* reached Ardrossan, in Scotland, at the end of a very long round voyage. Her apprentices had not been home for years. Everyone else was paid off but, as unpaid labor—Stewart indentures stipulated that their apprentices should receive no pay at all, though many companies paid a few pounds over the four years—the apprentices were kept aboard. There was plenty of hard work for them. After a while, a request for leave to go home was met by the owner's demand that, provided their parents agreed to pay for "runners" to replace them, they might go home for a few weeks!

"My parents were not well off," said the captain, half a century later. "But they paid. So did the others. But we never forgot that act of supreme niggardliness."

How anyone could feel loyalty to such employers, or continue to serve them at all, is hard to understand. But it was 1911 when young Course signed: life was hard then. The young had to "serve their time," observing their agreements, though this was more than many owners did. The indentures bound owners to "use all proper means to teach the said Apprentice or cause him to be taught the business of a Seaman"—wide enough, but also vague. The "proper means" was generally construed to be the ship herself, assisted only by the loud voices of those harrying the apprentices to assist in working her, and doing more than their share of the heavy labor of working her cargo in and out in the remoter ports.

A further meanness in Captain Course's indentures stipulated that, should his four years' servitude expire at sea or abroad, he must "remain by the ship until her arrival home at a port of discharge in the United Kingdom or Continent" at fixed wages of £2-10 a month. This meant that the apprentice might be in the ship many months or a year or more bound to work as A.B. for £2-10 a month, though the proper A.B.'s wages then might be twice as much.

The apprentice, to present himself for the official examinations, required good references from all the masters under whom he had served. So he had to toe the line.

"Any good apprentice worked as an A.B. within a year of going to sea," said the captain. "So the owners got three years out of him as A.B. for nothing anyway, after his parents had paid a premium of £40—a lot of money then."

Other companies, especially some Scots and a Liverpool firm known as Corsar's, charged less—one or two charged no premium—and gave better conditions. A few—very few—masters took a real and active interest in the welfare or instruction of their apprentices. All expected them to back up the afterguard in any and all cases of crew trouble, however caused. Many exploited them heartlessly as unpaid A.B.'s at sea, cargo workers in port as required, and convenient boat's crews for their personal use when not doing anything else, day and night, regardless even of their meal hours. Their assistance in "winning" a little coal or such from the cargo was taken for granted, when this was possible, and the profit from this went to the master.

By and large, apprenticeship was exploitation, relieved by the good spirit and the hardihood of the apprentices themselves: it provided the British Merchant Service and its ancillaries with many splendid men in peace and war, and Australia, New Zealand, California, South Africa, and Puget Sound with many excellent new citizens. The apprentice who became a no-good was quite rare. Those who stayed at sea often became leaders in their profession.

I was reminded of this recently when Captain Course invited me to one of the weekly coffee mornings of his Dorset Cape Horners, at the Swiss Restaurant in the heart of Bournemouth. Eight wonderful old boys turned up in that sunny south-coast town so remote from Tierra del Fuego, most of them octogenarians except one aged ninety-two, all with the stamp of the sea still upon their open faces, the snap of command in the old blue eyes. The talk was of great ships long gone and ships and shipmates claimed by Davy Jones half a century earlier, the hardness of the brassbounders' life and the astonishing way it worked out. All had been apprentices (one was in hoys and brigantines before that): most had been second mates in sail: all had their master's certificates before they went to steam. They'd been Royal Mail, B.I., Union Castle senior masters, Trinity House pilots, surveyors, London dock masters, insurance appraisers, examiners— the cream of the profession.

The names of ships great and small, forgotten guano islands where once four-masters scraped foul cargoes from the burning rocks, arid nitrate ports, sunlit coves in Sydney and San Francisco, Rio and Puget Sound were bandied between them like a list of bus stops on the way home. Highly respected elder citizens recalled weeks aboard hungry limejuice barks where their principal occupation (as well as loblollying for the master) was the felonious extraction of sufficient coal from the cargo to keep the galley and the bogeys going for the following twelve months.

"We 'won' and hid coal every way we could," said a venerable old gentleman. "We leaned heavily on the baskets as they were weighed. I remember we won fifty tons and then the captain bought that much less ballast, so he made money on both. We didn't get any of it.

"There was only one tally clerk. We had to fill baskets, heave them up by hand, put them on a primitive scale where the tally clerk weighed them, then empty them overside into a lighter. It was tough work—six twelve-hour days a week, less feast days and surf days. The crew got one Sunday's liberty when it was done. No wonder they were—well, wild. To us, winning a bit of coal was a game, a spot of relief: and we thought we were helping the ship."

"When I went in my first ship I had not the slightest idea what I was taking on," said Captain Course. "None of my people had been to sea. I'd read a book called *Sail-Ho, or a Boy at Sea*— absolute fiction. When I got my outfit list from the owners before joining my first ship, I was surprised to see no mention of a telescope. There *was* mention of dungarees. What were these? I found out—cheap working clothes for dogsbody jobs. When I joined, the mate said, 'Get into your dungarees and sweep the decks.' I asked him where I disposed of the rubbish I swept up.

He said, 'Poke it through the scupper-holes.' The ship was in London docks. Soon a big policeman came aboard demanding to know why the ship was littering the docks, against the by-laws.

" 'That bloody boy again!' yelled the mate, cuffing me a good one over the starboard ear. The satisfied constable departed, giving me the sort of look which I was sure established me in the police record for the rest of my life.

"Then the mate told me he had to stage his act, or the ship could have been fined. But he hadn't hit me hard. I was glad he told me. I hadn't noticed that. Whenever I cleaned up decks after that I took a good look round to be sure there were no policemen about, even at sea."

They all agreed that the sailing-ship apprenticeship system, though mean in many ways and often indefensible, somehow worked. They suggested that it should be reintroduced, indeed, as treatment for demonstrating students and other misled layabouts, for there were no such in their day.

In the first decade of the twentieth century, many British merchant shipmasters were very badly treated by any standards, especially in sailing ships. Poorly paid, without security of any kind or hope of earning enough to provide their own, they were members of an oppressed class, and so of course were their officers and crews. The results are obvious in a study of the records, particularly of the surviving official logs, the reports of inquiries, and the general tidings reported in Lloyd's messages, and the contemporary shipping newspapers. Many masters write "the ship" in the space provided in the log for their homes, having no other. Many were younger sons with no inheritance. When the master's wife of the *Fifeshire* dies as the ship puts into the Falklands to get medical attention for her, and her husband has to record the fact in the heartless log, the poor man cries out on the cold page. Her home "was on board the barque *Fifeshire* for the past ten years," for she also had no other. Many masters' wives die, by no means all of them old women. (Mrs. Caddell of the *Fifeshire* was thirty-eight.) Another far from old wife died in the *Port Elgin* on passage from Antwerp toward San Francisco in

'04-'05. She was Frances Hand, aged thirty-seven. "My dearly loved wife passed away after an illness of 34 days," the master had written. "As far as my opinion goes, cause of death was lung infection. I have caused the body to be preserved in spirits and, God willing, I intend sending her back to her friends in Australia. I followed the treatment for acute pulmonary consumption."

The poor man wrote "affection," not infection. It certainly was the sick woman's love for her husband which killed her. A sailing ship off the Horn was no place for the consumptive.

Far more masters died: how old they were nobody but themselves knew, for many went by fictitious ages for years. Who cared, so long as they sailed with their cargoes aboard and the ships came in again, in due course, to the ports to which they were bound? Seamen were not documented before the First World War, and not overmuch then. They required no passports, for they went with their ships and the ship's papers covered them. So long as they could stand up they went to sea.

In a sailing ship, the traditional organization—indeed the only practical effective means of control—was that the master was (or should be) the brains, the ship-handler, the sailor, the decision-maker. He had assistants (mates, usually two, of whom the first was much senior to the second: tradesmen in their own departments: a steward for the important matter of food) but he had no substitute. The others were his temporary eyes as watchkeepers, his specialized supervisors of detail. Traditionally he kept no watch, but the conscientious were in fact on watch all the time: and so the strain on them could be tremendous. He could not really learn to be a master while he was a mate. Command was flung at him suddenly. He had to rise to it and live with it (in those days) so long as he had a ship, with such respite as his own efficiency, skill, and capacity to create and maintain harmony in his ship might make possible. Nobody had *all* the desirable qualities; not many had even the essentials on the twenty-four-hours-a-day basis the sailing ship demanded. The low emoluments kept many fine men too long at sea until they were quite worn out.

There was, for instance, old Captain Thomas England

Parker of the four-masted bark *Holt Hill* of 2,400 tons, who suddenly dropped dead in the saloon of that vessel while preparing data for longitude sights one morning. How old he was no one knew: his age is penciled in as seventy-three on the record of his death in the official log. But he had celebrated his eightieth birthday some years before and the event was publicized, for he was a fine, tough old shipmaster, well known. In 1885, he had had the odd experience of having his ship, the *Ellenbank,* destroyed when in ballast off Cape Horn in a calm. Apparently she was caught in *two* heavy swells left by recent storms, one westerly, the other southerly, and with no wind in her sails to steady her, the bewildered ship flung this way and that, rolled right over. After some days—no one knew how many—a passing ship picked up the sole survivor. This was Captain Parker, sitting on the upturned keel. He was well past sixty then.

Calm destroyed several other fine ships in the same area, but not by rolling them over. They got ashore, like the *Bidston Hill,* or were dismasted by the violent rolling, like the *Fitzjames* when she was the German *Pinnas:* nobody sat on her keels. But the oddest loss in calm was probably that of the Norwegian bark *Alexandra* which was stuck in calm and current around the Galapagos Islands for so long that her crew of twenty had to abandon her just before she put herself, slowly but finally and very firmly, on the rocks of Iguana Cove at Albemarle Island. The *Alexandra* was bound with bunker coal from Newcastle, New South Wales, toward Panama and was then over six months out. She had been drifting about for weeks in a windless backwater of the Humboldt current, and had run out of food. The crew took to the boats, and some of them rowed and sailed to the coast of Ecuador, over 600 miles away. The sluggard bark broke up and sank.

As for that remarkable veteran Captain Parker, he had been forced to take the *Holt Hill* in temporary distress from the Horn twice since 1900. On the first occasion, some years earlier, the London shipping journals remarked that "Eighty-year-old Captain Parker had been in command for over half a century . . . Such a record of continuous service is probably unique."

It was common practice in those days for older masters to

transpose the digits now and then when they passed seventy. For instance, at seventy-six, they would switch back to sixty-seven by convenient "error" and start again from there. Old Captain Davies was still doing just that when the ship *Monkbarns* had to put into Rio in 1926. He was seventy-six, but became sixty-seven again, still in command of the *Monkbarns,* when he died there.

The ship *Monkbarns* survived to become one of the last five British deepwater square-riggers, but she was hard on her masters. Among casualties aboard was Charles Robinson, master, aged an official fifty-two, of "general breaking-up, heart and lungs." Captain Robinson was a North-countryman who would not have broken up all that easily. The *Monkbarns* was on the long run from Hamburg toward San Francisco when he died. The mate had previously treated him off the Horn for frostbite and failing eyesight. A later diagnosis—still the mate's—mentions beriberi, severe pains in the legs, tightness in the stomach, etc. Treatment, "various embrocations," all useless. Apprentices took turns keeping constant watch. The Golden Gate was almost in sight when finally the broken-up old man died, probably of old age.

How old really was Captain Thomas England Parker when he died? No one will ever know. Some who knew him said he was born well before 1820. Perhaps he had switched the digits once or twice long before the quiet morning in the northeast trade winds, over five months out of Glasgow on the long, long drag toward Victoria, B.C., when he heeled slowly over upon his chronometer, dead. He had got some sights from the poop, and was then reading the chronometer while the young second mate got some more. He had been complaining a little of his health for a week or two, which was unusual for him. He'd told the mate and the steward that he had "congestion of the lungs," and was trying to doctor himself out of the *Ship Master's Medical Guide.*

"The steward called me and told me he thought the master was gone," wrote Mate Alexander Anderson in the official log. "I came aft and found him dead. He was buried with all honors the following day." The mate then quietly assumed command and sailed the *Holt Hill* on to Victoria.

There was no retiring age for masters. There was, indeed, no retiring age for anyone. The casualty rate both before and abaft the mast was heavy: prospects for retirement, if any, were a minor matter. In the logs of Cape Horn ships on voyages in 1905 surviving at the Hayes Repository in 1970, one noted at least thirty-three in which the masters had died on the voyage, or been killed. Casualties to apprentices were sixty-nine; the number of masters' wives whose deaths are recorded is five. To these figures must be added all who were in ships which went missing, probably an average of at least thirty masters and five hundred men a year (in all British sailing ships, for it is not possible to know where most such ships were lost). The number of wives lost in these is also not known. Many owners did not like the idea of wives and families going to sea with their masters, holding that they could interfere with efficiency. They could. Just how many poor women were suffering off the Horn in any winter it is now impossible to discover, if it ever were. Official logs and Articles are sometimes kept in a slipshod manner. Unless the wife dies, she often is never mentioned, possibly because she could be there without owner's permission—or some woman could.

The masters of the *Celestial Empire, Blythswood, Annesley, Englehorn, Eskasoni, River Falloch, Ancaios, Bluebell, Samoena,* and *Travancore* all died or were lost. Captain Charles Thomas, aged fifty-five (at least as recorded by himself), was lost overboard from the *Annesley* in an odd way. The official log lists him as "drowned" and states very baldly that, in an October gale while all hands were getting sail off the foremast, one of the crew "thought he saw a man overboard." The second mate sent a man aft to report this at once to Captain Thomas in the poop, but the master was not there. (The *Annesley* missed him, for she struck the Tuskar at the end of the voyage and foundered in deep water.) The *Annesley* had run from the Horn back to Montevideo in distress on a previous voyage. Her master, Captain Andrew Culbert from Broughty Ferry, who admitted to being fifty-nine, died off the Horn then, and the ship was over a year reaching San Francisco from South Shields. The cause of Captain Culbert's death is given (by the mate) as heart failure, which he was trying to treat from the brief guidance available in his *Ship Master's Medical Guide.* The carpenter and sailmaker took turns at nursing him, while the mate sailed the ship.

The master of the *Eskasoni* was lost in an even more unusual way, for he fell out of the fore rigging. The oddly named *Eskasoni* was an iron full-rigged ship of 1,715 tons built in 1886, and the dead master was a Canadian named Thomas Townsend, from Sydney, Nova Scotia, whose age is listed as fifty. Down off the Horn, plugging along to the west'ard on passage from Antwerp toward California in the winter of '05, another ship had been sighted. There must have been something unusual about her, for Captain Townsend climbed to the fore upper tops'l yard to have a look. She might have been the *Deudraeth Castle.* Coming down, he missed his footing coming over the foretop, and fell to the deck "breaking both legs and hurt internally." Here the ladder of the stepped rigging led inward, *away* from a man's feet and out of sight. Long custom led the groping foot to the right spot for foothold without thought: but captains were not usually to be found aloft. Old feet and hands could lose their skill: any slip could be fatal. Captain Townsend was dead within half an hour. The carpenter made a watertight casket lined with cement: in this the captain made the rest of the voyage under the shelter of the forecastle head.

In the *River Falloch*—another 1905 battler—the cause of Captain Charles Sherwood's (age unknown) death is given as "consumption": the mate gets on with sailing the ship and writes little. Captain Richard Cautley (allegedly only forty-one) of the *Celestial Empire* died from—or with—"cramps in the stomach," poor man. A probable cause is in the entry that he "had been taking medicines of his own prescribing freely all the passage for indigestion of long standing." Captain Cautley was a good man. In a "mod. gale increasing with rain at 0400, ship making 11 knots" one morning near the Horn, I. Lundström, A.B., was tossed from the mainyard by a blow-back of the sail and fell in the sea.

"Backed mainyard. Away boat with 2nd Mate and 4 A.B.'s: soon lost to sight but recovered. Man not seen again: gale increasing."

These few terse words cover a fine feat of seamanship and indicate a well-run ship.

The voyage of the bark *Bluebell*, 845 tons, from Liverpool to Liverpool in late 1903–1905 by way of Durban, Delagoa Bay, Calcutta, and Demerara, caused the deaths of two of her masters. The first was Captain W. H. Luke, aged forty-two, of "heart disease," the second Captain James Donaldson, aged fifty-six, of "Berri Berri." We get no details about this or its cause. Donaldson had been mate. Four men were landed "sick" at Demerara: and this is one of the very few mentions of scurvy, alias beri-beri, I came across in all the logs. Limejuice really must have been an effective antiscorbutic, though ships of several other nations kept the scourge at least dormant with more intelligent diet, better prepared and more liberally served.

Even in the brief pages of the dusty official log, the story of the death of Arthur Newnham, Irish mate of the smart four-masted bark *Chiltonford* of Glasgow, at sea on passage between Tacoma, Washington, and Callao, is quietly moving. Mr. Newnham was one of the many mates who had been master himself in former days. His age is listed as forty which could be thirty years or more wrong. He had been a good mate in the *Chiltonford,* and the three years voyage was long and varied. Captain Thomas Atkinson comes from his log as a fine master—with little to say and none of that carping stupidity or fatuous exhibition of his own inadequacy as a leader. The mate becomes ill after two years of the voyage—South Shields–San Francisco–Newcastle–Antofagasta–Tacoma–Callao–Newcastle—where the log ends: quite a round.

"Inflammation of the brain" is diagnosed: bathing the temples with vinegar and a dose of salts with quinine every four hours is the treatment. This is no help, but the mate tries to get back on deck, perhaps to escape it. Cold brandy replaces the vinegar, a mustard plaster on the neck takes over from the salts with quinine. None of this helps, but there is no delirium. In a few days, Mate Newnham, who had been sleeping peacefully, opened his eyes, saw the captain there with him, pressed his hand, and died.

His wage of £8 a month included an allotment of £5, presumably to a wife. His excellent kit included his master's certificate, charts, copies of Findlay's *Ocean Directories and Light Lists* and so on—the equipment of a good master.

James Frazer, from Aberdeen, admitted age fifty-eight, could have avoided death in the Glasgow bark *Heathfield* on her voyage from Chile toward Egypt in 1906. He had stopped the steamship *Ocean* off the Azores and the M.O. wanted to take him aboard. (The doctor's diagnosis was dropsy, rheumatism, dysentery and heart disease.) But Captain Frazer would not leave his ship, sailed on and died.

An old A.B. in the *Heathfield* who died, admitting sixty, left a bottle of black hair dye in his kit, which indicates one of the methods by which these ancient mariners stayed at fifty-five or sixty for a decade or two. At the auction by the mainmast, a shipmate gave 1/6 for the dye, probably with an eye to future use.

Captain Owen Barlow Pritchard, forty-three, from Caernarvonshire in Wales, died in the *Blythswood* from "inflammation of the bowels caused by acute rheumatism." The ship was then out of Haiphong, on the Gulf of Tonkin in what was once Indo-China, bound across the Pacific toward Victoria, B.C. She had been four months at Haiphong and Captain Pritchard, according to the log, had contracted rheumatism there. It must have taken more than this to kill a good Welsh shipmaster.

When Captain John L. Boyce of the *Samoena* died aboard his ship from fever at Acapulco in 1905, aged forty-seven, he was the first of five to lose their lives that voyage. An apprentice and an A.B. were later washed overboard, another A.B. killed on deck, and the steward—a German named Dinchel—died of fever. An odd note states that Dinchel's "Masonic papers were not sold," when his kit was auctioned. Another master who died of fever at Acapulco in 1905 was Robert Crosby, aged forty-four, of the *Leicester Castle,* which like so many sailing ships of that period had brought coal from Newcastle, New South Wales. Acapulco then was far from being the fashionable resort it has since become, but it was a convenient bunkering port for steamers on the Panama-California coastal run. Trains had long been bringing passengers across the isthmus.

Captain Crosby's effects included "1 chest containing 80 charts, 1 Zither and music, 1 China Coast Manual." It was never customary to offer a master's effects for auction at the mast, mainly because no one aboard could afford to buy them. So the zither was locked away and wasted. Probably the essential charts were kept in use. There would be no others.

Like several of these stout-hearted old masters, Captain Edward Hill Lovitt, Bluenose master of the *Engelhorn,* got his big ship safely to port before he died, though he had been ailing the whole round voyage to Chile and back to Hamburg. "Stomach trouble and general debility" had accounted for an A.B. aged forty-five: there was no debility about Ed, even at sixty-five. "Inflammation of the lungs" is the official cause of his last departure. If he had stayed with the *Engelhorn,* he was doomed, anyway, for she went missing not long afterward.

"Cause of death—Drink," stands boldly in the logged record of sixty-two-year-old Captain George Colville from Bexhill, England, who died at sea in the bark *Invercoe* outward bound for Australia in 1905. "Capt. been indulging rather freely . . . went below, and has kept himself in a continual stupor," writes the mate with unusual verbosity and candor, adding that his captain "was more or less sensible all the time, and died peacefully asleep in his bunk." A merciful end, all things considered. His kit was locked away to be sent home.

"Dropsy" is a strong favorite in the "cause of death" columns, but one is forced to conclude that its meaning, if any, is that the deceased had dropped dead. Frequently another cause (or guess) is bracketed with it. Captain Richard Davies, aged forty-three, of the bark *Killarney,* died aboard on passage Callao toward Europe in 1905 from "dropsy and general debility," according to the log entry. So feeble at forty-three, and a Cape Horn shipmaster? The age was probably fictional, too. Sailors of all ages, real and imaginary, died from this "debility," but there was little pretense that the ages listed for them were real.

According to the mate of the four-masted bark *Kate Thomas* —another of the '05 battlers off the Horn—Captain Charles Hughes of that vessel was debilitated enough to die from that cause alone, at the age of thirty-two. The *Kate Thomas* was bound from Iquique homeward to Leith at the time, but poor Captain Hughes managed to fight back his senility until he was within sight of the Firth of Forth. His "legs swelled and he had a sore throat." Treatment was "plenty of limejuice and quinine," but his weakness could not be checked. Able Seaman Frank Wilson, an admitted sixty-three, died on the same voyage of "old age and senile decay." He was probably over seventy.

The only persons aboard who were invariably free of symptoms of senility and never seemed to die from "dropsy" were the apprentices, but the casualty rate among these could be appalling. They were tossed out of the rigging or washed overboard and left behind in what seems almost a careless profusion. If there were carelessness it was most likely to be their own. Boyish optimism was no use against the relentless risks of work aloft in bad weather or good, and the main deck of a deep-loaded sailing ship fighting for her life off the Horn was a constant death trap. On deck the work came first, not men's safety. Only the German idea of the man-saving life net stretched above the bulwarks in the waist saved life when the great seas stormed aboard. The square-rigged ship fought with the sea with her whole being: who helped her fight was vulnerable. Other nations' ships seemed to avoid the use of those rigged-up "sailor-straining" nets because they were a reminder and an admission of vulnerability in a profession which did not like that. The nets did not protect the whole waist, only the worst, the lowest, part of it. Back ropes were very rarely rigged on yards perhaps for the same reason (and for gear-saving) though they could also help to save men's lives.

"One hand for yourself and one for the owner" just didn't work aloft: it was both hands for either as appropriate, coupled with a degree of infallible judgment the lads did not grow old enough to acquire, iron nerve, and level heads *all* the time. Those lads did men's work but they had not men's backgrounds, nor bodies: the majority came aboard man-killers without the slightest prior experience, pre-sea training, or much else other than optimism and a mistaken idea that the sea life had "romance."

The drunken master of the ship *Aberfoyle* was by no means the only captain to take to the drink so thoroughly that he fetched up killing himself. He had an excellent mate, who normally looked after the ship for him, but when the *Aberfoyle* sailed from Fredrikstad in Norway bound for Melbourne in January 25, 1895, she struck bad weather in the Atlantic and the mate was washed overboard. The master, as usual, had been drinking heavily. There was some question at least in the crew's mind that the entry in the official log regarding the mate's death was falsified by the master, and those asked to witness the entry refused. This seemed to rankle in the befuddled mind of Captain Robertson. Just what had happened to the mate will never be known but, in the finer weather, the master began to harass the crew, going into the forecastle on several occasions shouting at them. They were all Scandinavians who had hitherto had a high regard for British ships, but Captain Robertson was too much for them. On the third occasion that he chose to come for'ard and assault them, they clapped him in irons.

Somehow the *Aberfoyle* felt her way around the north of Scotland, through the North Atlantic and the South Atlantic without hitting Brazil or the Cape Verde Islands with the master drunk, the mate dead, *and no other navigator at all.* This seems incredible, but it is possible. An accurate dead-reckoning must have been kept and the standard compass must have been in excellent state. Why the second mate could not navigate was never said, but it was not unusual to sign a good bos'n for this berth. It was uncommon for the second mate to be required to navigate or, indeed, even for him to be allowed to see a chart, unless he had the good fortune to be with one of the more unusual masters.

No log of the *Aberfoyle* exists for this voyage, but the case came to general notice when the ship, complete with ironed master, stopped a steamer named *Tagliaferro* on May 16, and made the unusual request for the loan of an officer to navigate the *Aberfoyle* on to Australia. She was then almost four months at sea and was presumably not far from the Australian coast. A newspaper report says the ship was "close in by Gantheaume Bay flying signals of distress." The steamer obligingly loaned her second mate, a Mr. Amery (sail-qualified, like all deck officers then) and, fifteen days later, the *Aberfoyle* came into Melbourne. At some time before this, Captain Robertson had killed himself. The whole odd business came before a court in Melbourne on July 2, 1895. Here the strangest character of the whole story suddenly makes a brief and final appearance.

"Call Seaborn Robertson," shouted the court flunkeys, in the usual manner. "Seaborn Robertson!"

In walked a little four-year-old girl. She "gave evidence to the court" on behalf of her dead father, produced by some counsel presumably on the grounds of failure to find any other witness to say a good word for him.

Seaborn said her piece and departed: the court found for the seamen. On the face of it, they could have been in serious trouble, admitting to have risen against their lawful master and put him in irons. They could have killed him, too.

But their innocence showed as clearly as little Seaborn's. She had smiled to them all. They had tried to preserve the captain's body for post mortem, but it was not possible with a timber cargo. With nitrates, they might have managed.

There are some odd points. Surely the child Seaborn was not aboard by herself. Her name indicates the probability that the *Aberfoyle* was the Robertson family home. Where was her mother? Just how had the ship managed to get from south Norway to within a fortnight of Melbourne, if no one had ever fixed her position since shortly after she sailed?

The *Aberfoyle* makes one appearance in the retained official logs at Hayes. It is not for that voyage but for another, made ten years later from London to Port Pirie, on to Callao and a Peruvian guano island, back around the Horn to Antwerp. She lost one able seaman who fell from aloft in port while bending sail, and broke his neck.

Almost any strange character may suddenly appear in any of these logs, without listing or previous mention. In a ship named

OFFICIAL LOG of the *Grace Harwar*

from *Tocopilla - Chili SA* **towards** *Newcastle NSW*

Date of the Occurrence entered with Hour.	Place of the Occurrence, or situation by Latitude and Longitude at Sea.	Date of Entry.	Entries required by Act of Parliament.	Amount of Fine or Forfeiture inflicted.
			he is now a deserter —	
			C. P. Hudson Master	
			J. A. Hughes 1st Mate	
18/6/07	Tocopilla	18/6/07	William Tyrrell OS is from this date promoted to the rating of AB at £3.00. Three pounds per month instead of his wages as per ships articles —	
			C. P. Hudson Master	
			J. A. Hughes 1st Mate	
5.30 am. 22/6/07	Tocopilla Bay	22/6/07	Ruth. Geraldine Hudson wife of the master died this morning at 5.30 a.m. of tuberculosis of the larynx and affection of the lungs. The body has been imbalmed here and will be taken to Australia —	
			C. P. Hudson Master	
			J. A. Hughes 1st Mate	
17/9/07	Newcastle NSW	17/9/07	I. E. Gates James took over command of this ship "Grace Harwar" this day, having been duly entered on Register & Ship's Articles — these documents having been handed with Crew's Accounts	

N.B.—Every entry in this Log Book required by the Act must be signed by the Master and by the Mate or some other of the Crew : and every entry of illness, injury, or death, must also be signed by the Surgeon or Medical Practitioner on board (if any) ; and every entry of wages due to, or of the sale of the effects of, any Seaman or Apprentice who has died must be signed by the Master and by the Mate and some other member of the Crew ; and every entry of wages due to any seaman who enters His Majesty's Service must be signed by the Master and by the Seaman or by the Officer authorized to receive the Seaman into such Service.

NOTE.—Reading over Entries of Offences.—The Master's especial attention is called to Section 228 (b) (c) and (d) of the Merchant Shipping Act, 1894, which will be found in Notice 1. prefixed to this Log.

One page from the Official Log of the ship GRACE HARWAR *for the 1907 voyage with the entry about the death of the master's wife and his intention of taking her body to Australia, which he did—the origin of the 'yarn' which put something of a hoodoo on the ship.*

The ship GRACE HARWAR

More or less standard British Cape Horn cadet's Indentures, virtually an acceptance of a sentence of four years' hard labor plus the grave chance of being drowned, or flung out of the rigging—a mean document and a mean servitude, but served loyally by some thousands.

I.

ORDINARY APPRENTICE'S INDENTURE.

This Indenture, made the *Eleventh* day of *February* 1911 between *Alfred George Course*

aged *Sixteen* years, a native of *Hammersmith* , in the county of *Middlesex* , now

residing at *No. 97, Letc.* of *97 orchard Avenue London E.C.* , in the county of *Middlesex* , of the first part, and *John Stewart &Co.* of the second part, and [1]

Herbert Edwin Course of *Ilfyston* , in the county of *Worc......* of the

third party WITNESSETH, That the said *Alfred George Course* hereby voluntarily binds himself Apprentice unto the said

John Stewart &Co. , his Executors, Administrators, and Assigns, for the term of *four* years from the date hereof ; And

the said Apprentice hereby covenants that, during such time, the said Apprentice will faithfully serve his said Master, his Executors, Adminis-

trators, and Assigns, and obey his and their lawful commands, and keep his and their secrets, and will, when required, give to him and them true

accounts of his or their goods and money which may be committed to the charge, or come into the hands, of the said Apprentice ; and

* Full Address.

he consent to any such damage being done by others, but will, if possible, prevent the same, and give warning thereof ; and will not embezzle or waste the Goods of his Master, his Executors, Administrators, or Assigns, nor give or lend the same to others without his or their licence ; nor absent himself from his or their service without leave ; nor frequent Taverns or Alehouses, unless upon his or their business ; nor play at unlawful games : IN CONSIDERATION WHEREOF, the said Master hereby covenants with the said Apprentice, that during the said term he, the said Master, his Executors, Administrators, and Assigns, will and shall use all proper means to teach the said Apprentice or cause him to be taught the business of a Seaman²

and the Master also agrees to provide the said Apprentice with sufficient Meat, Drink, Lodging, Washing, Medicine, and Medical and Surgical Assistance, and pay to the said Apprentice the sum of £ _____ in manner following ; (that is to say).*N.B.* *Should the term of this Indenture terminate when the vessel is on a voyage, or in a port abroad the said Apprentice shall remain by the ship until her arrival in a port of discharge in the United Kingdom or on the Continent of Europe. All foreign wages at the rate of two pounds ten shillings (£2.10.) per month*

the said Apprentice providing for himself all sea-bedding, wearing apparel, and necessaries (except such as are herein-before specially agreed to be provided by the said Master) : AND IT IS HEREBY AGREED, that if, at any time during the said term, the said Master, his Executors, Administrators, or Assigns provide any necessary apparel, or sea-bedding for the said Apprentice, he and they may deduct any sums properly expended thereon by him or them from the sums so agreed to be paid to the said Apprentice as aforesaid ; and for the performance of the Agreements herein contained each of them, the said *Alfred George Course* and *John Stewart & Co* doth hereby bind himself, his Heirs, Executors, and Administrators, unto the other of them, his Executors and Administrators, in the penal sum of £10.0.0. ;³ and for the performance of the covenants on the part of the said Apprentice herein contained, the said *John Stewart & Co* , as surety, doth hereby bind himself, his Heirs, Executors, and Administrators, unto the said *John Stewart & Co* , his Executors and Administrators, in the penal sum of £10.0.0. : Provided, that notwithstanding the penal stipulations herein contained, any Court, Magistrate or Justice of the Peace may exercise such jurisdiction in respect of the said Apprentice as he or they might have exercised if no such stipulations had been herein contained.

In witness whereof, the said parties have hereunto set their hands and seals, the day and year above written.

Signed, sealed, and delivered, in the presence of

WPHSharpe
3, Fenchurch Avenue
London. E.C.
Clerk

E.A. Mansell
14 West Lodge Avenue
Acton. W.
Clerk in H.M. Colonies

John Stewart & Co ——————— (Master.)

Place of the Seal.

Alfred George Course. (Apprentice.)

Place of the Seal.

Herbert E. Course ——————— (Surety.)

Place of the Seal.

Registered at the Port of ___London___ this ___13___ day of ___February___ 19¹¹

Signed ___George___ ___per Registrar General___

26/28 Billiter Street

London 8 March 1916

This is to certify that Alfred George Counce has served his apprenticeship on board the Barque "Loston" of Liverpool, and, Barque 'Edinburgh' of Glasgow and the Captains have reported to us that he was a sober active and willing seaman, and could Confidently recommend him to anyone requiring his services

He has served his apprenticeship to our entire satisfaction

Jno Stewart

The Reference, signed by John Stewart with standard lack of enthusiasm, was a 'must' or the Indentures could be wasted.

the *Isle of Arran,* James Patterson, master, Mrs. Patterson suddenly turns up—in the log—to nurse her husband homeward bound off the Horn, Melbourne toward Dunkirk, in that nasty winter of 1905. The second mate, twenty-four-year-old Ernest Grove, "stricken with paralysis during a fierce hail squall" has already died. The master gets his ship past the Horn and then is forced to his bunk by heart disease. Despite all his wife (aided by one of the apprentices) can do, he dies, aged fifty-seven (in the log). "All hands mustered to view the body to satisfy themselves that life was extinct," Mr. Webb, the mate, wrote in the log. Presumably all satisfied, the late master was sewn neatly into a combination shroud-and-coffin of new canvas, and buried from the poop. The mate sails the ship on to Dunkirk without fuss or incident: Mrs. Patterson, poor woman, disappears.

Masters' wives seem to have been especially vulnerable. Jemima Emmett, wife of Captain A. W. Emmett of a four-masted bark called the *Mooltan* which had previously been a P. & O. liner —a fast, narrow-gutted vessel for a square-rigger—was only twenty-nine when she died aboard the ship, on passage from Newcastle, New South Wales, toward Acapulco in May, 1904. An Australian, she had been married less than a month. According to her husband's entry in the official log, she knew that she was suffering from "Bright's disease, anaemia, and a weak heart," but two doctors had "advised her going to sea as the trip would probably do her good." She was married on May 16, signed on as "stewardess" in the *Mooltan* May 24, sailed three days later, and was dead two days after that. Those doctors could never have tried the Tasman Sea.

Mrs. Emmett's was an unusually brief marriage, but another Australian woman, married to Captain C. S. Hudson of the ship *Grace Harwar,* did not do much better. Ruth Geraldine Wrigall, aged twenty-eight, married her captain at Newcastle, New South Wales, early in 1907 and sailed with him in the *Grace Harwar* on a voyage to Tocopilla, Chile. She had tuberculosis: nobody seems to have told her that to make the eastward passage across the South Pacific in a full-rigged ship in winter was not really the place for a consumptive. She steadily weakened, and died as the anchor went down in Tocopilla Bay.

I had heard of this case. When I joined the *Grace Harwar* at Wallaroo twenty-two years later, in 1929, there was a yarn told by some aboard that she was a "hoodoo ship" and had been that way since a master had buried his wife in the ballast. He had killed her, of course (or there wouldn't be a yarn) and the crew was determined that he should be brought to trial. Just why in these circumstances he should choose to carry the evidence against him in the ship, nobody said: his case (according to the yarn) was that the evidence would clear him. The substance of the yarn was that her ghost walked and put a curse on the ship, or something: the ship killed someone every voyage.

This last statement, unfortunately, seemed to be true. She did lose people, and that voyage was to kill my shipmate, young Ronald Walker. But I was surprised, going through the official log at Hayes, to find there was some truth in the yarn. Captain Hudson records that he had had the body embalmed at Tocopilla and would carry it in the ballast back to New South Wales. The ship sailed empty back to Newcastle for another coal cargo to Chile (in the absence of a nitrate cargo at paying rates to Europe): she had about a thousand tons of ballast. At Newcastle, Captain Hudson left, with his wife's remains. She had probably asked him to take her back to Australia, after the wet misery of the Roaring Forties run from New South Wales to Tocopilla, though her husband drove the full-rigger across in little over six weeks.

Perhaps the oddest cause of death, and one of the strangest incidents mentioned in the logs, are both in the entry for the wife of the master of the ship *Scottish Moors,* on a long passage from Swansea to San Francisco in 1905. Like so many, this is not a well-kept log, by no means clearly written by an educated man. It says little and that badly, as if the master regretted the necessity to write in it at all and left everything possible unsaid—not such a bad idea when writing for bureaucracy. In one of the hard blows off the Horn that winter, the cook—a Swedish youth aged nineteen—is washed right out of his galley, swept overboard and drowned. As no one expected a cook to be lost in this way and there was much difficult sail-handling going on at the time, no one saw the cook go. He was missed when, hours later, an ordinary seaman came along to collect the meal. The galley was empty of meals, utensils, and cook.

The next death is listed as "Rose Tedford, 23, Stewardess, Irish: cause of death, over-excitement causing fit from which she never regained consciousness."

It appears that the cause of the fit was something the cabin boy did, exactly what is by no means clear. What on earth could a cabin boy do? What cabin boy? It was unusual for such ships to carry one. None was on the Articles. She had died within thirty minutes "from the time she fell over unconscious, caused by the over-excitement, until heart and pulse stopped." The *Scottish Moors* must have had an extraordinary cabin boy.

Indeed she had. The only cabin boy on the crew list was Captain and Mrs. Tedford's baby son.

NOTE: SOME FURTHER LIGHT ON THE *Aberfoyle* MYSTERY IS SHED BY CAPTAIN H. STRÖM, MASTER OF THE STEAMSHIP *Tagliaferro*, IN A BRIEF ARTICLE PUBLISHED IN THE "ANNUAL DOG WATCH" FOR 1970 BY THE SHIPLOVERS' SOCIETY OF VICTORIA, AUSTRALIA. CAPTAIN STRÖM RECALLS THAT HE WAS BOUND ALONG THE WEST COAST OF AUSTRALIA TOWARD DERBY TO LOAD LIVE CATTLE WHEN HE SIGHTED THE SHIP CLOSE INSHORE, UNDER A PRESS OF SAIL, OFF GANTHEAUME BAY. WHAT ANY BIG SQUARE-RIGGED SHIP COULD BE DOING THERE HE COULD NOT IMAGINE, AND THOUGHT FIRST THAT JAVA FEVER OR SOME SUCH INFECTION MUST HAVE DECIMATED HER CREW. BUT SHE WAS FIRING DISTRESS ROCKETS. HIS BOAT WENT, TO DISCOVER THAT ALL SHE NEEDED WAS A NAVIGATOR. SECOND MATE AMOS (NOT AMERY), WHO HAD BEEN A SAILING-SHIP MASTER, AT ONCE VOLUNTEERED AND WAS PUT ABOARD, WITH LOCAL CHARTS OF THE DIFFICULT AREA SHE HAD SAILED INTO. THE MASTER'S WIFE HAD IN FACT DIED BEFORE THE SHIP LEFT NORWAY: NOT ONE BUT TWO LITTLE GIRLS WERE ABOARD, WITH THE STEWARD'S WIFE LOOKING AFTER THEM. THE MASTER HAD GOT THE SHIP PAST THE CAPE OF GOOD HOPE AND ON COURSE TOWARDS BASS STRAIT FOR MELBOURNE BEFORE TAKING SO THOROUGHLY TO DRINK THAT HE KILLED HIMSELF, BUT NO ONE ABOARD HAD KNOWLEDGE ENOUGH TO KEEP THE COURSE CORRECTED FOR VARIATION AND OTHER COMPASS ERROR. SO SHE HAD RUN IN ON THE WEST AUSTRALIAN COAST SOME 500 MILES NORTH OF HER COURSE, AND WAS FORTUNATE NOT TO HAVE PILED UP.

"I SHALL ALWAYS REMEMBER THE STRANGE ENCOUNTER," WROTE CAPTAIN STRÖM, "THE GROUP OF DESPONDENT FACES WHICH CHANGED AS WE GAVE THEM HOPE, THE TWO PITIFUL FIGURES OF THE LITTLE GIRLS STANDING WITH THE STEWARDESS BY THE RAIL. . ." BUT IT WAS SECOND MATE AMOS WHO CAUSED THE MASTER'S BODY TO BE BURIED AND SO DESTROYED THE EVIDENCE OF HIS SUICIDE, CAUSING THE CHARGE AGAINST THE *Aberfoyle's* CREW AT MELBOURNE.

Chapter six

THE HARSH FACTS OF ECONOMICS

THE STRAIN was on good sailing-ship masters (and bad) in port and at sea. The life was not one for elderly men, but recruitment of younger masters had virtually stopped.

The deep-sea square-rigged ship became unattractive as a career for the ambitious when the lines went out of business, and the opening of the Suez Canal—with the consequent steady improvement in the economy and performance of deep-sea steamships since there were obviously many excellent trades they could capture—spelled the end for them. Jute, rice, and the other useful cargoes of the East and the parcel trades as well went to steam, naturally. The better sort of steamship, reasonably dependable in its loading and arrival dates and preferred by merchants, financiers, and insurers alike, was a sure winner in all regular trades. First India, then all the East went to the powered ships: then the passenger and cargo-liner trade to Australia and New Zealand, and soon a considerable share of the bulk cargo trades too. (A cargo liner is one of a fleet of vessels loading and sailing regularly, at advertised intervals, from a range of ports at one end of the world—or side of the Atlantic—and returning regularly to another.) The Glasgow *Lochs* were the last sailing cargo liners and excellent ships they were, well sailed and well run. As a young child, I can remember being taken to the Victoria Dock in Melbourne to see five of these graceful vessels alongside together there about 1907. That was the last time such a sight was available.

Riding on its dirty great coal fields and red-brown iron ore, exploiting its hordes of pale workers, its underfed women and children, and its mechanical and inventive genius, Britain concentrated on the steamship and made a world success of them. She had the wherewithal to build them and provide them with cargoes too, and she had accumulated capital to finance them. For a while, a few tramp sailing-ship "lines" kept going, such as Weir's big *Banks* and Law's *Shires* of Glasgow, and Milne's *Invers* of Aberdeen. The handy little *Inver* barks were soon too small to earn their keep and replacement costs. The *Banks* and too many of the *Shires* (to judge at any rate by performance and the surviving official logs) were often badly handled both in the matter of crew relations and their sailing. None of these lines survived the First World War more than a year or two, and then only with remnants. World War I gave them freights briefly but its aftermath quickly killed them.

Any man of foresight knew that British commercial sail must soon be finished, by the turn of the twentieth century. It is no wonder that younger British officers refused to stay with the ships though many grew to respect and admire them, heartbreaks as they so often were. It was no wonder, too, that so few masters were able to manage anything like comfortable retirement, or that so many died in harness. The Norwegians, Swedes, and to a less extent the Danes and Finns (flying the flag of Russia until the Revolution) kept many going with small companies which really ran and managed them, without benefit of so-called "managing owners." If they had such persons at all (some laws required them to be appointed) they were old shipmasters: and all these Scandinavians maintained their tradition of treating their masters, officers, and crews reasonably well. They still had considerable fleets of small fry to provide the best type of recruit, long after Britain's and America's fleets of these had declined.

As for the French and Germans who both maintained effective fleets until the First World War (and the Germans, starting again, for years afterward, keeping a vigorous remnant at sea until the Second World War), these were in a way special cases. German tramp sailing lines inevitably went the way of all flesh in due course, like the British and American. Where they differed, and strikingly succeeded, was in building up and maintaining an excellent cargo-liner sailing-ship trade, right at the end of the sailing-ship era.

In this, the professional German attributes of devotion to hard work and efficiency, clear-headed business acumen and the encouragement of the good workman greatly helped (and more about this later).

The imaginative and practical French, with rich colonies scattered about the earth (from New Caledonia to Indo-China, Madagascar to Tahiti, the West Indies to South India) had plenty of bulk cargoes to be moved and efficient sailing ships could move them, while at the same time maintaining a large reservoir of seamen of use to her Navy. So France encouraged the Cape Horn ship and her men, and produced both by the hundred. There were bounties for builders, for owners, for ships—tonnage bounties and mileage bounties among others, so that *good* ships could still be built and could afford to go seeking cargoes, properly maintained and manned, when they were built.

Both the French and German twentieth-century Cape Horn fleets were extensive, efficient, and included some magnificent ships. They were maintained fleets, their owners building replacements. The last German Cape Horner was built in 1926, the last French in the first decade of this century, the last British in 1905. Apart from the Danish four-masted bark *Viking*, built by Burmeister and Wain at Copenhagen in 1907 partly as a school ship, the Scandinavians built few if any big square-rigged ships this century. When those built elsewhere were worn out, they could provide no replacements. The French bounty system collapsed (with so much else) after the First World War, and soon the splendid great French sailing ships—apart from a few gallant survivors like the Helsingfors school-ship *Fennia* ex-*Champigny* (which in 1970 was still a hulk in the Falkland Islands and is scheduled for restoration in San Francisco) and a bark or two in the West Indies logwood trade—were no more.

The last handicap against the powered ship was Cape Horn. The great length of any sea passage from Europe to anywhere on the west coast of the Americas, no matter how reached, was a great bar, aided by the lack of facilities for maintenance, refueling, boiler and engine repairing, berthing and rapid cargo-handling in ports which were mainly open roadsteads. The sailing ship could stand these things, with her low capital costs and overheads and ability to use her own crew for all purposes short of dry-docking. She was a penny-pincher: a few pounds could take her a long way. But she was no longer worth replacing: sentence of her inevitable banishment shone from her white sails.

The last sail-banisher was that Horn-dodger, a working Panama Canal, and that was on the way.

At the turn of the nineteenth century, Chairman James Lilburn of the Clyde Sailing-ship Owners' Association, was still telling a meeting of that body that the general situation for big sailing ships was good. Freights were good, he said (possibly because of the South African—the so-called Boer—War on at the time): nonetheless steamers of large tonnage were being built increasingly, but no British sailers. Many large French ships were being added to an already considerable fleet annually, aided by their bounty system, and these would be "formidable rivals in the West Coast and San Francisco trades" (coal out and nitrates back from Chile, coal or general out and grain and general back from San Francisco and Puget Sound).

His listeners heard, and went away and ordered steamships. Britain had well over two million tons of sailing ships at the turn of the century. Far-seeing businessmen reckoned that was enough. What was to come when the Boer War ended? There was the flare-up of the Russo-Japanese War, indeed, which provided a few charters for nitrate cargoes from Chile to Japan, and maybe a chance to try to run the blockade to Vladivostok—but not this for sailing ships. It had little profit for any ships. And that nagging idea for the Panama Canal was more than coming up again after the French failures. If those United States engineers got *that* going, it meant the end of sailing-ship trade from Europe to the West Coast of the Americas. Anybody could see that!

There would still be the Pacific cross-trades—coals from

Newcastle, New South Wales, to Chile and Peru, Mexico, California: lumber from Puget Sound to Australia: some transpacific grain from good harvests—and a short-cut through Panama might take a long time to have serious effects on the bulk trade to and from Australia, nor was it likely to bother the case-oil business between the eastern ports of New York, New Jersey, and Pennsylvania and the Far East. This kept a fleet of large sailing ships busy. But some far-sighted oil companies were already planning transport by tank ships, and bulk installations ashore. The sailing-ship cargoes were dependent on donkeys' backs for shore transport, with a case of two tins of kerosene slung either side. When donkey transport went, so would the sailers.

Sailing-ship owners, on the whole, put the problem into the backs of their minds. After all, since man had learned to get about the world in reasonably free trade at all, there always had been sailing ships. For a great deal of the time there had been no other ships. Man had accumulated a tremendous know-how in the matter of the use of ocean winds and currents for the making of sea passages and the handling of big square-rigged ships without engines. In the preceding half-century ships had increased in size and both capacity and earning possibilities as they had never done before in all history. It was reasonable—if superficial—to conclude that as there had been work for them in the past, there would be in the future, and that neither owners nor seamen would ever be so stupid as to throw away all the tremendous knowledge so painfully accumulated in their safe voyage-making. (Safe? Well, reasonably so. The seas were always dangerous and the coming of great canals to pamper the power ships by no means robbed them of their capacity to rise up and smite proud vessels almost anywhere, at any time. They still do.)

But the conclusion was more vague hope than reasonable belief, based on comprehension of the full logic of the situation. Many able sailing-ship operators had long given them up and gone over wholly to steam: several great shipping companies, indeed, coming in with power (like Cunard and P. & O.) had never used them.

So old masters died in the ships they served, aware they were both on the scrap heap. Old mates stayed with them: young did not. What alternative the masters had to death in harness it is difficult to say, on their wage of £150 or so a year, with keep. In the larger ships their quarters were spacious, self-contained, and more or less livable. They had a sort of flat occupying the after third or so of the poop, with a large sleeping cabin on the starboard side usually fitted with a double bed and some cupboard wardrobes, a fixed sofa, and some chests of drawers. Off this opened a sort of bathroom without water other than a small tank of sea water filled daily (by an apprentice usually) and a much smaller tank holding a few pints of fresh water above a hinged washbasin standing in a slim, vertical contraption which used to be an important part of most ships' passenger cabins. On the port side were a couple of small spare cabins. Between the two sides was a spacious saloon with six or eight screw-down swing-chairs, a fine big table and a large sideboard, often ornate with polished mirrors, mahogany, and brass-railed marble top.

There was usually a small bogey-stove that could be rigged in cold weather, if the ship had been carrying a recent coal cargo and the small galley coal bunker was more or less full. Above the saloon was a large skylight for light and air (and sea water in large and unwanted quantities). Here hung a large brass swinging lamp, surrounded by geraniums which could stand anything but too often repeated douses of Cape Horn sea. These quarters could be made comfortably livable, and always were if the master's wife was aboard. Abaft the saloon, where those noble lights the stern windows used to be in ships not so deeply laden, was a large compartment where the master kept his slop-chest goods, his sea chest, spare charts (if any) and medical stores, which took up little room.

If there was a charthouse on the poop (there often was not, for such a useful shelter cost money) there were a chart table and sets of chart drawers in there, but many masters kept their working charts below, with the chronometer. For some absurd reason, the position of the ship was often kept as the master's secret. Judging by the frequency with which their odd landfalls wrecked them and mid-Pacific (or any other) islands got in their way in

Last of the American square-riggers and laid-up Alaska Packers ship at Alameda, late 1920's.

Becalmed in the Sargasso Sea—the HERZOGIN CECILIE. In a calm sails slat and bang—you can do nothing.

"Senorita"

The old SENORITA, once well known out of Sydney, was a typical Tasman Sea trader. These South Pacific barquentines were popular with deep-sea seamen.

Edward Sewell.

The big EDWARD SEWALL was an American Cape Horner.

later days, one wonders whether the ship's position was a secret from the master, too. It was an unusual ship which encouraged an interest in navigation by the mates.

In such quarters, older shipmasters, often with wives and families, lived and died. A few drank themselves to death—surprisingly few, considering the low cost of duty-free liquor even to a man on £12 a month, the temptation, and the long periods which could be spent with insufficient to do (as on a westbound Pacific crossing from Valparaiso, say, to Sydney). Even fewer shot themselves. If they survived long enough, most just wore out and quietly died.

When the well-known Maryport master, Captain W. A. Nelson, arrived at San Francisco in August, 1903, seventy-two days out from Newcastle in the ship *Acamas,* he had to lay the ship up when the coal was out, joining many more British ships. Some of them, he noted, had already been there for two years. The British ships, he said, could not accept the low rates of freight being offered—17s 6d a ton to Europe. Their minimum was 21s. But there were many subsidized French ships "busy loading grain for Europe at 17s 6d for lower hold stowage and 10s 6d for the 'tween-decks, which the Britishers could not compete with." The French mileage subsidy allowed them to undercut. The logical French held to their enacted view that the shipping bounties were necessary, both for ship-building and operation, as part of the defense of the country as well as of the national prosperity. Their merchant service was an adjunct to the state arsenals, helping to support men and make possible a navy. Its trained seamen formed a reserve which helped in the defense of French colonies. The Bounty Law of 1881 had useful results—for the merchant fleet of 735 vessels grossing 312,000 tons then grew in the following ten years to 1,157 ships of 520,000 tons—so they kept it.

The *Acamas* had been one in a congested harbor full of ships at Newcastle, New South Wales, too, all waiting to load—the big sailing ships lay there three and four deep on both the Stockton and Carrington sides of the harbor. She waited for over two months, because of labor troubles in the coal industry. She got out of San Francisco with a load of lumber from Oakland for Fremantle on a "lump sum" basis—not a large sum, but accepted in the hope of picking up grain homeward to Europe from Australia, and so showing an eventual profit on the voyage. But there was no grain: the *Acamas* had to buy ballast, sail round to Newcastle, and wait there three months for another load of coal to San Francisco. Arrived at San Francisco, once more the ship had to lay up, reducing crew to her apprentices, officers, sailmaker and carpenter. This sort of thing—long detentions, poor freights and far between—put many British sailing ships out of business. Most were sold for a third or a fourth of their building costs: though many then were between ten and fifteen years old and still had long lives before them.

For a well-built steel sailing-ship hull, forty years was not a long life, with fifty years or more for iron ships—strandings, wreck, and costly dismastings being avoided.

There was always *some* useful work to be done, at a price: the difficulty was to gear good ships down to an economy low enough to afford it and not to finish a long, hard voyage having—in effect —paid merchants for carrying their cargoes. As sailing ships became older, they had to pass more severe surveys at regular intervals in order to retain their "class," which was their authority to remain working ships carrying insured cargoes. This could be costly. Owners increasingly sold their good ships to other flags when they became due for reclassification, for such surveys were onerous. Older ships cost more to insure. When scores of sailers found themselves without cargoes to load at ports like San Francisco and Newcastle, New South Wales, it was no use to go seeking elsewhere, to make voyages of thousands of miles on chance. The number of trades open to them became more and more limited. Seasonal conditions affected grain, industrial unrest affected Australian coal, earthquakes at Valparaiso and San Francisco led to temporary boom conditions followed by slump. British ships had to beat competition from the subsidized French, from their own ships sold foreign and often better operated at less cost, especially by the Scandinavian countries and the enterprising Germans. Other factors working against them were the increasing size, range and efficiency of steam tramps, the loss to power of almost all of their own good apprentices and young officers as soon as they were qualified, and the steady progress in the cutting and building of an effective Panama Canal. By the end of the first decade of the twentieth century, this last was a certainty.

In 1906 there was still a certain attachment to the big sailing ship both in Britain and (perhaps to a less extent) in America, and a real reluctance to discard ships brought to such a stage of splendid development. In the United States, big wooden sailers were being sold cheaply for conversion into coastal barges for towing in strings. A correspondent on January 14, 1910, was pointing out that the American square-rigger was then making a last stand, instancing the sale of three 2,000-tonners from the Pacific Coast to New York, to become barges. At the same time, he said, many good British ships were being sold and delivered abroad as coal hulks. He instanced the *Samuel Plimsoll* sold to Fremantle, *Loch Tay* to Port Adelaide, and the *Scottish Isles* to Gibraltar, all as coal hulks. At least thirty of the surviving large British steel sailers were being sold foreign annually, and none had been built since 1905.

"In a few years the metal sailing ship, as far as the United Kingdom is concerned, will be but a memory of a glorious past."

In fact, her disappearance took another twenty years.

The earlier tramps were decidedly unlovely vessels and could be dangerous, too, with vulnerable engine-room skylights, heavy and inefficient hand steering, scarce power enough to get out of their own way in fresh head winds. Of thirty-four vessels posted missing in 1906, eight were steamships. The big French bark *St. Donatien,* the Britisher *Drumcraig,* the German ships *Rodenbek* and *F. Fischer,* the Norwegian barks *Jorden Bang, Columbia,* and *Coimbatore,* and the Nova Scotian barkentine *Milton* were among the missing sailing ships, though there was little doubt about the fate of the *Coimbatore.* The British bark *Zinita* had sailed into another square-rigger off the Australian coast: in the brief moment while the riggings were locked, a Norwegian deck boy leapt on to the deck of the *Zinita*. He said he was from the *Coimbatore*.

In December, 1906, a writer in the *Shipping Gazette Weekly Summary* noted that many Scots square-rigged ships were sold during the year as the owners were going into steam. "I would sooner buy six sailing ships like the *Saxon* which changed hands at £6,000—half her building price thirteen years earlier—than put £50,000 in one steamer," he says. He appreciated the difficulty in getting good officers. But he argued that there could still be a handsome return on investment in sail. San Francisco, Tacoma, and other Puget Sound ports had been fixing freely for wheat and lumber—30s a ton from San Francisco to Antwerp was typical of the year—and Australia-U.K. grain was also good. But Chilean nitrate was offering only 15s: here outward freights in building materials to Valparaiso had helped. "Union" ships had bound themselves not to accept nitrates at less than 21s 3d the ton, but they were being offered only 15s.

This "Union" was an international body of owners formed to stand against uneconomic freights, but it did not last. Sailing ships had many troubles. Apart from the missing vessels, forty-three sailing ships, each of more than 1,500 tons, were involved during '06 in casualties serious enough to cause them to be written off—driven aground in hurricanes, smashed up off the Horn or wrecked round Vancouver Island, dismasted, knocked down by steamships or by another sailing ship. Masters and officers were justly complaining over their wretched pay and conditions. Pleas for better treatment of apprentices were frequent, for the lads were "still suffering from poor food, indifferent accommodation, professional neglect" and plain exploitation. They "come from good homes, some with professional education from the school ships *Conway* or *Worcester*. Once the premium is paid, they are assured a berth to sleep and their allowance of food. The owner hands them over to the captain, the captain to the mates who could not care less," complains a parent in the *Shipping Gazette*.

"My boy coils lines, sweeps the deck, lights the binnacle, keeps time"—and, he might have added, it is entirely up to him whether he learns anything besides how to extract eggs while keeping the hens silent in the captain's chicken coop, raid the steward's stores (if any), or find his way in the unlit hold on the rare occasions when his ship might have a little foodstuffs in a general cargo.

The gentleman who preferred six *Saxons* for his £36,000 rather than one steamer for £14,000 more could have been fooling himself. Absence of depreciation, though helpful, was not vital. Steamers could earn more. It is true that 1907 was a reasonably good year for the sailing ships, but the very wet summer in Britain that year was a factor in this. It improved grain freights from Australia and California. The selling rate of good big sailing ships stood at round £3 a ton: the demand even at that low figure was not great.

By 1908, there were still 9,660 sailing vessels of 1,575,379 tons gross on the British registry, compared with 11,400 steamships of 16,501,427 gross tons. That total of near-10,000 sailers included small fry like the Devon schooner *Isabella,* 46 tons, built in 1865, and then still making at least three tough North Atlantic voyages a year and several U.K.–Spain runs as well—these in winter. Her '08 Atlantic voyages were done in an average two months and six days. She was a good old-timer of the best sort and she would work until she quietly dropped: but no more of her kind were being built.

That same year, though the White Star Line commissioned the ship *Mersey* to train forty of their own cadets, the question was being asked at Lloyd's and elsewhere whether "steam-trained juniors aren't sufficient for all purposes." And the Foreign Office was being asked—very unusually—to organize a search of the Cape Horn islands for possible survivors from yet another quartet of large limejuice missing ships including the *Toxteth, Carnedd Llewellyn,* and the *Falklandbank.* A search was organized (one of the lost apprentices must have had a relative in Parliament) but nothing found.

Also in 1908, the *Shipping Gazette and Lloyds' List Weekly Summary* (dated January 3), noted the rise of the steamer with unveiled hostility.

"Steamers can now be built at less cost than sailing ships," it reported, "and the great size of the modern tramp, with its economic consumption of coal and its enormous bunker capacity, renders it the most formidable competitor even where formerly it hardly dared show its black sides and ungainly form." Up from 5,000 to 7,500 tons and 8,500, with the same number of crew as a sailing ship half the size, doing its work on the same routes in half the time, easily and cheaply insured, spending much less time in port, the hated steamer "also carries its own appliances for rapid loading and discharging."

This was a formidable array of telling advantages. The steamer also had reasonable regularity and predictable dates of arrival. The value of the steamship's big hatches and array of easily swung cargo derricks, each served by its own steam winch, was considerable. The big sailers fought back with a donkey boiler and one or two winches, which were a help particularly if the for'ard winch could be geared or led to the windlass for anchor work on sailing day. The lower yards could be manipulated to serve as derricks, but the square-rigged ship's own standing rigging was a considerable impediment to the idea of rapid cargo working. For the whole fabric of that apparent maze had been evolved down the centuries to do the work it was designed for—to support masts and yards and facilitate the setting, trimming, and working of sails, permitting maximum manageable sail area to do maximum effective work. That creation must stand the most violent gale yet permit sails to draw driving power from the lightest air. Cargo working was not just secondary. It didn't enter the plan at all. The stuff had somehow to be put aboard despite the rigging—big balks of redwood through holes cut in bow and stern; slings, baskets, nets of stuff hauled above the rail from a whip at a yardarm block, threaded among or beneath the rigging, and lowered gently through a small hatch into a tremendous hold. Coal could be shot in one hatch at a time.

So it took weeks, sometimes months, to discharge and load even in some large ports (like Newcastle, New South Wales). If there were any "power" to assist sailing-ship cargo-handling, it was provided by one old horse, tramping up and down the wharf just enough to haul a sling of bags or basket of ballast up from the hold. Being a well-trained Australian horse, such a dobbin knew the ship's bells very well. At eight bells he stopped work and trotted off for his midday meal. At two bells, he came back very slowly. And he never took a step more than enough.

Even ships which were equipped with donkey boilers and a winch or two used the one-horsepower method of getting out their ballast and replacing it with a sufficiency of coal to keep the ship stable. It was cheaper, and there was usually considerable delay while waiting to load, caused by industrial trouble or just plain congestion, or both.

Looking at the tiers of big sailing ships at such ports as Newcastle, Iquique, Valparaiso, Talcahuano, the anchored dozens waiting for orders at Falmouth or at Queenstown, Eire, the dozens more which often assembled at ports like Melbourne, San Francisco, Cardiff, Buenos Aires, Noumea in New Caledonia, Hobart in Tasmania (bounty Frenchmen in for orders there, as it was so convenient), it was difficult to realize that the whole of that enormous fleet—still a thousand strong at the end of the First World War—was on its swift way from the face of the sea for ever: as indeed it was. It was obvious enough that many could be earning little if any profit.

Chapter seven

"TREATED AS PER MEDICAL GUIDE"

THIS *Ship Captain's Medical Guide* (or *Ship Master's:* same thing) could be a very useful publication, properly used in conjunction with a chest of drugs, dressings, etc., as laid down in the "Medical Scales for Merchant Ships Not Required to Carry Surgeons." One difficulty was that when needed, no instruction was available in the use of either. A sort of elementary knowledge of first aid was required later, almost as an afterthought, in examinations for officers' certificates of competency. This amounted to about Boy Scout standard. After all, sudden death was far more common than death by illness: less than a fourth of all casualties received any treatment at all. Putting the fallen together again, or rescuing those gone over the side in severe weather, were beyond the wit of any man: and the unfit did not survive for long at sea. (There was—still is—the excellent idea that sea voyages are "good for the health" in themselves, but such voyaging is not done by professional seamen. The real benefit of such voyages is in bringing a regular way of life and plenty of unpolluted air—in a sailing ship—to those perhaps unaccustomed to either; and an absence of stress. Simply to be without a daily newspaper even in the "good old days" could be a help.)

Ships which took persons to sea for their health carried medical men, for they were usually passenger vessels. In merchantmen, the rule really was not to be sick. There was no medical examination required for British merchant seamen before they signed on. The all-important qualification was the possession of a continuous discharge book (in which were listed the

121

ships in which an applicant had served, together with formalized appraisals of his conduct and ability) or a certificate of discharge, which was a similar piece of paper from his last ship only. If the applicant could walk, even unsteadily, to the signing-on table bearing one or other of these, and having signed the Articles joined the ship afterward, that was enough. There was a sort of tradition that unfit seafarers were all dead: illness was a luxury they could not afford. There was something in this.

But masters did their best to cope at sea with the sick and the surviving injured. Simple surgery was no great problem, for handymen like the carpenter and sailmaker could help with this. Many of the older masters had been one or other themselves (like old Captain Nelson of Maryport, master of the *Acamas,* who served seven years' apprenticeship to sailmaking before going deep-sea at all: he was highly expert at putting in stitches). But correct diagnosis of illness was quite another problem. How could the master (or anyone else aboard) cope with this? What "opening medicine" of sufficient potency or the current treatments for venereal disease could not cope with remained uncured, if nature did not take a hand. Symptoms as described in that sea-going *Medical Guide* were vague and indiscriminate. So, often, was treatment, especially in the earlier editions.

When I took the ship *Joseph Conrad* of Ipswich on a voyage around the world—57,000 miles of it, around Good Hope and the Horn, with the Coral Sea and more than enough Melanesian islands thrown in—of course I carried the faithful *Guide,* then in its nineteenth edition. Its first (and possibly best) advice was that "no vessel should haul out of dock without robust and healthy seamen." To ensure this, I had the lot medically checked before leaving. As the ship had been the Danish school-ship *Georg Stage* for eighty boys before I bought her, I had her medicine chest from this career too, with far better stocks than the British flag asked of me, and a better book. I had, by God's grace, only to cope with the usual run of lesser accidents, and outbreaks of malignant malaria in the New Guinea Islands, and the Solomons, and those nasty running infections on feet and shins caused by some tropic coral. Accidents, I'd learned, are best coped with when they arise: no seaman can foresee the varied injuries they cause and it is of little use to study books beforehand.

A great asset to recovery is the healthfulness of the sailing-ship life. One day a seaman had a nasty cut on the upper arm. Some of the muscle was bulging out. (He had a lot.) Of course I put it back in again, added a few stitches, bound the arm with good Stockholm tarry oakum, and he went back to work. He was a healthy chap, and Stockholm tar is pure stuff—or was then. There was nothing in my nineteenth edition of that *Medical Guide* to give guidance for this particular accident. As for the nasty type of malaria we picked up at Guadalcanal, it took the tropic experts at Melbourne to cope properly with that. The coral infections were a matter of constant care and clean dressings, with a refusal to be deterred by the apparent lack of progress.

I was fortunate. The average age of my whole crew was about seventeen, as in most of the Finnish grain ships where I had recruited the professionals. There was more trouble from bad teeth than from illness, and there was nothing in the *Medical Guide* about teeth. They were probably assumed to be good, to cope with the sea diet of the day—hard pantiles and harder salt beef.

But there is plenty of evidence in the official logs I studied to show that the deepwater masters made good use of the *Guide,* though its shortcomings frequently almost defeated them. A very few had wives aboard signed on the Articles as "Nurse," like Mrs. A. Keibyson, wife of the master of the ship *Clackmannanshire* of Glasgow on her round voyage from South Wales to Antofagasta, on to Portland, Oregon, and back to Cork, in 1907–'08. The nurse could have been busy coping with lesser ills, but the casualties in those ships were usually too gravely injured for any nurse to help them. An apprentice was washed off the forecastle head —that most exposed of all places—and a young A.B. was pitched from an upper tops'l yard. They got the apprentice back, which was smart boat work: he is logged for working at the bow without the life line his captain's orders called for. The A.B. went in the sea, by night, in a howling gale off the Horn: aged twenty-one.

Many masters were presented with medical problems which

would have been difficult for trained medical men to solve. Captain W. S. Procter, of the Liverpool ship *Dynomene,* had his hands full when the ship was partially dismasted off the Horn in the winter of 1907 while on passage from Tyne dock toward San Francisco. Falling rigging killed nobody but badly injured four seamen, three of them A.B.'s and one ordinary seaman. They were all carried into the cabin: two had severe head injuries; one a crushed knee; the fourth, crushed hands. Sending for the carpenter (for splints and other useful woodwork) and the steward, Captain Procter "did the best I could for them," setting the bones, patching the hands, putting the leg with the crushed knee into splints. "All did well" except the O.S., whose name was Hendrick. He had "something wrong I cannot make out." The *Dynomene* at the time had only a third of her foremast standing, and soon lost another A.B., so back they sailed to Montevideo to patch up her seamen and her rigging before taking on the Horn once more. This she did: the second time she made it, though she was over ten months out from the Tyne when she finally reached San Francisco, with those four seamen fit and well.

The listed kit of A.B. Jansen (who was killed) included "1 blanket, 1 towel, 8 bars Sunlight Soap, 2 plugs tobacco, 1 Book of Psalms, 1 box with few photos"—a pitiful collection of belongings for a man to take on winter off the Horn, and a two-year voyage. The soap and the plug tobacco were bought from the slop chest aboard. He could scarcely have joined as a "pierhead jump," with his psalms and his photos: that must have been his idea of the essential kit.

Many of these men took on the world with next to nothing. For example, Bos'n Mike Flaherty of the *Kate Thomas*—a ship which was fatal to many seamen, in the end taking her whole crew down with her when a steamer blundered into her in the English Channel—left "1 clay pipe, 2 singlets, 2 blankets" in a very small kit, when he was swept from the foc's'l head off the Horn. He was supervising the rigging of a preventer foretack (an extra heavy wire to hold down the wind'ard corner of the foresail) to the cathead. Flaherty's age is given as thirty-two. Those tough Irish often began long voyages with no warm clothes, little bedding, almost nothing at all. Nor did they patronize the master's slop chest, except for plug tobacco. There are many entries of seamen who left no salable kit, and some who left literally nothing, but these were mainly pierhead jumps or the desperately stranded who had stowed away.

In the *Cambrian Princess*, Captain William Roberts (an Abersoch man) could get no lead from the *Medical Guide* nor from anyone aboard in the case of a seaman who, straining at sail-handling in a gale aloft, climbed painfully down the rigging holding his crotch. Examination showed that "both his testicles were shifted together in the right scrotum." The resourceful Roberts "tied them up in a bag" and arranged a sling, put the man on light work and hurried on toward Taltal, Chile, to land him for treatment. Another A.B., an American named John Shepherd, had fallen out of the rigging. A shipmate beside him on the yard said that Shepherd "had a sudden fit." No treatment was necessary.

An unusual accident to George Mason, cook of the beautiful ship *Loch Katrine*, defied treatment. Near Cape Horn on passage from Melbourne toward the Channel for orders in 1907, the "ship rolling heavily threw the cook down in his galley and he having a wooden leg it got knocked out of its place" and pierced his stomach with considerable force. Poor man, there was nothing in the *Medical Guide* for this, though Captain Anderson (from Park House, Skelmorlie, Scotland) did his best. The cook's internal injuries were too serious: down there, there was no place to land him. After a few days, "he quietly died" when the ship was off the pitch of the Horn.

Cook Mason's kit included "2 wooden legs, 1 axe, 9 sox odd, 1 shoe-horn," a few items of clothing, mending gear, "1 book Bogatsky's Golden Treasure, 1 pack playing cards, 1 marline spike, 1 watch." He must have been an old sailor.

There was no known treatment, either, for one E. Stanistreet, A.B., in a ship called the *Ardnamurchan*, who died, apparently, of being "stabbed by a native woman in a brothel three times" at Taltal. This might be regarded, perhaps, as a hazard of the profession, but the case of the A.B. in the ship *Toxteth* who "died of privation in the desert" seems odd even for such an inveterate wanderer as a Cape Horn able seaman. The official logs for that voyage (which began, apparently, at Antwerp on June 2, 1902, and ended at Antwerp on April 15, 1907: a voyage so long that a second Articles of Agreement had to be opened for it and a new official log begun, at Newcastle, N.S.W., on July 6, 1906) are most interesting, especially as the *Toxteth* was posted missing on her next voyage. The A.B. who died of privation was a deserter named as M. J. Marsh, from South Wales. He had been jailed at Caldera, Chile, for refusing duty aboard—the duty at the time was working out Newcastle coal twelve hours a day—and had escaped. Some days later, he was found "beside the railway in the desert, almost starved to death." He had been staggering along with the tracks to guide him, wanting only to put as much distance as possible between the ship and himself. The Chileans who picked him up offered to take him back to the *Toxteth,* but he refused. He was taken to a hospital where he died. He was almost dehydrated.

Able seaman Marsh must have felt strongly about the *Toxteth* to prefer death to return aboard. She had made a tremendous voyage, beginning under Captain Thomas Motley with a passage from Antwerp to San Diego direct. At the California port another A.B. died in the hospital. (Pinned in the log is a receipt from the Sisters of Mercy of St. Joseph's Sanatorium at San Diego, dated Dec. 10, 1902, for $25 for "care of a seaman landed ill 10 days at $2.50 per diem," and a bill (paid) for Johnson and Connell, funeral directors, for another $63 for burying the man. This includes $25 "for burial case and box," $10 for the hearse, and $5 for the priest. It was very expensive for poor sailors to be buried ashore.)

From San Diego the *Toxteth* sailed to Puget Sound, thence to Port Adelaide, probably with Oregon pine. The voyage continues with transpacific hauls—Port Adelaide–Newcastle, N.S.W.–Caldera–Sydney for orders Newcastle–Valparaiso–Newcastle–Caldera again: and here Marsh could take no more, and ran. It was a pity, for he had then only a year or so to go. It took three masters to stick out the *Toxteth*'s long voyage: poor Marsh had done well.

Sailing-ship seamen, of course, would desert anywhere. But what so perturbed the ship *Castle Rock*'s ordinary seaman James B. Smith, an American aged seventeen, that after an unsuccessful attempt to desert in a barrel off the Hawaiian Islands—he was rescued and put in irons until the islands were out of sight—he contrived to make himself a small raft from "a bucket rack and some small planks" when his ship was sailing through Torres Strait, and got away with this frail contraption? Why? He could not hope to get far. The *Castle Rock* could not have been that bad, on that long passage from Port Townsend, Washington, toward Fremantle. The ordinary seaman was not seen nor heard of again. He launched his raft in bad weather off Double Island in Torres Strait, a wild spot in those days. A preference for the delights of Hawaii rather than the hard life of the limejuicer is understandable, but Torres Strait then was a coral-strewn labyrinth unfit for ships or men. The *Castle Rock* was safely anchored, hanging on by her two best bowers.

In a comparatively small ship called the *Loch Trool*—of Liverpool, not a Scot—the master is listed in the official log as having died of D.T.'s. The mate's treatment was "castor oil mixed with brandy," which he says was "according to the *Medical Guide*." A rather odd incident aboard the *Loch Trool* that voyage (Bunbury toward Gravesend, November 5, 1904 to March 14, 1905) might have helped lead to those D.T.'s. The official log, in Captain R. Mainland's writing (apparently), records the sudden disappearance of Able Seaman Rudolf Anderson. His shipmates said he had a revolver. This was gone, along with one bullet. There was also a line hanging over the bows. Anderson was a "moody man who kept himself to himself." After a while, watchmates from New York (where that round voyage had begun) said he had "shot a man in Boston some years back." Suicide while of unsound mind, said the log.

But four days later, R. Anderson was found staggering about the foredeck, "thin and emaciated and covered with rust." He could not or would not say where he had been. He denied he had taken the revolver, declaring that he had sold it in Newcastle, N.S.W. He "had been in a trance," writes Captain Mainland, obviously mystified.

Some weeks later, Anderson was paid off (by mutual consent —that save-all phrase) before the British vice-consul at Valparaiso. Nothing was said about murders. Probably he was still in a trance.

That *Ship Captain's Medical Guide* was no use aboard the *Almora* of Greenock on her Australian voyage of 1904–05, for the treatment of one "A. Turple A.B. effected [*sic*] by the moon," and because of this had been using insolent language to the afterguard and calling the master a "pimp." No evidence is written explaining the connection of these proceedings with the moon, other than Captain Nicolle's remark that he did not think Turple was "accountable for his actions at all times." A belief in the power of the moon at the full to pull sleeping mariners' faces out of shape was held by some older seamen aboard the *Bellands* in 1921, but the countenance of the ordinary seaman used as evidence appeared to me to be lopsided anyway. Driven out of the foc's'l in the tropics by bedbugs, most of us slept in the open. I took the precaution of keeping my own face out of the moonlight, when I thought of it.

There was no treatment specified for Mr. Swan, the second mate of the *Lindfield*, who—according to the log—was poisoned by a cat bite. How this was suffered is not recorded, but it must have been quite a bite. He was taken to a hospital at Newcastle, N.S.W., for treatment, as the poison had affected a whole arm. This *Lindfield*, according to her official log for a voyage lasting from her sailing from Antwerp on April 18, 1903, to arrival at Queenstown, Ireland, on June 29, 1906, had all the standard troubles of the average British ship of those times—loggings for everybody (a hundred men pass through the Articles), desertions everywhere, too many entries for men "returned to ship from jail," and so on. She spent two years of the thirty-eight months commission on the transpacific trade and was in San Francisco and Newcastle twice, notorious ports for inspired desertion, "crimping," and so forth. But it might not have been just the saloon cat that was poisonous. The general pattern of the men's behavior—and often the apprentices' as well—in too many limejuicers of that period is deplorable, at least as reflected in their surviving official logs. There was obviously something drastically wrong in the way in which many of the ships were run.

The four-masted bark *Jordanhill* had more or less constant trouble between crew and master about food during a two-year voyage between September 2, 1904, and August 29, 1906. She lost five men killed or died: three more successfully deserted by self-made raft at sea, somewhere near Simbawa Island (led by one Gilbert Kennedy, O.S.) and another got away by swimming ashore off Mollendo, Peru. Even the steward's wife, aboard as a real stewardess, was in trouble for not having the master's breakfast ready smartly enough, and she and her husband were put ashore at Hong Kong.

At Hong Kong, too, suddenly some light is thrown on all this deplorably bad morale and unrest. Captain Kennedy is summoned to the Mercantile Marine office ashore. There is an investigation into the constant complaints of insufficient food. It is found that the crew were on short rations for eighty-four days during the passage from New York because the master was using false weights. A note in the official log (on page 24) orders him to "make compensation at the rate of 1 *d* a day to each member of the crew."

Seven shillings each! It would scarcely buy them a good dinner in Hong Kong, even in 1905. The troubles continue. The penalty imposed was derisory. How long had the skinflint captain been using these false weights? Probably for years. It may seem incredible that shipmasters should think such meanness worthwhile or practice it on an organized scale when it must profit them little and be fatal to morale. They were so poorly paid themselves that they *had* to make something on the side. Unlike so many of the seamen, they were not drifters but most were qualified, stable men capable of good service if such were appreciated. The managing-owner type had not the slightest interest in them except to harass them. Over a long voyage, many petty thefts could amount to considerable sums: a ship chandler's bill for a voyage was a large item. The meanness aft in some ships could be extreme, not only toward the mariners but to the officers and afterguard as well.

Joining the ship *Terpsichore* at Port Talbot, Wales, in 1910, a new second mate found the afterguard at tea in the saloon. Invited in, he sat down, absentmindedly picked up a ship's biscuit and began to butter it.

"Turn that biscuit over!" shrilled the captain's wife.

The bewildered officer did not at first grasp what she meant. But, looking down, he noticed he had been putting a scrape of butter on the side with holes in and so, he realized, possibly causing the tooth-breaker to absorb a quarter of a milligram more butter than the smooth side could.

So he turned the biscuit over, and he did not sign in that ship. Mean masters he was used to but the prospect of a voyage with a mean and noisy wife was too much. Some such wives used to supervise the steward at his weekly issue of stores to be certain that not an extra grain of sugar nor anything else reached anyone.

(Poor women, their attitude is understandable: they wanted a home ashore someday, too, and they were just as hard on themselves. They had learned that they had to be.)

The mate of the big full-rigged ship *Wiscombe Park*—a slow, wall-sided brute which ended her days as a German named *Greif* (according to some it should have been *Grief*) knew better than to accept his captain's treatment out of the *Medical Guide.* Laid up with severe stomach pains on an Australian voyage in 1905–'06, the log records the mate's refusal to accept such treatment.

"I gave him the book to read for himself," writes Captain Maurice L. Power (a friendly Irishman), "and he offered to take Mixture No. 6."

So Mixture No. 6 it was. It must have been quite wrong, for the mate grew steadily worse.

At Melbourne he was taken to the Royal Alfred Hospital. He said he had gallstones; the hospital said jaundice. Anyway, in

The work aloft called for clear heads, no 'nerves.'

Aloft in a small gale

*The accident! (A boy was in trouble high aloft. H[...]
survived.)*

It was a long way down.

OFFICIAL LOG of the *"Zinita"*

from *Wallaroo S. Australia* **towards** *The Channel for Orders*

Date of the occurrence entered with Hour.	Place of the Occurrence, or situation by Latitude and Longitude at Sea.	Date of Entry.	Entries required by Act of Parliament.	Amount of Fine or Forfeiture Inflicted.
4 P.M. 7. 2. 06	Lat. 48.38 S. Long. 170.0 E.	4. 3. 06	**Sale of Effects** Part of Effects of Albert J. Pretty Apprentice (who fell overboard on passage to Melbourne) Sold by Auction & the amount obtained for each Article.	

½ doz curtain rings) 2 bunk Curtains	2/-	1 Uniform Cap & cord	0.10.6	1 Tam O'shanter	0.8.0
top coat	1.0.0	1 suit serge	1.5.0	2 mufflers	0.5.0
Reefing Jacket	1.01.0	1 serge coat. vest. & pants	1.0.0	6 Hankerchiefs	0.1.6
suit oilskin & southwester	0.5.0	2 white suits	0.17.0	1 Cap -	0.3.0
				2 pair braces	0.3.0
long oil coat	0.9.0	1 Guernsey	0.18.0	2 rubber fronts)	
pair sea boots	2.10.0	9 Shirts	1.6.0	3 " Collars	0.5.0
pair boots	4.0	2 Sleeping suits	0.17.0	1 " Cuffs	
				4 linnen Collars)	
pair shoes	1.6	10 pair socks	0.18.0	4 Ties	0.8.6
hard felt hat	1.0	2 pair mits	0.6.0	1 Silk Hankerchief	0.2.0
cloths brush) shoe brushes)	6.0	1½ Bars Sunlight soap) ½ " White Soap)	1.0	2 paws 2 sail Hooks) 4 needles in cake)	0.3.0
5 Pkgs Matches	2.0	1 Cake Exsamie soap)		1 tin tooth powder	0.6
1 Pkg Writing paper)	1.0	4 pair drawers.) 9 singlets —)	1.18.6	1 looking Glass	0.6
Pkgs envelopes) 2 small bottle ink)	0.6	3 pair stockings)	0.9.6	Blanket.	0.2.0
	£ 6.3.0		£ 10.6.6		£ 2.2.0

	£	s.	d.
	2	2	0
	10	6	6
	6	3	0
	Total £ 18.11.6	

Ludovic Scheyrens Apprentice

F. W. Macdonald Master

C. D. Watson Mate

A page from the log of the ZINITA listing the effects and auction prices brought for the effects of a lost apprentice. This sale and list were required by law.

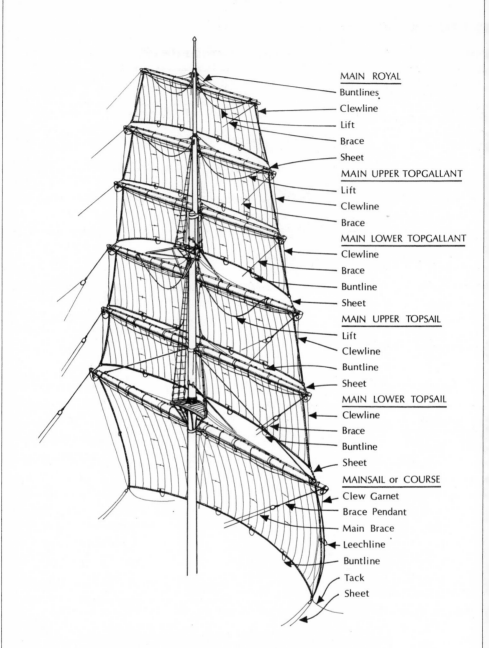

MAIN ROYAL
Buntlines
Clewline
Lift
Brace
Sheet

MAIN UPPER TOPGALLANT
Lift
Clewline
Brace

MAIN LOWER TOPGALLANT
Clewline
Brace
Buntline
Sheet

MAIN UPPER TOPSAIL
Lift
Clewline
Buntline
Sheet

MAIN LOWER TOPSAIL
Clewline
Brace
Buntline
Sheet

MAINSAIL or COURSE
Clew Garnet
Brace Pendant
Main Brace
Leechline
Buntline
Tack
Sheet

The steel main-mast of a modern square-rigger

hospital he stayed, his effects landed with him and his salary at an end including the £5 monthly he had allotted to his wife. (His kit is listed as "1 Sea Chest, 1 Bag, 1 Bed, 1 Umbrella, 1 Walking Stick.") What happens to these sailors who are forever being thrown on the discard, left ashore through no fault of their own? Some countries insist on at least some subsistence money being left for them and also a minimum fare back to the United Kingdom, if unfit to follow their profession again. Australia does not seem to be one of these: there is no evidence of anything but the strictly kept account of wages for the discarded mate, in the official log records. What about his wife, too, when her alloted 25s a week suddenly stops? She has to fend for herself. The threat of the poorhouse must have been very real to these people, officers abaft the mast and men before it, though there was at least one charity which tried to do something for some of them, and did.

The lovely old clipper *Ariel*—a real clipper, not a model for pretty Christmas cards but a wood-and-iron-and-fiber beautifully modeled, graceful and sea-kindly ship—turns up in the dusty boxes of the official logs at Hayes, too. Her log is there for a round voyage begun in London on July 28, 1905, and ended at Yarmouth, East Anglia, eleven months later, by way of a passage around Good Hope to Hobart and Launceston, Tasmania (probably with general cargo), thence to Port Broughton, South Australia, and homeward around the Horn with grain. Her master was Thomas F. Beadon, of Dartmouth, Devon—a good man. There are very few desertions, no nonsense, no crew troubles. The *Ariel* was 117 days to Hobart and 124 days from Port Broughton to Yarmouth—no clipper passages, but she was an old race horse then, fighting hard to earn her oats. There was neither sense nor profit in trying to drive her, and she hadn't a racing crew. Sailed as a cargo carrier, not a clipper, she was handy enough.

An A.B. named Arthur Wadsworth, from Goole, in the east of England, aged forty-nine (more or less) died at sea from kidney disease (master's diagnosis). Here was another stalwart who would have nothing to do with any concoction from that *Ship*

Captain's Medical Guide. The log records that he came aft in the northeast trades not to report sick, but asking Captain Beadon for "Dutch drops," which he said were for stones in the bladder. There were no Dutch drops aboard, and the *Guide* had not heard of them. Captain Beadon offered any other treatment from the *Guide,* but it was Dutch drops or nothing. So it was nothing. Wadsworth had to lay up, first in his bunk for'ard, then in the spare cabin aft, still demanding his Dutch drops. He declares he will not take anything else, "not for a £10-note," saying he will soon be better. He isn't: he weakens. The master treats him for Bright's disease according to the *Medical Guide*—saline mixture and a "good linseed poultice round his loins," on a diet of arrowroot and beef tea. The log continues: "Sept 1 7 p.m. Temp. 101° gave two purging pills: threw up pills so I gave him one more. He threw that up too. Sept. 2. Died. Buried."

His death seems to have taken Captain Beadon by surprise. He had been doing his best, but he had never heard of Dutch drops. It probably would have made no difference if he had.

The balance of wages shows a credit of nil—earned £3.14: advance £3, slops 14/-. Effects delivered to George Hawthorn, shipping master at Hobart, included unusual signs of affluence —"2 suits, 3 pr white cuffs, 5 white fronts, 7 white collars, 5 neck ties, 3 brushes, 1 cloth overcoat, 2 woolen sweaters" and a small supply of working clothes but no oilskins or sea boots or sou'-wester, or sailor's gear at all. Who was this Arthur Wadsworth? Was he choosing this passage as A.B. to immigrate to Tasmania? He was or had been a real A.B.—no doubt of that—but he must have been something else, too, despite his affection for "Dutch drops." No one aboard ever found out what they were.

Now and again, strange characters emerge from the pages of the official logs. Who, for instance, was George Warburton, signed as A.B. in the ship *Bardowie* on her voyage from South Shields toward San Francisco (by way of a call in distress at Cape Town en route)—a passage which took exactly twelve months? Mr. Warburton, aged fifty-three, died at sea of consumption, according to the log. He left the kit of no able seaman, for it included items like "1 soft felt hat, 10 mufflers, 4 pillow-cases, 1 bundle cloth patches, 1 housewife, 2 Bibles, 9 neck-ties, 1 looking glass, 1 bank-book and marriage certificate." He may have been a passenger, but it was not usual to sign these as able seamen nor was it lawful to do so. Able seamen were qualified persons, in accordance with the Act. Passengers were usually disguised as pursers, or as stewardesses if female. The well-equipped Mr. Warburton departs this life, and that is the end of him—and the beginning too, as far as the log is concerned.

A Welsh A.B. named Daniel Edwards who died on the *Port Caledonia* about the same time was certainly not an A.B., for he was reduced to O.S. as soon as the ship sailed. His ignorance showed up immediately, for the sailing-ship A.B. learned his way around the rigging of *any* ship within five minutes. So Edwards —if that was his name: he might have had someone else's papers, for he would need only one certificate of discharge to sign on— sat on the main hatch a few days later and died. "Heart failure," says the log. He left a large kit which included (in 1903), "1 tooth brush" (the first and only mention of such a thing in any list), "20 handkerchiefs, 1 dictionary, 2 pair leggins, 1 magnifying-glass" —a very odd lot. This is the one and only listing of handkerchiefs, too. Real seamen like one John McClillen, A.B., who died off the Golden Gate, left items like "2 fids, 1 box sail needles, 1 dittybag, 1 small pricker, 2 sou'westers, 2 jerseys, 1 palm."

Of course, work went on in bad weather or good without accident or thought of accident as the normal thing. At least three-fourths of all the big sailing ships caught off the Horn in 1905 lost no lives. Men and lads knew their way and their work aloft without thinking about it—watching that they took no missteps, hauled on no slack gaskets, trusted life to no lines—and climbed up and down to wind'ard with the aid of the ship's leeward rolls, and swung with that natural rhythm and balance on the high footropes which they had so quickly to acquire. On deck, they made their way never far from the life lines, ready to leap and hang on, legs swinging, watching the weather rail—sometimes more wary than others, depending on who had the helm. For there were men (and lads) with a sort of natural touch there who could somehow keep the worst of the seas off the deck, and others whose grip of the spokes made a bitch of the ship at once.

Sometimes one finds log entries like "Logged for striking so-and-so helmsman, blamed for bringing a dangerous sea aboard": though such entries are rare. In the bark *Conway Castle,* R. V. Jones, master, an A.B. named Swanson "struck A.B. Griffiths in the nose causing bleeding because Swanson got wet through water coming aboard while Griffiths was at the wheel. Fined 5*s.*"

This *Conway Castle* does not come from her logs as a happy ship. Naked men chase the mate around the deck. An A.B. named Lionel Toynbee gets a month's jail for deserting at Albany, Australia. An apprentice dies of "having his leg caught in bitts when lowering the t'gallant halliards." The leg was mashed and infected, causing "lockjaw" within a few days: the *Medical Guide* could not cope with this.

All falls from aloft were not fatal, though the vast majority were. I came upon a few cases where the fallen had lived, more or less miraculously. A Liverpool able seaman with the unusual name (in a Cape Horner) of Mahomed Abdullah had a most unusual escape from death when he fell from aloft at sea in the *Leicester Castle,* in the course of a long voyage which began in Dublin on April 4, 1905, and ended at Wallaroo, Australia (at least in the surviving official log) some three years later. Mahomed Abdullah fell overboard while furling the fores'l, "striking the rigging and sail in his fall." Picked up smartly, he complained that his legs were "strained." A brief period off duty to recover their use, and he was soon at work again. His captain (Robert Crosby) had died of fever at Acapulco earlier.

In the *Port Crawford,* of Greenock (Captain F. W. Tode), an A.B. named H. Haakoven fell from the main yard to the deck and escaped with some bruises. He was taken aft for treatment "in accordance with the *Medical Guide"* and survived that, too, although lame for two weeks.

D. Nielsen, A.B., was lucky to survive his fall in the *Ventura* (on one of those long, long passages from Hamburg toward Puget Sound which took almost six months in 1907). Pitching from the main t'gallant yard, the clewed-up weather side of the mains'l flapped as he reached it and picked him up in its fold. (It was customary to haul up the weather side in a fair wind and leave the lee side set, to allow the wind to reach the fores'l better. This made a sort of big bag.) Hauled up on a buntline, he went into the forecastle for a drink of water and was back at work "within ten minutes as if nothing had happened," though sleepless for a day or two afterward.

Rankin, fourteen-year-old ship's boy in the *Saxon* on her passage of over six months from Liverpool around the Horn to Victoria, B.C., in 1905, had a particularly solid head, was extremely fortunate, or was exceptionally well looked after by Captain Thomas W. Smith of Greenock, the *Saxon*'s master. Near the Horn, on June 9, 1905, while up on an all-hands job furling the fores'l in a stinking gale—and it *was* a gale when they furled the fores'l—Rankin was pitched or blown or fell off the footrope. Fortunately, he was at the bunt of the sail (the men would not allow him to go farther out on the yard) and he fell inboard. Otherwise he would have gone in the sea. It was night.

He was "supposed to have landed on his head and shoulders," writes Captain Smith in the log. "No bones broken: carried aft, put in the mate's berth, gave dose of Brandy and Laudanum: rubbed him with liniment." For a while, he complained of severe pain in the shoulders, but recovered on a diet of "beef-tea, toast, port wine," and was soon "taking his food regular and with appreciation." And so back on deck for deck boy Rankin.

The foreyard was the closest to the deck, but all such falls were usually fatal. There was luck in it, too: Rankin may have fallen into three or four feet of sea, may have broken his fall on some of the gear, or may by good luck have fallen like an acrobat.

In the *Cromdale*, which was once a smart and well-known ship often in the Australian wool run, Frederick Day, A.B., was knocked from the foreyard by a carried-away gantline when changing to lighter sails in the tropics.

"He picked himself up and sat on the fore hatch. Told mate he'd be all right in a few minutes. He walked aft to see the captain but suddenly collapsed at the cabin door. Put on a bunk and rallied: said he would be all right if he could only get his breath.

Died." He had no broken bones and there was no sign the master or mate could see of internal injury.

Those masters could cope very well, usually, with broken bones. When C. Harris, A.B., in the ship *Bardowie* had his collarbone fractured and shoulder dislocated, Captain Joseph Suiter (of Liscard) made so good a job of it that surgeons in the next port complimented him.

Treatment for Apprentice J. Fielding's T.B. in the big four-masted bark *Sofala* is "quinine three times daily and tincture of steel," which must have been Captain Moore's idea. It was wrong: the lad quickly died. The *Sofala* was a particularly hungry ship that voyage. When she moved from the Cardiff coaltips to Barry Roads to prepare for sea, the freshly signed crew began at once to complain of the "bad and inadequate" food. Captain Moore —a Falmouth man—offered to sign another cook but it was the food, not the cook, the crew wanted changed. The log laments that they "surely could make a good meal of hash, biscuits, butter and tea, as they were not getting worked too hard." (But what sort of hash, how hard the biscuits, rancid the "butter," washy the "tea"?) The crew do not agree and refuse work until they get more and better food. They are paid off, but the new crew is worse.

The *Sofala* was at the Falkland Islands in distress from the Horn in '05, and the cook was changed there. Later in the same voyage James Doyle, sixty-one-year-old A.B. from Dublin, died of "tetanus as result of accident." It appears that he had his "fingers crushed between the wharf and the ship while painting ship alongside the South Wharf at Melbourne." The ship sailed for Newcastle. Doyle came aft complaining of "stiffness of jaws." Treatment was a "dose of Black Draught and advice to keep warm." He grew steadily worse and died of tetanus in the hospital two days after the ship reached Newcastle.

Three able seamen died in the big four-poster *Pegasus* on her Hamburg-Honolulu passage of 1905—all of sickness. They must have been elderly men, as their admitted ages are given as forty-eight, forty-five, and forty-eight. They are said to have died of erysipelas, dropsy, and stoppage of bowels, and all stoically accepted treatment from the *Medical Guide*. They *might* all have died genuinely of old age. It may seem strange that so many of these extremely hard and heavy-working ships included old seamen in their crews, but the fact was that such old-timers could be—and usually were—wonderful men, skillful and resourceful, indefatigable aloft, wonderful at the helm, respected and steadying in the forecastle. No Cape Horner went to sea without one if she could help it, while the supply lasted.

The treatment for Charles Row, A.B., in the Glasgow ship *Loch Carron* (Captain Stainton Clarke) on the usual Autralian voyage in 1907–'08, certainly came from no *Medical Guide*. Row came aft with ringworm, was sent back for'ard with a bottle of ink. Perhaps Captain Clarke thought this was based on gentian violet, but it was no use. Carbolic acid lotion apparently did better. This cleared the ringworm but the A.B. developed spots on his body. Diagnosis: "blood out of order": treatment not stated. Row recovered in due course, or perhaps became discouraged in his quest for a remedy from the *Medical Guide* and reported aft no more.

The *Guide* had no useful advice to offer in the case of Bos'n Robert Wesley, aged thirty-eight, who died of "shock" on the *Puritan* of Glasgow. The bos'n's shock was caused by being struck by one of the big bower anchors, while catting it at sea. It fell on him. The shock was sudden and final. An anchor fell on the mate of the *Criffel* in much the same circumstances, except that its fluke fell only on one of his hands when the ship was in port at Mollendo, Chile. The difficulty there was to get him any treatment at all. It took Captain Billet five days to find a surgeon.

In by far the greater number of accidents in sailing ships at sea, anything published in the *Medical Guide* was superfluous. Men (and a few boys) went overboard three and four at a time, and it was very unusual to rescue even one. The Scots four-masted bark *Hougomont*, in 1910, and the ship *Ancenis*, in 1905, were just two which washed out three or four men with one scooping aboard of a malignant sea—the *Hougomont* over her stern, the *Ancenis* in the waist. She rolled her side into a breaking sea while the men were bracing. Four went over, but the mate hung on to a brace and was swept back aboard at the next roll. The *Hougomont*'s pooping took four (not known until a muster, held immediately the decks cleared) and injured Captain McNeil as well, as well as damaging all the boats. The *Hougomont* was what sailors called a "wet" ship. She'd washed a man from her bowsprit in vile weather not long before. He was the sailmaker, trying to repair a jib. She plunged; he was not seen again.

But it was apprentices, in a way, who were the saddest casualties and at times the most frequent. In 1905, for example, thirty-six of them went, not counting all those in the missing ships—five washed overboard, twelve died or were drowned, nineteen fallen from aloft. *Nineteen!* It is a lot, even from a thousand.

Apprentices were not meant to be particularly expendable, but in fact they were so. They died of typhoid fever: they fell out of the rigging: they went overboard and weren't missed until it was too late to go back to look for them—not that that ever had much hope of success. One reason for this was that so many of them came so raw to the harshness of the big sailing-ship life where a slip, a misstep, a slippery hitch, even failure to gauge the height of a big sea coming at the ship could so easily mean sudden death. Many came from families with no seafaring tradition. Some were misled by books' overplaying the "romantic" aspect of the sailing-ship life—an aspect only appreciated ashore.

In the four-masted bark *Levernbank,* running east in the Roaring Forties on passage from Newcastle, N.S.W., toward Valparaiso midwinter 1905, no one had any idea when Apprentice Alfred Thompson, of Hull, was lost overboard, or how, one morning watch. There had been some sail-handling and he was there. There were seas lolloping aboard as usual. At the change of watch at 0800, the watches mustered; Apprentice Thompson was not there. With the attention of all on the job in hand and that always dangerous, no one was his brother's keeper. In hard weather gear of oilskins, sou'westers, soul-and-body lashings, etc., all looked alike.

There was a gale, the ship running heavily. It was not possible to go back: if she did, how could she hope to cover again the track she had sailed over?

William H. Raeside, bos'n, aged nineteen, is listed also as losing his life that voyage in the *Levernbank*. Bos'n at nineteen? He turns out to be an apprentice, too, promoted for his skill as a seaman. But there were points he had no time to learn. Working aloft on the foreyard, he was repairing the heavy steel fish-tackle block, and tried to haul in the block on its pendant to the yard the better to work at it. But he misjudged the weight, slipped, pitched into the open hold.

From the *Serena,* running hard to round the Horn with a cargo of wheat from Melbourne, four went overboard with the one sea when Captain Dagwell tried to bring the ship up, to heave to, in an increasing gale. He chose noon, with all hands on deck. As she came up to the wind a huge sea struck her. She rolled toward it, filling the decks. When they could see again, *seven men* were overboard. Two kept desperate hold of loose ends of gear trailing outboard. The rolling smashed them against the side, but they were hauled back. A third climbed back (for the ship had little forward way: they'd gone over to leeward and she drifted to them). The sailmaker, a Norwegian aged thirty-nine, a Danish A.B. aged twenty-one, a Swedish A.B. also aged twenty-one, and an Irish apprentice named Charles Lilley, aged seventeen, were not seen again.

"A squall of hurricane force and one mountainous sea did the damage," says the log. The *Serena* was near Diego Ramirez at the time. Always an apprentice. . . .

The Scots *Kirkcudbrightshire,* 1,582 tons, of Law's "Shire" line, was a goodlooking full-rigged ship, and Captain David Roberts, of Dolgelly, Wales, was an excellent master. Young Tom Maltby, from Leytonstone, London, must have been pleased to be appointed to the ship when he signed his indentures in early 1907. But she was a big ship for a small boy, and he didn't get much chance to grow bigger. Less than two months out on passage from Rochester in Kent with bagged cement for Talcahuano, the ship was on the line—with quiet sea, beautiful weather, no prospect of squalls. It seemed the perfect day to grease down the t'gallant masts. This was an apprentice's job— what greasy job wasn't?—so the mate sent young Maltby up on the fore. He gave him a gantline, a pot of grease, and, presumably, a bos'n's chair.

But he had to rig the gantline block right at the masthead to grease down the high mast. All sail was set. There was little to help even an acrobat to shin up the royal pole. He "got on to the royal tie and made an attempt to climb up to the royal yard but slid down again . . . about 2 feet . . . he was seen to apparently turn giddy."

The cook had been watching the lad, as he leaned over the galley half-door. The bos'n and he saw the lad falter, seem about to fall. The cook was nearer. He had never been a rat line off the deck in his life, but now he rushed for the rigging. The shrouds and rat lines shook as he pounded aloft, the bos'n after him.

They had no hope. Maltby, giddy with the bird's-eye view of the sail-clothed masts and the decks so hopelessly far below, feeling the sway of the ship up there, fainted.

Aged fourteen.

The list of his kit takes two log pages. "Three doz. brass buttons . . . Box of Chessmen and 2 boards . . . Sheets, oilskins, seaboots, woollens, a uniform . . ."

He had only one uniform, for his mother knew he would soon grow out of it.

Chapter eight

EVIDENCE FROM THE LOGS

ALTHOUGH IT WAS no one's intention that it should be so, a fairly good idea of the manner in which at least some deepwater square-rigged ships were operated emerges clearly from a study of the surviving evidence in their official logs. It is sometimes fragmentary evidence; to know more we should have the deck logs, the account books, the owner's correspondence files, the files of cases held before naval courts and the like, and some evidence of contemporary informed opinion as to the worth of the masters, especially in the eyes of other masters. In any case we have only a selection of the British vital-statistics logs—the so-called "death logs." Any ship could lose life, the best-found as well as the worst. Even a ship which seems to lose some of her crew almost every voyage could be herself at fault, perhaps, particularly prone to pitching her bows into the sea or exceptionally hard to steer when running free, or have a very heavy rig and an accumulation of bad habits which made her especially vulnerable. There were such ships—more than enough of them. Sailors grew to know them and the experienced tried to avoid them. Yet the best of masters could tame them too, by careful study of and attention to trim, and good handling of ship and crew.

Too many shipmasters seemed almost to look for trouble and some created it when it was not there. Those masters had tremendous power for good or evil in their ships, and the evil came more readily to notice. In Britain, after all, a world-wide tramping merchant service was, historically speaking, a comparatively new development, sprouting in great measure on the

141

back of the Industrial Revolution—and that had brought little joy to the lives of most British ashore. English long-voyage merchant sailing had been a gentlemanly profession in the days of the great monopolies such as that of the Hon. East India Company, where a few voyages could bring a captain fortune. Then, officer recruitment was from the great public schools, with good prospects and chance of fortune to the captains and officers, and no bad life for the worthy mariners who managed to survive. Coasting and the short voyage trades were quite another matter. Then almost suddenly came expansion, wealth, vast increase in trade, dispersal of time-honored monopoly, the pampered, overlauded clippers briefly, on their few specialized trades, the "far-flung Empire" forever expanding, the thin high funnels of the steamships forever belching more and more smoke into the sea air while iron bows, blunt and sharp, thrust the sea aside, aided by the latest ditch at Suez; and the great fleets of the iron and steel windjammers hauling bunkers for the steamers, serving the ports they could not reach—the dull stuff of this earth, paying lowest freights, demanding longest voyages with ever more emphasis on the fight with Cape Horn, the one war it was no sense for the steamship to enter.

For the sailing ship, there were no more bonus cargoes. For the masters, no fortune; for the men called upon to work heavier, larger, more lightly manned ships-of-the-wind than had ever before been sent to sea—the sea-wallowing molloths of the ugly new age: what chance for them? It is remarkable that they did so well for so long, that masters were available to sail the ships so well and thrash them past the Horn so long after they were obviously outmoded, that enough good seamen were always at hand to man them and stay with them no matter what they did to them.

There were enough indifferent masters, and their sins are more fully recorded than the deeds of their better brothers. There were "sea lawyers," and troublemakers in some forecastles, but, considering the oppression that was too often accepted as their normal lot—they had signed for it, hadn't they? Those Articles of Agreement were almost holy writ—the malignant rabble-rouser was a rare bird indeed. One reason was the absence of rabble, for the sea life (with its obvious need for thorough discipline) gave men common sense.

But there is evidence in some of their own official logs that there were masters who goaded their crews to near-mutiny, and the principal reason seems to be their own stupidity. It surely was unpardonably asinine behavior on the part of Captain H. H. Dexter, a Nova Scotian, master of the *Samaritan* of Liverpool, to throw his crew in jail merely because he thought it desirable to prevent desertion on their part, in the course of a long voyage which included a passage from Tampa, Florida, to Yokohama during the Russo-Japanese War. There were demands by some seamen for extra pay for war zones, but this was mainly in tramps trying to run the Japanese blockade to Vladivostok. Desertions at Tampa would mean engagement of replacements at higher wages, so the Bluenose master claps ten A.B.'s and three ordinary seamen in Tampa jail "for safe keeping." They are brought back by the sheriff in time to sail, and promptly refuse duty. They are then ironed—handcuffed—"under H.B.M. Consul's orders," says the log. They still refuse to sail. The wind is fair. Bluenose Dexter has an afterguard of nine, including himself. (No apprentices are listed or mentioned, but five or six could have been there: they did not sign Articles nor appear on all lists of crew, being indentured.) At any rate "it is enough for the time being." The weather is good. Dexter sails, the ironed band still refusing duty.

"Hoping the men would return soon to their duty," writes the captain, giving them "the usual fare under the circumstances"—hard biscuits and water, which was not much inducement. Four were chained in the sail locker aft, the other nine for'ard. They remain adamant. The four in the sail locker get their irons off somehow and throw them overboard. They are still locked up. So things continue for a week of good weather, while the skeleton crew work the heavy 2,000-ton ship around Florida and into the North Atlantic, to begin the long passage toward Yokohama. The weather worsens. Captain Dexter needs his crew. He removes all the irons and unlocks the quarters. But the seamen, bloody-minded from their incarceration in Tampa and aboard, and hungry, tell him to continue sailing the ship himself. They take the view that they are now a shanghaied crew, kept under duress in a ship under a master they have learned to despise, on a voyage they do not intend to help. So the *Samaritan* has to go into Bermuda, for seven seafarers plus one cook and one steward make no fit crew for her, with or without a few apprentices. At Bermuda, early in February, 1903, the recalcitrant thirteen get another four weeks' jail. This time they are paid off and a fresh crew engaged. At least they are finished with their Bluenose, and Bermuda jail was no worse than his ship.

At Yokohama Captain Dexter has more trouble with desertions and other difficulties. He ships Japanese for the ballast passage to Puget Sound. Here they take the first opportunity to desert, and Dexter is superseded. His only achievement had been to turn what should have been a profitable voyage into a loss.

The state of affairs reached aboard the Anglo-American Company's steel four-master *Lyndhurst* of London, Capt. P. H. Parnell (his home is given as New York), off the Horn on passage Rotterdam toward San Francisco in 1906, is perhaps understandable, after studying a few hundred contemporary limejuicers' logs, but thoroughly deplorable. Captain Parnell writes of "mutiny." If he writes mutiny, it is legal mutiny anyway until an authority higher than his own disproves the charge. Any combination of men (or some of the men) to cease duty is "mutiny." There doesn't have to be anything else. They have no arms. They can be asking for a proper issue of the food to which the Merchant Shipping Act entitles them, and, being consistently refused, fed with "substitutes at master's option" and too little of these, arrive at the point of desperation. No seaman wants to sail in a vulnerable ship, and a square-rigged ship at sea was obviously in a dangerous state without effective crew. Those Anglo-American case-oil sailers were well found and properly stored, but there was something seriously wrong aboard the *Lyndhurst*.

"With a large ship on the high seas . . . I am bound to take strong measures," writes Parnell in his log in the 40's in midwinter, as he irons a couple of ringleaders named Reimer and Van Apern. But he has to take stronger measures as he works south, for all hands refuse duty. He irons another half-dozen and locks the lot in the foc's'l "without food until they resume duty in the proper manner." (The mate and second mate witness these entries, as they must.) The men hold out a week, the afterguard, tradesmen, and apprentices meanwhile working the ship under very easy sail. Then all agree to work again except Reimer and Van Apern, who stay in their irons in some locker until the ship is in the Pacific trade winds. Here, apparently, they go quietly back to work, and desert the first day in San Francisco. So do most of the rest of the crew, but this was normal.

At no time does the captain indicate the grievances of his crew: properly stated, these could be a reflection on him. Whatever induced such a state of bloody-mindedness in them that they would no longer work the ship at all must have been serious. The conditions were savagely grim. On 55.30° S., 75° W., early in August, "Kannute Johanessen [Knut Johansen] furling the main upper tops'l apparently lost hold through cold: nearly fell on the lookout man on the midships house. Killed instantly": because he could not hang on with his frozen hands. One wonders how well Johansen (aged twenty-two) might have been nourished.

That passage to San Francisco took 166 days, which was a long time. It was, one might think, an insufferably long time to be badly fed—unnecessarily badly fed. Just how intolerably mean some of those ships could be would be incredible if it were not so well documented. An interesting book called *The Last of the Cape Horners,* part written and part edited by the late Commander Claude L. A. Wollard (and published at his own expense because no regular publisher was interested, though the work is a valuable documentary) presents evidence enough. The bark *Powys Castle* is one among many ships mentioned here where the half-starved crew, homeward bound from Peru, never even get a drinkable mug either of tea or coffee nor a properly prepared meal of tolerable food. It was the cook's practice—by order from the captain—to prepare their tea with the used leaves from the cabin pot thrown in and boiled, and the "coffee" had a base of inferior beans ground together with burnt ship's biscuit. The bread and biscuits were iron-hard, the beef and pork "as salt as

Lot's wife's ass" (as the old sea chantey has it), and always served half-cooked because, the cook explained, if he cooked it any more it would shrink to nothing. To still the constant pangs of serious hunger, the sailors were accustomed to grind up some grain from burst sacks in the cargo to make watery gruel. They ground the grain with the galley coffee mill, and were expected to be very grateful for the loan of this.

The real reason for this criminal penury, almost always, was that a proportion of the money provided by owners to buy food was siphoned away: in those days many owners provided the bare minimum and any misuse of that meant near-starvation for the crew. It was not ship chandlers' fault: they served shipping as they found it. Commissions, kickbacks, false bills were not their idea. They needed business and their "runners" had to get it somehow. Sailors generally vented their wrath on stewards, and indeed a bad steward could waste food and the odd one be dishonest. But close behind a bad steward there was generally a drunken or at least neglectful master. Most stewards were excellent hardworking men.

My experience was that most ship chandlers gave good value at fair prices: if I were dissatisfied there were always markets to keep the ship going on a fresh-food basis in ports. It was the meat selected for the nonrefrigerated ship, put up in heavy brine casks, which could let one down. That might not be the chandler's fault either. After all, there was no market for salted prime cuts.

Some masters could have taken a doctorate in calculated, continuous, and comprehensive meanness, if such were offered. There was a master in the four-masted bark *Beechbank,* for instance, who was not just a tyrannical penny-pincher with the food. When sails were repaired and hands were called on to assist himself and the sailmaker, he calculated the amount of sail twine necessary for each seam and issued that much and no more, so that no one could "win" enough to sew a button on his pants. When old rags were served out from a bale for paint-washing and the like, he saw that every rag was holed beyond use by stabbing holes in them, to make sure the sailors couldn't patch old shirts and would have to buy from his slop chest, at his prices.

There were other masters who gave their seamen good canvas and twine enough to make themselves sea bags, and the
wherewithal for eyelets and securing line too. But the harm done
by the stupid could be cumulative—and, unfortunately, slip into
long memory.

Putting seamen by the dozens into jail was commonplace in
many limejuice ships. There was a limit to the capacity of ill-paid
and worse-fed seamen to accept intolerable conditions stupidly
enforced on them in badly run ships. The *Celticburn,* a big steel
four-masted bark of Greenock, J. S. Davidson (whose address is
"ship: no home"), sends an A.B. to a month's jail at Port Pirie:
another A.B. hangs himself in the forepeak. (Another is aft complaining of sickness in his penis, caused by "heavy strain in the
performance of duty. Treated him for Clap as per *Medical Guide,"*
details unspecified. He recovers.)

The *Iverna* of Glasgow (Thomas Hodge, master), staggers
about the sea on a long, meandering voyage begun at Barry
Dock, South Wales, in July, 1902, jailing her people, disrating
seamen, losing an eighteen-year-old A.B., leaving seamen behind as deserters, having trouble even with those stalwarts the
apprentices. She sails to Cape Town first (Boer War freights were
still up), thence to New York and on to Shanghai (this New
York–Woosung passage took almost five months). From China
she crosses the Pacific to Port Townsend and Port Blakeley for
a cargo to Callao: thence to Tocopilla for nitrates around the
Horn to Hamburg. She reaches the Elbe on February 2, 1905,
four months out from Chile: and at Hamburg the survivors of the
tough thirty-one-months voyage pay off and thank God.

By then Mr. McMurty, the mate, has doubtless forgotten the
incident at Cape Town when—according to a long entry in the
log— he stamped into the saloon "intoxicated and shouting filthy
language calling me a dirty stinking S.O.B. and S.O.Whore and
a mean bastard, etc. etc. too bad to mention." The mate apolo-
gized when he sobered and the entry was canceled, Mr. McMurty
leaving soon afterward. To judge by the sad state of discipline in
the ship, there was possibly truth in his descriptions. The new

mate (also logged) is soon thinking up some of his own—"an old sod and many other names too bad to mention," and so forth.

Three A.B.'s are arrested and get fourteen days hard labor for breaking out of the ship at Shanghai: more desert at Port Townsend, Callao, Tocopilla: more are jailed. The third mate and the cook are in trouble with the Chilean authorities for smuggling their plug tobacco to get a little spending money and it costs the ship $50 to get them out of jail. An American A.B. aged eighteen falls out of the rigging and dies, leaving the usual incredibly small parcel of "effects" which got these wanderers past the Horn and around the world—"2 old serge suits, 1 old suit oilskins, few rags, 1 chest," the lot priced at £1–5–0. An apprentice named Flack demands two dollars a week for working cargo (instead of nothing). He is offered one dollar and is soon absent without leave. The crew complains of the cook's "bread" at Tocopilla. A loaf is sent to the consul, who says he can find no fault with it. (How much did he try? Was it specially baked? He had other things to eat, anyway.) The complainants refuse duty: another dozen go to jail.

So it goes, voyage after voyage, in so many ships. Evidence from a mixed bag such as the ship *Claverdon* and the four-masted barks *Dundee, Inverness-shire, Dumfriesshire,* and *Beechbank* is rather depressing.

The state of discipline aboard the oversized full-rigged ship *Claverdon* (Captain David Thomson of Montrose), on her three-year voyage which began at Antwerp in June, 1905, can be described only as deplorable. On the previous voyage she had taken 218 days from the Elbe to San Francisco, after losing five men overboard in her fight off the Horn, turning away eastward and encircling the world. For the mileage covered, perhaps, seven months was not so bad, but her insurers were bothered about it and had paid 65 percent for fresh cover. (That is, they got rid of the risk but had to pay 65 percent of the ship's insured value to do so, so pessimistic was the market about the chances of her arrival. This reinsurance rate could get as high as 90 percent, and was a gamble. The *Claverdon* was a known sluggard, or her rate would have been higher.)

Captain Thomson was one of the older masters who made his whole career in deep-sea sail. He had had command of a fine ship, the *Euphrosyne,* in his prime, from 1892 to 1902, and had got consistently good passages out of her, some of them outstanding. For some reason, he appears to have gone from the well-behaved *Euphrosyne* to the bitchy *Claverdon,* and he did not take his good luck with him. Probably no one could. Those ships were rather like race horses: some of them nobody could make go. But they lasted much longer and made far more trouble.

David Thomson had command of the four-masted bark *Garthpool,* the former Dundee jute man *Juteopolis,* in her last days, and lost her off-course in the northeast trade winds in 1929 on the Cape Verde Islands when bound in ballast toward South Australia. He had the smart bark *Garthneil* before that and did well with her. The *Garthpool's* full sister was the well-known *Lawhill,* the ship which Captain J. C. B. Jarvis ("Brace-winch" Jarvis) had for several years and always found tractable. The *Lawhill,* after an excellent career under the British, Russian, Finnish, South African—in part of World War II—and the Finnish flag again, was one of the last of the real, old Cape Horners left on earth. She fell to pieces slowly in a creek near Lourenço Marques, Mozambique, in the 1960's.

The *Claverdon's* log surviving in 1970 is a sad document, a dispiriting account of crew troubles badly dealt with, refusals of duty, striking of mates, desertions (including yet another attempt by crudely constructed raft), replacements by unqualified crimps' men, "mutiness conduck" (master's spelling) of all descriptions. The sailmaker—who was ordinarily one of a Cape Horner's trusted servants—became so incensed that once he "struck the Master to the effusion of blood and ran along the deck crying Come on boys I have got him now." He is ironed for this "conduck" and kept handcuffed for a week, in port.

The case for the seamen is never put in these logs, though entries against them were supposed to be read to them and their comments recorded. The general rule is no comment—what use was it?—though one irate able seaman once told his captain to "fill the bloody log and continue on the backs of the charts." At

Antofagasta, the sailmaker had been required to work cargo.

There was plenty of sailmaking to do and he was a petty officer, but was disrated to A.B. and "run in" to the consul. The consul supported Captain Thomson, who was within his rights under the Merchant Shipping Act. Consuls very rarely took time to investigate such matters properly, in any case, and seamen were usually either incoherent or belligerently maudlin when brought before them. But a few consuls *did* try to look after them.

The easiest course was to take such action as got rid of the ship, and them, as quickly as possible.

That voyage of the *Claverdon* lasted three years. Eighty-eight seamen passed through the ship to keep her crewed, and this was about the average wastage. The first leg was a passage of five and a half months from Antwerp around the Horn to Seattle, in 1905 (she lost a Russian A.B. named Pahsch from aloft). From there, she wandered from Tacoma to Antofagasta with lumber, from Junin to Kahului in Hawaii, from Honolulu to Sydney, Newcastle to Portland (Oregon), Astoria to Falmouth. She was four months on the last passage. In those three years she rounded the Horn twice, once each westward and eastward, but for the rest there were many months of trade-wind sailing, "flying-fish stuff" as the old sea dogs called it. Much of that Pacific voyaging could have been pleasant despite the *Claverdon*'s big single t'gallants'ls and workhorse rig, if only there ever was harmony aboard. Harmony went with well-disciplined ships, well run, no matter how rough the men. A master who could not get along with his stalwart tradesmen was scarcely likely to get the best out of his crews.

The sailing-ship tradesmen—sailmakers and carpenters especially—show a high standard of devotion to duty almost invariably. They were also poorly paid for a twelve-hour day, though highly skilled men. Both served seven-year apprenticeships before going to sea, for their work was vital. Ill-cut sails would drive no ship and were a waste of canvas. As a misstep could kill a seaman, a mis-stitch could blow out an expensive sail just when it was most needed. Carpenters were expected also to be skilled blacksmiths: all the complicated ironwork aloft (and its repair) was in their hands. They were responsible (under the mate) for fresh-water tanks, anchors, the windlass, capstans, dolly winches, if any, the hatches and their security, the tightness of the hull. They were as skillful at turning out a cradle for the new baby aft as a new fore t'gall'nt mast when needed. Both sailmaker and carpenter were privileged folk aboard the well-run sailing ship, often the master's friends. He could work and yarn with them if he wished, and favor nobody. They often shared a minute cabin (in one of the deck-houses), and were privileged to take their meals seated in the galley, with plate and pannikin on their knees.

It was a fool master who made enemies out of them.

The *Inverness-shire* was a clumsy-looking bald-headed four-masted bark with a high jigger mast which had no gaff. She was "jubilee"-rigged, with a squat, square rig without royals, a wall-sided sailing warehouse of such a sort that, if there were any other square-rigger in port, a sailor's eyes would not linger on her. She was a tramp "windbag," and she looked it. Her name *shire* deserved a far lovelier model, as many of the other Shire ships were. When she was built in 1894, in a sense she already had a poor future, though she might have had—with tolerable passages and freedom from accidents—ten or fifteen good or reasonable earning years, at the best. At 2,307 gross register tons, she was on the small side to earn on low freights, but the stump t'gall'nt "jubilee" rig made her easier to work and easier on her sails. After a career which included more than sufficient long passages, a complete dismasting (except for the jigger mast) in the south Indian Ocean, a change of name and flag to Norwegian, she went missing in 1920. Perhaps having seen enough of her, the sea took her with all hands.

The official log of her voyage begun at London in April, 1904, and ended at Southampton in February, 1906, is preserved, and sorry reading it is. The voyage was from London to Philadelphia, thence to Japan (four months, twenty days on passage, probably with case oil), from Kobe to Newcastle, N.S.W., for coal to Valparaiso, thence to Iquique for nitrates to Antwerp by way of a distress call at Southampton—three cargoes in twenty-two months and crew troubles all the way. This was no manner to earn a dividend.

The master was T. E. L. Tindale, and there were eighty-seven crew changes, not reckoning the apprentices (the usual excellent lot Law's Shire ships somehow attracted.) An A.B. fell from aloft overboard and the second mate died of smallpox. The ship doesn't get very far before it is horribly obvious that Tindale is a Tartar. Desertions begin at Philadelphia, and the first away is George Murray, the cook. He is picked up, the city police charging $23.38 for arresting him and for his board in jail. The second mate is disrated for alleged incompetence: the third mate is soon in irons, on bread and water, with two apprentices and an A.B. to keep him company. Refusals of duty, refusals of "lawful commands," etc., blight almost every page of the log. In Japan the story is of constant troubles—all of the poorly run ship type which becomes so clearly recognizable after a brief course of reading these logs. The master issues warrants for the arrest of the bos'n and others, who have deserted. Other deserters include two apprentices, and warrants are issued for them too. Changing the mates becomes a more or less constant exercise.

Entries are read to men concerned—just about the whole crew including the officers and apprentices—and the charges denied by all of them. The denials are recorded, but nobody's defense. The second mate is ironed, said to be suffering from delirium tremens. (These limejuicers must have carried large stocks of irons.)* In Newcastle, at sea toward Valparaiso, in

* In the outfit list of the new four-masted ship *Falls Of Clyde,* contracted for in January 1878 and launched from the Tail of the Bank on December 12 that year, the following appears:
GUNS

To	1	pair Revolvers 6 Chambers and 100 cartridges	£1	15s
	2	lbs powder 1 Copper Powder Magazine		13s
	12	pair handcuffs	1	6
	12	Rockets in metal box	1	2
	12	Blue Lights in do.		6s
			£5	2s

The rockets and blue lights were distress signals. These details are from the copy of the *Ship Cost Book* still in the possession of the builders.

Valpo—everywhere the same. Megalomaniac Tindale is against the world—his world, anyway. The apprentices are goaded into making formal application for their release (or at least transfer to another of Law's ships) on the grounds that they "are unable to get on in this one." Tindale's answer is to order them into the forecastle. They refuse, very properly—so he puts them on bread and water while they are helping to work out near 4,000 tons of coal, as well as rowing him about at the tyrant's whim. More deserters follow. All this nonsense puts up the ship's costs, delays her turn-around, achieves nothing but harm.

The sad ship shifts up to Iquique at length, to load homeward. The change of scene brings no change of action. Twelve of the crew refuse duty because of poor food, and are jailed forthwith. (Their refusal is the crime, not the incompetent master's persistent goading them into it.) An A.B. is logged for using "contemptable [*sic*] language to the Master—viz. 'Why the hell did you take me out of the calaboose?' "—life being better there. There are more desertions. The ship is anchored not far out: they swim, or hide in returning nitrate lighters—anything to get away. The mate—he is the third replacement as such—is "informed that he was quite incompetent to fullfill the duties of 1st Mate" and told his wages are reduced.

(Here the consul or shipping master, unable to accept any more of these diatribes, has placed a heavy red entry "NOT ENFORCED.") The mate's answer to his captain is "Go Ahead."

In due course, the *Inverness-shire*—then 140 days out—drifts back to the English Channel, toward the end of February, 1906. At 2 A.M. on the twentieth of that month, off the Isle of Wight, the "1st Officer used insluting langue (*sic*) to the Master namely . . . etc., etc." The entries are becoming somewhat incoherent. Stress of weather forces the ship into Southampton. (What stress is not described: and why Southampton?) Here the owners can take an active interest in her. Complaining still of more refusals of duty, "contemptable and filty [*sic*] language," T. E. L. Tindale departs from the scene (it is to be hoped, from all ships forever) and the unhappy, lumbering four-poster staggers onward to Antwerp under tow.

Poor *Inverness-shire:* poor crew! Some years ago, the deputy librarian at Christ Church, Oxford, confided to me that he had been an apprentice in the *Inverness-shire,* but when I asked about his experiences he only looked pained. And no wonder.

The kindest explanation for his behavior on that long and hellish voyage—perhaps the only possible one—is that Captain Tindale was mentally ill. It is a pity that he does not record the crew's complaints. A near-starvation diet (through no plan of the owners, who wanted economy but not starvation) had a great deal to do with bad conditions in many of these ships. Other masters admit as much. Many try to do something about it, aware perhaps that at least in part shortages were their own fault. In the *Simla,* another four-masted bark, Captain G. T. Casson writes clearly that the crew are complaining "at not getting their whack," both at sea and on arrival at Hong Kong. He discovered that the steward had been stealing much of the sugar rations with false weights, when that skinflint absconded at Hong Kong.

But it was far more than short shrift of sugar the *Simla* mariners complained about. Planned short delivery aboard against falsified bills was a deeper cause of sailors' hunger, and this sort of thing could not be carried through by stewards. It would appear that it was a practice of the trade manipulated at the expense of seamen over many years. The deep-sea sailing ship was particularly prone in the days of poor communications, and the obvious inability to carry stores from a home port sufficient for her often unpredictably long voyages. The appalling turnover of crews helped cover up misdeeds, for half-starved crews melted away. It was rare to have attention paid to their often justified complaints. For one reason, they were generally drunk when they made them. Lesser officialdom turned deaf ears, for the wild "crowds" of sailing-ship crews were easily dismissed as unstable wanderers. After all, they always melted away, usually fast. Sailors' boardinghouse keepers and other crimps saw to that.

The little barks and barkentines sailing out of Australia and New Zealand in the South Pacific did not have these troubles, though they were manned almost exclusively by deserters from the big ships and a sprinkling of young so-called Colonials. With smaller crews, shorter voyages, far more frequent returns to home ports, perhaps they could afford to be more human. They fed crews properly under the reasonable rule of "sufficient without waste" and no "whack" system, and they treated men as men. Since there was no sense in deserting from them, the problem did not arise. Members of the afterguard were properly paid and owners and agents could supervise things thoroughly. The nastiness of "making" on crew's food did not arise, either.

Deepwater seamen often deliberately deserted to join ships of the intercolonial fleet, as a welcome change, and there settled happily for the rest of their seafaring lives, giving no trouble at all.

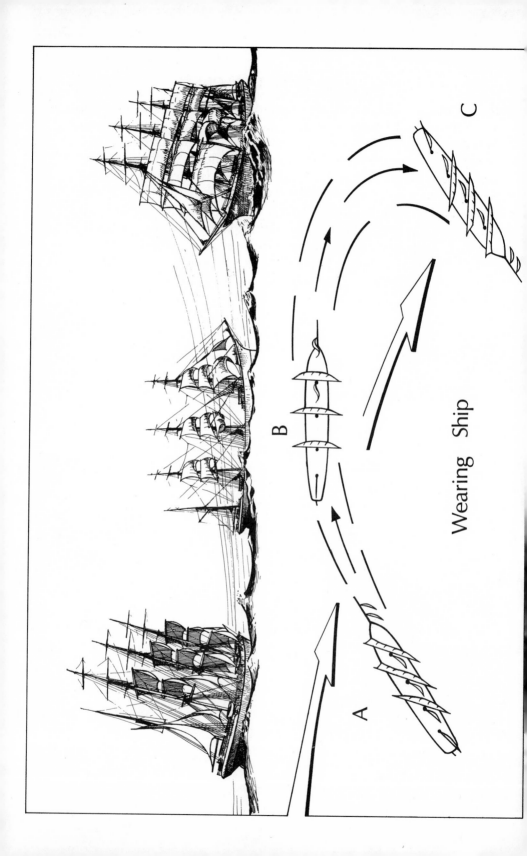

Wearing Ship

The big four-mast bark INVERNESS-SHIRE *looked ungainly, and sometimes was.*
Published by permission of the Trustees of the National Maritime Museum.

Fresh water was always scarce. Rain was saved for bathing in the Doldrums squalls.

Stowing the fore royal. The sail needs repairs and is to be sent down. Otherwise two hands would suffice.

Wet work in the waist. The net is to keep the boys inboard when she rolls. This is a watch, less helmsman.

A page from the BRITISH ISLES' Articles of Agreement giving the Scale of Provisions as allowed by Captain Barker. It was unusual to fill in the section hopefully entitled Bill of Fare.

SCALE OF PROVISIONS
TO BE ALLOWED AND SERVED OUT TO THE CREW DURING THE VOYAGE.

.—There is no scale fixed by the Board of Trade. The quantity and nature of the Provisions are a matter for agreement between Master and C The scale agreed upon is in addition to the Lime and Lemon Juice and Sugar, or other Anti-Scorbutics, in any case required by the Act.

ROVISIONS.	Quantity	Sunday	Monday	Tuesday	Wednesday	Thursday	Friday	Saturday	Weekly	PROVISIONS.	Quantity	Sunday	Monday	Tuesday	Wednesday	Thursday	Friday	Saturday
... ...	Qts.	3	Daily							Condensed Milk ...	oz.							
... ...	lb.	1								Tea	„	$\frac{1}{8}$						
... ...	„	$1\frac{1}{2}$	$1\frac{1}{2}$	$1\frac{1}{2}$		$1\frac{1}{2}$				Coffee Beans (roasted)	„	$\frac{1}{2}$	Daily					
... ...	„		$1\frac{1}{4}$	$1\frac{1}{4}$	$1\frac{1}{4}$					Cocoa	„	.						
red Meats ...	„									Sugar	„	2						
red Potatoes ...	oz.									Dried Fruit (Raisins, Currants, &c.) ...	„							
red Vegetables...	lb.									Butter	lb.							
... ...	„	$\frac{1}{2}$	$\frac{1}{2}$	$\frac{1}{2}$						Marmalade or Jam ...	„							
... ...	Pint	$\frac{1}{3}$	$\frac{1}{3}$	$\frac{1}{3}$						Molasses	Pint							
nces	„									Mustard	oz.							
... ...	lb.						$\frac{1}{2}$			Pepper	„							
al	„									Vinegar or Pickles ...	Pint							
... ...	„									•								
Fish	„																	

James P. Barker
Master

• Other articles may be inserted here.

SUBSTITUTES AND EQUIVALENTS.

At Master's option
No spirits allowed

BILL OF FARE.

NOTE.—The Act does not require these particulars to be given, but the Table may be filled up if desired.

	BREAKFAST.	DINNER.	SUPPER.
lay ...			
lay ...			
day ...			
nesday			
sday...			
y ...			
day...			
es sup-l daily			

The Mate

Working clothes: no brass buttons for them. 3rd Mate, Master, Mate, ship GRACE HARWAR

Chapter nine

PENNY-PINCHING TO MUTINY

IN 1906 there was at least an attempt to improve the standard of food served in British ships, steam as well as sail. Contemporary steam tramps were run on lines of rigid economy with the two-watch four-hours-on, four-off system on deck (three watches in the minimum-manned stokeholds and engine rooms) too, but this was owners' controlled economy which at least was not greatly worsened by chicanery in the ships. It was "pound and pint"— bare allowance, taking the scale laid down as maximum: but at least a pound was a pound and a pint a pint, and, as time went on, an icebox helped a little on short passages though it might be sparsely stowed with neck ends, bullock heads, and such. From 1906, British ships of more than 1,000 tons were supposed to carry certified cooks, but the certificate was granted on a some-what low standard since the victuals scarcely called for exceptional skill—or any. An amendment to the Merchant Shipping Act then required sea cooks to be able to pass a test in cookery.

A typical test, as outlined in the *Shipping Gazette Weekly Summary* of November 9, 1906, mentions the preparation on an ordinary galley stove of "pea soup with sippets, baked beef and Yorkshire pudding, baked potatoes, curry and rice, plum duff, and tapioca pudding." The "baked [?] beef and Yorkshire pudding" was for steamships only, or perhaps a very occasional meal in port aboard a sailing ship; and there was no way known to man or woman to make even a palatable curry from poor salt beef. At the same time a school of sorts was opened in London's East End for training sea cooks (there had been a voluntary school at the

Well Street Sailors' Home for the preceding fourteen years).

"It seems almost certain that Jack will fare sumptuously every day," chortled the popular press, noting that "British seamen will be enjoying the luxury of half-a-pound of compressed vegetables a week." Luxury? If any cook anywhere could make B.O.T. compressed vegetables edible he wasn't a cook but a magician. This and other improvements—unspecified—were going to cost British shipowners half a million a year, said the same newspapers, but a week later the estimate was halved.

The weekly rations were still the standard eight or nine items plus fresh water—1 pound of "bread" (vague term, construed usually as elderly, very hard biscuits), 1½ pounds of beef or 1¼ pounds of pork daily (more vague terms: very salty and usually elderly, chosen for the utmost economy and put in casks of heavy brine), ½ pound of flour or ⅓ pound of peas on alternate days except Saturday, on which there was ½ pound of rice, ⅛ ounce of tea, ½ ounce of coffee, and 2 ounces of sugar daily, most of these three items and all the others except "bread" being issued to the cook. In fact, the sailor was better off in 1890. The list of items required to be issued to the men of the Glasgow ship *Ardencaple,* for example, on a Calcutta voyage that year, add up to nineteen, including raisins, butter, dried apples, and marmalade. In some ships one noticed, the crew signed for "as much as could be eat, without waste," but such generosity was reserved for run crews, on very short passages. All that could be "eat," of course, was from the usual provisions put aboard.

In the meantime some ignoramus of even higher—or lower —standard than most, signing himself George Bull, produced some doggerel for the *London Sphere,* supposed to be based on the musings of one Valparaiso Bill.

> We ate so much when outward bound
> Of bread and jam and fish and beef
> That soon we grew so plump and round
> We couldn't get aloft to reef.
> The wheel we never could get near
> Enough to reach the spokes and steer.

Very funny, no doubt: at least the "poem" got Mr. Bull, one hopes, the price of a meal of pantiles and compressed vegetables, with snippets made of ship's bread fried in a sea cook's rancid fat. In fact, the new statutory scale of provisions in Mr. Lloyd George's revised Merchant Shipping Act made little if any difference. Late in the previous year, in November, 1905, the Norwegian Ministry of Commerce, Navigation and Industry had increased the already adequate amounts of their seamen's *minimum* rations. It was required that each seaman in Norwegian ships must have at least 500 grams of fresh butter a week (or margarine, failing butter) or, failing both, half a liter of olive oil: 350 grams of sugar (sugar and butter used in cooking NOT to be included), 3,000 grams of fresh potatoes (or yams), 150 grams of condensed milk, plus raisins, dried fruit, coffee, vegetables, meat, fish and all the rest, weekly. Limejuice must be served daily "if the fresh potatoes or yams run out or spoil, or scurvy or beriberi appear."

The Norwegians further required that "the main dish for dinner must be fish or meat, and not fish more than twice weekly, unless fresh. Fresh bread must be issued three times a week. A soup or porridge made with sugar and fresh or preserved fruit must be served at least once a week . . . and the victualling is *not to be limited to the scale laid down."* This was the vital difference.

No Ole Bull wrote an ode for Valparaiso Olaf or commiserated with the vast expenditure forced on reluctant owners required to keep their sailors properly fed. By this time, Norwegians were increasingly buying excellent British ships, and somehow running them successfully, while the British shipping press still deplored the perennial shortage of officers, bad treatment of apprentices (not only in sail), the endless increase in the habit of deserting, the large numbers of foreigners in British ships, etc. The Scandinavians found need to enlist few foreigners, were not short of officers, and had no premium-paying apprentices in their sailing ships at all (until later, when the ship *G .D. Kennedy* and the four-masted barks *Beatrice*—both former limejuicers—*C. B. Pedersen,* and *Abraham Rydberg* were commissioned as Swedish cargo-carrying school-ships largely manned by cadets, when commercial square-riggers had become too scarce to provide experience for the yearly intake of embryo deck officers).

Perhaps poor British standards of sustenance at sea reflected poor standards ashore, at any rate for the "working classes." Little was asked, but too often much less was given.

There were official inquiries from time to time, of course, in the usual manner on the well-established principle that the certain means of delaying the making of any decision was to set up a commission (or any other sort of inquiry) into the possibility of making a decision at all. A committee of thirteen (including Mr. Thomas Lane Devitt, Sir Walter Runciman, and Mr. J. Havelock Wilson, M.P., all excellent fellows in their own right) considered the matter of recruitment endlessly, while smug and ignorant asses like "George Bull" added to the general confusion, and the secretary of the British Merchant Service Guild threw cold water on them all with his curt statement that the "sea life is a dog's life: all respectable boys who know anything of the conditions shun it." He added that of the two master mariners appointed to this particular commission, "one had experience only in liners and the other had not been at sea for thirty years." This was typical of such commissions.

The "dog's life" was not wholly true, of course, but a lot nearer truth than a million George Bulls (and far too many John Bulls) would ever get, for they had an infinite capacity for taking their ships and seamen for granted. They took good care that their roast beef and Yorkshire pudding was *not* prepared by any Lloyd George–certificated sea cook.

As for apprentices, there were no signs of any shortage of adventurous youth willing to try the sea life, though the wastage was enormous. Many who became qualified officers gave up the profession as soon as they could. In August, 1906, the secretary of the Mercantile Marine Service Association recorded (in the *Shipping Gazette Weekly Summary* for August 3) that a list put up in the Association's employment bureau requesting applications for 156 deck officers drew eighty-one applicants. Pay for a sailing-ship master then offered was as low as £10 *a month,* and the Association was still vainly trying to get owners' agreement to such elementary conditions as three watches for officers (in steam: this was never achieved in merchant sail), the right of officers to defend themselves when charged with misdemeanors and not to suffer immediate discharge unheard, reasonable tenure and some leave, and the principle of one officer, one room. For apprentices, they tried—unsuccessfully—to have premiums abolished and some instruction made obligatory.

As for the seamen, Messrs. Davies, Jones & Co., Shipbrokers, wrote to the *Shipping Gazette* on July 27, 1906, proudly announcing that "We have a sailing-vessel in port manned by eight hands, all staunch teetotallers and everyone a Britisher! They have sailed in this ship for some time. This may be a rare instance, but it is a fact."

Rare instance? It was obviously unique. No one else ever wrote in to dispute such a record. Most ships—certainly the larger—were doing well to keep the same crew for half a voyage.

In the United States there was already a noticeable growth in the attitude of more or less scorn for merchant shipping, almost as a whole. The Department of Commerce and Labor in Washington, D.C., reported in July, 1906, that "the number of ships built for the Merchant Service last year is ridiculously small for a country with the coastline of the U.S.A." The number was twelve steamships of 5,000 tons or more, and two hundred vessels of all descriptions, many of them for service on the Great Lakes. But nobody seemed to care, for there was no war coming up at the moment.

British sailing-ship masters often complained about their officers, just as sailing-ship owners might have complained (and doubtless did) about the masters themselves, with greater cause. One wonders why the despised foreigners continued to ship in limejuice vessels, in which they provided at least half of all the crews throughout the period from 1897 to 1915, mostly Scandinavians, alleged Russians, and Germans. I asked my friend Captain J. B. Junker (Master of the Danish school-ship *Georg Stage* for many years, and a highly respected shipmaster) why young Danes went in British sailing ships, himself included.

"They went in German ships, too," he told me. "But that was not for me. I was born in South Jutland in 1879. Among my earliest memories is of our family trek from our home at Rodding when the Germans chose to drive us Danes out. I can see now that long row of farmer wagons which took us from Rodding to Vejen on October 1, 1884. It was the only time I saw my mother cry . . . No, not German ships for me. But if I was to make the sea my career as I intended, then I must serve at least four or five years in big sailing ships. Great Britain had plenty of them: their reputation as ships was very good. I didn't know about the starvation.

"So I went to Liverpool when I had finished my training cruise in the old *Georg Stage,* in 1896, and I got an ordinary seaman's job in the bark *Minnehaha,* of Londonderry. Sometimes the *Georg Stage* went specially to Liverpool at the end of the summer's sailing, to find jobs for the boys. There was a good demand because we were properly trained. We were glad to go because Denmark herself had not enough deep-sea ships for us to go in. We were rather more on an agricultural economy then, but the Germans had taken our land."

The *Minnehaha* was tough. He made two Atlantic voyages in the bark, then went to the big steel *Austrasia* for a round voyage to San Francisco and back—outward with a capacity cargo of coke, fire clay, and bricks for a smelter on the Sacramento River; homeward with grain. The *Austrasia* was a hungry ship. Able Seaman Junker paid off from her at Hull night-blind as a direct result of the bad diet. Good shore food with plenty of fruit put his sight right, but spoiled vision was too high a price to pay for time in limejuice ships which ran out of limejuice and had little or nothing else. So he shipped thereafter in Americans and French Cape Horners.

"The good wine and the spirits ration in the French kept scurvy away," the captain told me. "The Americans fed well. You were all right in them if you knew your work and did two men's share of it. I had no more trouble with my eyes."

By late 1904 he had been at sea eight years. It was time to go home to Denmark and begin at navigation school. Qualifying there, he chose a career with the United Danish Steamships Co. which led, in time, to selection first as mate then master of the *Georg Stage.* Here I met Captain Junker, when I bought the ship in Copenhagen in 1934.

The answer of the deepwater sailing-ship man to intolerable conditions was to desert. This was a crime: he could be arrested, jailed, and brought back to the ship. But first he had to be found. He soon became expert at melting away in big ports: some persons ashore, unfortunately for him, became far more expert in disposing of him (at a price) while pretending to assist him. It took a sober, determined, and level-headed man to desert successfully. There were plenty of them—in a ship named the *Sutlej,* for instance, the log of which I found at Hayes. It was her official log for her 1906-'07 voyage, which began with a four-and-a-half-month passage from Antwerp to San Francisco where her crew were soon at their usual practice of deserting—wholesale if possible, but getting away by any means. As far as one may judge, she must have begun with a good crew, for apart from finding the second mate drinking steadily through a case of gin going down the Scheldt (something which could happen to almost any mate or second mate who started too early on his sea stores), the *Sutlej* sailed the whole 142-day passage round the Horn to California without a single log entry. At San Francisco the second mate— out of gin by this time—led twelve of the A.B.'s ashore. Another died there of T.B., and his account of wages is charged with:

> £7. 4. 4 to burial
> £1. 0. 7½ ambulance to hospital
> £1.19. 9 St. Mary's Hospital fee

This left him (with some slop-chest debits) 18/- in debt to the ship. A crimp provided replacements at San Francisco. (Captain J. Parry of the ship *Monkbarns,* on a voyage from Hamburg to San Francisco and back to Flushing between February 17, 1906, and March 20, 1907, questioned six men put aboard by a crimp at San Francisco as alleged able seamen. Two, named Kohlmann and Kolloff, said they were "stokers," one August

Assa was a blacksmith, one Wood a stonecutter, one Edwards a seaman, and George Anderson was a "candy-maker." The "seaman" was from the Great Lakes. All were reduced to ordinary seamen, but told that "if they learned to work as A.B.'s they would be paid as A.B.'s." Assa lost his life from the rigging, the candymaker learned nothing, but the others settled down and did well.)

Whatever happened to good seamen kidnapped, misled, or otherwise induced to desert from limejuice ships in West Coast ports, they never seem to be sold back to other limejuicers. The *Sutlej* gets a dozen hopeless duds. These and six others of the crew remove themselves at the next port, which is Chemainus, B.C. More crimps' men (at the standard rate—legally fixed—of $30 a head plus expenses) are put aboard: next stop, Caleta Caloso, Chile. Here seven slip away in the night in the ship's work boat, but are met on the harbor by the master and mate being rowed out to the ship by four apprentices, and shepherded back aboard. A night or two later, some of them are discovered making a raft with the ship's timber and cordage. This time they are put in irons for a while. No sooner are the irons off than they are away again, leaving "bowlings and downhalls [*sic*] over the bows," having apparently swum.

Homeward bound at last with a fresh crew supplied expensively by the seamen's boardinghouse keepers of Callao (she had loaded guano at a Peruvian island and got crew from Callao), once again the *Sutlej* seems to be well-manned. Perhaps only real seamen were to be found at the time in Peruvian seamen's boardinghouses. Their spirit was good, and Captain Touzel (his wife and small son were aboard) must have been a good seaman. The ship is on half rations homeward bound "through the miscalculation of the steward or means unknown to me"—this is a lapse, for George Touzel was certainly responsible. He tells the crew they must go on half rations of bread, beef, and peas (which wouldn't leave much): they accept this as they "will be recompensed," except for D. Desmond, A.B., who demands his whack according to the Act. The ship "at the time being dangerously surrounded with tremendous large icebergs," Desmond lays up complaining of a sore throat. On the Line, they put up a hoist of flags to the German steamer *Rheinfels,* which stops and "supplied us with all stores required, viz. bread, flour, beef, rice, sugar, potatoes, veg., etc."

And so on to Nantes where they arrive on January 29, 1907, 135 days out from the guano island—not good but not too bad either, for the bottom of the *Sutlej* was foul with barnacles and sea grass before she left Peru. At Nantes all hands pay off cheerfully, declaring that they wanted no compensation for their weeks of hunger. Strange men, those international wanderers of sailing-ship seamen: a little human treatment and consideration, and their morale is excellent. Obviously, they had learned to like and respect George Touzel: cheerful refusal of the few daily pence for their loss of victuals was the only way they could show it.

All except D. Desmond, of course. Refusing to be paid off, he would not leave the ship. He stood by awhile and then deserted.

The more or less wholesale exodus of British sailing-ship crews at San Francisco, Puget Sound ports, and (on a slightly lower scale) at Melbourne, Sydney, and Newcastle, N.S.W., was a regular feature of limejuicers' voyages. With so many willing deserters, there were inevitably opportunists who saw profit in "helping" them. The form was to go aboard newly arrived ships as quickly as possible, with liquor, and set up an instant—and utterly false—camaraderie with glib talk of great times ashore, good jobs and all the rest. The bodies did not have to be carried: that came a night or so later, when they were delivered to other vessels, outward bound—at a price, paid to the crimp not to them.

The "trade" seems to have prospered most—or first—at San Francisco, but all the worse American ideas inevitably cross the Pacific to at least eastern Australia. The whole sordid business presents a fascinating if depressing field of investigation for the industrious sociologist. It would seem that there were deserting seamen before there were crimps. There was, after all, one reason for the costly wastage from the sea, and that was oppression in some form or other in ships. If the seaman had little or nothing to lose, why stay? If he were reasonably treated, why desert, and leave his payday (often his kit as well, such as it was) behind him?

Mr. Lloyd George said, during a discussion in the House of Commons on a Merchant Shipping Bill in 1906, that there were "probably 27,000 cases of desertions from British ships in a year." The British Consul at Portland (Oregon) was happily reporting a "welcome decrease" in the number of desertions from British ships calling there, in May, 1906. The figures, he said, had declined from 40 percent of all crews in 1903 to 21.26 percent in 1905. But he had to admit that the French rate was a steady less than 7 percent. French ships, he said, were diligent in pursuing deserters and fighting off crimps. The crimps' charge for supplying seamen was £6 each.

He might have added, if he knew, that there was a world of difference between the treatment of her seamen by the average French ship and that habitual in many British. There was also a very great difference in the treatment of seamen ashore. *All* French seamen, naval, merchant ship, fishermen, were regarded alike as national assets and treated as such. They had a contributory pension fund. They were assured of a place ashore or at least, at the age of fifty, something of a pension from the state. If they wished to better themselves, the state freely provided instruction of all the principal ports in the professional subjects the seaman had to master. French ships had no need of the mean apprenticeship system of the British, which meant in effect that after four years of callous exploitation the time-served young man had then to finance his own crammer, having prepared himself as unpaid A.B. to the state where the minimum cramming could help him. The Frenchman was subject to drafting for government service, but this was no hardship. France had considerable reserves of good seamen, particularly in Brittany and Normandy.

A French deserter had more to lose than a miserable balance of wages, shrunken by slop-chest charges real or imaginary, swollen "tailor's" advances, charges for "substitutes" and fines (these at least a consular officer or shipping master was supposed to approve) and advances of pay. Too often the seaman in the British ship had little to lose by desertion and, if only he wasn't shanghaied, could easily better himself. But in some large ports he was an item of barter: he was shanghaied because he was a salable commodity when Cape Horn ships had to go to sea, and money could be made out of him by unscrupulous and useless persons.

Mr. Lloyd George hinted that desertion could, perhaps, be profitable to seamen and owners. An editorial (in the *Shipping Gazette Weekly Summary*) commenting on this said that desertion in fact costs owners large sums. The paper quoted statistics from fifty-three ships in which 548 deserters left behind a total of £3,826 in wages (lost by them to the ship) but the "extra wages and other expenses incurred in consequence of these desertions was £6,000." Ships had to pay "blood money" to crimps at so much the body, and the seaman also lost at least his first month's wages to his "supplier." But no breakdown was given for that £6,000.

The figure of 27,000 desertions would be officially supplied to Mr. Lloyd George, who was president of the Board of Trade at the time, and should be reliable. The round figure of £10 a head lost on all deserters may be more questionable, although it amounts in fact—offsetting the forfeit wages—to about £4. The constant changing of crews was of benefit to nobody other than those who made that change their business.

This business of driving seamen *out* of ships, as Mr. W. S. Lindsay indicates in Vol. III of his four-volume *History of Merchant Shipping and Ancient Commerce*,* grew as a habit from American legislation first enacted in 1790 which provided that if any seaman deserted or "absented himself for 48 hours without leave from his ship," he forfeited at once his wages and all his gear and kit in the ship. The idea of this was to prevent desertion, or at least to deter deserters. The effect was to encourage unscrupulous owners and masters to drive men *out* of their ships, if they had a good credit balance, so that the money could be purloined and new men shipped at lower wages. To mark a seaman as "deserted" on the Articles or in the log was sufficient to condemn him. There was built up a trafficking in seamen and alleged sea-

* London: Sampson Low, Marston, Low and Searle, 1876.

men which, having begun and prospered, was very difficult to put down. In Britain, in time, rigorous prosecution of any who sought to induce seamen to leave their ships, or pretended to supply them, at least drove the business underground and confined its possible profits to the take-over of the supplied man's advance note, for his first month's pay. Merely for being found aboard without the master's permission, talking with seamen in the forecastle of the *Star of Scotland* before the ship paid off, while she was lying in the Victoria Dock, London, in mid-1908, two men were given three months jail each. They were described to the court as "known crimps."

The deliberately brutal treatment of seamen in many American ships, called hazing, designed to drive them out of the ship without their pay, is well documented in the "Red Record," a sort of supplement of maritime evil published periodically in the *Coast Seamen's Journal* of San Francisco, over a long period. The "Record" was kept by a Scots American named Walter MacArthur, who had served in hellships in the 1880's. Though he lived quietly alone in San Francisco until he was well past eighty, he never forgot the brutalities of the callous buckos. For several decades, from the '80's to the early years of the twentieth century, he compiled case histories of indefensible nastinesses perpetrated against deep-sea seamen serving in American ships, with names, dates, witnesses: but it took a long time for the appalling facts to arouse any interest ashore. It was 1915 before some abuses were corrected by legislation. By that time, many of the deep-sea ships were gone. MacArthur plugged away with his "Red Record," living quietly in his later years in the Terminal Hotel on lower Market Street in San Francisco. Here Captain Harold Huycke, well-known American and international maritime historian, knew him. Files of the *Coast Seamen's Journal* are kept at the San Francisco Library and in the Maritime Museum of that city. MacArthur died unnoticed in the early 1940's.

There is no doubt what upset morale and led to many desertions in the four-masted bark *Dumfriesshire,* a skysail-carrying steel vessel of 2,565 gross tons built in 1890, with the new idea of the "Liverpool house," like the *Pegasus.* This incorporated accommodation for the master, officers and crew. There are few logs for the *Dumfriesshire* still surviving, which is a good sign: I found only one at Hayes, in 1969. This is for a California and Puget Sound voyage in 1907-'08 under Captain R. W. Furneaux, of Totnes in Devon, a well-known master who had the ship for some time. She was 170 days sailing from Newcastle, England, to Los Angeles, and almost the same from Seattle to Falmouth for orders—over fifteen months for one round voyage, with two cargoes. Fortunately, she carried a lot. She lost her Scots cook and a West Indian A.B., both to illness. Eleven A.B.'s and the second mate deserted at Los Angeles, and an apprentice deserted at Newcastle. The unfortunate cook was found collapsed in the snow on deck off the Horn and never rallied: he had no kit at all. The West Indian was badly affected by frostbite off the Horn but lived to be buried at Santa Monica.

There were other desertions. It took seventy-six men to keep the ship provided with twenty A.B.'s, so that at least fifty additional persons must have passed through the ship during that one round voyage. Though by no means exceptional, this does not speak well. No explanation is hinted at for the rapid turnover in ports. One can learn about this from Captain F. Miners, who was an apprentice in the *Dumfriesshire* and wrote of his experiences in Captain A. G. Course's little journal, the *Cape Horner.* (This is the journal of the British section of the International Association of Master Mariners—Cape Horners—an organization based on St. Malo. It is not a body of Cape Horn master mariners, for in 1970 there is not a single one of those left from merchant ships in Britain. Its members in the United Kingdom include former apprentices and others who served in Cape Horn ships, and went on with their sea careers very wisely in steam, as well as many who were passengers in later days, and other honorary members.)

Captin Robert Furneaux had a "frightful mean streak," wrote Captain Miners, "especially where the food rations were concerned," and he blames this for most of the crew troubles. The ship herself was well found (and reasonably well sailed) but for the crew it was "strict Board of Trade scale, and less if the steward could get away with it—an appalling system . . . just about sufficient to keep one alive." One item was an issue of one pound of fresh bread each three times weekly. Many of the apprentices —there were ten—would "sit down and eat this at once," though they well knew they would get little else. As soon as the ship was clear of the land "the crew began to give trouble over the food. They made frequent trips aft to register their complaints to the captain, but nothing was done and troubles increased." At sea and in port, all hands remained on bare subsistence diet. "Food was taken aft [as inedible and far from sufficient] almost daily and with arguments over this and money, tempers rose on both sides." The mate, a Bluenose, shot a sailor dead at Rio (where the *Dumfriesshire* discharged coal) but was exonerated at a perfunctory local inquiry.

This voyage continued from Rio round the Horn westward in ballast bound for Puget Sound, and more misery with inadequate food, more troubles. Through all this the captain remained aloof, never sparing a word even for the senior apprentices whom he was supposed to instruct (there was no instruction which was not provided in the performance of their work or through their own efforts), never permitting the slightest variation in the inadequate rations of wretched food. A shower of iron belaying pins descended out of the rigging toward the mate one dark night off the Horn, but all missed him. The captain never left the poop.

The crew of the *Dumfriesshire* was then fourteen A.B.s, ten apprentices, a bos'n, carpenter, and sailmaker: obviously the apprentices were an important—an essential—part of her complement. It was at best foolish to keep them and everyone else undernourished: but it was the way of many British ships then. It was owners' policy (forced on them) to run their ships with strict economy, but not to starve the crews nor to keep them so on the breadline that poor morale became bad for the ship's efficiency. Away from home ports, owners did not buy the food and did not usually have their own agents. This—and handling the money—was the master's duty.

Captain Furneaux, writes Captain Miners, "was prepared to do nothing, expecting, no doubt, that the entire crew of sailors would desert as soon as the ship arrived and he would make a fresh start." At what, starving another lot? At Puget Sound he knew very well the crimps would induce his crew to leave. He was a good ship-handler, a good sailor: he usually made reasonable passages. But what satisfaction could there be in commanding a ship manned by disaffected, half-starved men? No fault was found with those seamen. The most stupid aspect of the whole business was that, provided the money allocated to food was spent on food with no kick backs or other nastiness for anybody, even the skinflint allow ances of those days was sufficient to keep men's bellies de cently full and themselves happy at their work. All the good masters managed it. Even in the 1930's, we managed it very well in the *Parma,* on 1s 1d to 1s 3d a man a day—paltry sums to try to "make" on.

Arrived in Puget Sound, his indentures being then expired and "feeling I had had enough of the old man and his mean ways," young Miners left, with his four-years balance of pay of $6, to find his own way back to Britain. He had the good fortune to get a berth as second mate almost immediately in the American four-masted schooner *Aloha* at $60 the month, no nonsense about inadequate food, and a harmonious afterguard of young Scandinavian Americans. An excellent colored cook-steward served magnificent meals, coffee, hot rolls, and everything else as required.

The *Aloha* was the antithesis of the hungry *Dumfriesshire*—a happy ship, not well manned numerically, for she had only four hands (one to a mast plus minimum afterguard was her manning scale): but these four hands were the best young able seamen from the *Dumfriesshire.*

They had had enough of mean ways and discord too. They were decent young men: but they never shipped in a British ship again. They took American nationality, in due course, and established themselves in excellent careers under the Stars and Stripes. Britain's loss was America's gain.

There was a sort of mutiny aboard the Glasgow four-masted bark *Beechbank* (John R. Bremner, of Wick, master) after she arrived at Santa Rosalia from Hamburg in 1903. The voyage took four and a half months: she was to wind'ard of the Horn before the worst of the winter months. Santa Rosalia could be a difficult port to make. It was about halfway up the eastern coast of Baja California, across the Gulf from Guaymas, and big square-riggers bound there were often beset by baffling winds and harassed by calms. In those days, it was not much of a place when reached. Its smelters could make good use of special fuels imported from Hamburg, and—as far as seamen were concerned—this was the only good point about it. Obviously, this was the sort of difficult trade the Cape Horner could keep, at least until the Panama Canal was in operation.

The *Beechbank*'s log is reticent. An A.B. is lost from the rigging off the Horn. An apprentice reports V.D.: he is "treated with caustic and black wash" and is quickly back at work. The master has malaria. Then suddenly the police flags are flying. The officers arm themselves, after beginning to lose a fist fight with some of the crew. "Have mutiny aboard," says a hoist of flags in the international code. No one pays attention. Captain Bremner is ashore, trying to get treatment for his malaria. The officers fire shots in the air. Still no one pays attention.

Apparently, no one ever pays attention. A few shots in that part of Mexico meant nothing then: neither did a limejuice hoist of flags. After sunset, a couple of A.B.'s row away in a ship's boat. The log declares that one Nelson, A.B., was ringleader of the flare-up, without recounting the evidence. Perhaps he was one who rowed away—they were never found—for things quiet down to the usual wordy discord after that. There is no more open mutiny, though the troubles continue to fill pages of the log.

There was no British consul at Santa Rosalia: the ship had to look after herself. In due course she staggered off in ballast to Port Townsend, where most of the seamen deserted. (Crimps supplied replacements at $20 a month: outside Captain Bremner disrates these to ordinary seamen at $10, with good cause, which meant that as the crimps took the first month's advance at the higher rate plus blood money, the shanghaied men worked at least for the first two months for nothing. Such matters do not make for harmony.) At Port Adelaide, Port Pirie, and Melbourne there were more wholesale desertions. Eighty men pass through the ship—all named in the log—to keep her crewed, though almost half the crew were premium apprentices. Since she carried only fouteen able seamen, this meant a turnover of approximately six men to keep one aboard. Apprentices did not usually desert and casualties were not replaced among them until the ship reached her home port, unless some young optimist came forward in Australia or the United States. Optimists of that magnitude were scarce in both countries: they had, perhaps, better outlets.

The *Beechbank* was back in Antwerp from that voyage in February, 1905.

Some further light is shown on the state of things aboard the *Beechbank* in a log kept by the young second mate a year or two after this Mexican voyage. The second mate was Harold W. Green, later Captain H. W. Green, D.S.C., a highly respected shipmaster, an R.N.R. commander, and a member of the British branch of the Cape Horners' Society. When he joined the *Beechbank* Captain Green was no stranger to tough conditions in Cape Horners, for he had been in the wreck of the Bristol-built bark *Powys Castle,* a vessel which was supposed to be "unlucky." She was certainly unfortunate with her last master, for he managed to lose her in the breakers on Tierra del Fuego homeward bound with a fair wind and—for those latitudes—good weather.

The master was from Fishguard in Wales which has produced many good seamen, but that voyage the mate (from Nevin in N. Wales) was the better man. Perhaps realizing and resenting this, the master paid no heed to the mate's counsel. He cut the corner round the Horn inside Diego Ramirez, the wind jambed him, he was embayed, flung ashore and lost his ship and several of the crew. Fortunately it was midsummer; after some time, the survivors were rescued by the Argentine government's vessel *Ushuaia.* Captain Green finished his apprenticeship in the *Conway*

Castle, but he never forgot the lessons he learned in the *Powys.*

Some years later, appointed second mate of the *Beechbank* with his new certificate scarcely dry, he presented himself aboard at Port Talbot where the ship was loading coal for Chile. It was quickly obvious that young second mates rated low indeed: so did stewards, and the steward left after less than twenty-four hours of the *Beechbank* and her master. There were eight apprentices. Before she slipped from the loading berth, four of the newly signed A.B.'s decided, like the steward, that the *Beechbank* as commanded by Captain Bremner did not really appeal to them. Pierhead jumps (rarely the best form of recruitment) replaced these, and off punched the *Beechbank* into a hard sou'wester to get an offing as quickly as she could. It was bitterly cold, the decks were in a mess and the crew, for the moment, likewise. These were tough times for old sailing shipmasters and very new second mates, and mates as well. The afterguard was not an harmonious team, but the four-master got along and was soon down in better weather.

The ship hadn't gone far before there was trouble about the food, the for'ard hands bringing bad salt meat aft to ask for better. They got short shrift: soon they were back again, but they got no concessions. They got nothing and they became hungrier. By the time they reached the Line there were hard words: the men's spirit was deteriorating. It became obvious that the master and mate did not approve of each other, and the second mate was no admirer of either. But the ship sails steadily down both Atlantics with considerable friction, but no serious trouble, despite her hungry crew. Approaching southern latitudes, the captain amused himself by shooting albatrosses.* They were off the Horn in March, with other big sailing ships sighted daily. The ship was making reasonable progress, but that nagging matter of the starvation rations kept spoiling morale. The crew discovered somehow that the ship was south of 60° S.—the legal limit their articles bound them to—and complained about that. This got them at least one decent meal, but only one, and so the poor morale continued. The two mates were the principal sufferers

* See note at the end of the chapter.

from this: whatever they did could never be right. Men laid up
with frostbitten feet—"Cape Horn fever," says the second mate.
Northerly and northwesterly winds forced the ship south. Master
and mate are often at loggerheads. The crew take turns at laying
up. There is the usual abundance of all-hands work. In eleven
days the ship made 270 miles of westing, and lucky to do that.
The wind stayed north of west: she made leeway farther and
farther to the south.

So Easter came, cold, gloomy, wretched, the ship beset by
nature's hard head winds, the ship's three officers in a sort of
truce, the for'ard hands in a state of constant discontent over the
food. Poor ship! But in time she was far enough south and sufficiently to the west'ard and south'ard for a shift of the wind to
southwest to be favorable. When such a shift came, after weeks
of misery, she scudded along.

"Oilskins are giving out . . . The cargo has shifted a little
giving her a list. She is more like a submarine than a ship. Heavy
snow squalls all night"—so reads the second mate's diary. But
she was making northwest and, by God's grace, past the Horn.
Not long afterward it is fine and warm, and the hands are strop-
ping ballast baskets getting ready to work out the coal. Ninety-
three days out from Port Talbot, the *Beechbank* is at Iquique. A day
or two before that, the second mate notes "the captain writing in
the official log all day"—from memory? If so, it seems a vindictive
memory, for all things considered the crowd has worked well
despite their miserable rations: except for the mate, bos'n and
carpenter, everybody is "logged," even the second mate. He
learns this for the first time when all are mustered to hear the
entries read out publicly.

In Iquique there was constant trouble, though the hands
were given some concessions in their twelve-hour day, six-day
week of working out the *Beechbank*'s big cargo of patent fuel, such
as a ten-minute "smoke-oh" spell in the afternoons. Regular full
rations of reasonable food would have pleased them better. They
try to steal a boat to get ashore. They demand to see the consul.
They refuse duty. They desert. They cut up some of the more
expensive of the ship's running gear. They dump the starboard

sidelight. Six are removed ashore to the calaboose. . . .

So it goes, day after day—the whole fault bad morale, the principal reason stupid meanness over food, the principal villain very obvious.

It took two months to get the *Beechbank*'s cargo out, another month and a half to load nitrate for Europe, which was slovenly progress. By that time the whole of the foremast crew had been changed: but little else.

His captain might have had some reason for not being wholly pleased with Mr. Green as second mate. He was very young (he had his twenty-first birthday aboard that voyage) and his previous experience was limited to the usual four years apprenticeship varied by being wrecked near the Horn. He had a brand-new certificate as an officer. Although apprentices joined ships as embryo officers few shipmasters offered them the slightest training (or indeed much example) in officer duties or qualities. A lad moved aft and suddenly took charge of a watch, perhaps bewildered: ship, trade, attitudes aboard could be quite strange, but he was expected at once to be half the ship's watch-keeping strength, efficient as leader, disciplinarian, eagle-eyed watcher of the wind and judge of weather present and probable, possible and impossible. For the first time, he had to handle *men:* his half-deck training, far too often, had set his mind against them, which was a pity.

A kindly and efficient master would keep a helpful eye on new, young second mates, but such masters were rare. The majority scorned and showed their scorn, seeming to resent the appointment of the youth—any youth—as an affront to themselves. Perhaps they were reminded that their own youth had gone, and were well aware that young second mates would not tolerate the Cape Horn profession a moment longer than they needed for advancement toward their master's qualifications. That gained, they would go into steam—a step the old boys had to scorn. They knew very well that it was the only intelligent thing the young could do: it was too late for them, despit the fact that the *Beechbank*'s owners were already then becoming interested in steam.

There was an enormous and unnecessary gulf between mate and second mate, too, especially when the mate was some old passed-over or tried-and-found-wanting ex-master. After a round voyage in a ship like the *Beechbank* (where despite his obvious faults the master as a sailor was well worth understudying) a bright ex-apprentice like Green would be an excellent officer: but by that time it was far more usual that he had had enough of deep-sea sail to last his lifetime. He had by then a year or more or experience as certificated officer in charge of a watch, and that took him on to his next certificate, a mate's. Qualifying time on the way up had to be spent *in charge of a watch,* to ensure experience with real responsibility. Some young men went back with their first mate's certificates to serve sufficient time to qualify as master, for many of the better steamships lines required that deck officers should already have their master's certificate before they would recruit them. Either way, the former apprentice generally served abaft the mast in sail only as long as it suited him, if he intended to follow a useful career at sea.

Most continental seafaring nations had only one stage before master, and that was mate: but the schooling ashore for this was long, comprehensive, and thorough. For many, including Scandinavians and Germans, the navigation school curricula included meteorology studied thoroughly, and far more ship construction, stability, treatment of sickness and injury, seamanship and navigation than the British did. Even when I went to sea it was customary for ambitious lads to study quite well by themselves—perhaps I should say "cram"—for the second mate's examination from a couple of question-and-answer books, not at all formidable to anyone with reasonable maths and a good memory. Unlike many continentals, all Britishers then had to finance their own schooling.

The captain of the *Beechbank* was over sixty when young Green was his second mate. He had been at sea since before 1860 when, in some ways, things were even harder. He was a dyed-in-the-wool conservative in all matters relating to merchant seafaring: he was a sailing-ship sailor—as such, indeed, a very good one, for he handled *ships* well and made reasonable passages.

What he never appreciated was that men needed good handling too—mates, second mates, stewards, apprentices, seamen. He never learned, being well content with his own standards.

So in due course the ships disappeared from under him, and all his kind. The *Beechbank* and the *Inverness-shire* were both sold to Norway (like many good British sailing ships) and the *Claverdon* to Italy.

NOTE : LISTED AMONG THE KIT OF ABLE SEAMAN CHARLES BENNETT, AGE UNKNOWN, WHO DIED VERY QUIETLY WHILE SITTING ON THE MAIN HATCH WITH HIS WATCH DONE, WAS THE ODD ITEM OF "4 BIRDS' FEET," AS WELL AS "1 PR. EYE GLASSES" AND THE MORE USUAL "SHEATH-KNIFE, A FID, A MARLINSPIKE, 4 PIPES, 2 PALMS IN DITTY BAG," ETC. PROBABLY THESE WERE ALBATROSS FEET FROM WHICH REAL ANCIENT MARINERS SOMETIMES MADE THEMSELVES TOBACCO POUCHES, REGARDLESS OF THE VIEWS OF SAMUEL TAYLOR COLERIDGE. COLERIDGE WAS A LANDLUBBER WRITING FOR OTHER LANDLUBBERS, AND THEY PAID LITTLE ATTENTION TO HIM. MASEFIELD'S DAUBER WAS DIFFERENT. IT WAS OBVIOUS TO THEM IN EVERY LINE THAT THOUGH GIFTED AND HIGHLY IMAGINATIVE, LIKE CAPTAINS J. CONRAD, D. W. BONE, AND F. RIESENBERG, JOHN MASEFIELD HAD BEEN IN SAILING SHIPS, AND NOT JUST FOR A DOG WATCH.

PERHAPS IT WAS A NARROW VIEW, BUT SAILING-SHIP SAILORS RESERVED THEIR SEAL OF APPROVAL STRICTLY FOR THOSE WHOSE ACQUAINTANCE WITH THEIR CALLING WAS OBVIOUSLY REAL. SO THEY MADE POUCHES FROM ALBATROSS FEET, AND DRIED ALBATROSS HEADS TO PRESENT TO DISTINGUISHED CITIZENS KNOWN TO THEM AS OF REAL WORTH, LIKE BARMAIDS AT CHARLIE BROWN'S IN LONDON'S DOCKLAND OR BIG NELLIE'S IN NEWCASTLE, N.S.W. THEY CAUGHT THE ALBATROSS EASILY IN CALMS, ON CRUDE TRIANGLES OF WOOD AND WIRE BAITED WITH SALT HORSE. SNAPPING FOR THE BAIT, THE ALBATROSS WAS HELD BY THE CURVE OF HIS BEAK, AND HAULED ABOARD. THE FRENCH ATE THEM, AFTER MUCH PATIENT PREPARATION. SAILORS KNEW THAT THE ALBATROSS WENT FOR THEM IF THEY GOT OVERBOARD. HIS SOARING FLIGHT WAS MAGNIFICENT, BUT THEY HELD THAT HIS SPIRIT, IF ANY, WAS THAT OF NO SAILING-SHIP SEAMAN. IT WAS MORE LIKELY THAT OF A MANAGING OWNER.

Chapter ten

CASE OF THE BARK *CRAIGMULLEN*

I HAD received an object lesson on the harmful effects of bad masters once, on a long passage of five months from Melbourne to St. Nazaire in a big English four-masted bark named the *Bellands* (ex-*Forteviot*), in 1921. Having previously served only in our own "colonial" barks under the Australian flag, the style of things aboard the *Bellands* was a shock, and a grievous disappointment too. I'd been in a half deck of cadets in my first ship, the Sydney bark *Rothesay Bay,* but we were not fee-paying apprentices indentured to the owners but five lads, aged fifteen to eighteen, on the Articles of the ship. Our quarters included a six-berth sleeping cabin and a messroom that we could study in, and the senior was already a failed second mate sent back to sea for more study. We were not there as a sort of class-backing for an inadequate afterguard against the foc's'l men: such an attitude didn't enter life at all, for there was no need of it where men were treated properly.

I found the *Bellands,* which was a splendid strong ship, run curiously indeed. But she *was* a sailing ship, so three or four of us joined together from the bark *James Craig,* in order to continue our qualifying time and to gain knowledge toward the acquisition of a second mate's certificate. There were in fact few English in her apart from the afterguard, galley crew, and apprentices. The voyage had originated in Norway and the "crowd" was international, mainly Scandinavian. The apprentices had their own quarters, kept themselves to themselves, looked vainly aft for a little instruction, and we were sorry for them. The senior was a very new second mate (he had finished his time and qualified while the

179

four-master had slowly handled Norwegian timber out and bagged Australian wheat in at Melbourne): neither he nor the others had any privileges, though he lived in the worst cabin aft.

The master was not seen until the ship was ready to sail, for he had lived ashore in the city. When loaded, the ship wasted a week at anchor in Port Philip Bay, towed down the bay with a fair wind, anchored at Melbourne Heads another week, towed to sea from there. Why? I wondered. Scandinavian, American, French deep-sea sailing ships came in and out without tugs while we languished. It was midsummer, the weather glorious. The *James Craig* and the *Rothesay Bay* had sailed when they were ready, their masters and crews aboard always. What was the matter with this *Bellands?* She was large, certainly. Was she also unhandy?

We learned that she was not. It was *spirit* she was lacking: that was not her fault. There was an attitude of hostility between poop and forecastle, which was new to us. It came from aft, not for'ard. We had managed without that sort of thing in our colonial barks. Perhaps I had been lacking in observation—I was still sixteen at the time—but I had not noticed such an attitude ashore in Australia or New Zealand either.

Well, there we were. We made the best of it. Beyond a stupid incident at Melbourne which involved the removal of one of the few Englishmen from the foc's'l—a Cockney A.B.—to jail, for alleged refusal of duty, etc. (he had asked for a larger kettle to hold the limejuice issue for his watch) there was no active oppression, nor need for such stupidity. The *Bellands* made a long passage homeward around Good Hope, shortening down at any drop in the barometer, coming across the Indian Ocean in flying-fish weather, around the Cape in the Agulhas current, through the South Atlantic in the southeast trade winds. She more or less ambled along by herself as if she were trying to do her best, and was as bewildered as we were when she was halted and shortened down.

We were three months to the Line, another two months from there to St. Nazaire. Captain Mann never once tacked the ship—put her around in the classic manner, head thrown across the wind. He always ran off and wore, the wasteful way meant for

severe weather, because of his distrust of the Jarvis brace winches. They would "take charge," he said. We thought it was a pity
he didn't, thinking of Murdo' Murchison sailing the *James Craig*
like a yacht in the Tasman Sea come what may, and his brother
Finlay getting the bark *Wathara* past the Horn with half her main
backstays gone. Ah! those boys were *sailors.* There in the *Bellands*
we hadn't even a has-been: he was what Captain David W. Bone
called a "never-bloody-was'er."

So we were five months. Arrived at last, the big ship was
immediately paid off, reduced to a care-and-maintenance basis.
She had good owners, but she lost money despite the two good
freights. Tugs, dilatory discharge and loading, master's expenses ashore had eaten away the hope of profit. She had an
excellent crew with A.B.'s paid £12 a month (reduced to £1-10 for
her next—and last British—voyage). She had excellent apprentices and a good young second mate, but the mate was indeed a
has-been, a wonderful old man with ages of experience, reduced
to impotence by feeble eyesight and lack of faith in all promoted
apprentices and most other persons under seventy.

I learned a great deal about how *not* to be a sailing-ship
master, in the *Bellands.*

There was one curious yarn the apprentices passed on which
the captain had told them, for he used to yarn with them sometimes and, indeed, had given them some useful navigation instruction on a previous voyage. The yarn was of an experience
he said he had had in a Liverpool bark named the *Craigmullen,*
when he had brought the bark single-handed into Callao after all
hands, or almost all, had died on some drifting match of a passage between Siam and Peru. It was both highly colored and, we
thought, highly improbable. Whatever happened was supposed
—in the *Bellands* at any rate—to have been extremely harrowing,
affecting Captain Mann for the rest of his life. All I noted at the
time was that the captain had left the China coast in a bark and
all hands died of some fever, except himself and one hand.
Caught in calm for one hundred days, the bark eventually drifted
quite close to the port to which she was bound. When a steamer

put a boat aboard in quest of salvage, only Mann was left conscious to thwart them. He had had to watch all the others die—the yarn went something like this.

Looking at him, I wondered why the Lord had acted so strangely—if there were any truth in the yarn. I discovered later that a version of it had been published in 1920 in the Pacific Steam Navigation Company's house journal, *Sea Breezes*, which at least tried to present authentic sailing-ship news. Here the version had the *Craigmullen* adrift on passage from Bangkok toward Pisco. I read:

> The passage took 260 days! 260 days!! Food and water ran out, and luckily the cargo was rice. For upon rice all hands lived and with what rain-water they could catch.
>
> Of other ships they saw nothing. Solid weeks of calm, burning decks, illness, and madness, and death. Every man suffered, severely and with courage whilst he had the strength, but at length overcome by weakness, gloom, and despondency. The carpenter went mad, raving and dancing, and denunciating in the cabin. Eventually he died, followed by the cook and four sailors. The burying of them was pathetic and terrible to those who remained.
>
> No one was able to go aloft, no one was capable of setting or shortening sail, and as time went on and nothing showed up on the Pacific the crew stared at one another, and wondered, and dazedly held to drifting life. Canvas aloft hung from untrimmed yards and the running gear rotted against the shrouds and was left standing where it carried away.
>
> Two hundred miles from Pisco a ship was sighted. The *Craigmullen* hoisted a distress signal to the gaff peak. A big German full-rigger swung slowly down and gave them a supply of food and water. And this supply alone saved what hands were left. A week passed before the *Craigmullen* anchored in the port.

Further investigation showed that the story had been published much earlier, with wide variations: our friend Captain Mann had indeed been aboard. A highly colored version of the yarn had been published in August, 1908, in a curious English magazine called *Wide World*, which allegedly dealt in "true sto-

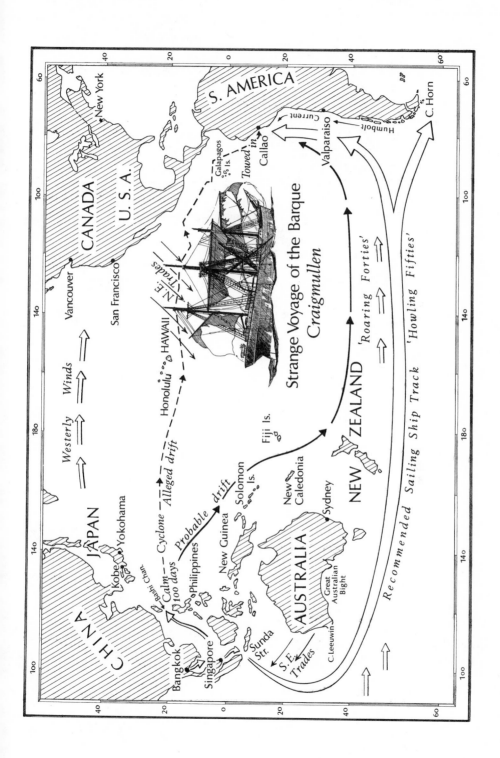

Strange Voyage of the Barque *Craigmullen*

The BELLANDS *leaving Melbourne*

The abandoned bulk of the LYSGLIMT

ries," mainly written by former elephant hunters, gold-seekers, minor district officers, recruiters, and other such worthy types from the frontiers of the British world.

Here the *Craigmullen* became:

The Ship That Disappeared
As told by Captain Edmund G. Mann
And Set Down by J. O. Grey.

This was "the tragic story of the British bark *Craigmullen* which sailed from Singapore in 1895 and mysteriously vanished. Nearly a year later she reappeared under dramatic circumstances with three unconscious men on board in place of a crew of twenty-five. The full narrative of her dreadful voyage is here set forth for the first time by the *Craigmullen*'s C.O., one of the only two survivors."

A hundred-day calm in the Bashi Channel—between the Batan Islands north of the Philippines and Formosa (Taiwan)—merely started things. A typhoon, dismasting, crew troubles, over twenty deaths followed in melodramatic sequence. Why a master tried to reach Callao by this north-about route was not explained: the sensible way was to get south to the South Indian Ocean and thence to the South Pacific, below Australia, Tasmania, and New Zealand, running east in the strong west winds down there, to come in on Callao eventually with the help of the Humboldt current.

But sea sense had nothing to do with this story. The postcalm typhoon dismasted the ship, bashing her up in the Bashi Channel to such extent that she could no longer sail properly anywhere (as told by Captain Mann and set down by J. O. Grey).

"First to die was the youngest apprentice, a boy of fifteen, and one who, by his kindness of disposition, had endeared himself to all of us. He died on Christmas morning. The Captain was the next. He died raving. After that not a week passed without one man dying. Sometimes they went with quiet fluttering of the heart and a sigh; at others shrieking in maniac fury and cursing with foaming lips. I buried them all in the same grave beneath the oily surface of that leaden sea . . ."

And so forth and so on for the rest of the hundred days. "Wither we drifted all this time I knew not nor cared." Navigation was given up, the chronometers run down. The calm ended with a typhoon, of course. The bark was left a "hopeless wreck." The fourteen survivors were "abject specimens of starving humanity . . . whose wild staring eyes showed the terror through which they had passed, and fear of the death awaiting them."

With still almost the whole of the Pacific Ocean to cross, scurvy followed, and more deaths. This was not enough. A slow virulent fever set in. So all "sat down to await the fast approaching end. My own strength gave way." There were seven left. Acting-Captain Mann brought the survivors aft. In another week there were three. He saw visions, lay on the poop to die. But, *mirabile dictu* (according to Mann as told to Grey), he awoke to hear the voices of strange men aboard.

"She's salvage right enough," they were saying. "They're all dead."

"Not all," the indomitable "captain" managed to get out: and lost consciousness. He had thwarted the salvage claim, almost with his last breath.

Not a German full-rigged ship but a P.S.N. coasting steamer had picked them up, drifted miraculously to within three hundred miles of Callao! The undistinguished old bark, "dismasted and derelict, had drifted right across the Pacific" (against the trade winds?) to arrive more or less off the port to which she was bound —a remarkable yarn indeed, even if true. The *Craigmullen* had been ten months at sea: the two (or was it three?) survivors took months to recover at a hospital in Peru (as told by "Captain" Mann).

With so many deaths aboard that *Craigmullen,* surely, I thought, the official log of the vessel should be at Hayes. Search failed to find it, but the Articles were there. These list with a more certain accuracy even than the log the fate of all persons on board, since consular officers supervise and attest the entries. The men's own signatures are there, or their "marks." Consular entries record deaths, if any: such matters are investigated.

There are no voyage details, but what does emerge is that the longest she could have been at sea was 229 days—long enough (though not much longer than the German ship *Susanna*'s passage from Port Talbot to Chile in 1905) and considerably shorter than the 260 of the *Sea Breezes* account and Mann's own 310. The elapsed time between the last date-stamped consular entry at Singapore and the first at Callao (not Pisco) I made 229 days— from June 30, 1895, until February 13, 1896. A good many big sailing ships were at sea longer than this without suffering any hundred-day calms, on passages from northwest Europe to San Francisco or Puget Sound, for instance, or when driven away from the Horn and compelled to go east-about, almost around the world.

There were two deaths only reported to the consul and so entered on the articles—Thomas Callister, steward, aged forty-five, and Charles Kerr, carpenter, aged thirty-seven. Everybody else is alive enough to sign his name or make his mark. One seaman was brought to the hospital with scurvy on arrival at Callao, and another followed later with fever. The mate, Edmund Griffin Mann, was paid off at Callao, "discharged at this port on the alleged ground of mutual consent," Acting Consul George Wilson has written in, adding that he has "inquired into the matter and finds the allegation true and the grounds sufficient."

This "mutual consent" could mean anything: usually it meant that for some reason or another, both the master and the leaver were glad to see the last of one another. Perhaps Captain Loades, the hale and hearty master of the *Craigmullen,* felt that the bark might do better with a less imaginative script writer as her mate. This W. Loades must have been a good master, for fourteen of the original crew signed off the Articles when the twenty-eight-month round voyage ended in November, 1896. With the three apprentices still aboard (none had died), this was unusually good in those days of considerable crew wastage and many desertions.

Script writer Mann was an odd shipmaster, indeed. Perhaps he was before his time—but not as a shipmaster.

What really was the matter with him? Was he suffering from some compelling dissatisfaction that set him to living in an odd dream world of his own, like Barker of the *British Isles* and his romances? They seemed to share much the same attitude toward crews, simply because they were crews. There was that callous incident on the *Bellands* voyage when the young second mate and his watch sighted the Danish bark *Lysglimt* on fire at the edge of the northeast trade winds, and Mann refused even to run off a mile or two to offer help. I was in the second mate's watch. We saw rockets in the night, the billowing smoke among the sails in the morning. It was good weather, the wind favorable to go to the burning ship.

"Huh, auxiliary steamer," scoffed the mate, who didn't like his young colleague and couldn't see, anyway.

Mann didn't come on deck until long after daylight. He took the mate's view, too: though there hadn't been such a thing as an auxiliary steamer belching smoke then for years.

We sailed on, the second mate, crew, and apprentices distressed. What could we do? It was only after reaching London and checking at Lloyd's that we learned that the Danish bark *Lysglimt* had been abandoned on fire close to our position that day—May 4, 1921, 28° 26 N., 41° W.: she was abandoned on 27° 55 N., 41° 01 W. The crew took to the boats and were eventually picked up, after many days, by the French steamer *Souivah* and landed in France at the end of that month.

What did Edmund Mann really think the burning bark could be, the ghost of the libeled *Craigmullen?* Observing these seniors of the *Bellands* afterguard and Mann's reaction to his second mate's report, I wondered whether this scornful attitude of pig-headed seniors toward whatever their youthful juniors said or did hadn't something to do with that tragic incident when the master of a steamer named *Californian* (as the Courts of Inquiry were told) paid no attention to his second mate. The young officer had tried to tell him about some rockets, too, one night in 1912. No one on the *Californian* knew then where these rockets came from: but they were a ship's distress rockets, like the *Lysglimt's*, and the *Titanic* was in her death agonies not far away, at the time.

What the *Bellands* needed was someone with the competence and guts to sail her. Other masters did better. Captain John Finlay had her for several years as the *Forteviot* and he made quite reasonable passages. An official log of his covers a voyage made between July 21, 1906, and October 19, 1908—Finlay took her from the Tyne to San Francisco and back on the voyage prior to this, sailing outwards in late May 1905 which brought him off the Horn while Barker was there in the *British Isles,* but he had no trouble—and gives the following passages, all direct (more or less:

Hamburg to Seattle	150 days
Port Townsend to Adelaide	91 days
Newcastle to Valparaiso	50 days
Caleta Buena to Dunkirk	98 days

For a wall-sided big sea-basher carrying well over 5,000 tons, these passages are not bad. She was free of accident and must have paid quite well. The voyage turnover of foremast crew as recorded in the official log (kept because one died) was eighty-seven, to keep her going with twenty-four. This was good for a vessel which had spent months that voyage round Puget Sound and Australian ports, both noted at the time for the success and industry of their sailor-stealing crimps. There is only one spot of bother mentioned in the log, when the watch below expressed reluctance to come back on deck to get the fores'l off her one stinking night off the Horn. Such an attitude, though understandable, could not be accepted. Old Finlay marched at once into the foc's'l supported by his mate and threw the ringleader out. The rest followed.

Mann's successor on the *Bellands'* last voyage under the British flag was Captain David Williams, from St. Dogmaels in Wales —the same Dai Williams who had shown what sort of seaman he was by his splendid handling of the four-masted bark *Medway* on Cape Horn voyages through most of the First World War. Old Dai warmed the big four-master up forthwith, and chased her from France out to Sydney and back to Falmouth in less than eight months, bringing 5,600 tons of grain homeward round the

Horn on the way. He had plenty of time to take a fatherly interest in his apprentices and the colonial lads as well.

Steward Claude Locke, the only member of the *Bellands* crew to be in the ship when Captain Williams came—she was laid up for a few months—gives a memorable picture of the great little captain. "He was a real sailor and a gentleman," he said in a letter to me the other day. "I never had a wrong word out of him. . .He made that old ship do 13/14 knots watch after watch, bound out in ballast for Sydney. An old homespun overcoat to keep him warm, a soft hat for sou'wester and a bit of binnacle wick lashed across it to keep it on, on that poop he stayed hour after hour while the ship charged along. Squalls, sleet, hail—the lot didn't bother him: he just had the ship in his hands while the water streamed from him. Must say I wondered how he stood it, but he was tough. What a quiet little hero he was!"

It is given to few shipmasters to be heroic in their steward's eyes. The *Bellands* was the only big limejuicer I sailed in. She was enough. But I wish Dai Williams had been appointed a voyage earlier.

Chapter eleven

FOUR MASTERS

ONE MUST NOT be led to imagine that all the big sailing ships left in the Cape Horn trade in the first decade of this century were run in anything approaching the rather stupid manner so obvious in some of the surviving official logs. After all, there were only two hundred-odd sailing-ship logs left for all 1905. The majority of the other eight hundred or more British ships (and hundreds of German, French, Scandinavian, Russian, Latin and American then still in that tough trade) made their voyages successfully and quietly, lost nobody, met no trouble they could not themselves handle, and came and went about their business with no publicity and no notice taken of them at all. One wonders, too, how *any* man in a responsible and difficult position like that of a Cape Horn shipmaster would come out of it if he had been required to keep something like an official log of his proceedings, to be read half a century or more later and a judgment pronounced on that evidence. For that matter, what other profession equaled, or even resembled his? His battle was on his own, his forces for the fight by no means always the best that could be assembled, the hour of his hardest "actions" never by his choice, nor his lieutenants'.

The great majority of those Cape Horn men were splendid and they did magnificently. *Any* might lose men: any could have a serious accident. It was the plainest common sense (and also elementary survival drill) for the badly damaged, the too savagely handicapped ship to turn away from Cape Horn if she could. Some masters were lacking in leadership. Many were past their

189

prime. A few seemed unable to comprehend their own faults, which could be so much more serious in their effects than in almost any other profession. These were a product of their times: such still exist by the million, probably, and always will, but there are no longer the exacting, demanding, dangerous sailing ships to try them and—sometimes—find them out. Just as good sailors and bad were shown up publicly among their shipmates by the manner in which they went about and accomplished their exacting work, good and bad shipmasters showed their qualities among their contemporaries, too. Among them all flourished an absorbing, almost a passionate interest in their profession, and the behavior, the qualities, and performance of sailing ships.

One does not at all rely on those logs for data to present a balanced portrait of those times, nor upon the majority of the books written during or about them. The great part of these about British ships are written by former apprentices, naturally, as these were the loquacious, the observant, the more gifted in the field of writing. As far as I know, no genuine, thoroughly experienced foremast hand from this era, of any nationality, has left a published book or the wherewithal to produce one, and extremely few masters, I mean masters in sail. I can think of only two, very different but each invaluable—Joseph Conrad (in his books about the sea) and James Learmont. These commanded working deep-sea square-rigged ships and sailed them on their voyages, Captain Conrad briefly, in one small and lovely bark, Captain Learmont for years in full-rigged ships and four-masted barks. The briefness of Captain Conrad's command was no handicap to the intensity of his powers and his perceptive genius: in his works, *all* has been said, and with brilliance. In Captain Learmont's one straightforward *Master in Sail* is a picture of what a good, thoroughly professional Cape Horn shipmaster should be and Learmont himself was. He *knew* he was and is quite unashamed about it; and there in great part lies his documentary value. For with him are no shams, no heroics, no play whatever for alcoholic or otherwise induced imaginary performance, ultrafast or catastrophic voyage, or episodes. James Learmont tried to be a good shipmaster—this book proves it. Under God, he was: and he had good ships. His record stands.

I have been fortunate in knowing masters like Learmont and J. C. B. Jarvis, David Williams, T. C. Fearon, W. A. Nelson, Murdo' and Finlay Murchison, the Americans P. A. McDonald, Ken Reynard, and Fred Klebingat, the Finns Reuben de Cloux, the Sjölunds, and Gunnar Boman, Mattsson of the *Olivebank,* the Germans Robert Miethe, Hermann Piening, Robert Claus, Adolf Hauth, and several others. I have written something of Learmont earlier and of Captain Fearon in another book,* long out of print. I came to know him after sailing in the ship *Grace Harwar* in 1929, as he had been master of her during her British days. Like many other good shipmasters, Captain Fearon was a Cumberland man from the north of England, where the toughness of the land made many adventurous lads take to the sea. (Captain Nelson was also a Cumberland man. Captain Learmont was from just across the border in Scotland.) Apprentice in a Cape Horner at fifteen— Fearon's first passage was in an 800-ton bark with a cargo of steel rails from Newport, Monmouthshire, nonstop to Portland, Oregon, and back with grain to Liverpool, two 16,000-mile runs with Cape Horn to defeat on each—he was second mate at nineteen, mate (and wrecked) at twenty-two, master at thirty, and thereafter for the rest of his sea life (except for one period of about a year) master in deep-sea Cape Horn sail. The odd period was in 1886 in steam which he soon gave up as having many of the disadvantages of sail and others of its own.

"My first steamer was the *St. Ronans,* in 1885," said Captain Fearon. "She was rigged as a four-masted jackass-barque (a vessel with two square-rigged masts followed by two fore-and-aft rigged), on the Liverpool–New York run. I'd had command of big sailing-ships but I had to start as 3rd mate of the steamer. I left sailing-ships at the time because my owners would not allow my wife to sail with me. We did more setting and taking in sail in eight months in that steamer on the Western Ocean than I ever did in any eight years in a sailing-ship. I gave it a fair trial and made mate in about a year. But I'd had enough of steamers and went back to sail. Steamers just weren't interesting enough."

* *Sea Dogs of Today* (London: George G. Harrap & Co., 1932).

So back to sail it was, in command of several excellent ships of the White Star Line. In one of these, the *Dawpool*, Captain Fearon sailed from Liverpool to Melbourne in eighty-one days (belting along at 10.4 knots for twenty-one consecutive days in the Roaring Forties) although the best day's run she had was only 290 miles. The *Dawpool* was not a "clipper"; Captain Fearon got good passages out of her in the same manner that Captain Learmont got them from the *Brenda* and the *Bengairn*, by running a well-disciplined, contented ship and sailing her thoroughly well all the time, which meant endless attention to *all* detail, not just belting along when a favoring gale chanced to turn up. Fearon sailed the *Dawpool* from San Francisco round the Horn to Queenstown in ninety-seven days, and that was 16,000 miles.

He was as good and as consistent in the four-masted bark *General Roberts* and the ships *Fitzjames* and *Grace Harwar*. He had the *Fitzjames* fighting to the west'ard off the Horn in the winter of '05 with a heavy cargo of cement from London for Talcahuano, but did not mention it. It was bad, but the *Fitzjames* had no damage to speak of and lost nobody. The only accident which really worried Captain Fearon in the *Fitzjames* happened after loading general cargo at New York for Melbourne in the winter of 1906. A savage northeast gale which jumped suddenly to northwest with even greater violence knocked the ship down until her lee rail was under water. The triple tarpaulins on the main hatch had been put on frozen, but now the slightly warmer water (with a touch of Gulf Stream drift) thawed them. This made them slightly loose. The wooden wedges were washed out on the lee side and the tarpaulins began to work adrift. The ship was still underwater on that side. Though the tarred canvas had thawed, it was icy cold, but captain and mate led the men into the sea waist-deep, with lifelines on to keep them inboard, and they worked until the hatch was again secure.

"Either we did that successfully or there'd be another missing ship," as Captain Fearon said. "We secured that hatch or foundered."

For twelve years of this sort of thing Mrs. Fearon had been with him. When he took over the *Grace Harwar* from the *Fitzjames,* she went along though she had no love for the sea and was always sick in bad weather. This was after Mrs. Hudson had died in the *Grace Harwar:* Mrs. Fearon knew very well about that, and the death of young Captain Hudson which had followed not long afterward. The *Harwar* was already then a ship with a bad name. On Captain Fearon's second voyage with her, a near-hurricane blew suddenly into Iquique Bay where she was loading, causing a devil's own mix-up of the nitrate-loading ships moored in the usual tiers. In the morning, some ships were ashore, others sunk. The *Grace Harwar* had collided with a large steamer which knocked her bowsprit hopelessly askew, damaging the heavy steel spar beyond repair.

"There was no chance of getting a new bowsprit at Iquique," said the captain. "So I decided to sail home without one. It should mostly be a fair winds passage. After all, this time we were going round the Horn the down-hill way."

So this he did, very quietly and effectively—no deserters, no irate, underfed sea lawyers shouting to see the consul. There were no such fellows aboard. All hands buckled to, set up the forestays in the best way possible to give the foremast full support, contrived a temporary rig for the inner jib and fore topmast stays'l, and sailed like that for 12,000 miles. The only thing they could do nothing about was the figurehead, which had been destroyed in the collision, and all hands were perturbed about losing this.

This was Captain Fearon's thirty-sixth Horn rounding. He and Mrs. Fearon decided that it would be their last: this time they meant it. The captain had been at sea for more than forty years during which he had been responsible for the safe propulsion of big sailing ships over some 900,000 miles, only by the wind. No official log of his is on the records. No fantastic claims nor apocryphal yarns cling to his name. He is indeed infinitely more the typical Cape Horn shipmaster of his day—if there were a "type" —than some of the others.

I asked him once about westward roundings of the Horn— "a hard fight at any time," he said, offering a little advice in the form of some really obvious rules. Here they are:

Prepare thoroughly for the fight beforehand.

See the rigging is well set up, the best sails bent and *well* bent: the running gear overhauled.

Rig lifelines in good time.

See the hatches and other deck openings are made secure.

Be sure the crew are well and warmly dressed (from a good slop chest at reasonable prices).

Feed the men well, with plenty of hot coffee at nighttime; and a good stove with plenty of coal in the forecastle and half deck.

"Having done all these things, *carry all the sail it is possible to carry* as long as possible, at all times. Do not spare the crew or yourself. After shortening sail, *set it again* the moment the wind moderates by day or night. Don't wait to see whether it will blow again. Of course it will: the important thing is to make use of *every moment* when you can sail. Put the ship round—tack or wear her —the moment you know she is on the wrong tack, even though this is heavy work.

"Remember, perseverance wins. Dodging along under easy sail waiting for the weather to get better will not do it. Use what you get *all the time* and you'll get better."

Captain Fearon reckoned Horn windward roundings as some 1,300–1,500 miles at least—"the toughest bit of sailing in any part of the world." The best time he'd ever managed was fifteen days in the *Dawpool*, eighteen in the *Grace Harwar*. If he managed within three weeks he thanked God: indeed he thanked God and a good crew at any time.

Captain W. A. Nelson, of Maryport in Cumberland, was famous to an older generation as master of the steel-four-masted bark *Auchencairn*, a fine vessel of over 2,000 tons which was built by the side of a river at Maryport in 1891 and launched by being pushed and hauled sideways into it, and of the ship *Acamas*, built and launched in the same way in 1897. Messrs. Ritson were the builders: they built good ships and Maryport gave them good masters. Three times in two years Captain Nelson sailed the *Auchencairn* between Britain and Puget Sound, and once to San Francisco, in less than four months when others were taking five, six, and even seven. His best passage was 108 days to Portland, Oregon, the "poorest," 116 from Fleetwood to the same destination. A lucky fool might make one good passage, but only an outstanding shipmaster showed consistency. Like Learmont and Fearon, Nelson looked after his men *all* the time, in port and at sea. He was a career man with his roots in the port whose ships he sailed, and townsmen he knew sailed with him.

Born in 1840—his father was at Ecclesfechan Academy with a local boy named Thomas Carlyle, who did not go to sea—he served a seven-year apprenticeship to the skilled business of sailmaking before going to sea at all, for those Cumberland men were thorough. He served then in some terrible ships, beginning in—of all things—a steam-auxiliary bark named *Imperatrice,* 570 tons and 80 horsepower, in the American trade at the time of the Civil War. One voyage was enough in this abortion. Nelson did not care for sewing sooty sails and the *Imperatrice* was a bit of a failure anyway. So it was "pure" sailers for him after that, throughout a long lifetime—a wooden bark of Jardine's to the East first, with fever and leaks and terrible food, poor officers and all the rest.

"The salt beef was as hard as teak, the pork a greasy mess of blubber, the hardtack made from mixed flour and bone-dust and full of maggots," the old man recalled afterward. "As sailmaker I shared a small wooden compartment secured over a hatchway with the cook, with no bunks or anything."

There were many good Jardine ships but the *James Jardine* was not one of them. In those days, deepwater sailers were mainly elderly wooden ships of a few hundred tons. By 1880, the Captain and a brother bought one for themselves, the wooden bark *New Brunswick,* built in New Brunswick in 1860, of 611 tons, and he took command. The first thing he did was to see her stocked with good food—plenty of fine Cumberland hams and good potatoes and vegetables. At twenty, she was already elderly for a softwood ship, so the brothers kept her timber droghing on the North

Atlantic, where the hams kept very well. But the North Atlantic summer and winter was a tough trade. After seven years the bark quietly opened up. She didn't sink, for the timber kept her afloat, but the seas washed over her and she had to be abandoned in a winter gale.

This was in 1887. Now Captain Nelson, already past his mid-forties, began his real career in good Cape Horn ships. He took the 565-ton composite bark *Mary Moore*—a former China trader then nineteen years old, a beautiful little vessel which could easily make nine knots on a wind and thirteen before it—in the trade around the Horn to the West Coast of South America. A seaman used to winter crossings in the North Atlantic had nothing to fear from Cape Horn: Captain and bark took that tough trade in their stride, with occasional round voyages to Australia as vacations. (This *Mary Moore* was still a hulk in Melbourne when I was a lad: though cut down to a coal lighter, black and unadorned, her lithe grace of hull shone upon the dark Yarra.)

In the West Coast trade at that time was a fine tradition of little Welsh wooden barks known as the Swansea "copper-ore men," which sailed year after year from South Wales round the Horn to wind'ard, laden with coal, with their Welsh masters and crews, and brought back ore to be smelted at Swansea. Captain Nelson joined these with the wooden bark called the *William Ritson* and then, in 1889, with the iron bark *Rising Star*—his first metal vessel—of less than 1,000 tons. He found her slower than the wooden and composite ship, and more readily fouled below the waterline by sea growth. Yet on her first voyage he made Valparaiso sixty-seven days out from Antwerp, with general cargo.

"She wasn't particularly fast but she hated to stop," said the captain. "So I kept her going."

He did indeed. And he went right on doing just this in ship after ship—always getting bigger and bigger—for the rest of his career. Ice, gales, furious storms became routine to all masters on the Cape Horn run: so did coping with near-fatal accidents such as having their ships flung over upon their beam ends, within an ace of capsizing, with cargo or ballast shifted. Then they had to be somehow straightened up again—if they remained afloat—and sailed on. Here good discipline, good morale showed their worth: but these could not be created when desperately required. They had to be in the ship as the spirit of the ship *all the time.* It was grand to make good passages, to keep lovely ships spanking along upon their voyages, pleasantly, stirringly, and accident-free, but there was one way only to do that. Master, crew, and ship in sail were *one.* . . .

None of these ships that W. A. Nelson sailed so well was a "clipper" (the *Mary Moore* came nearest to that but she was a carrier too, or Maryport would not have bought her). They were working ships, long-haul cargo-droghers of coal and grain, lumber, nitrate, cement, railway iron: and the good passages were part of their economy. The *Auchencairn* never did a better day's run than barely over three hundred miles, yet she ran 7,100 in thirty-one days on a two-and-a-half-month passage to Australia. She made San Francisco sixty-one days from Port Pirie, far up Spencer's Gulf in South Australia. She consistently moved big cargoes through the great seas at economical speeds on worthwhile voyages, and the grace with which she did these things appealed to master and ship's company. He was a *satisfying* master to serve with, *all* his ships were satisfying ships. The Horn in the winter of '05 his ship (the *Acamas* then), her master and her men took in their stride, though they sheltered a day or two against one mighty gale in the lee of Staten Island, off Tierra del Fuego. To save the helmsmen from frostbite that very cold winter, Captain Nelson had a tub of straw beside the wheel for them to put their sea-booted feet in: he had none of the troubles which so filled the logs of the *British Isles* and too many other ships. That voyage his *Acamas* was 109 days from the Bristol Channel to Pisagua, despite the day or two behind Staten Island. (That was a very good idea—far better than costly runnings for distress ports: he wasn't in distress anyway, for it cost nothing and allowed the crew to get on with repairs and urgent maintenance in reasonable conditions. Some of the smaller "P" ships of Hamburg did the same thing, at times. A master had to be a good navigator to tuck his ship in away from the wind around Staten Island: at that time, a great many were not. They allowed themselves to get rusty: some never had been very bright.)

Captain Nelson was an extremely thorough man. He had learned to be in the very first month of his forty-seven years at sea. Typical of his thoroughness was his habit of going aloft regularly to examine everything up there himself. Another habit he followed at sea throughout his long career in command was to remove his clothes, whenever he turned into his bunk, and stow them in the proper order for putting on again in a hurry when called, or when an increase in the wind's noise, or the swish of water past the hull or the ship's motion roused him. This was to allow him to dress rapidly without light, and come on deck with full night vision. For there were no floodlights nor any other lights on the deck or in the rigging of Cape Horn ships. To emerge from the companion suddenly on to the reeling, sea-swept deck of the lurching ship with the scream of the wind in one's ears and the thundrous roar of some blown-out sail striking a hellish cacophony could be nerve-racking, even alarming. Who is in command must see!

Learmont, Fearon, Nelson—these were sea *men.* There were others, such as J. C. B. Jarvis, that great innovator who refused to accept the idea (always held by generation after generation of old seamen each in their era) that the seagoing sailing ship was incapable of further improvement. He believed that she was and did something about it: but (as far as British ships were concerned) it was in vain.

When I think of Captain Jarvis, I see a thin, tall man, straight as a topmast, strong of countenance and dignified as an elder don. He and I are walking along the old Shore Road in Brooklyn beside the Narrows of the harbor of New York. It is 1930 or so: in the harbor we still may see the occasional three- or four-masted down-East schooner, a little Svendborg t'gallants'l schooner or the Spanish bark *Guadalhorce,* a 350-ton Majorca wanderer in the West Indies trade. For the most part it is all steamships, tankers and Staten Island ferries, liners and tramps,

The sailor liked his figurehead female, buxom, and strong-featured—figurehead of the bark
KILLORAN.

Full of the free, untaxable wind—it seemed impossible that all ships would ever abandon its use.

Behind a friendly sea—Trade Winds view of a bark.

Until the end of the 19th century and in the beginning of the 20th century, very small square-rigged ships continued to make long ocean passages. A New England brigantine and a Yankee whaling bark leaving Honolulu.

The only "engines" were the sails. There was no auxiliary. It made no sense. But such sails were enormous and demanded skillfull handling.

Outward bound—she leaps and frolics to be at sea.

barges and Moran tugs. I am telling Captain Jarvis about the
Lawhill, a big four-masted bark he made famous with his inven-
tions and sailed successfully for years. I was in the *Lawhill* in the
early '20's, with Captain Reuben de Cloux.

Captain Jarvis pulls a slim pamphlet from a coat pocket and
hands it to me. "Wrinkles and Suggestions for Sailing Vessels,"
I read, "By Captain J. C. B. Jarvis," and published by himself
through William Kidd, printer, at Dundee, in 1897. This I know
is about his brace-winch invention and other "wrinkles"—now
called gadgetry—for the simpler working of big sailing ships
retaining the orthodox rig. The *Lawhill* was full of his wrinkles,
and a great deal the better ship for that. I knew that very well, for
I had been able seaman in her, aged seventeen, with an incredibly
small crew of Finnish and Swedish lads in 1921, and we all
thanked God for those wrinkles. That *Lawhill* was a big four-
masted bark, and she looked a workhouse. She would have been
one if Captain Jarvis hadn't fixed her.

"Deep-sea sailing ships could still offer a career in the twentieth century," said the captain. "I believe they could find useful
work to do at sea so long as sea transport may last. The trouble
at first was that the more conservative shipowners didn't seem to
realize that they were threatened. When they did—around the late
1890's and the turn of the century—they panicked. They thought
that only steamers could be improved. So they exercised the
wrong economies. They cut wages, stores, even provisioning one
way or another. They shipped lots of so-called apprentices but
did little or nothing to train them. They cut down on anything
and everything, but it never occurred to them that their sailing
ships were machines and they could be made better.

"I had to take them as I found them and do what I could to
simplify the rigging as I found it, concentrating on real man-
power savings. The brace winches did that. So did the patent
leech lines, which smothered sails so they could not blow back as
the men clewed them up. Blowing-back sails knock men from
the yards and kill them. My other improvements were of lesser
importance, like bringing all sheets to the deck. No one was
interested. I suspect that seamen had been against all improve-

ments ever suggested since Noah built the Ark.

"So I never got anywhere with my real idea. That was to develop a big square-rigger where all the gear could be operated without going on the main deck at all, if necessary. More men were lost from the decks than from the rigging. I felt I could stop that and make the ship more efficient too."

I gathered that the general principle was to design a ship with simplified working gear beneath a sort of shelter deck—the brace winches were only a part. There were to be halyard winches, too, and better gear on the sails to snug them up without going aloft at all, as Chinese sails are snugged down. Simplified masts and rigging would permit the vessel to lie closer to the wind, making better to windward, and the snugged-up sails would be finally secured by short lengths of line—gaskets—passed over the top and secured to a second jackstay along the yard behind it. This idea of the double jackstay was the only one ever taken up. It worked very well. But to the average master, the very fact that Captain Jarvis even thought of improving well-tried rigging and sail-handling methods made them regard him as decidedly odd, another fey Scot.

In fact, Jarvis was an unwanted genius. Perhaps they are all fey. The real trouble was that he came too late. His vision of a handier, safer ship—with strong three-island hull, protection for the crew to work on deck, brace winches, halyard winches, simplified gear of all sorts useful, power winches for working cargo and for driving the windlass, good boats the sea would have difficulty in destroying, strong hatches stoutly defended—was in large part achieved by the Germans, but his own countrymen would have nothing to do with it all. Jarvis lost a lot of money over his brace winches: he could not afford to carry on that sort of investment. No other British interests considered the Cape Horn ship worth bothering about. The Americans' big ships were laid up, and the French had given up their efforts and were building no more ships. That left the Germans. They took up the brace winch wholeheartedly and found it invaluable, but Captain Jarvis told me that there was some flaw in his contract with the German manufacturers and he received no royalties.

What the Jarvis brace winch did was to take 90 percent of the danger and 80 percent of the back-breaking out of bracing, which had been the work most frequently necessary and often most difficult and dangerous aboard square-rigged ships. They trimmed their sails very largely—exclusively, except for the courses, which had tacks and sheets to capstans on deck: all other sails were sheeted to the extremities of the yards (called the yardarms) immediately below them—by trimming the yards, and this was done by braces of strong wire and tackles with the hauling parts of all the heavier braces led to the upper bulwarks and inboard through lead blocks to large belaying pins. So the braces had to be worked, often, in the most dangerous part of the ship. She rolled her rail down and the haulers leaped for their lives or some went overboard, particularly in the waist. (Lighter braces, royal, skysail if any, t'gallants, led to the fife rail, a strong pin rail in by the bole of the mast and therefore safer: these were much lighter and so were boys' work.) It called for good beef to haul taut the heavy braces, squaring in. The mate slacked alee and the beef hauled aweather, and the mate's skill was in slacking just the right amount on each brace so that when the hauling was done, the sails all set into the most perfect airfoil possible for maximum use of the available wind. The master kept an eagle eye on the whole proceedings.

With Tayport (also called "Bracewinch") Jarvis's winch, three or four men and boys could do the work of a whole watch, or even of both watches. Whips at the rail were eased and set up briefly afterward for perfection of trim, and the bracing was done by long wires led ingeniously—all part of the Jarvis patent—from each tops'l and course yardarm to the mast abaft, thence to the conical drum of the six-drum winch, so designed that braces were paid out and hauled in to just the proper amounts by a few hands turning the two winch handles. The winches were on the ship's center line, just abaft the fife rails. Here the lads worked inside the lifelines: with the brakes slammed on the winch, they could jump on the fife rail or leap for the lifelines, where the seas could not knock them down. (The sea coming over the side both knocked them down and made it impossible for them to get up again, very often, before a roll swept them over the side.)

The advantages of the brace winch, indeed, were so obvious that only a dyed-in-the-wool conservative or very stupid master (or penny-pinching group of sixty-fourther one-ship owners trying to get a dividend or two from some cheaply bought old-timer) could fail, or not bother, to see them. There were unfortunately many such, toward the end. In the *Bellands,* which had been German for some time after twenty years as the limejuicer *Forteviot,* the Germans had installed brace winches, but her master when I was there declared them too dangerous to use and would not tack ship because he feared that the swinging yards would take charge.

There was no danger in them at all. All he needed was the competence to use them.

Captain Jarvis was one of the last sailing-ship cargo-liner masters. When he commanded her, the *Lawhill* carried case oil regularly from eastern United States ports to the Far East, China and Japan. She sailed for the Standard Oil Company at times but was owned by the Anglo-American Oil Company. So was the four-masted bark *Alcides,* which he also commanded. He was the only seaman I knew personally whose career dated back to the command of immigrant passenger-sailers in the Australian trade. He had command of several fine ships in this business, the last the bark *Cicero* in which he took 368 men, women, and children to Port Adelaide in 1883. Masters and surgeons (no *Ship Master's Medical Guide* then) were paid a good bonus for landing healthy migrants, and paid reasonable salaries too.

Captain Jarvis was an upright and very intelligent shipmaster: he knew how to sail ships, look after crews and passengers, and the "bawbies" too. He'd had command since he was twenty-three. He told me the best day's run he had ever made under sail was 346 miles noon-to-noon (in an old stern-windows ship called the *Earl of Dalhousie*) though he "logged" 403 miles one day in the *Cicero.* This was a necessary log entry to bring the ship's noon position up to date after running for ten days on dead reckoning, with no reliable fix at all. The ship had never sailed at such a rate. The 403 miles included all the underestimates of the preceding ten days—perhaps a gross of nearly a hundred miles. (In such manner were some "records" claimed.)

The passage between New York or Philadelphia and China or Japan could be difficult and was always long. A look at the map of the world (disregarding the Panama Canal) shows the immense distances involved.

"If we could get through the China Sea," the old captain told me, "then I went the Good Hope way. It was shorter and kinder to the ship. I would make for south of Good Hope the usual square-rigger way, and run east as if bound for Australia, then make up the Indian Ocean with the southeast trade winds into the Java Sea by the Straits of Sunda and up through the South China Sea to Hong Kong or wherever I was bound. But if I doubted I could get that far while the favorable monsoon blew, I'd take on the Horn.

"Then I'd have to beat past, of course. I'd plan on spring or summer for that if I could. It was a long way, but once well past the Horn I had the whole trade-wind system of the Pacific Ocean in my favor. It wasn't the miles that counted in deepwater voyages: it was making best use of the ocean winds."

Indeed it was—fair winds, not fewer miles. But it was an immense way to induce, cajole, drive a big heavy-laden ship moved only by the wind. A sailing-ship master had to know his geography.

"The best passage I made was New York to Hong Kong in 108 days, in the *Lawhill*, the worst, 176. That was homeward bound, not outward. I had bad weather in the North Pacific, calms in the South. I crossed the Pacific three times that passage looking for wind. It was the worst passage I ever made anywhere. But there was no scurvy."

The ineffective ship-waster in the *Bellands* in 1921 was, by God's grace, relieved by David ("Dai") Williams, of pretty little St. Dogmaels in West Wales where the River Teifi flows into the wild waters of Cardigan Bay and men in 1970 still fish the salmon in prehistoric coracles. Dai Williams took over the big four-master in St. Nazaire and chased her in ballast out to Sydney, filled her with 5,700 tons of grain in sacks, and romped home again around the Horn to the Channel for orders in little more than ninety days out and a hundred days back again. He was no driver of ships or men, just a *sailor*—not a sailor *born,* for there are no such and never were, but an intelligent, clear-minded, reasonably gifted man brought up to the sailing-ship sea, as so many good youths were from West Wales and all Wales. For here the last of the ancient Britons stand, the stalwart, hardy remnants of Boadicea's tribes who stood against Caesar's legions—harried, driven westward from the good lands to the mountains of Wales and beyond to the sea. And so down the centuries, nurturing their independence, fostering their great abilities, while they made a hard living from the hard land, they turned to the sea and made that domain their own. Along the coasts of Wales the Atlantic gales blow out with such strength that all the trees and bushes grow leaning from them, toward the east. Along the lovely coasts and at the river bars and tides rage and race and boil. To make to seaward here calls for strength of body and of mind: so nurtured, the seamen of West Wales were early Atlantic wanderers —just how early the academics argue but the seamen *know,* for the tradition of good seafaring has been handed down among them for countless generations.

There are some who have detected Welsh words in use among American Indians, who speak of transatlantic voyages from Wales long before the Columbus publicity—be these things as they may, it is certain that the Welsh play a great part in keeping British shipping going and have done for centuries. Take all the Lloyds, Llewellyns, Lewises, Hugheses, Davieses, Williamses, Owenses, Jenkinses—or only the Joneses—from the British merchant service and more than the half of it would come to a full stop. Considerably more than half the Cape Horn ships would not have sailed.

From this tradition came that pleasant, gentle, supremely competent little man, David Williams: and he lived up to it in full. I did not know him when I was at sea. I was an ordinary seaman, then A.B., when he was a master. I knew of him as war-time captain of a handsome, well-behaved four-masted bark named

Medway, a working, cargo-carrying, Cape Horn school-ship which had sailed successfully, doing excellent work with large crews of boys, throughout the First World War—mainly in the Chilean nitrate trade—until the palsied hand of the impossible bureaucrats fell upon her at the end, ripped off the masts and yards, mangled the stern frames to thread a shaft through to an unnecessary, noisy engine room, "converting" her to be fit for a war which by then was over, in fact destroying all her usefulness for any purpose at all. For some overlarge committee of talkative nincompoops, pencil-pushers on the edge of shipping, had made a "minute" that good sailing ships sould be converted into powered oil tankers: they had no knowledge of sailing ships, but the good record of the *Medway* had come to notice. So they'd heard of her.

I met the little captain at his cottage called Cannon House in St. Dogmaels, across from Cardigan. He was well over eighty then. He was up on his roof doing some repairs, and some neighbors were in their gardens watching with obvious concern, expecting him to come pitching down at any moment. He was a small, lithe sort of man with peace in his countenance and a smile on his face. He looked almost too gentle to be a Cape Horn shipmaster: but I thought the gentleness had come through, perhaps, since he had left the sea. Perhaps not: it looked as if it had been there forever.

"They don't know what it is to go aloft at sea," said the old man, smiling happily from the rooftop, patting the sturdy tiles. He looked after the shipshape cottage himself, a widower with his children grown up and married best part of half a century earlier.

Like so many of his countrymen, David Williams was born to the sea. His father lost his life off the Horn in the Swansea copper-ore bark *Georgina* on a Valparaiso voyage before David was three years old. This was in 1879. Perhaps because of the early loss of his father—who was only thirty-seven—the young David was set to teaching first, as a pupil teacher at St. Dogmaels Board School, aged fifteen.

"But that wasn't for me. I wanted to go to sea. So a neighbor of ours named Morgan got me a berth in a London bark called

Cathaya in the trade to the Brazils and the River Plate. That was 1893. She was a handy bark. I liked the life. So I stayed in sailing ships until I got my master's license, in 1902."

Before the *Cathaya,* he had been to sea during school holidays, in the Welsh wooden tops'l schooners and barkentines to the Mediterranean and Newfoundland, where his poor mother hoped he would soon sicken of the hard life. Instead, he thrived on it. After he had qualified as second mate, he served in that capacity on a round voyage U.K. to Puget Sound and back in the big *Forteviot* (twenty years later under his command as the *Bellands*) and was mate of the *Garsdale* the voyage before she threw her masts out off the Horn. But in 1902, a qualified master mariner aged twenty-six, mate of a bark, never having been in steam, he made the sensible decision to change over to steam before he grew too old. So he joined the White Star Line as a junior officer, took his extra master's certificate (a sort of doctorate in the sea profession) a few years later, and set out to work his way up slowly in the big line. He was married then: he didn't want his wife to be left at home waiting while he was off on round after round of tremendous voyages while their lives flowed along in separate streams, slowly at first then rapidly toward a retirement he would have no wherewithal to face, nor did either wish that she should be cooped up for years in the master's quarters of big sailing ships cut off from her kind.

In those days, the White Star steamers made long enough voyages, many of them in the Australian and New Zealand trades. David Williams rose slowly, as is the way in big ships and big lines —fourth officer (nothing so lowly as mates) in the *Arabic,* third officer of the *Arabic* a year later, second of the *Ionic* by 1910. But about 1910, believing in sail-trained officers but not optimistic about the supply of qualified apprentices from limejuice Cape Horners, White Star bought a full-rigger of their own, renamed her *Mersey,* manned her with sixty cadets, and appointed Captain Williams to be "Chief Officer"—mate. The *Mersey* proved expensive to run and didn't last long as a White Star school-ship: soon she was sold to Norway and he was back in the company's big steamships as first officer—junior to the chief but senior to all the other deck watchkeepers. The *Mersey* had shown him a career in sail that he wholly liked. At the time, Messrs. Devitt and Moore, of London, operated similar ships, among them the excellent four-masted bark *Port Jackson,* and the beautiful ships *Hesperus* and *Harbinger.* When they bought a handsome bark which they renamed *Medway* in due course, we find David Williams appointed to her command. He had written offering his services: Devitt and Moore knew a good man when they saw one, just as Captain Williams knew good owners and a good ship.

Those older cargo-carrying school-ship Cape Horners were unique. They were, in all fundamentals, plain working sailing ships, not to be confused with the much smaller auxiliaries of one sort and another—many excellent: a few scarcely operated as sailing ships at all—called school-ships in 1970. Their masters and officers were the best of experienced merchant seamen. The ships had no power, no improvements (never even a Jarvis brace winch), no special fittings. Devitt and Moore crews were usually premium-paying apprentices, paying the substantial sum of £200 for four years' indentures. But they were *trained,* properly instructed in their exacting profession while being also ordinary (and, in due course, able) seamen. A proper staff of instructors was carried, under watch officers who, like the master, were interested in the lads all the time, at sea and in port. The cargo-carrying was real, to earn the keep of real ships, and the boys as crew were real too. But the ships were very expensive to run. Big staffs cost money. Good upkeep, good feeding cost money.

In the back of one of Captain Williams's *Medway* workbooks (which he lent me), as well as extracts of many splendid globe-circling voyages, is a list of menus he worked out and applied, one for port (with fresh food), the other for sea, without. It would make any poor mariner in the average early twentieth-century limejuicer stare in disbelief, for meals are diversified, generous, and good. Here is a sample day, marked for "Sea," fifth voyage, arranged for the three messes into which the big crew was divided:

Sundays Saloon	*Cadets and P.O.'s*	*Crew*
	Breakfast 0720 to 0830	
Rolled oats, milk and syrup	Rolled oats and syrup	Dry hash
Ham & eggs, or ham & kidneys or sausage	Bacon and eggs (or rice cakes)	Rolls
Dry hash or fried potatoes	Butter, marmalade	Butter, marmalade
Rolls, toast, preserves	2 hot rolls each	Coffee
Coffee	Coffee	
Mondays	*Dinner Noon*	
Soup	Soup	Soup
Minced collops & mash, 2 tinned veg.	Sea pie & veg.	Sea pie & veg.
Plum pudding	Plum duff	Plum pudding
Biscuits & cheese Coffee	Fruit & nuts	

Chief Cadet in charge of lime-juice issue.

The *Medway* worked magnificently until those unforgivable bureaucrats came along. What they destroyed was never put together again. The combination of Messrs. Devitt and Moore, the four-masted bark *Medway,* and Captain David Williams was unique.

By the mid-1920's a handful only of undistinguished square-riggers still flew the British flag, the best of them the little old *Inverneil.* There was some competition for the title of worst. All carried apprentices, several of them ten or twelve, but none offered training or instruction that the ship's own hard work and the sea's challenge did not provide. Some excellent masters survived to serve them. By 1929 all were gone.

By that time the requirement—another effort of the impossible bureaucrats—that in British ships *one year's* experience as anything in long-voyage sailing ship was sufficient to carry applicants brazen enough to claim it through all grades of certificates of competency to master in sail and even extra-master, had made a mockery of the whole business. For it meant that anyone who had ever been on the Articles of a deep-sea square-rigged ship for twelve months as a deck boy could qualify to take command, first, of a watch and then—though without having served in charge of a watch at all—as a sailing-ship "master."

The truth was that, true to the best traditions of bureaucracy, the qualification still mattered technically—for certain shore appointments, examiners of masters and mates, some pilot services—though real long-voyage sailing-ship jobs under the British flag were nonexistent. Which could have been just as well.

Chapter twelve

THE THOROUGH GERMANS

THE GERMANS came late into the field of the long-voyage world-wandering sailing ship, but they more than made up in thoroughness of professional approach for any experience they might at first have lacked. For that matter, they were excellent Baltic, North Sea, and short-voyage sailors with stout, hard-working ships long before they began to sail deepwater, with special interest in the Melanesian islands of the South Seas, the rice and other trades of the Far East, and the West Coast of South America. This last they made particularly their own, especially with the Hamburg fleet of the House of Laeisz, the famous "P" ships the names of which all began with the letter P (for no other reason, apparently, except that a favorite early ship built for the Ferdinand Laeisz company was named *Pudel,* because this was Mrs. Laeisz's pet-name). Their Southern American trade was a logical process born of commercial enterprise and need, fostered by sustained scientific investigation, inquiry, and analysis, and well served by able men.

Who can sail engineless ships in narrow waters can also sail deep-sea—indeed, the more easily, for the making of long voyages is in some ways simpler than constant passage-making in the same waters. The short-sea man must put up with the whole winter: the deep-sea man soon leaves it behind. He knows the delights of trade-winds sailing and the mighty stimulus of running four, five, or eight thousand miles driving his well-found ship before the wild west winds as they circulate round the watery world south of latitude 40°S. He does not contend with the buffet-

211

ings of local vagaries, but uses the ocean winds by principles of voyage-making discovered or chanced upon centuries ago, and well understood. Those redoubtable mariners, the Portuguese, laid down the best square-rigger route to India in the time of Bartolomeu Dias (for the Atlantic section) and Vasco da Gama (the whole way) and much else besides. Their Ferdinand Magellan, sailing for Spain, knew both where the straits now named for him were to be found and the trade-winds sailing route across the Pacific. Somehow Columbus took the most sensible square-rigged route to the West Indies when he went that way in the *Santa Maria* in 1492, and a good sailing route to the nor'ard and eastward back again too, though whatever else that strange man was it is highly unlikely that he was a working shipmaster. That leaves him, like Magellan, profiting from others' knowledge—the silent, probing, unknown seamen slowly or boldly extending the limits of trade.

Whether Germany, as such, was late in the field of commercial maritime enterprise or not, the Germans quickly became outstanding. They had plenty of tradition of hard seafaring and tough sailing in smaller ships. As the nineteenth century went on, they bought and they built larger, deep-sea square-rigged ships —many acquired from Britain—and soon the flag of their merchant service was known in the ports of the world. There was no shortage of able and enterprising German masters, seamen and owners. Noting in due course the advantages of the so-called "Liverpool house"—the British "three-island" hull for Cape Horn ships—and the Jarvis rigging improvements, they took these up and soon were building all their larger sailers with big midships houses and rigging them with brace winches, halyard winches, and at least one powered winch for every cargo hatch. They established excellent nautical schools for officers, and *ab initio* sailing school-ships for boys and working-cadet ships for embryo officers of some of the greatest lines. They made the most thorough study of ocean sailing conditions ever undertaken (not forgetting the pioneering Maury), requiring masters to keep meteorological logs, sending them in after each voyage. The broad principles of passage-making (using the winds and currents systems) were already understood: they got after details. Hydrography, oceanography, cartography, seamen's health and diet—no aspect was neglected.

The thoroughness with which these things were done and the resultant knowledge organized and put to use came to my notice when a small group of us bought the Laeisz four-masted bark *Parma* in Hamburg in 1931. When you buy a ship, you buy also her inventory as a ship—that is the law. That inventory in a big Cape Horner includes many things: her anchors and cables, sails, lights, galley equipment, bells, barometers, capstan bars, hatch covers and tarpaulins—the lot. In the *Parma* it included also the publications her masters had used to aid their passage-making, right back to her British days (when she had been the Anglo-American Oil Company's case-oil carrier *Arrow*). These last were a few old Findlay's Directories, of the South Pacific, South Atlantic and Indian Oceans—fascinating historically and good reading, but the *Parma*'s copies dated from the 1870's and '80's. The Germans' shelf included several large tomes of most useful information for the making of modern sailing-ship voyages, compiled by Deutsche Seewarte, a 560-page work on the Atlantic and 900 pages on the Pacific.* In both were large stores of the most valuable information, carefully assembled from voyages and skillfully dissected by meteorological experts, designed to assist square-rigged shipmasters in working their ships through such diverse and difficult zones as the horse latitudes, the doldrums, the Straits of Le Maire, and to wind'ard past the Horn. There were other, smaller books which showed how German ships had fared, where they had found and lost the trade winds at all seasons, how they'd felt their way past icebergs or through field ice and fought their way around the Horn, or "run their easting down" with the westerlies behind them.

Here it all was, and all relevant. There were also several deck logs from the *Parma*'s postwar German voyages showing how the

* *Segelhandbuch für den Atlantischen Ozean:* Herausgegeben von der Deutschen Seewarte (Hamburg: L. Friederichsen & Co., 1910). *Segelhandbuch für den Stillen Ozean:* Herausgegeben von der Direktion der Deutschen Seewarte (Hamburg: L. Friederichsen & Co., 1897).

information had been used there. Here I came across the name of Nissen. (I knew that he had been one of the very few masters of the great ship *Preussen:* I paid special attention to him.) The point about all this information was that it made possible the planning of long voyages with reasonable expectation of good sailing winds and help from ocean currents, instead of impediment. It was never possible, of course, to plan perfectly for voyages from northwestern Europe to ports in California or Oregon when the ship had the whole Atlantic and much of the Pacific to sail through on the outward passage, with four lots of trade winds, four sets of the baffling conditions called horse latitudes, and two lots of far worse called doldrums with perhaps a winter wind'ard rounding of the Horn thrown in—at least 16,000 or 18,000 miles of the lot, and only the wind for power, the set of the sails and the skill and nerve of the master for speed. Indeed, to make such a tremendous passage at all was enough. Many ships took six or seven months over it. But there was a great difference between the slovenly amble of the misguided ship drifting into zones of calms and baffling winds through plain inability to avoid them, getting too far south of the wintry Horn and stupidly, stubbornly staying there (or running away), and the determined follower of the planned course of most reasonable fair—or at least usable—wind expectation. This latter is the way the Germans most diligently tried to sail.

Nobody had the wind laid on, though it was said some could *troll,* like the Ålands Finn de Cloux, who always got the best passage out of any ship; or were in league with the devil, like Hilgendorf of the Flying P's—a childish libel on a great sailor. Analysis of long passages attributed to excessive calm generally showed more than enough slovenly sailing, somnolent watch-keeping, failure to use every air as it offered. Captain de Cloux had been making good passages before we found that Deutsche Seewarte information in the *Parma:* he made even better afterward, like hustling that big, open-deck four-master from anchorage off Port Broughton to anchorage at Falmouth in eighty-three days, after her Plimsoll line had been officially moved up a few inches and the average age of his crew of thirty was between seventeen and eighteen, for the majority were young cadets on their first voyage. The best speed our *Parma* could do deep-loaded was about 12 knots. Her merit (under de Cloux particularly, and a few others like Nissen before him) was that she slipped along even in light airs. The flap of her sails gave her steerage way, when sailors were steering.

The *Parma* had all the standard German improvements in her rigging—brace winches, halyard winches, and so on—and life nets above the bulwarks for bad weather, but she was not built as a three-island ship. Her main deck was wholly open to the sea. Some ships, fortunately, sail drier—or less wet—than others, through some difference of design: our *Parma* was comparatively dry, handled well, steered well, seemed (unlike the *Pamir* which we were offered and did not buy) to like sailing.

The winter of 1905, except for the partial dismasting of the *Pitlochry* and the long westward passage of the *Susanna,* went practically unnoticed by the German Cape Horners. The other fourteen Laeisz ships thrashed around with neither damage nor delay, and so did the other Germans bound for Chile, Peru, Mexico, California, or Puget Sound. There were at least two hundred German square-riggers on Horn roundings of some sort or other that year. They did not only pay regard to scientific information, assembled and tabulated, but they paid strict attention to the weather patterns they observed at sea. Once in port, they focused their attention and their efforts on those other vital matters of fast turn-around, good turnout of cargo, and keeping good morale among efficient crews. There was not a brass-bound apprentice in the lot, excepting only the Norddeutscher-Lloyd school-ship *Herzogin Cecilie,* and they were not missed. There were many scores of good young seamen serving in their forecastles, who were excellent officer material—and the better with their men later because they *had* begun their service with them. There were indifferent German masters, too, and the odd drunk. But there was none among them who was master in sail as a has-been, an embittered old-timer unemployable elsewhere.

The majority of those German ships were line ships, both

from Hamburg and Bremen, belonging to companies like F. Laeisz, Siemers, Vinnen, Schluter and Maack, Knör and Burchard. Many of these offered careers for their officers in power as well: the fate facing the unemployed master was not the scrap heap or going third mate of some tramp. Conditions of employment were reasonably good although employers varied. Laeisz, for instance, when the company began to include some powered ships and after the First World War built up a fleet, gave its Cape Horner masters command of them, direct. It had shore appointments, too—banana plantations in the Cameroons (and a fleet of fast ships to serve them), business interests in South and Central America and elsewhere. It had its own cargo superintendents to see its ships had fast turn-around, and marine superintendents to look after the ships down to the smallest detail.

For Laeisz, a good master was employable in associated fields: a bad master they tried not to appoint. Where British ships were usually months in Chilean or Peruvian ports, the Laeisz ships romped in—generally to the best berths, alongside if there were any, paying extra dues—whipped their cargoes out (usually all general, or some fuel and some general), whipped coastal cargoes in for the move up to nitrate ports like Iquique, sailed there with the same dispatch they'd brought the European cargo with, and straightway began the loading of nitrate homeward. This cost money, but it earned money, goodwill, and steady employment.

German ships served German merchants ashore as well as Chilean: there were many in Chile and elsewhere in South America. Germany needed nitrates. German ships paid a bonus for fast dispatch, regarded time as important, treated their crews well and kept them. The Laeisz ships had practically no deserters. Indeed, desertion at these West Coast ports was the act of the desperate, the poorly treated and the poorly led. Able seamen in Laeisz ships received a 20-mark monthly increase in pay when they signed for a further voyage. Crews mattered, and knew this. Masters were required to report on everybody. No man was unimportant. Stupidity over food, incompetent cooks, penny-scraping stewards (or masters) were not wanted.

Selection of officers was done with care. Men marked for early command—and, really, this Cape Horning was not for abandoned old men who switched the digits until they died— were appointed mates of the ships they would later sail, particularly the two big five-masters and the awkward ships like the *Pampa* (which in some trims was very tender, with her unnecessarily massive rig) and the *Pamir* which could be wet, stubborn and bitchy. The idiosyncrasies of big sailing ships varied greatly and could be learned only by sailing in them. Deutsche Seewarte could not help here.

The spectacle of one of the big Germans storming with the afternoon wind into Valparaiso was unforgettable, magnificent and moving, and was meant to be. In she'd come, the great bark *Potosi* or the ship *Preussen*—or the graceful *Pitlochry,* the sleek *Pinnas,* the strong *Peking*—under every stitch of sail, swinging with a swishing of the sea along her sides, a roll of foam tumultuous at her cutwater, the wind singing in the mighty rigging and the swollen sails alight in the afternoon sun. On she'd race unchecked, as if she meant to crash all that great instrument of ordered and efficient beauty on the Chilean beach. Not a line was touched except the braces as strictly necessary, not a hand was yet aloft. No one was in sight except the master and the helmsman on the midships deck before the charthouse where the big double wheels stood. There was no shout of orders; no whistle blew. Was she really going to cast herself ashore, picking the way among the anchored shipping by herself?

At the last moment, around she would come! Spanker to wind'ard, jibs down on the run, royals, six (or eight, or ten) t'gallants hauled up as if they were great white blinds, courses and lower tops'ls clewed, around she swung with the upper tops'ls backed, taking the way off her perfectly just as she dropped into her place in the tier. Down came the great anchor with noisy rattle of chain, down came the upper tops'l yards: and there the great sea bird stood while her sailors raced up the rigging, spread out along the yards to fist and stow the canvas she so magnificently used. Seventy days or less from Hamburg! And past the blasted Horn as if it were not there—well, almost.

No huge crowd of seamen manned those yards, though the envious and the inefficient declared it was "all done with Prussian discipline and crowds of cowed boys." Few if any Prussians sailed in Laeisz ships, though the greatest was named *Preussen:* Prussians were not particularly popular among merchant seamen. The German discipline was based on respect for the good workman, the discouragement of the brash and reward of the efficient. Ships' boys and ordinary seamen were required to doff their caps when they entered the forecastle as a sign of respect to their elders. Bos'ns, sailmakers, carpenters, senior seamen had their special bonuses and privileges as a mark of the ship's need of and regard for them. Most of the crews were German, chiefly North Germans. There were also many Danes, experienced seamen from a still largely agricultural Denmark which had few Cape Horners of its own then to employ them. Even the giants *Preussen* and *Potosi*, with their maze of yards, acres of canvas, miles of wires and cordage, carried crews of just over forty of whom no more than four were ordinary seamen and boys. The rest were able seamen—*real* able seamen.

Nobody cowed them. Nobody was required to do so stupid a thing. As regular traders, the men had their perquisites, too, their own ventures in items such as good cigars which seamen from other ships came to buy. The sailing liners made fast and regular voyages—two a year was the rule in the nitrate trade. (Three in two years was good for Santa Rosalia or the California voyage, with its greater uncertainties.) This brought masters, mates and men regularly and predictably home, which allowed them to lead something of a reasonable home life. This helped to keep good men with the company.

And nobody had to "win" the galley coal, or food from the cargo, or cheat on the stores, take chances with the ballast to collect commissions dishonestly "on the side." Laeisz superintendents watched everything: the company suffered neither knaves nor fools. Nor did it allow women on its ships—no wives, no children—for these were at best in the way aboard hard-sailed ships and at worst could be an abomination.

All this, of course, until 1914–18: during those years the

Big Cape Horners found many cargos on the Pacific Coast until the Panama Canal was opened—loading lumber at Port Blakeley. From the collections of the San Francisco Maritime Museum, by permission of the Director and Trustees.

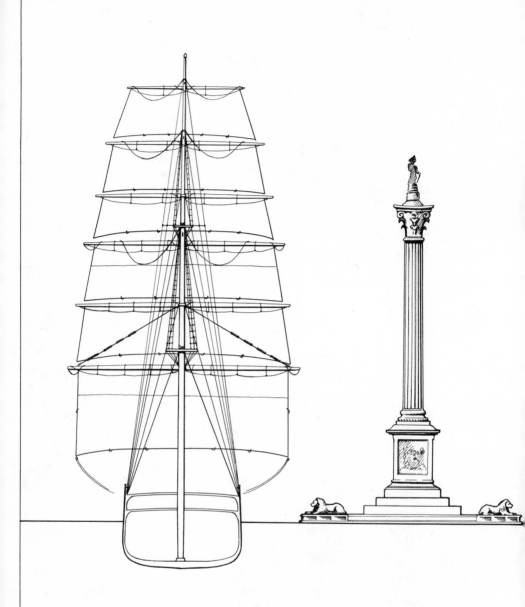

The four masted barque PASSAT   200 feet
compared with Nelson's Column   145 feet

The four-masted bark PARMA was the Anglo-American 'case'-oil carrier ARROW. De
Cloux sailed her from South Australia to Falmouth in 83 days.

The German four-master PEKING under Captain H. Piening, outward-bound. Published by
permission of the Trustees of the National Maritime Museum.

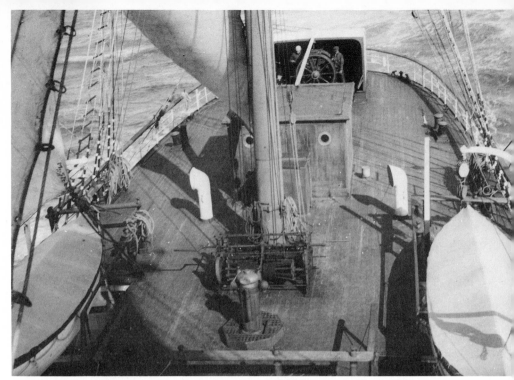

Coming the other way was easy—eastwards toward the Horn in the PARMA. *Steel open-fronted wheelhouse protected the helmsmen. (Note Jervis brace-winch at foot of the mast.)*

In a Cape Horn blow—the four-masted bark PARMA *could be very wet.*

France

Maria Rickmers

Potosi

R.C. Rickmers

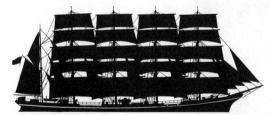

France II

København

Comparison of the world's five-mast barks

It seemed incredible that they could all disappear—and fast. Sail at Hamburg, early 20th century.

new-old Germany was destroyed, at least temporarily. During this time, too, the British in their own way were organizing and increasing their world-wide powered shipping, in which they'd had a head start. The Germans were busy in this field, too, but perhaps the British, taking a long view, could afford to let their sailers go.

After realizing something of the German contribution, I took a continued interest in this field, and met and talked with many masters. Some outstanding "P"-ships men and others I grew to know fairly well—men like Captains Hermann Piening, Robert Karl Miethe, Fred Krage, to a less degree Robert Clauss and Adolf Hauth. Miethe was—in 1970 still is—the last of the five-master captains, Piening the record-breaker with the *Peking* and last of the sailing-ships marine superintendents, Krage a school-ships man and world wanderer, Clauss and Hauth the last sailing record-breakers to sail in the Cape Horn business. It was Hauth who made the shortest westward 50° S. to 50° S. Cape Horn passage on the record—five days, fourteen hours with the *Priwall* outward bound to Chile in 1939, Clauss who sailed the same ship to Australia in the clipper time of sixty-five days in 1933 with Jürs in the *Padua* beside him. Clauss went straight into the Gulf from sea despite bad visibility: Jürs stood off a while to be sure.

In 1970 Miethe, Hauth, Clauss still live, Miethe at Quilpué near Valparaiso, the others in Germany. Several other outstanding shipmasters live in the Woermannhaus on the Palmaille in Hamburg, among them Captains Richard Sietas, Hans Rohwer, Richard Wendt. Captain Hauth, born in 1899, is the youngest among the survivors; Miethe, born 1876, the doyen. Piening died at the age of eighty in February, 1968. Like them all he had been through two World Wars, had twice lost all he had: in addition he was badly wounded in the second when he also lost both his sons.

I used to visit him in the Laeisz offices and, later, at this little home on von Hutten Strasse in Hamburg-Bahrenfeld, to talk and learn about ships. He was a quiet man, strong-faced, gray-eyed (one eye was of glass), with the powerful voice all Cape Horn masters are born with or develop. He had sailed a while in Australian ships when young—ships I knew. There were hard German ships as well as properly run fleets of them, and once, before he was seventeen, he ran from one of these. Some German seamen used to do this in order to improve their English (which Piening spoke and wrote perfectly): a clash of temperament with the mate could speed an exit, too. But they usually went back to Germany. Piening, like most seamen, was a member of the German naval reserve, but not at seventeen.

I asked the captain to tell me of a typical voyage in the 3,000-ton four-masted bark *Peking* from Hamburg toward Chile with general cargo. He chose one he made in 1928. After preparations of a thoroughness new to me, including a personal inspection of the ship alow and aloft by the master and mate, missing nothing, and a good briefing on weather prospects, the big four-master towed down the Elbe, shook her thirty-three sails free and sheeted them home off the Elbe 1 lightship near its mouth, and made out to sea.

"We have to start from the furthest leeward corner of the North Sea. First problem is, which way shall I try to go, passing to the north of Scotland or take on the English Channel, full of hurrying steamers and maybe westerly winds? I have forecasts. I have a good barometer, a small wireless, battery-operated. But really I am on my own. Nobody else has quite the same concern with the wind as the big sailing-ship master. I have data. I have my eyes, my judgment—my luck, too, if you like. But I'm not going to ride that.

"Despite the wireless and the forecasts, I'm not really much ahead of Columbus. It isn't the handed-out data that matters. It's how I construe it. For that I have also my eyes, my ears, my understanding based on years of watching the clouds and the sky and the face of the sea—and, if you like, my nose. Maybe my sixth sense. I can't spell that out, but I'd better have it and put it to work. So I do just that, and forecast that if I make for the Channel I may have to fight a foul wind its whole length. The old crews have changed. Now I have half a crew of raw young lads. The north of Scotland can be as bad as the Horn. I can have a tough slog on my hands up there, too: but I'll have sea room. It is a little longer: it has an even greater certainty of bad weather: but it should be the safer way. As far as any of us knows, we haven't lost a ship up there. We have lost enough in that Channel—all through collisions.

"But winds and weather change rapidly in these latitudes. I sense a hope of easterly, then northeast, then north. All these will shove us through that Channel fast. The Channel it is: let her go!

"The easterly came, but it also brought fog. All around us buzzed the whistles of the steamers. We had no whistle, only a hand-operated foghorn blowing a signal meaning here is a sailing ship with fair wind. But who may listen, in the enclosed bridges of the steamships? Or listening, understand? We were obliged to hope, with beating hearts, that the greyhounds and powered sluggards would hear us and make way for us in time. I sail on cautiously. It is silent aboard the *Peking*. I can hear the too-close steamers. I know that not all nations train their ships' officers in sailers, as we still did then in Germany. On many a steamer the men on the bridge have never put foot in a sailing vessel nor learned about them. We have lost several of our best sailers to such steamers, sometimes in blind collision, as with our beautiful *Pitlochry;* sometimes through misjudging our speed with good winds, as in the knocking down of our great *Preussen.* True, some of our sailers have sunk the steamers which collided with them—once a big P. & O. liner. But we don't want that. We only want to sail upon our way. International rules of the road prescribe our signals and require all powered vessels to keep clear of us, except when we overtake them."

The stronger wind came back, the fog blew away, and the *Peking* bounded on outside the Bay of Biscay clear of all shipping lanes, on the long sailing route toward the Horn.

Past Finisterre well out, the big four-master sailed, Captain Piening carefully watching the meterological data, making his swift appraisals of the best way to make use of depressions to keep his ship moving in the desired direction at best speed. He had no weather maps, of course, and no great store of new information—soon none. His own eyes and brain, nourished by experience, provided data for the weather map that was in his head.

He picked up the *nortada* off the Portuguese coast, well out to avoid both steamships and the land's interference with the sea winds. And then the trades! That remembered paradise of the ocean sailing-vessel life when all the hardships are forgotten.

Through the blue sea the keen cutwater of the sleek, big *Peking* rips day after beautiful day, scaring the wide-eyed flying fish with the roll of foaming water that forever races at her bow. Here the sailor may feel the essence of harmonious beauty between his ship and the sea. But nothing lasts. The doldrums come, with their nervous cat's-paws of fleeting airs, their sudden swift squalls, their deluge after deluge of almost solid rain.

"You are not to think that we are dealing here with a domain of absolute lack of wind," says Piening. "That seldom exists, for even slight variations in pressure must always result in movements of air. But the wind is uncertain and faint here. The navigator who is not continually ready to make use of even the lightest breath can spend weeks in this uncomfortable hothouse. There is no rest for the sailors. There are watches in which they hardly get off the braces for ten minutes. And what these Johnny-goodfellows can find use for here in the way of forceful strong speech goes far beyond all that our pseudo-writers are capable of with their stupid 'Oddzooks! Foresails and topgallant shrouds!'*

"There is only one pleasant thing about this region: it rains frequently. In a compact mass, the water falls from the blue-gray sky. Everything and everyone aboard revels in soap and water, for the fresh-water store of a sailer is limited and the duration of the passage most uncertain. A sort of madness seizes everyone. Clad only in a cake of soap, the whole crew leaps around and lets itself be washed clean by the lukewarm ablution. Filled with envy, the helmsman looks at the laughing foam-snowmen into which his comrades have transformed themselves. Everyone pulls out whatever he can wash and lets the sea salt get rinsed out thoroughly. By night the heavy lightning flashes of this region present a splendid show. Often the heavens flame copper-red and sulphur-yellow, and hardly for a second is the vessel sur-

* A quote from a "sea" novel.

rounded by complete darkness. At times St. Elmo's lights dance upon the yardarms.

"Sailing through this region makes special demands on the shipmaster. To a high degree, it depends on his knowledge and his experience how long the passage will be delayed here. The belt of calms lies diagonally across the Atlantic like a wedge with its broad end on the African coast, narrowing toward the west. Once through the wedge, he will find the southeast trade wind; but there are currents in this doldrums zone, too, and they can set me toward Brazil. A square-rigged ship can steer into the wind—"sail by the wind," we say, only up to a certain angle, say about 65° at best. If I foolishly allow the ship to get too far to the west, working through this calm belt, I can find the bulge of Brazil getting in my way and have to work back before sailing south again. I must avoid that! Vigilance is the answer— the endless wariness, the correct (well, mostly) interpretation of the met. factors the good Lord puts before you, added to diligent study of the doldrums data in our books and voyage records. You will get no all-night in—not before you make port. You need luck, too. No use denying that—the more good luck the better.

"The southeast trade winds come. You bound along, approaching the coast of South America once you are well past its bulge, because you are making now as direct a course as practical toward Cape Horn. In the area of the estuary of the great La Plata River—the River Plate—we keep wary watch for the first sign of those overheated violent bursts of pampas winds sailors call *pamperos*. Again the best sails are bent, all examined carefully during the passage through the trade winds while old sails were temporarily aloft. Everything must be ready—not just the sails and all their necessary gear, but the footropes (soon now to be slippery with ice) where men swing and balance and work without thought of danger, the beckets where in violent rolling they may thrust an arm, the gaskets they must haul upon to smother a skinned-up fighting sail—all must be fit for their work. There must be certainty that where a man takes hold he shall find secure grip: where he stands nothing shall break, though thirty men swing upon the footrope while the torn sail thunders and blows back over it, trying to force them off.

"The days fly past. All things are done. We watch for the telltale sausage-like cloud bank which briefly seen turns rapidly into the dangerous *pampero.* Just note the ends of that sausage cloud begin to droop like a Chinese mustache: then stand by the halyards! Lower the royals, the upper topgallants! Furl all kites. Getting the best out of your ship does not include taking foolish chances. For the *pampero* comes with a mad haste that frightens the sea itself so it lies flat, as if all the wind on earth had struck it at once like an enormous roller flung along at 100 knots. On we sail, forever wary: soon there is a nip in the air, as if these west winds bring the sting of Andean snow this far to sea.

"We approach latitude 50° S., the threshold of the Horn. From 50° S. in the Atlantic to 50° S. in the Pacific is the windy corner we must now take on, in a wide swing south of all the land and its offshore islands as far as Diego Ramirez, down to 60° S. if we must go that far (but unwillingly, for there the Antarctic ice is much too close: we can have frostbite). Now I have no weather information. There is none (not in the sailing-ship era). I watch the clouds if I can see them, the signs in the sky and sea. I study the barometric movements, for their data is all-important.

"Down here is generally a realm of low pressure. In southern latitudes the winds spiral clockwise toward the center of the low as they rush round the tip of South America. I have to use that spiral to get west, hundreds of miles. It is not an afternoon's sailing. The passage, I know, has been done in little more than a week—and in months. I have been here as a boy in the *Susanna* twenty-five years before, for three months. Often the best of ships have been defeated altogether. Well, I don't know *that* experience, thank the Lord: in all our Laeisz sailing only one of our ships was ever driven away, and that case was understandable.*

"My company regulations require me to give the dangerous coasts here a sufficiently wide berth, especially all southwest Chile: I must not cut corners, lest the ship be caught fatally unable to claw off an unlit lee shore. I must not ask too much of

* See note on the *Pellworm* at the end of this chapter.

my ship in this way, by getting her through chance-taking in a dangerous corner. A lot of ships have never been heard of again after taking on the Horn, especially in winter—literally some hundreds of them. Only one is from our company. I shall not— I hope—begin a fashion: yet I know that the utmost care at all times may not be enough. There can also be ice. Down here there can be tremendous seas, particularly over the shallower water inside Diego Ramirez. In winter I shall not press my *Peking* in there. I shall stay in the deeper waters. There are chances it is foolish to take.

"My interpretation of the evening sky, my graph of the barometric readings, tell me to stand on, to get south of the low and take advantage of the easterly I *should* find down there. But here lows race furiously one after the other: who in a 12-knot ship shall be certain of the way between? Here, too, such gales pay little attention to the man-held theories: they care nothing for the dogmas carefully laid down in his learned tomes. I know that I am little better off, in fact, than Magellan was, except that we take James Cook's advice and have sea room. No twisting, mountain-lined, squall-filled Strait of Magellan for us!

"I make first for the Straits of Le Maire, between Staten Island and the eastern end of Tierra del Fuego. That's different. They are very short. Here I go warily, for this shortcut is deceptive though it is twelve miles wide, and can save me a hundred miles where I most need it. What can be so risky about sailing through a short strait twelve miles wide? One cannot understand what a Strait of Le Maire passage means until he has sailed through it with a big ship. Under full sail, we are sailing southward before a stiff north wind. Like a small dark-blue cloud, something rises to starboard out of the sea—Cape San Diego, our turning point. Soon land comes into sight on the port side also. At first it is a low blue streak, soon the most comfortless shore imaginable. It looks as if a giant's child had thrown his building blocks at the sea in anger. To starboard, blue mountain ridges rise above the cape. Before our prow, between the two land's ends, the gateway opens through which we are to pass— we hope. All right, let's go. But we need to get through with the one tide. The current in the strait can have a speed of six knots.

"Just what this current can do to the southbound vessel one first learns by sailing there. This mighty swell of waters which giant forces press through the gate between Tierra del Fuego and the island, this crowding together of millions of tons of turbulent water, creates a sharp piling up of eddies and backwaters in which the largest ship can become unmanageable. It is too late to find that out in such a confined place. Current fights swell, and the rocks wait with the cold sea snarling impatiently around them. It is not an ordinary ocean swell rolling on and on as one is accustomed to see. These waves rush perpendicular as if cast up by an invisible power, and fall to run again on the same spot —savage ship-stoppers going nowhere but all 100 percent against me. The natural motion of the vessel ceases. She no longer rolls or pitches. The sails belly full before the north wind; we steer south but our course made good is something else. I realize that, seized by hidden forces, she is hauled now to one side or the other, now backward.

"In a flash, the reports of the many strandings in this passage come before my mind with ghastly clarity. What am I doing here? Vessels have been stranded in every strait of the sea, but those here are counted in dozens. The patent log shows 10 knots, yet after three hours one still has land on both sides. We have sailed through thirty miles of water but twenty of those miles were over the same bottom. No wonder the old seamen gave to the southern doorpost on the Tierra del Fuego side the name the Cape of Good Success. Pass that safely, and you have come in through the back door to the Horn. Fail to pass, and the chances are you will not be knocking on any door again.

"Now a large swell rolls up from the southwest. This reminds me to push on: the north wind will not wait. Suddenly it turns toward the west. Thank the Lord we are out of the narrows! The swell grows longer, higher, dirtier-looking. The barometer shows a rapid drop. I furl the higher sails right away, while it is light. Quick and threatening the night falls on the sea. The wind increases. Now I head into it. The cold sea smashes over the whole foredeck. Well, we are ready. I call out all hands to take in the fore and mizzen upper topsails, then reef the mainsail and crojack. The wind grows heavy with noise and power: but our *Peking* carries all-steel rigging from deck to truck. Hard though it blows, the wind is still usable and the *Peking* can stand this canvas in a gale. Sailing is our job. We have confidence in our ship. She lurches over, sails with a list and a crashing of seas through the gale's roar, and a hellish concert clamors in the rigging. The seas break and roar over the rail, strike the deck threateningly, wash violently around hatches and capstans, and run off in thwarted fury through all the wash ports. When the squalls hit, our vessel buries her lee bulwarks deep under the waters that rush by. A broader stripe of spray shimmers blue-green in the inky darkness of the night. Then she rights herself a little in a slight easing and rushes on to the south. I must try to find, on the south side of the storm's center, the wind with east in it that will then carry us to the west past the cape of storms.

"When morning comes hesitant in the shrieking wind, many of our boys look anxious. In endless procession the watery gray-blue mountains march upon us from the west. From their summits blow flapping manes of blinding spray which the storm tears to shreds. The black-gray clouds ride upon the sea. A universal, endless roaring fills the air of such strength and continuity it seems to stop the ears as if with sand. When the squalls strike, a man must turn his head away in order to breathe at all. The excessive pressure of rushing air forces itself through mouth and nose into the body, blows up the lungs until they are no longer in condition to breathe out. Rain and hail come, bringing a strange hissing and singing to mingle with the roar. The air is gray with flying water and opaque as milk glass. In the lee of the charthouse stands the watch, or behind the awning of strong canvas which is secured to the weather rigging of the main.

"Most of them are young, hardly twenty, the youngest fifteen. This is postwar: there are no longer pre-1914 crews. It is good that they are here at the end of the world. Here is the right school for them if they want to be seamen. They learn there what no university may teach them—that the Lord God gave man two hands to take hold and work with and two legs to keep his place.

And with these a body and a will that do not need to go to pieces at the first scream of the wind or the last. When they haul on the impossibly hard and frozen gear to haul up some great fighting sail that thunders its defiance, when they stand shoulder to shoulder on the footropes aloft to tear yet another sail out of the fury of the storm, they learn the most important lesson of all—that they are not alone, that when worse comes to worst, the individual can achieve the impossible when true comrades are standing by his side, each with his will set firm no matter what. In a Cape Horn ship, this works, though it may take all night to fight one sail. Once having learned these lessons, their value stays through life, not only in ships.

"With the ship shortened down to storm canvas but by no means hove to—it isn't *that* bad: the *Peking* is strong—we drive on. I send the watch which should be there below, to rest them. There is hot coffee for everyone, braced with a little kümmel for the over-eighteens if they want. Our galley is not washed out, thanks to our big midships house. It is warm and dry there. The crew can rest. My rig now of lower tops'ls and reefed courses can stand a lot. The center of effort of that sail plan is low and good. I have storm stays'ls set too, of course: she balances well, is not pressed down, keeps good speed. The *sound* of the wind can't hurt us. I am driving her to get under the belly of the depression, to find the wind working abaft the ship's beam. I drive her to 56°, 57° S. Already I am clear of the Horn—south of it. That's not the point. I have to get my ship with the winds God gives me to the place where she may use them all to make north again. I must exploit the situation as I find it, outguess the wind. Even in murk and utterly stormy shouting sky, there shall be signs and I must interpret them. If I lie here and wallow under too little sail to advance, all I achieve is to wait for more storms, right in their path.

"So I figure, and I watch, catnapping a bit in the daylight hours on the charthouse settee. I have excellent mates. No man may stay alert all the time.

"I reach 58°. Now it is cold—very cold. The short days are shorter. I watch for frostbite, try to expose nobody. I do not want to get beyond 60°, not just because there is a company rule against going avoidably down there. It is rarely good sailing sense. On 58° S. the gale which had been west swings to south —this is it! Swing the yards, trim the sails to accept this useful wind from the port side! Shake out the frozen reef points! Give her the three upper tops'ls! Lose no chance, waste no mile, for she is sailing westward now—west she runs and west I drive her with the brave wind abeam. These breaks are brief. Soon the west and west-southwest winds will return, roaring to stop my way. Out in this frigid down-south waste I must have sea room to keep to wind'ard. Make west now! Make west! Degrees of longitude are shorter here. I race across them. The wind is soon southwest again, but the *Peking* lies a good course to wind'ard of northwest with that, until I am far enough into the Pacific to know I can keep clear of all the southwestern Chilean shore, the labyrinth of rocky islands flung in the turmoil of the sea's rage there. No bad chances taken, no good chances lost—these are the watchwords for wind'ard roundings of the Horn. Use the situation that comes to hand while it is there. For God's sake, *use* it.

"Soon I may use the southwest as fair wind. I am across longitude 75° W. to the west of it. Ten days after passing through the Strait of Le Maire I cross 50° S. in the Pacific, beyond 80° W. longitude. Already I feel the help of the beginnings of the north-flowing Humboldt current. Once again my Cape Horn rounding is done. Very quietly but in a real way, I see not just relief in the lads' faces—not relief at all as we'd known twenty-five years earlier in the *Susanna*. I see a new sense of manhood. We anchor at Corral in the Bay of Valdivia sixty-four days from the English Channel. That passage is over. Now to get the cargo out, shift north for nitrates, and begin another."

But there were in fact not many more voyages for the *Peking:* she was sold by the Laeisz Line in 1932 to the British Shaftesbury Homes and Training Ship organization, which rigged her down until only three yards remained aloft, converted her into a sort of stationary training ship, and renamed her *Arethusa*. Looking fine below but like the skeleton of her former self aloft (the charity operating her has no money to keep up expensive and to them unnecessary rigging), in 1970 she still lies at moorings in the River Medway in southern England, doing good work.

During the First World War the sailing-ship trade to the west coast of both North and South America suffered blows from which it never recovered. A way was discovered to produce nitrates artificially, the Panama Canal was opened, and even in the Culebra Cut its high sides did not slip into it (as some sailing-ship men hoped they would), and the South American republics excluded foreign-flag ships from their coastal trade. They also developed the manufacture of cement and other things which had given sailing ships many outward cargoes from Europe, and several formed their own shipping lines. The replacement of coal by oil had begun, perhaps assisted by recurring industrial trouble on the New South Wales coal fields; and more and more efficient steamships and motor ships picked up all the general cargo available. The great reservoir of experienced sailing-ship masters, officers, carpenters, sailmakers and seamen had gone forever, and so had much of the ancillary services—the builders, rigging lofts, rope walks, and all the rest—on which the essential flow of new ships must depend. There were no new ships, except the *Padua* (in 1926) and an auxiliary square-rigged school-ship or two. There were some good men still available for a while, but they had to find careers elsewhere.

For a very few years after the end of the First World War, there were plenty of cargoes to be moved: but only for a while. Slump soon came: even the most poverty-stricken sailer could not hope to pay, and the slump seemed endless. The last big British sailing ship was lost in 1929; the last German handed over at the end of the Second World War; the last under the Finnish flag went in 1950, having done very well to sail that long. One speaks of sailing ships, not auxiliaries: no real sailing ship needed engines. The last Finns were the four-masted barks *Viking* (Danish-built) and the former Germans *Pamir* and *Passat*. There were no Finnish-built Cape Horn ships.

The last Portuguese was none other than the old Jarvis *Lawhill*, which rusted slowly away in a creek near Lourenço Marques in Mozambique a few years ago, after brief ownership by a Portuguese Goan citizen. She had sailed for South Africa during the Second World War, when the *Pamir* sailed for New Zealand—a country which still could man her properly thanks to her former fleet of colonial sailers.

The United States emerged from the First World War with a considerable fleet of sailing ships, both her own and handed-over German square-riggers, as well as large numbers of big wooden schooners, many of them built on the northwest coast almost like Liberty ships. They did not last long. It was an economic impossibility to operate them successfully under the American flag, though Captain P. A. McDonald did well for a while with the big four-masted bark *Moshulu,* the former German *Kurt.* She had to be sold to Gustaf Erikson of Åland (in 1935) to become viable. A full-rigged ship renamed *Tusitala,* which had once been the British *Sierra Lucena,* was the last working square-rigger to fly the American flag, using the Panama Canal route between New York and the Hawaiian Islands, which was scarcely economical. She was laid up during the Depression, which began in 1929. The last down-Easter, the ship *Benjamin Packard,* languished for a while as a sort of curiosity at a place called Playland, at Rye, New York. A "playland" was no place for a Cape Horn ship: she shriveled away.

Italy, Denmark, Peru, Brazil, Chile, Belgium, Argentina, Uruguay, and Russia operated a few square-riggers until the 1930's. Several fine large ships were built in Italy in earlier days and one or two in Denmark. The South American countries acquired theirs mainly from the First World War but kept several going into the second—among them Peru's former German four-masted bark *Omega,* Chile's *Calbuco,* and Brazil's *Tijuca.* Both Denmark and France (whose logical citizens never bothered again with the big Cape Horners when they realized that their day was done) kept a few smaller square-riggers in the West Indian logwood trade into the '30's. Italy kept beautiful small barkentines and brigantines going in the Mediterranean for a long time after her deepwater men were all gone, and square-rigged cod-bangers sailed out of St. Malo in France until the early '30's. The last square-rigger operating on the historic Grand Banks fishing grounds was the shapely Portuguese barkentine *Gazela Primero,* still afloat in 1970 and fishing until 1969. A handful of Portuguese schooners still sail to the Newfoundland and Greenland grounds, but the working square-rigged ship is gone from the world— even the last brig from the Maldive Islands, and the last Tuticorin brigantine.

All these, really, were no more than temporary lingerings. World War I effectively finished the Cape Horn sailing ship. Her last great era was from 1890 to 1915. After 1920, though several hundred put up a brave show of sailing under a dozen flags and a handful lasted another twenty years, they were picturesque remnants left by chance in a world that no longer needed or wanted them.

NOTE: THE ONLY LAEISZ SHIP WHICH EVER TURNED AWAY FROM CAPE HORN WITH HER MASTS STILL IN HER WAS THE *Pellworm,* A STEEL FULL RIGGED SHIP OF 2,270 TONS, BUILT AS THE FRENCH *Maréchal Suchet* AT ST. NAZAIRE IN 1902 FOR OWNERS IN NANTES. BECAUSE THE GERMAN MERCHANT SHIPS HAD MAINLY GONE AS REPARATIONS TO VARIOUS ALLIED FLAGS (WHERE THEY WERE VERY QUICKLY NOT WANTED), THE F. LAEISZ COMPANY BOUGHT THE FRENCHMAN IN 1924 WHEN SHE WAS LAID UP IN THE CANAL AT NANTES, AND CAPTAIN ALBERT WIST TOOK HER OVER THERE FOR A VOYAGE TO CHILE WITH THE BALLAST SHE HAD ABOARD. THIS WAS SAND, HAD BEEN IN THE SHIP FOR YEARS, WAS VERY DRY AND RAN EASILY. WIST ASKED FOR MORE BUT THE THEN LAEISZ MARINE SUPERINTENDENT, THE FRIESIAN BOYE PETERSEN, REFUSED THIS. THE COMPANY NEEDED TO GET HER ON HER WAY AS QUICKLY AS POSSIBLE TO HELP RE-ESTABLISH ITS BUSINESS. THE FREIGHT MARKET WAS GOOD, BUT WISE OPERATORS WERE AWARE THAT THIS WOULD NOT LAST. SO WITH THE NEW NAME, A QUICK DRY-DOCKING AND A GOOD REFIT, THE BIG *Pellworm* WAS HUSTLED OFF TO SEA.

AFTER THE 1914–18 WAR, THE SPIRIT OF HAMBURG SEAMEN FOR THE TIME BEING WAS FAR FROM FORMER STANDARDS. REVOLUTION AND HOPELESS INFLATION FOLLOWED THE LOSS OF THE WAR. INSTEAD OF GOOD MEN PROUD OF CONTINUITY OF GOOD SERVICE IN A GOOD LINE, NOW CROWDS OF BLOODY-MINDED, DISILLUSIONED AND DISPIRITED EMBRYO REVOLUTIONARIES DOMINATED MANY FOC'S'LS. SO IT WAS IN THE *Pellworm.* THE SAND BALLAST SHIFTED OFF THE HORN. SHE GOT OVER ON HER SIDE. THE CREW REFUSED TO TAKE ON THE HORN AGAIN WITH THAT BALLAST (THOUGH THEY GOT HER UP SOMEWHERE NEAR AN EVEN KEEL) AND THREATENED MUTINY IF THE SHIP WAS NOT PUT BACK TO MONTEVIDEO. BACK SHE HAD TO GO. SHE MISSED HER GOOD NITRATES CHARTER (ALL CHARTERS STIPULATE LOADING DATES) AND THE POSTWAR FREIGHT MARKET HAD COLLAPSED. HAD SHE ARRIVED IN TIME, THE ORIGINAL CHARTER RATE WAS 105 SHILLINGS A TON WHICH WOULD HAVE CLEARED SOMETHING LIKE £10,000. SHE WAS OFFERED INSTEAD 35 SHILLINGS, WHICH MEANT A SERIOUS LOSS. NOTHING ELSE OFFERED ANYWHERE. SO THE SHIP WAS ORDERED BACK TO HAMBURG, SOLD THERE TO THE ASSOCIATION OF HAMBURG SHIPOWNERS, RIGGED DOWN AND CONVERTED INTO AN ACCOMMODATION SHIP FOR AN EMPLOYERS' LABOR FORCE IN CASE OF NEED. WHEN TIMES IMPROVED SHE BECAME A YOUTH HOSTEL, BY NAME *Hein Godenwind.* ALLIED AIR

RAIDS IN THE SECOND WORLD WAR BADLY DAMAGED HER, LUFTWAFFE PILOTS USED HER FOR TARGET PRACTICE, AND THAT WAS THE END OF HER.

BROTHER SHIPMASTERS CONSIDERED THAT CAPTAIN WIST WOULD HAVE ROUNDED THE HORN AND KEPT HIS CHARTER, HAD HE BEEN ALLOWED THE BALLAST HE REQUESTED. HE HAD BEEN IN COMMAND OF THE LAEISZ SHIPS *Peiho, Pelikan,* AND *Parma* SUCCESSIVELY BETWEEN 1909 AND 1914, WHEN THE *Parma* WAS CAUGHT IN CHILE. HE MADE CONSISTENTLY GOOD PASSAGES IN THESE THREE SHIPS BUT, AFTER THE *Pellworm*'S TURN-AWAY, HE WAS FINISHED IN SAIL. HE WAS MORE OR LESS BANISHED TO THE COMPANY'S STEAMERS AND BANANA PLANTATIONS IN WEST AFRICA.

ONE WONDERS HOW CAPTAIN BOYE PETERSEN MIGHT HAVE GOT ON HAD HE TAKEN THE SHIP. HE WAS DOING HIS DUTY FOR THE COMPANY WHEN HE ORDERED CAPTAIN WIST TO SEA WITH THAT UNSAFE BALLAST, BUT IN FACT HE HAD SET HIM AN IMPOSSIBLE TASK.

Chapter thirteen

FIVE DAYS, FOURTEEN HOURS

ONE GREAT difference between German (and Scandinavian) and British sailing ships that very much helped morale and efficiency in the former was an absence of class-consciousness and a respect for the competent worker more or less along the old craft lines. Another difference was that the Germans and Scandinavians, though their shipping was closely controlled, were not harassed by bureaucracy in the sense that unnecessary regulation took the place—or tried to—of discipline and leadership by competence among qualified and trusted men. There was no need of a deckhouse full of exploited and unpaid youth as backing for a weak afterguard. There was no miserable division of the strictly rationed provisions into poor food and worse. A sufficiency of good-to-tolerable provender was served aft and for'ard, without the miserable economies of no galley fire at night (and no coffee or anything else) even with stolen coal. The oppression of the seaman as a seagoing serf was not continental European policy. Some ships and some companies were better than others, of course: there could be rascals or drunks temporarily in the afterguard of any ship, and a good master always made a tremendous difference anywhere.

"Small ships were better than large," Bos'n Charlie Müller —a man who went to sea in 1890 and is still fit and well in 1970 after fifty years at sea, *never* having served in a powered vessel at all, nor wanted to—told me. "The smaller ships were handier to work, weren't so long in ports or at sea, and often had a happier spirit aboard. The happiest days of my life were in the inter-

235

colonial barks and barkentines of the South Pacific, out of Australia and New Zealand. Of course, in our German ships, a green lad had to learn respect for the calling he'd taken on, and for his elders in it—doff his cap when he came in the foc's'l, fetch and carry for his watch, look after his gear and everything else. That way, he learned that his own competence would mean something, too. Once he was A.B., he was a man among men, even if he was only seventeen and a half or eighteen. He didn't get to be an A.B. easily.

"We had very happy smaller sailers in Germany, too. I remember one I sailed in from the Friesian Islands, sailing out of Hamburg in the Atlantic trade. She was about 600 tons, rigged as a four-masted tops'l schooner. The captain had his wife aboard and a small baby, and we crew had our meals aft at the same table as them—real family style. She traded to the Caribbean and Central America, with cargoes like dynamite to La Guaira, redwood to San Pedro in Santo Domingo and so on, finally loading mahogany logs somewhere in Yucatan for Le Havre. This was 1919–20. She was a good ship with a nice crew. There were plenty such ships about then, but they didn't last long after that—not in the South Pacific either. Maybe another five years. I missed them."

Some big Finnish ships had something of a family spirit, too, though the seamen lived and ate in their fo'c'sle. In the *Lawhill* of Mariehamn, the mates knew all the Åland Islands crew by their first names and used them, when I joined in 1921. She was a happy big ship.

Not being committed as an apprentice to one owner and one ship as so many British lads were, Piening gave himself a wide career without any emphasis on just getting four years' service in somehow or anyhow, and then sitting for his first certificate as officer. The *Susanna* experience had been exceptionally tough, too.

"The ship reached Caleta Buena on a Sunday. That day we cleared up everything, rigged the cargo gear, and unbent most of the canvas. This took all day," he said. "I felt a bit starved, and as if I'd been through something. But on the Monday morning it was turn-to in the hold at six o'clock and start with the discharge of our 3,000 tons of Welsh coal. We had to put the lot in sacks and heave it up by the old-style hand-operated dolly winch, a real back-breaker. That went on all day. Then as a first voyager, the other lad and I had to hurry on deck, clean ourselves up, and fetch and carry the meal for the A.B.'s. Then we got our own.

"After that, very often, the two of us had to row Captain Jürgens ashore and wait to row him back again, though it was usually after midnight when he came. Like all captains then, he seemed to have little consideration for the boys. The following day began at five-thirty as usual, setting table for the A.B.'s before the turn-to at six again. A boy had a hard life, though it was only for one voyage. Maybe the idea was to try us, or impress on us our foolishness in going to sea, but it didn't do that to me. I *knew* this was my career. Perhaps a truer notion was that boys must come up the hard way, knowing the value of doing all things thoroughly and well even though you felt you could drop. There was no such attitude as 'Take it easy.' "

There was typhoid aboard, treated by a shore doctor but not as typhoid. It was Captain Jürgens who realized the real nature of the illness when eight of his crew were laid up. He rushed them to Iquique hospital by tug, but the other ordinary seaman died. Having lost her homeward nitrate freight, the *Susanna* sailed to Puget Sound in ballast, to load timber at Port Townsend back for Chile. Arrived at Port Townsend, young Piening decided that he was fit to sign as A.B. in any other ship, and he had had quite enough of the tough *Susanna.* So he quietly asked the leading crimp of the port to find him a ship as A.B. Maxie Levy got him away in the old Norwegian iron ship *Hovding,* bound for South Africa. (Although such crimps stopped at nothing to supply bodies more or less alive to ships needing crews, they also worked honestly with seamen wishing a change of ship. Why not? They gained the blood-money either way—for "supplying" Piening to the *Hovding* and, in due course, a replacement for him to the *Susanna.* Blood-money was still $30.)

After this, Piening wandered the sailing ship's lonely world for years—in the wooden down-East skys'l-yarder *Henry Failing,* a near-2,000-ton wanderer quarter of a century old when he was in her; the Peruvian bark *Nora*, a slip of a bark carrying some 500 tons which a German crew of eleven all-told sailed round the Horn to Callao, then worked the cargo out before handing her to new owners; the ketch *Dashing Wave* on the Australian coast and the old wooden bark *Daniel* out of Sydney, sailing in the Tasman Sea. Large or small, skys'l-yarder or 100-ton ketch, any language, any trade, Piening served them all, always learning. With years of this sort of thing behind him, home he came at last to Hamburg and navigation school. Graduating finally as master *summa cum laude*, he then joined Laeisz, working his way up slowly because of four years in naval service during 1914–1918, followed by service in Laeisz steamships in the absence of sail. Offered command of a small wooden bark in the Atlantic, he took that temporarily—his first command. She was the 688-ton *Yildiz*, built of wood at Arendal, Norway, in 1881, as the *Royal* of Fredrikstad. In forty years of hard seafaring she had been known also as the *Freya, Amphitrite,* and *Wehrwolf.* She had leaked the worse with each change of name. When Piening had her, her main pumps were geared to a windmill which rose from the main deck like an odd, ungainly extra mast, and clanked around whenever there was wind, while the clear water ran across the decks.

"I got to know the North Sea very well in that ship," said the captain. "We must have pumped most of it through her at least twice, though the windmill handled most of it."

The Laeisz Line came out of the war with two big sailers, the *Pola* and the *Priwall,* but the *Pola* had to be given to France and was soon afterward lost as the French *Richelieu,* burned at Philadelphia. Ordered in 1914, these fine ships were completed during the war but could not sail then. While the *Pola* went to France, the *Priwall* in 1920 was sent off to Chile with the oddest "cargo" any Laeisz ship ever carried—240 bloody-minded roughnecks, flotsam from the war but all sailing-ship seamen, going out to man the interned German ships left there to sail them home for handing over to other flags. The 240 had far too little to do in the *Priwall* and no satisfactory future; what a voyage! Even that rugged Friesian Boye Petersen, sent in charge, had his hands full with the impossible job: but he did it. At least, he got most of them to Valparaiso. On the way some deliberately wasted fresh water stored in extra tanks, forcing the ship into Montevideo for more. Here the worst of the gangsters melted away.

Piening had to wait until 1926 for his first Laeisz command. By that time, the sailing-ship line was established again with half a dozen fine four-masters bought back from nations which had no use for them, and the new *Priwall* and the newer *Padua*— ordered in 1925 and built in 1926, last real engineless Cape Horner launched. Piening took her over after two years in command of the *Peking,* which was bought back from Italy. He proceeded at once to carry on the tradition of the wonderful Laeisz sailing records in the Cape Horn trade—sixty-four days outward in the *Peking,* seventy-one days Hamburg to Talcahuano, seventy-two days back from Mejillones to Terneuzen in the *Padua.* The way square-rigged ships must go to get best use of the wind, these are tremendous distances to cover in ten weeks, requiring the big ships to be moved through the sea by the wind at an average thousand miles a week.

Piening was in the company's steamers and motor ships too, handling these with distinction. He was promoted marine superintendent of the fleet in 1936. After the Second World War (through which all Laeisz ships were lost once again), the *Padua* was allocated to the U.S.S.R. as a school-ship: in 1970 she still sails, now as an auxiliary manned by Russian cadets. The *Priwall* was lost by fire as a Chilean school-ship under the name of *Lautaro* in 1945.

It was Captain Adolf Hauth whose duty it was to turn over the four-masted bark *Priwall* to Chile in 1941. Caught in Chile in his first ship, the Laeisz four-masted bark *Passat* during the First World War, he had the considerable misfortune to be caught there again in the second, this time as the *Priwall*'s master. It is this same Adolf Hauth who holds the record for the fastest passage ever made under sail for the classic westward rounding of the Horn, from latitutde 50° S. in the Atlantic to 50° S. in the Pacific, passing south of Diego Ramirez and keeping out to 78°

and 80° W. from the lee shore of southwestern Chile—five days and fourteen hours! And no doubt about it. His ship then was the *Priwall,* the year 1938 when the 3,100-ton four-masted bark was some twenty years old—except only for the *Padua,* the "youngest" Cape Horn ship in the world: and Hauth (born in 1899) was then the youngest of the real Cape Horn masters. The *Priwall,* built by Blohm and Voss at Hamburg during the First World War, was a very strong ship but not the fastest. She could stand a lot of hard driving, but it was not this which made the fast passage possible. It was plain good sailing in a great tradition by a good shipmaster who recognized the best way to use the good conditions offered, and did just that.

As was the custom in the very few surviving Laeisz ships in the late 1930's, the *Priwall* then was in part a training ship, with seventy-two hands all told. Few of these were the old dyed-in-the-wool tough mariners—very few. Fifty-five were cadets, thirty of them on their first voyage, sixteen on their second, only nine on their third. All embryo deck officers for the German merchant service then required sailing-ship experience. There were the usual excellent Laeisz officers and tradesmen. Hauth himself, at thirty-nine, had twenty-five years' sea experience, though six years of that were largely lost between 1914 and 1920. More time was unavoidably lost in the postwar depression. Like many others, Hauth had to serve where he could—home to Germany at last in the *Peiho,* then a while in Baltic schooners, followed by a wretched voyage in a 2,000-ton steel full-rigger named *Bertha* where only three for'ard hands had been in sail at all. The *Bertha* staggered in 1922 as far as Calcutta, taking 145 days and losing half a mast in the process, thence to Newcastle, N.S.W., in seventy days, and a long wait there for a coal cargo to Callao. Another seventy days saw the *Bertha* in Peru.

Here Able Seaman Hauth learned that the German inflation had robbed him of all his wages: he was working for nothing. Not only that, the whole nine years he had spent in ships had been for nothing, and he was still an able seaman. He had planned that the *Bertha* voyage would finance him to mate's school: but the dispiriting *Bertha* would be lucky to get herself and her penniless crew back to Germany at all.* At Callao, Hauth walked ashore. The American steamship *Memnon* was in port, short-handed: he stayed with this vessel and as bos'n of another American, the *Horace Luckenbach,* until he had saved enough real money for that school. Then home he went, took his mate's certificate, spent sixteen months in North Sea and Baltic steam until the Laeisz Line had a berth. His ambition was still to be master in sail: but first he had to serve as watch-keeping mate in a deep-sea square-rigger. His chance came as third mate of the *Priwall* with Captain Jürs, then second in the then new *Padua* under Captain Piening, from 1926 to 1928. Jürs and Piening were the real stuff: this was invaluable experience. By May, 1929, he had taken his master's certificate—properly qualified at last! It had been a hard fifteen years, much of it almost embittering, some near to soul-destroying. Hauth's internment aboard the *Passat* during the First World War was at Iquique, where for some reason conditions in the German ships were much more rigorous than among the considerably larger number held at Valparaiso. It was a hard time for a young fellow to live through and keep his spirit and his hope.

And now came the worst depression of all. The Laeisz Line had built up slowly to six big sailing ships again and a small fleet of fast motor-ship fruit carriers: they had struggled hard to win back trade, to restore at least some semblance of the old order of things to the West Coast of South America despite trade difficulties, nitrate difficulties, political troubles. Crew troubles had smoothed out when some stability returned to Germany: international trade was another matter. The four-masted barks *Parma, Pamir, Passat* and *Peking* all had to be sold, for very little, for the Åland Islanders were the only buyers. Only the new *Padua* and comparatively new *Priwall* were kept going. Half the banana ships were laid up, their masters ashore on half pay. Even the two four-masted barks still in commission had to make their outward passages in ballast, for it was no longer possible to round up general cargo for them. Only two fast fruiters remained in service, the motor ships *Puma* and *Panther*. Sail-qualified Laeisz

* In fact, she did not. She went missing homeward bound from Jacksonville, Florida, toward Hamburg. Only a small boat was found.

officers had to change from sail to power or back again as required: a competent master could serve equally well in both, despite the different problems facing the man with an expensive cargo of fragile bananas to race to market at the proper time. So the newly qualified Hauth had to take second mates', then mates' berths in the motor ships for the following six years. He knew he was fortunate to find employment at sea then at all.

In February, 1937, he achieved command at last—of the *Priwall*, outward bound for Talcahuano and Valparaiso with such general as could be assembled, homeward with guano from Peru. She made Talcahuano in seventy-two days from Hamburg, which was good. Homeward she was ninety-two, for it took time to get away from the light winds and calms which so often were found around the rainless guano islands. Captain Hauth took over the *Priwall* from the veteran Captain Jürs, who was very ill. The second voyage was much like the first—eighty-one days, Hamburg to Corral, eighty-nine days back from Iquique—except that she managed to get a nitrate cargo homeward. Despite the success of the artificial stuff, there were still advantages in the real, and some market for it. For instance, it was good on Egyptian cotton fields where it killed the boll weevil, which flourished on the artificial nitrates. Many farmers still preferred *nitrato de Chile* as a fertilizer. On the third voyage—his own third in command —Hauth made that remarkable rounding of the Horn. Again he had a good trim with general cargo from Hamburg toward Talcahuano: again the whole passage was done in the excellent time of seventy-two days.

But the passage of the Horn was phenomenal. It was no "romp" before following winds which changed conveniently at all the turning points, as some said enviously: the Horn does know some good weather, of course, but remains tractable for no man. Rather was it the last in a long line of good Cape Horn shipmasters finding *at last* a wonderful chance, interpreting it correctly in all respects and exploiting it with a good ship, to the full.

"It was early in November," said Captain Hauth. "I got through the Strait of Le Maire all right with a strong northwesterly, and drove along before that almost to the south of the Horn. Then we had a day of light easterly, sometimes almost calm, as one does get in the summer. The wind shifted to south, strong and squally. I could use all that under full sail, pounding along. Next came southwesterly winds but by the time the wind shifted to that quarter I was far enough round to use it very well. It worked to the west'ard, of course. I stood on, but I was never near cutting the corner on the Chilean islands. I crossed 55° S. latitude on 75.37° W. longitude, and 50° S. on 79° W.—plenty of sea room.

"These are my noon positions by observation during those six days:

	Latitude	Longitude
Oct. 31	49.55° S.	65.53° W.
Nov. 1	56.08° S.	66.34° W.
2	56.54° S.	69.15° W.
3	55.32° S.	75.37° W.
4	52.22° S.	77.11° W.
5	48.20° S.	78.25° W.

"I looked up the best records in my copy of the *Segelhandbuch* for the Pacific which was aboard, and the best passage recorded there was one of six days and twenty hours by the bark *Parnass* in 1884, and the second best was a week in the *Parsifal* with Robert Hilgendorf, in August of that same year."

Even the redoubtable Hilgendorf, who sailed every ship he was in better than any other master ever had, had never done better than that. Hauth's feat was astonishing. Robert Miethe, last master of the *Potosi,* was in Chile when Hauth came in from his record run.

"I could scarcely believe it," Captain Miethe told me afterward. "At first I thought the reported time of five days, fourteen hours was a newspaper mixup for fourteen days, five hours. When I knew it was not, I wondered, had he cut the corner? It seemed incredible that, at such a late stage, along should come this young fellow with just a good-to-average ship and do better than the lot of us. I went aboard his ship and looked at the charts and the met. records. He hadn't cut any corner. He'd made the best use of the wonderful chance he got, and there he was."*

It was just in time. The *Priwall* sailed back from Iquique to Hamburg in ninety-nine days, taking it easy for that very last homeward run. The next outward passage—Captain Hauth's fourth with her—she came to Chile in seventy-eight days, and reached Valparaiso on September 3, 1939. There she stayed, idle, until June, 1941, when the German ambassador handed her over to the Chilean navy to be a school-ship. By that time only the master, Mrs. Hauth (who had managed to come from Germany after war began), the third mate, the carpenter, and a couple of boys were aboard. The others had melted away, some back to Germany early by devious routes through Japan, others to run the blockade—or try it—in escaping steamships like the *Frankfurt* and *Erlangen.* Many lost their lives.

As for Captain Hauth, he spoke Spanish perfectly from that earlier Chilean sojourn. Ever resourceful, he became port captain of Chile's whaling fleet based on Valparaiso, and stayed with his wife at Viña del Mar until 1953. There were no more sailing ships. This time when he reached home again, he got command of the Laeisz banana motor ship *Pelion,* and stayed in this service until he retired to his native Rendsburg, by the Kiel Canal.

There I found him, waiting for me at the crowded railway station one summer day in 1968. I had not seen him before, but I knew the sailing-ship master at once in all the crowd. Such a man stands out, the strong character in his face developed through much testing of a sort the more ordinary citizens will never know. So I looked at the crowd as I walked along the platform and I saw the *Priwall's* master at a glance. He was a quiet man, well-built to stand the buffetings of wind and sea, a man who didn't need to say anything to establish power of command. I noticed the big, practical hands of the sailor, the firm look in the gray-blue eyes. We walked to his apartment where he lived alone, for Mrs. Hauth had died recently, from cancer. A ship's barometer, a painting of the *Priwall* are the only maritime touches. Outside the windows an endless pageant of shipping passed along the Kiel Canal, mostly motor ships large and small.

* See note at the end of the chapter.

"The pilots tell me that aboard some of those ships there's scarcely a man who can steer," said Captain Hauth. "The officer of the watch has to do the job."

I knew that Captain Hauth came of Mecklenberg seafaring stock. I knew that an uncle, Captain Joachim Hauth, had once sailed the *Seestern* from Newcastle, N. S. W., to Valparaiso in twenty-five days. This was in 1911. A year or two later, he sailed the same ship from the face of the earth—more likely, below the face of the sea—for she had been missing with all hands since 1913. I'd read that, in the Book of the Dead German Seamen—*Ebrenmal Deutscher Seeleute*—in the Hamburg-Altona Museum (a good place to study ships). In that book, published in Hamburg in 1939, are 363 large, closely printed pages, full of the names of Germany's merchant seamen lost in her merchant ships at sea—wrecked, foundered, missing—often by the shipful. When his uncle died, Adolf Hauth was eleven or twelve years old, already determined on a sailing-ship career. His father sailed a 400-ton brig for Laeisz in the Pacific in the 1870's and '80's. His brothers were already at sea.

Well, he didn't regret it. It had great compensations. After all, he was still alive. He told me about the *Bertha,* missing in the North Atlantic since January, 1924. The master was Heinrich Groth, aged thirty-six, his wife, Emilie Elisabeth von Rodden, aged thirty. There was a baby son. They were nice people. Probably some wartime mine still drifting in the Gulf Stream had got them. Several large sailing ships were posted missing about that time. He'd had no presentiment when he cleared out. It was just that it seemed no sense to stay. A man had a sort of sense of living on borrowed time after he knew he had narrowly escaped going missing, especially when others in the family hadn't.

"I was astonished myself at our good fortune with the *Pri-wall*'s good Cape Horn rounding," said the big man, quietly. "We were lucky, of course. When that southwest wind changed to west, it forced me closer to the Chilean coast than I'd have preferred. It came from west with some very heavy squalls. I lowered the tops'ls at times but I set them again immediately the wind allowed. I had to keep her going. The least water I had to leeward was seventy miles. I passed the Evangelistes at the Pacific end of the Strait of Magellan about a hundred miles off.

"We didn't have any single days of great sailing all that voyage. The best twenty-four hours was 236 miles. The *Priwall* was not the fastest ship. When I was with Captain Piening in the *Padua,* she sailed better. But it seemed as if this time the *Priwall* was determined to get past Cape Horn as if she never wanted to be taken there again. From 40° S. in the Atlantic to 40° S. in the Pacific, we were only eleven days. If *that* isn't also a record, I don't know what is.

"I had a lot in my favor. It was summer. She was in nice trim, not down to her marks, loaded with coke and general cargo. I still had a stiffening of the good old sailors—six A.B.'s, four mates (one was mainly instructor for the boys), a carpenter, sailmaker, blacksmith-donkeyman, and bos'n. Up to 1938 we still had some seamen who had never been in a steamer. They knew the sailing-ship work and life, and they preferred that. They were not so old either. Our bos'n in the *Priwall* was a man of fifty or fifty-five. He'd been in sailing ships since he was fourteen. You'd generally find that men like that began in smaller vessels, in the Baltic or North Sea. There you learned thoroughly, the old ways first. After that, Cape Horn was a bit of a break in a pleasant voyage. They didn't like steamers or motor ships. There wasn't enough sailorizing work. It was all hurry-up and worry about the cargo.

"My nineteen passages round the Horn aren't much. The longest I ever was going to the west was nineteen days. The Laeisz ships were strong and properly kept up: you could ask a lot of them and they'd give it."

It was odd that Captain Hauth—who, beyond doing the best he could with his ships, had never particularly sought any records —should be the man in the end to defy the mighty ship-destroying Horn. If the sea gods were moved by thought of such things as justice or the reward of merit long sustained, there were other candidates. Robert Hilgendorf was one, surely, for he was the most consistent among the able earlier masters, the first master of the big *Potosi* which he sailed for her first ten voyages.

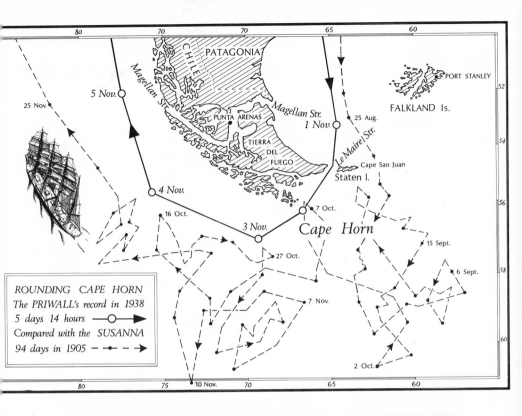

ROUNDING CAPE HORN
The PRIWALL's record in 1938
5 days 14 hours ——◯——▶
Compared with the SUSANNA
94 days in 1905 — •— — —▶

80   70   70   65   60

PATAGONIA
CHILE

5 Nov.

25 Nov.

Magellan Str.

PUNTA ARENAS

Magellan Str.

1 Nov.

25 Aug.

FALKLAND Is.
PORT STANLEY

52

54

TIERRA
DEL
FUEGO

Le Maire Str.

Cape San Juan

Staten I.

4 Nov.

16 Oct.

3 Nov.

27 Oct.

7 Oct.

Cape Horn

15 Sept.

6 Sept.

56

58

7 Nov.

2 Oct.

60

80   75   10 Nov.   70   65   60

Captain Adolf Hauth—Five Days Fourteen Hours!

Making 10 knots. It took time to stop a ship running like this.

Happy Finnish A.B.

The sea rages but the main deck is dry—aboard the JOSEPH CONRAD.

Frömcke, who drove ships so hard he drove himself to madness; that tough Friesian Boye Petersen, who had the *Preussen* first, and little Hinrich Nissen who followed him; big Jürs from the *Peking* and the others; Miethe from the *Pitlochry*, Scots-built, loveliest Laeisz four-master of them all—why not one of these? They all tried manfully, as required in the ordinary process of their voyages. Or that gentle man, Hermann Piening? The outstanding nature of their gifts caused several of these to be moved ashore, to the most difficult administrative post of marine superintendent, while they might still have had many years of useful battle with the Horn before them. Nissen and Miethe were also appointed to the giant five-masters, which must have been trying to sail at any time, with the knowledgeable eyes of the international sailing-ship world focused upon them. To handle them *at all* was the challenge. They had the power and a little of the glory, but they were huge, heavy, outsize to the point of inhumanity. And they both had sailing quirks that made them hard to hold.

"There were times when I felt the *Preussen* was sailing me, not I the big five-master," said Nissen ruefully once. He took the huge ship over from Boye Petersen in 1909, coming from the almost equally huge bark *Potosi* which he had had then for five years—the only master to sail both the five-masters. (He was still in the *Preussen* in 1910 when she was lost, through no fault of his.)

Nissen was in command of eight Cape Horn ships between 1898 and 1925, including the fast *Pitlochry* and the tractable *Peking*. He'd had Laeisz ships in other trades, too. Once he'd sailed a ship called *Parchim* 4,870 sea miles in nineteen days through the west winds, bound from London to Sydney in 1900. He'd been with Laeisz since joining as mate of the iron bark *Plus* in 1892, coming from Rostock ships. He was born at Heiligenhafen, the Baltic port of Holstein, in 1862: at thirty he'd had a great deal of varied experience.

He was a small man, as many of the older seamen were: maybe they'd begun at sea too young and didn't get much chance after that to grow up. Robert Clauss, of that sixty-five day run in the *Priwall* from the Elbe to anchorage in Spencer Gulf, South Australia, was another surprisingly small man—a fiery, whiskered cock of a man with an enormous voice. He, too, had the square jaw, the hard blue eyes, the big competent hands of the seaman. I found him in 1968, running his small farm at Heid-rege-bei-Uitersen, in pleasant country not far from Hamburg. He ran the farm as if it were a ship, and as a hobby made excellent rigged models, mainly the *Preussen,* which he put in bottles and mostly gave away.

Nissen was almost slight enough to be a jockey and he had power of command enough to scare the wildest horse. He had the right touch to get the best out of any ship. When I first saw him (he'd had the *Parma*) I had difficulty in imagining him in command of the big five-masters. I had a vision of him being swept along hidden among the cloud of tremendous sails somewhere on the midships house, a human fragment all but lost among the immense labyrinth of steel masts and stays and yards and sails, yet in unquestioned command and constant control of them all as the vast creation hurled itself along in the sea.

I learned a lot more of Hinrich (called Hein) Nissen later from my friend Herman Theilig, sales manager of the early American Airlines when I first knew him. (These Cape Horn men turn up anywhere. Many took up flying.) Herman was an able seaman in the *Parma* after his service in the First World War, when she was recommissioned as a Laeisz ship. She had been briefly under the British flag, as allocated in the "reparations" spoils, but was sold back as not required. The official temporary British owners are listed as the General Steam Navigation Company which operated in the short sea trades. What they could have used a big four-masted bark for, one doesn't know. These were troubled times: perhaps there was some idea of using her as a stores or accommodation ship somewhere.

So soon after the war life in the recommissioned *Parma* under the German flag was very hard. Herman Theilig sailed in her at a time when extreme care had to be used in the expenditure of every penny in case it was never replaced—not at anything like its old value, anyway. After the style of ships like the *Potosi* and *Preussen,* at the time she was a sad decline for Captain Nissen, though he knew that he was fortunate then to have a ship at all.

The *Parma's* long, open main deck and her quarters in (and control from) the poop made her not the first choice of senior Laeisz masters, used to the greater safety of their midships accommodation and better control of the ship from there. But she was a good ship with nothing brutish about her: she handled and sailed well, and got along if Neptune as much as drew a deep breath.

There was another reason for masters to worry a little about her, in the early 1920's. She was laid up at Iquique for six years because of the 1914–18 war. The sea grass grew on her. Some optimist got the idea of removing this by working mooring chains along the bottom, handling the ends of a bight of chain from the deck and dragging it along held against the hull. This knocked away some of the sea growth, the longer barnacles and such. It also removed much of the protective paint. Since she was not dry-docked throughout this long lay-up, this was a serious matter. The bottom plates became pitted. How good were they? Test borings showed a few millimeters of steel gone in the deeper pits, but sufficient seemed left to hold her together. (Indeed there was. We had her until 1937, during which time she was reclassed after careful survey. Of course the pitting, such as it was, had been smoothed over before we bought her. We were supposed not to know about it, but this, and the shipping slump, were the reasons for the low price we paid.)

Anyway, in 1921 Nissen took her, keeping whatever doubts he might have had to himself. His company was making a fighting gesture, he knew, in trying to pick up the pieces of its sailing ships again and rebuild their trade. Herr Laeisz had also bought back his four-masted barks *Pamir, Passat,* and *Peking,* and the ships *Pinnas* and *Peiho.* The *Parma* cost him £10,000, the *Passat* £13,000 the *Peiho* and *Pinnas* £6,000 each. At the time this (with the cost of the others) represented a considerable investment and quite an act of faith. There were enough good captains and officers available: crews were another matter. In the generally upset conditions of the times men continued thoroughly disturbed by the unholy mess their "betters" had made of the world: if somebody came along with what looked like a better system of life, they were for it. In the meantime they were not at all convinced that it was worth working again for those who had helped to raise so long and profound a turmoil. But they had to eat. The *Parma* found a crew of sorts, mostly green hands and one or two scallywags: not professional or determined troublemakers, for these could do better ashore. Among them were a few real sailors as essential stiffening.

With this bunch, off went little Nissen to take on the Horn once more. His greatest difficulty was the familiar limejuicers' problem—poor and not enough food. It was not so long since Germany had been close to starving: storing ships was still very difficult and expensive. Nissen faced such a test as he had never taken on before but, by dint of his competence and fairmindedness, and the 100 percent innate decency so obvious about him, he managed.

He had troubles. Herman Theilig, one of his real sailors, told me of them and how Captain Nissen came through.

"What I remember best of him," wrote Herman, "was his bellow. When he roared the guys on the royal yard had no trouble hearing him no matter how loud the wind blew. I always remember how surprised I was when I heard that big roar come out of that little fellow. I had good opportunity to watch him when I had the wheel. I don't remember him ever talking to anybody except the mates. He had a friendly and very intelligent face. He never made an effort to be tough, but everybody had a lot of respect for him as a man and as a seaman. We all knew that he had been in command of the *Preussen* when it went on the Dover rocks. It surely wasn't his fault, otherwise he would never have gotten the *Parma*. So, his main characteristic was that he was highly respected. The crew neither liked nor disliked him, but they were inclined to consider him a fair man. Under normal circumstances, I am sure he would have been not only a fair man, but also a kindly man. As things were he was a bit handicapped.

"The food aboard was goshawful! It seemed that we mostly ate *Doerrgmuese.* That means cabbage and other vegetables shredded and dried and kept stacked in warehouses until used. They fed that to the German population and the army during the war. Undoubtedly what we had on the *Parma* was left over from the war. It was bought up by Laeisz and that was our main fare. And then we had a sort of 'flour soup.' We could never figure out what it was, except that it had dried fruit in it, apples or pears with the seeds still in them. We liked that soup until one day, when one of the fellows cut one of the fruit in half while it was still in his soup, what was inside turned out to be a dead and dried-up mouse. A mouse might have been only in that particular piece, but that finished our appetite for our favorite dish. We would also now and then get a portion of hardtack. It was full of maggots. Of course we were fed salt horse, beef salted down and so old that it was absolutely black and stringy and tasteless. The best part of the salt horse was that it was full of maggots. When we got soup with salt horse in it, the top of the soup was a layer of maggots. We just ignored them and ate them as fresh meat.

"We had a young crew, with only a few having sailed on a square-rigger before. Quite a few didn't know a thing about splicing, tying knots, or handling the wheel. To make matters worse, we left Hamburg in early December and ran into tough weather in the Bay of Biscay. We didn't get any rest day or night, were wet all the time, and those who had some experience stayed up on the yards more often and longer than we had bargained for. In spite of all this I do not remember any of the first-timers being in the way, or being weak in their knees. All I remember is that the work got done. The bos'n and the mates must have sworn under their breath or loudly at all the work they had to do on account of an inexperienced crew, but I don't remember anyone griping at any time. On Christmas Eve, in the Bay of Biscay, the cook had prepared a punchbowl for the crew to celebrate with. As he was balancing it over the deck toward our deckhouse, a big wave happened to wash over the side and swept him and the bowl into the scuppers. That was our Christmas celebration. If I remember rightly, we were all called to the poop for a swig of rum. Then we got into the *nortada* and sailed in no time at all down the Portuguese coast. I remember a glimpse of the Canaries, I guess it was, or the Cap Verdes, or both. I am hazy on that.

And then we got into the blue skies of the trades. By that time we were a damn good crew.

"You know more about heavy weather at sea than anybody. So, I am not telling you about the Biscay in order to entertain you with the description of how one feels in a black night when you go aloft to secure a sail that somebody hadn't nailed down tight. I am going into these details to explain that Captain Nissen was a fine and most capable seaman. With a green crew, and just out of home port, caught in the Biscay with a four-masted bark, and we must have been there almost a week (at least it seemed that long), and I don't remember him ever losing his cool. I assume that the Portuguese *nortada* is a wind that is always there. Anyhow, he found it and it took us out of the tough weather and into the trades.

"As another example of his seamanship, after we had passed the Falkland Islands, he headed for the Le Maire Strait as a short-cut to the Horn. It seems to me that it was the first mate who told me about it during my turn at the wheel. Whoever it was mentioned that he hoped that the wind would stay fair. As we were in the strait, I could see why he was worried. We could see the ribs and what was left of other ships which tried to go through there and for which the wind had not held fair. As it would happen, our wind veered for the bad just as we were clearing the strait and we all breathed a sigh of relief. I believe that we had lost so much time in Biscay that Captain Nissen hoped to make up time by cutting through Le Maire. He made it by a hair. It showed to us that putting the *Preussen* on the rocks at Dover hadn't taken any wind out of his sails, and we admired him for it.

"Getting back to the trade winds, the weather improved, but the food got worse. It got so bad that the crew decided to complain to the captain. The crew really were a fine bunch of fellows then. Some were the sons of *Elbe-Lotsen* (Elbe pilots) who were going to become pilots. Others were from seafaring families. None were looking for trouble. All of this was something new to me, because I had just signed off a Danish bark on which I had made a five-month voyage to Santos, Brazil. Our food had been like heaven compared to what we had on the *Parma.* However, I had signed on for the voyage and I was going to see it through no matter what. So I wasn't in any particular mood for trouble. However, some of the fellows were breaking out with boils, and the bad food was telling on them. To make matters worse, there were some chickens on board. One by one they went on the captain's table. A small pig had been butchered but we saw nothing of it. Some of the crew started talking that we should complain to the skipper. Because everybody really was an all right guy, and because the complaint was just, we all went along and moved as a group aft to the poop where the skipper and the mates were standing at the railing.

"I don't know who the spokesman was; I have forgotten. Anyhow, somebody bravely told the skipper the story in a nice way. Gosh, you should have heard him explode. That big bellow of his simply roared out calling everybody a landlubber who couldn't splice, tie a knot, go aloft without breaking their necks —and now this bunch of landlubbers was complaining to him about the food. Well, I would have lived through the whole thing without batting an eye. But when he classified everybody as a landlubber who wasn't fit to be in a sailing ship, I raised myself up a bit and told him that there were some in the crew who had a right to resent that. With that he turned all of a sudden friendly and called some of us by name as being good sailors who had helped to get the ship out of Biscay. He just stayed friendly and promised that he would take a look a the matter and see what could be done about it. Yes, he was very fair. When he saw that this was not a ganging-up on the part of the crew, he immediately stopped barking and tried to be helpful. I thought that this was very good of him, and very smart, because he re-established the good feeling which he had had aboard.

"Thereafter the food did improve some. Best of all, we began right away to get a ration of lime juice—so much per head every day. That helped a lot. We all knew that the provisions were skimpy and that the skipper could not help that very much. Anyhow, we decided to do something in our own self-interest. One of the guys, as we were in the trade, with the hatches open for ventilation and to shift the cargo a bit better (we had coal and goods in boxes) whispered to us that he had found a way to the bulkhead behind which were the ship's stores. In examining the situation closely, it was found that one of the planks could be prised open wide enough for someone to slip in there and see what was in the storeroom. There was some cheese, some sausages, but it would be too obvious if any of those items should be disturbed. However, there were a number of five-gallon cans (I guess that was the size) of English marmalade. If one of them disappeared it might not be discovered right away. So one of them was extracted through the opening. Then the plank was put back in place and nobody could see that it had been tampered with. After dark the can was sneaked into the deckhouse. Everybody participated. We didn't have any bread or anything else to eat with the marmalade, but we all had our stomachs full of the sweet stuff—it was heaven! We hadn't had anything sweet for so long that it tasted out of this world just licking the goo off your hand.

"We never were quite clear as to whether the evaporation of the can was blamed on us, or whether the poop concluded the broker had cheated them. Anyhow, the empty can was silently dumped overboard, and everybody felt that some sort of justice had been done.

"Another innovation which was instituted by the skipper was that, if we would beat our hardtack into smooth flour, we could take it to the cook who would put some spices to it and bake it in the oven and make cake out of it. Of course, the "cake" was almost as hard as had been the hardtack, but we ate it and thought nothing tasted better. So the complaint to the skipper had some good effects. We were indeed a happy ship. We had a good cook, and he was on our side as much as he could be.

"You may remember from the logbook that it was a one-year voyage. In the meantime, everything had gone completely to pot in Germany. The inflation which was already bad enough when we left had really gone on a rampage. The German paper money was in the millions and was worthless. I remember that very clearly because when we got paid off in Hamburg my earnings for the year's voyage were a big wad of paper money for all of which

I couldn't even buy a pair of shoes. They paid us the amount in Reichsmarks for which we had signed, and they paid with inflated money. It was a bit scurvy on their part. Well, nothing could be done about it, and we all took it philosophically. It was then that I decided not to make the sea my career. So, it was all for the good. Of course, Nissen had nothing to do with that. In fact, he probably got paid in the same manner.

"At the time I felt badly about the line, but they were probably so broke that they couldn't help themselves. It was a matter of getting the ships going again from scratch. That was the reason for the bad food and skimpiness of reserve gear. Anyhow, I wouldn't take a million for the experience and the memories. The *Parma* was a great ship—not very fast but sturdy and good sailing. I remember quite a few times when we were in bad weather with the storm and the waves listing her to the point where she would hesitate and then one could feel her shudder as if one more inch would be the end of her, and then she would slowly, ever so slowly, come up again and stick her masts up into the howling storm to do more battle. Yes, she was a good ship.

"And Nissen was a fine seaman and a good master. In my book he was among the best. I have told you about bad weather to show him as a seaman who could handle the ship and the weather. When I mentioned the green crew, I did so because he changed them in no time into an efficient gang of sailors. As far as the food is concerned I have gone into detail to indicate that he had a tough assignment. In retrospect, I give Nissen a lot of credit for having been so patient and understanding on all occasions. There were many times when he could have been tough and when he could have given some of the fellows a black mark which would have haunted them for the rest of their lives. I am sure that he didn't do it because he didn't want to ruin anybody's future. Nothing ever happened which could be classified as a major offense. On the other hand, some of the situations which I have mentioned, and many others, could have grown to serious problems if it hadn't been for Nissen's kindliness. My reaction to him is based strictly on having been around him for almost a year. I never was very good in shining up to anybody on the poop.

I wanted to be a good sailor and be considered as such. If he hadn't been a fine sailor, an exceptionally good officer, and a kindly man, I would have smelled him out in no time at all."

"He was a splendid master and a hard driver," wrote Hermann Piening of Captain Nissen, "but one who always knew what he was doing, and was better liked by his crews than the average."

He died quietly in 1945, aged eighty-three.

The loss of the big *Preussen* off Dover was in no way his fault. It was caused by a piece of plain bad seamanship on the part of the master of the British cross-Channel steamer *Brighton* which, misjudging the five-master's speed and regardless of the international rule of the road which required him to give the sailing ship a clear berth, took a chance and smashed into the *Preussen*. There was nothing that Nissen could do to avoid collision. The wind was then light, his *Preussen* making only a few knots under all sail. Her few lights were burning brightly. The steamer was hurrying along at 17 knots, fully maneuverable. All he had to do was to alter course slightly, in time. But he did not. Even then, the hull was undamaged, but most of the foremast was brought down and the anchors made unusable. The *Preussen* could not be worked properly: she took the ground: tugs could not move her: bad weather came up, and that was that.

The loss of the *Preussen* before the war and the *Peiho* after the war, both full of general cargo meant for the Christmas trade in Chile, were serious blows to the Laeisz Line and its cargo service under sail. Merchants had relied on Laeisz. A valuable consignment of German pianos was lost with the *Preussen*, as well as all the lump sugar meant for Christmas. The *Peiho*, too, had grand pianos, as well as glassware, chinaware, furniture, thousands of cases of lump sugar, all sorts of supplies for druggists and chemists' stores and dispensaries, hardware, thousands of boots and shoes as well as tools, steel wire, foundry items, bathtubs, and a thousand tons of cement in barrels of 180 kilos each. She went in the Strait of Le Maire—that always menacing backdoor—and with her went the goodwill of a lot of shippers who had been served well by Laeisz for years. "P" Line sailing ships' advantages over power were good stowage (damage or loss to cargo was so rare that it was not even insured against) and, except for these accidents, good delivery. Both damage and pilferage were avoided by the use of the company's own permanent stevedoring gangs, and gear. Against them was the fact that filling up on loading berth in Hamburg could take four or five weeks, and steamers could make two or even two and half round voyages while even the fastest sailer was making one. So merchants' money was tied up longer in the sailing ships' cargoes.

NOTE: CAPTAIN LEARMONT CLAIMED A RECORD PASSAGE FROM 50° S. ATLANTIC TO 50° S. PACIFIC PAST THE HORN OF FIVE DAYS AND ONE HOUR, MADE IN THE *Brenhilda* BETWEEN JULY 9 AND 14, 1902. IF HE CLAIMED IT, HE MADE IT, AND IT *was* CERTAINLY A RECORD. HE GIVES ONLY TWO NOON POSITIONS—49° 50′ S. LATITUDE 65° 05′ W. LONGITUDE ON JULY 9, 50° 20′ S. LATITUDE, 76° 44′ W. LONGITUDE ON JULY 14. CAPTAIN LEARMONT WAS FREE TO SAIL HIS OWN ROUTE: HE MET FAVORING SOUTHERLY WINDS, FREEZING COLD BUT VERY USEFUL, AND LATER NORTHWESTERLIES WHICH HE TOOK ON HIS PORT BEAM TAKING SOMETHING OF A CHANCE OF BEING JAMMED ON THE DANGER-OUS ISLANDS OF PATAGONIA. LAEISZ SHIPS WERE INSTRUCTED TO GO TO 78° OR 80° W. AND NOT TO CROSS 50° S. (PACIFIC) TO THE EAST OF THAT. LEARMONT SAW THE LAND BUT STOOD ON "AS NORTHWESTERLY WINDS DO NOT LAST LONG ON THAT COAST." JUST AS WELL.

CAPTAIN HAUTH CROSSED HIS SECOND 50° S. ON THE PACIFIC LONGITUDE OF 78° W. HE CUT IT RATHER FINE BY LAEISZ STANDARDS, AS HE HAD CROSSED 52° S. ON 77° 11′ W. BUT THERE HE WAS WELL OUT FROM THE LAND, IN A STREAM ALREADY SETTING NORTHWARD.

IT IS ODD THAT, AS FAR AS ONE KNOWS, NONE OF THE GREATLY PUBLICIZED CLIPPERS EVER CLAIMED A FASTER 50°-TO-50° PASSAGE THAN SIX DAYS, AND ONLY THE *Young America,* APPARENTLY, EVER CLAIMED THAT (ACCORDING TO CAPTAIN ARTHUR H. CLARK'S BOOK *The Clipper Ship Era**). NO DATES OR DETAILS ARE GIVEN. IT IS NOT MENTIONED IN CARL CUTLER'S EXHAUSTIVE STUDY, *500 Sailing Records of American-built Ships,* PUBLISHED BY THE MARINE HISTORICAL ASSOCIATION INC. AT THE MYSTIC SEA-PORT. CARL CUTLER, AN EARNEST AND COMPETENT STUDENT OF SAIL WHO WAS ONCE A SEAMAN, DOES NOT DEAL WITH WEST-BOUND 50°-TO-50° "RECORDS" AT ALL, THOUGH HIS EXHAUSTIVE WORK MENTIONS EVERYTHING ELSE. PERHAPS THEY WERE MERELY INCIDENTAL TO CLIPPER PASSAGES, BUT IN THE NITRATE TRADE THEY WERE VITAL.

* G. P. Putnam's Sons, New York and London, 1920.

Chapter fourteen

FIVE-MASTER CAPTAIN

IN 1970 one last master survives from the handful of five-masted square-rigged ships the world has known. There only were seven —six five-masted barks (two French, both named *France,* two Germans of the Bremen Rickmers Line, another German built for the Laeisz Line named *Potosi,* and the postwar Danish school-ship *København*) and one five-masted full-rigged ship, the Laeisz Line's *Preussen.* Only the two Laeisz vessels and the first *France* had no auxiliary power. All seven came to bad ends. Three are missing, one burned, one was destroyed by collision with a steamship, one was wrecked, the seventh sunk by submarine in the First World War. The longest-lived and the most successful was the Laeisz Line's five-masted bark *Potosi,* of 4,026 tons, built in 1895 and burned out off the coast of Argentina in 1921, after being laid up in Valparaiso harbor throughout the First World War.

There was something odder than their giant appearance about these five-masters. I saw only one, the second *France*—the first vanished before I was born—towing up the Yarra into Melbourne docks about 1918. I was used to big full-rigged ships and four-masted barks, and I was familiar then with at least one six-masted barkentine (which resembled a five-masted schooner trying hopelessly to catch up with one lone out-of-place square-rigged mast). Maybe the *France* looked inhuman, at least as if one man ought not to be required to sail her nor seamen expected to handle all that multitude of sails—an unnecessary development, a riveted creation shaped like a sailing ship asking

259

too much of God and men. I watched her towed out of sight, still astonished, and I had no desire to go in such a ship at all.

Half a century later I met Captain Robert Miethe, the last surviving man who ever had to handle one of these monstrosities. He was the last master of the *Potosi* under the German flag, and he had commanded her for two voyages and a half in the Cape Horn trade. I sensed almost at once that he had some reluctance to expand about her. The four-masted bark *Pitlochry* he obviously preferred, even the heavy ship *Pampa* or the small, well-behaved bark *Prompt.* He had, he told me, asked to be excused from accepting the appointment when offered promotion as mate of the *Preussen* early in 1905—the biggest sailing-ship mate's job in the world. The owners were surprised, but they did not force the appointment upon him.

Perhaps not only I reacted oddly to these giant ships. I sensed, too, that a man appointed to command one of them must accept sharp focus upon his every deed and every passage from the eyes of the maritime world. He could and would do his best quietly in the other ships, but in either the *Preussen* or the *Potosi* he would have to make not only good voyages but the *best,* all the time. It could be impossible. It must be a great strain on a man. In 1905, the famous Robert Hilgendorf had recently left the *Potosi:* Hilgendorf was without doubt the most able sea warrior who ever regularly did battle with the Horn. He had a sixth sense for the wind. He was gifted, resolute, a man of steel. But the Horn had taken one ship from him, the bark *Parsifal* in 1886, when he had been very fortunate to get all hands safely away in the boats. He had the *Potosi* after that from the stocks for some ten years. That was enough for him. It seemed that he wanted no part of the *Preussen,* either. (By comparison with that five-masted full-rigged ship, the *Potosi* was a graceful slip of a ship, almost like a big clipper.)

Rather than take on the *Preussen,* Hilgendorf took himself ashore after the *Potosi*'s tenth Chilean voyage, aged fifty. For twenty years he had been defying Cape Horn with ships, barks, three-, four-, and five-masted, from 650 to more than 4,000 tons. He had done very well. He never said so, but it could be that he found the *Potosi* a handful and knew the *Preussen* could be worse. A five-masted bark, after all, is a lot handier than a five-masted full-rigged ship with *all* her huge masts carrying the full square rig. Perhaps he knew things about both ships that I certainly didn't—indeed, that few people ever had and no one alive now could possibly know, except Robert Miethe. Robert Hilgendorf was killed when a collision pitched him from his bicycle in the Hamburg streets when he was over eighty. His trail was cold long before I could get near it, after the Second World War.

I knew of Robert Miethe. All sailing-ship professionals did. I knew he lived in Chile, somewhere near Valparaiso. I heard that he was coming to Europe in 1968 to attend a meeting of the International Company of Cape Horn Master Mariners, as he is a member of the German section. So, indeed, am I (and of the Finnish). So I went to Hamburg to meet him and learn about those giant five-masters—learn *really* about them, I mean, not listen to a lot of second-hand and fifth-hand colored reminiscences passed on cheerfully by the credible, the gullible and the foolish who had not been there. They were a great technical achievement: that was obvious. Why then hadn't they been fore-runners of a dynasty? What was their effect upon *men?* Above all, on the men who had commanded them.

Captain Miethe, aged ninety, was still a square block of granite surmounted by a smaller block, the massive combination provided with long arms and carried squarely upon two sturdy legs. Kindly but penetrating gray-blue eyes looked quietly at the world, long ears that missed no note of the wind emphasized the broad brow: the close-clipped, grizzled white hair of a mustache was kept in firm order. The big hands of the practical seaman, the powerful, incisive voice of the man used to commanding by that alone the immense and noisy area of great square-rigged ships —these marked him out. He was not a tall man—these Cape Horners rarely run to height: perhaps the wind kept them down (or, more probably, the diet). He stood straight as the mainmast. He had no hearing-aid, no stick to lean on, no spectacles, no sign whatever of his score of years beyond man's allotted span. He looked well fitted for another score.

But for some time, he would not talk about those five-masters at all. All the others, yes, with obvious pleasure, even some which had been tougher than enough. But the *Potosi,* the *Preussen?* He remembered the names. A cold look came into his eyes at the mention of them. He talked of his career, of going to school in a Holstein village and shipping in minute Baltic craft as little more than a lad from his farmstead home on the Baltic side of Schleswig-Holstein, of seven years of deepwater wandering before the mast in the Cape Horn trade after that, of the long climb abaft the mast and the hard years before it, of his first command—the Laeisz bark *Prompt,* a German-built 1,500-tonner —at the age of twenty-eight, when he had been fourteen years at sea; of long years in tough "P" ships before that and afterward —the ship *Pampa,* a ship so temperamental that the company appointed no man to her as master who had not served in her well as mate: that other problem ship the *Pamir,* a sort of dog with a bad name though she was only six years old when he took her— heavy, sluggish in anything short of half a gale, fat in the buttocks and full of drag but powerful as a 3,000-ton elephant; with between the too-tender *Pampa* and the too tough *Pamir,* the Scots-built *Pitlochry,* the tractable, the faithful, the so-friendly and responsive ship, his great and lasting love. He had done well in them all, the young Miethe (for he was young as average Cape Horn masters go, only thirty-five when appointed to the *Potosi*).

Then suddenly he was promoted to sail the biggest Cape Horn ship left in the world—one of the biggest there ever was. (It was 1912: the *Preussen* was a wreck off Dover.) He was appointed suddenly, unexpectedly, because she had driven the redoubtable Frömcke mad. I realized for the first time what such a command could mean. Mates and masters had no periods of recuperative leave then spread through their years in hard-sailed company ships. For seven years he'd been a *driving* master, *required* to maintain fast passages and fast turn-around.

"My ships can and shall make fast voyages," read Herr Laeisz's personal instructions: he meant exactly what he said. The pressure was on all the time. It didn't mean so much in a *Prompt* or a *Pampa,* for the first was small and the second cantankerous, but a new master was watched closely by a shore staff who knew about ships, and cared. He soon showed what he was made of—the better a master was, the further he went. Seniority as such had nothing to do with it. The company had no commodores: it paid bonuses to all its masters for all profitable voyages, and switched them around from ship to ship. The larger the ship the bigger the bonus. So the *Potosi* was Number One command in Laeisz (and in the sailing-ship world, for the only other five-masted barks existing in 1912, the *R. C. Rickmers* and the second *France,* were both powerful auxiliaries).

Master of the *Potosi* at thirty-five? Miethe was not anything of a flamboyant character, as the Graf Felix von Luckner was, nor a cold, determined driving man like Hilgendorf or Boye Petersen, or the bull-voiced gale-riding little Hein Nissen—magnificent seamen all of them, but different. The *Potosi* would be a supreme test: and in 1912 she was seventeen years old, all 4,026 tons of her with that 366-feet-long by 50-foot-beam Tecklenborg hull, and the enormous masts that towered over everything in Hamburg's *Segelschiffshafen* and stood out boldly even against the backdrop of the Andes. For fifteen years a ship may hold her prime and another ten after that, perhaps. But just how good was the *Potosi* in 1912? She had driven the driver Frömcke mad: what had *he* done to her? Shipmasters—and seamen—talked, and they talked with knowledge. Frömcke had touched on Smith's Knoll with her deep-loaded, in the North Sea. Touched? How hard? There was talk that it was a real knock: she wasn't the same ship afterward though the same passages were expected of her. *Nobody* could go in either of the Laeisz five-masters (while the *Preussen* lasted) and not make outstanding passages in them—the *best* passages of all the fleets.

That was the myth, anyway. Robert Miethe had reason to know, better than anyone, that it was a myth, for he had twice sailed the *Pitlochry* back from Chile with better passages than the *Preussen,* once by twenty days. Sailing in early 1909 from the nitrate port eleven days after the giant ship, he had the *Pitlochry* in Hamburg nine days before she arrived. Nothing was said publicly about this at all. Nissen had the *Preussen* then. The logs of the voyages—deck, navigation, meteorological—were carefully examined and compared in the office. Nissen had done the best possible with the winds—and the ice fields—he met. Miethe did better with better winds and avoided much of the ice.

Nissen got in very light winds between Iquique and the edge of the Roaring Forties, and in an ice field north of the Falklands. So did Miethe, but he reached the ice later, managed to skim the field, and make maximum use of the winds off the South American east coast: he picked up better winds leaving the west coast, too. Some of this could be luck. A ship gains nothing by sailing early and then being becalmed: a later sailing might well bring the latecomer on the wings of a wind she carried with her to the heels of her becalmed rival ahead. (Not that Miethe's *Pitlochry* and Nissen's *Preussen* were rivals. Each tried to make the best passage possible, and on this occasion Nissen came off worst.) On this voyage, in late 1909, the *Preussen* was ninety-three days from Tocopilla to Cuxhaven, eighty-three to the Lizard, off Falmouth.

In the office, in the press, nothing was said about the *Pitlochry*'s better passage. But it was noted. On the very next voyage, Miethe beat the *Preussen* with the *Pitlochry* again, this time by six days. He was sent to the *Pamir* immediately afterward, to see what he could do with her. No one had succeeded in getting very good passages out of her: neither did Miethe. The trouble was that she needed strong winds to drive her: such winds can never be consistently expected over passages of eleven and twelve thousand miles. Perhaps the *Pamir* would have done better in the Australian or New Zealand trade, with the world to encircle in the wild west winds every voyage. (She did, later.)

Miethe had not succeeded in doing better with the *Pitlochry* than the *Potosi*, passage for passage. Perhaps she was a little more tractable than the *Preussen,* though both were Tecklenborg ships, built at Geestemünde. (Hamburg ships built by Blohm and Voss, like the *Pamir,* were usually considered to be a little heavier.)

How did he find the *Potosi* handled? Had Frömcke's mad driving affected her? (He would sail any ship on its ear, maybe lose three or four men washed overboard every voyage.) Was the

Potosi really a super-ship? I asked: but I had to wait until I could spend a little time on the Miethe *quinta* at Quilpué, on the Santiago-Valparaiso line not far inland from Viña del Mar, to find the answers.

First, I learned about his career.

Born in July, 1877, on a small farm at a little place called Lippe Kreis Plön in Holstein, he was the youngest of four sons of a small farmer who died not long after he was born. It was a wild, bleak place, especially in winter, not far from the sea. The boy Miethe could see vessels in Kiel Bay off the coast of Holstein. He was interested in these ships and early expressed the wish to serve at sea. None of the Miethes of his immediate family were seamen. His mother hoped he would grow away from this odd desire, for there was much to do on the farm. He did not give up the idea: at the age of fourteen he was off in a little thing called the *Emma,* a galeass, hailing from Laboe, not far from Kiel. Her living was made by fishing up stones from the bed of the Baltic left there by the ice in some glacial era of long ago. The little vessel's very small crew fished up the stones, and brought them in when they had a cargo to sell for lining the sides of the Kiel–North Sea Canal, then under construction. It was good business but hard. The crew of three or four did everything: it was a good school.

Widow Miethe prayed for the day when the canal would need no more stones, at least at the Kiel end. The day came in 1893 but, instead of quietly giving up his hard career, her Robert traveled to Hamburg—the nearest great port—and shipped away as deck boy in the Laeisz bark *Pamelia,* of 1,438 tons, built at Hamburg and then only five years old. The boy had been recommended to begin with Laeisz. They were as hard owners as any, but fair, and they always tried to employ the best officers, preferring those who had begun in coasters.

Though a giantess beside the stone-fisher *Emma,* the *Pamelia* was a handy bark where a lad could make a real contribution on the higher sails. The crew worked the usual two-watch system of four hours on, four hours off, with an unwelcome variation (common in German ships then) known as "ten and three." This meant that two hours were lost from the daylight watches below, for the eight A.M. to noon watch below had to come on deck to work until ten after half an hour for breakfast, and the afternoon watch below came on deck again between two and three P.M. after an hour off for their midday meal. Nobody got too much sleep, but the boys were allowed half an hour off—in the ship's time— to clear up after meals.

"I stopped this ten and three system when I got command of the *Pitlochry,*" Captain Miethe told me. "It was hard, and it wasn't really necessary as we had good crews—always thirty-two or thirty-four in a four-master, good men. Laeisz didn't exploit the British brace winches he put in the bigger ships to cut down on the crews. With the halyard winches, they meant that it was not nearly so often necessary to call out all hands. You could work the ship with the watch on deck—safer, too. When the decks filled up the few men at the brace winch could just jump up on it and hang on to the wires, first clamping on the brake which took a second. So you saved them. Nobody could keep on sailing a ship with worn-out men. If the sea washed them over, nobody could get them back from a running ship. It was a hard life still, of course. It just was that way, if you had to fight the Horn. But our owners installed everything that helped their crews in their fight."

But, he added, compared with common practices aboard some American ships and all Bluenoses, it was easy. He did not go in such ships. The only foreign ship he sailed in was a Norwegian named *Hera,* for a voyage to Japan. He was in no hurry to get to mate's school, and he wandered the world as able seaman in deepwater barks and ships for years, always on round voyages, usually in the trade around the Horn to Chile. He had to save money for mate's school, and that took time. He was young, and found always plenty to learn about seamen's work and sail-handling, about the stowage of cargoes, particularly nitrate; about the handling of seamen themselves, getting the best out of them. Sometimes he sailed with a bad master: then he learned what *not* to do. Some were drunks, a very few incompetent, even fewer both drunk and incompetent.

The last ship in which he sailed as A.B. was the same *Susanna* in which Captain Piening later began his career. I gathered that she gave Miethe a bad time, too. The master was new to the Chilean nitrate trade, his mates not. He considered the established method of stowing the heavy sacks of this stuff to be wrong. It was all stowed by one Chilean working in the hold, taking one 180-kilogram sack on his head at a time, as it was hoisted aboard, carrying it a carefully planned minimum distance and then, with a twist of his tremendous shoulders, dropping it in precisely the place where it should be, working always to a well-tried plan which gave the ship two-thirds of her cargo perfectly pyramided in the lower hold, and a third built up in the 'tween-decks, each bag fitting into its patterned place locked there and helping to lock others. Nitrates set hard and carried perfectly when stowed in this manner. Such cargoes were never known to shift, though being so heavy, they had plenty of room to shift in. But this fool forbade such stowage, demanding that the full cargo be in the lower hold.

He was the master and appeared to be sober. But the poor *Susanna,* working like a high-speed pendulum, didn't get far before she had to stagger back to port and have the cargo restowed properly, fortunate not to have flung half her spars overboard.

The *Susanna*'s voyage was long: Miethe had saved enough for mate's school. By the beginning of 1900 he had been eight years at sea and was twenty-two years old. It was time to move abaft the mast (an old British expression which meant nothing literal in the large German ships. In older sailing ships, officers lived in the poop behind the aftermost mast—hence the expression. Seamen lived before the mast—in merchantmen right in the eyes of the ship with the windlass: later, in a steel house on the foredeck still called the forecastle though no longer a "castle" of any sort. In warships they lived on the uncomfortable gun decks, while those abaft the mast had the commodious aftercastle for quarters. So the expression meant something then.)

His schooling at the village, though elementary, had been thorough, and Captain Miethe early acquired the habit of reading. He had studied English to read Dickens, whose books he loved. He had been able to study the theory of navigation at sea —not the practice, for many German ships followed the same ideas as the British with charts and instruments strictly the master's property. It was no problem. There was time at the well-run nautical school—at least six months—to get down to it properly. In due course, young Miethe took his mate's certificate at the first sitting.

Before joining the Laeisz Line, he decided to make an Australian voyage in a bark named *Apollo,* a former limejuicer of 1,170 tons built of iron at West Hartlepool in 1884. She was a handy bark and a good sailer, which was just as well, for, during the couple of years that Miethe was her second mate, she had no effective master at all. There was a master aboard, a man of fifty-nine who had just been promoted, in the absence of other applicants. After thirty-five years as a mate, now he could give undivided attention to his real career, which was drink. This he did. Unfortunately—or perhaps fortunately for the ship—this odd master had long grown far too accustomed to being mate and showed no inclination to act as master at all. He was "a 100 percent, soaked-in-the-barrel, hard-working professional drunk"—indeed, his two mates thought he probably had been born in a barrel, or reared from several. There were two mates only, the chief, named Battenberg (an excellent seaman, later prominent in the port of Bremen), and Second Mate R. Miethe.

"We became the watch-keeping captains," the old man told me. "It was the time of the Boer War and we had a couple of charters between South Australia and Cape Town. On some of these passages we did not see the master on deck at all, not from the beginning to the end. He just left us to sail the ship. It was wonderful experience for me. Of course, we tried to report to him every watch, but it was useless. He had a row of seven bottles behind the pillow in his bunk. I think they were of various strengths. According to the howling of the wind when we were east-bound, he'd reach for such and such a bottle. In a full gale he got to number seven and then he was unconscious!"

Battenberg and Miethe enjoyed the unique experience. It

Captain Robert Miethe, of the PITLOCHRY, PAMPA, POTOSI, *at the age of 93.*

The German five masted barque POTOSI

Adrian Small '70

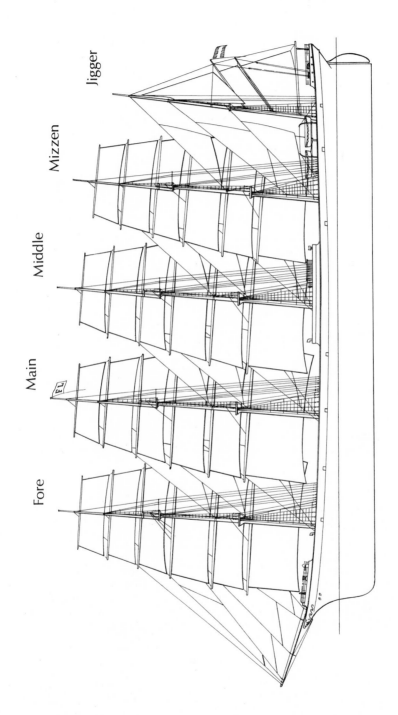

Fore   Main   Middle   Mizzen   Jigger

Sail plan of the POTOSI, built in 1895

Adrian Small '70

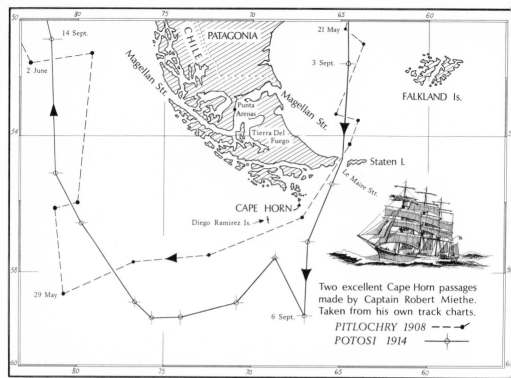

Two excellent Cape Horn passages made by Captain Robert Miethe. Taken from his own track charts.

PITLOCHRY 1908 — – – •
POTOSI 1914 ——○——

14 Sept.
2 June
21 May
3 Sept.
FALKLAND Is.
Magellan Str.
CHILE
PATAGONIA
Punta Arenas
Tierra Del Fuego
Magellan Str.
Staten I.
Le Maire Str.
CAPE HORN
Diego Ramirez Is.
29 May
6 Sept.

The **POTOSI** *towing down the Elbe outward-bound to Chili. Dr. Jurgen Meyer Collection.*

CANADA

U.S.A.

75

45

15

50

Ushant

EUROPE

Azores

Canary Is.

25

C. Verde Is.

AFRICA

SOUTH

AMERICA

St.Paul
Rks.
Nov.7

. Mar. 19

0

Iquique

o Jan.30

Valparaiso

o Dec.17

25

. Mar. 1

Dec.1

. Feb. 22

Falkland Is.

Staten I.

C. Horn

Dec.7 .

50

TRACK CHART OF
POTOSI 1913-1914

Hamburg to Lizard	6 days
Lizard to Line	29 days
Line to 50° S.	24 days
50° S.–50° S.	10 days
50° S. to Valparaiso	6 days
Outward passage	75 days
Iquique to C. Horn	19 days
C. Horn to Line	29 days
Line to Ushant	26 days
Ushant to Hamburg	10 days
	84 days

Left Hamburg 3 Oct. 1913
arr. Hamburg 25 Apr. 1914
Capt. Robert Miethe

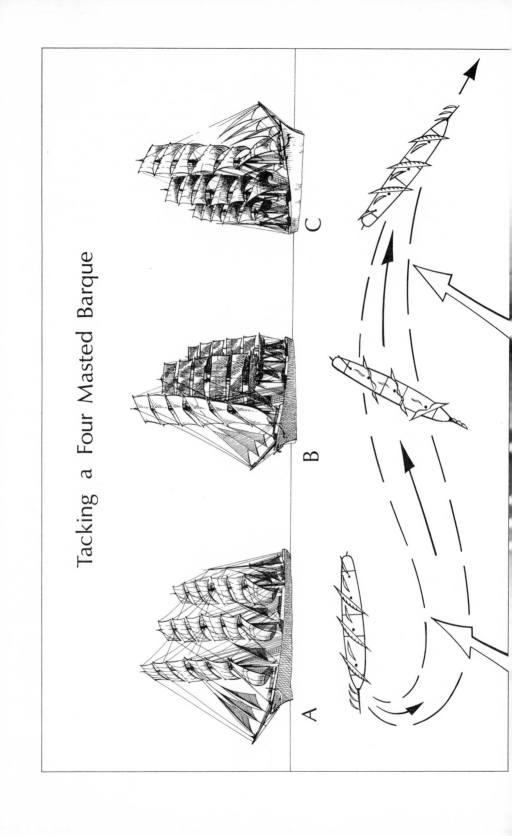

Tacking a Four Masted Barque

A   B   C

was no strain on them, though it lasted two years. They had an excellent crew. The real master sobered up a bit in port, but not much. He mishandled things there too. Leaving Cape Town once, he had grabbed another master's coat with the wrong papers in the pocket and, not once looking, did not find out until he reached Port Adelaide and tried to enter the wrong ship at the customs house. His papers were for a big Yankee skys'l-yarder, which had been held at the Cape until *her* papers were found, and the *Apollo* was held at Adelaide until a Blue Funnel liner brought her proper papers across. Of course, foolishness of this sort reached the owner's knowledge, for Battenberg and Miethe, mates and temporary acting masters, could not cover it up. There was a little score to be paid when the master got back to Germany. He was fired by the owner and fined heavily by the state.

But he did not seem to mind. He still had a few cases of number seven.

It was time to take life seriously after the *Apollo.* So Miethe joined Laeisz again, this time as an officer. Before long, he was appointed second mate of the ship *Posen,* a fine ship which was formerly known as the *Preussen* until that name was co-opted for the giant five-master. He must have been unusual as a second mate, which perhaps was not to be wondered at after his unique experience in the *Apollo.* Young Battenberg was a member of a prominent family: the matter had come to professional notice. After one voyage in the *Posen* Miethe found himself, after passing for master and doing his naval service, promoted to be mate of the *Plus,* a Blohm and Voss-built "P" Line bark of 1,270 tons. The *Posen* and the *Plus* were good run-of-the-mill Cape Horners, comparatively small, with no particular problems, but Miethe's next appointment was as mate of the *Pampa.* She was something of a dog with a bad name.

"She could throw a real scare into you if you didn't know her," said the old captain. "There wasn't anything wrong with her except that she had a lot heavier rig than she needed. She was tender and she could be cranky. That's why nobody went master in her unless he'd already learned her oddities as mate. So I knew that, if I kept my nose clean, here was one ship at least where I'd get command. I studied her all I could.

"Once we were discharging nitrate as usual, in Hamburg. She wasn't within 300 tons of critical stability, but a squall blew across the harbor and she listed heavily to it and hung there on her moorings. I knew she wouldn't go over any further, but the stevedores didn't, and they came rushing up from below, scared.

" 'She won't capsize, boys,' I told them. 'Not yet anyway.' But they were doubtful. When the wind eased, she stood up again. I put some stiffening into her pretty fast, of course. She was a good ship but heavy—not only aloft. She took a lot of driving."

The *Pampa* never did roll over. When larger ships made her uneconomical in the nirate trade, she went tramping under the Finnish flag and lasted for years.

After this, Miethe, still a mate, was offered the senior berth in that rank in the Laeisz fleet—in the *Preussen* with Boye Petersen. He was not alone in thinking the five-masted full-rigger something of an unnatural handful. It was common knowledge that the great Hilgendorf wanted no part of her. He stood by her building and rigging, and then quit the company and active seagoing rather than take her to sea.

"I've had the best ship," he remarked, referring to his many years in the *Potosi.* There was more than a suspicion that he was against the whole idea of the new five-master, holding the common-sense view that too little was known of the vagaries of an outsize ship with such a rig. She could be too big. She could sail badly. No man alive knew more about giant five-masters than Robert Hilgendorf. He was the only man who ever spent a decade sailing one, and walked away. The *Potosi* was a five-masted bark: it might seem a minor matter to change the rig of the fifth mast from the convenient fore-and-aft of a bark's after mast to the inconvenient square rig of a ship's. But Hilgendorf knew things about the difficulties of handling the *Potosi*—perhaps the alarm she had caused him—that no one else then knew. It was significant that he never took her through the Strait of Le Maire, that useful short cut to the Horn. Why? He was not a seaman who scared easily.

The *Preussen*, too, was heavier in the hull than the *Potosi*. Hilgendorf had set up a splendid record with the consistently good passages he'd made with her—outward and homeward to and from Chile two voyages a year for the best part of ten years at an average speed of better than seven knots. Even if he thought the *Preussen* could be driven to keep this up, how much strain would she put on him? On any man?

Miethe was to go as mate: well, he had one brute on his slate already, earmarked for his later command, under God. Maybe that was enough. He did not want to contemplate command of the *Preussen* too. So he put down his reason for declining the offered appointment as incompatibility with Friesians in general and perhaps Boye Petersen in particular, and politely asked to be excused. (As for Captain Boye Petersen, he undoubtedly was a very tough seaman and later became a very tough marine superintendent. It was no one's duty to love either.)

Miethe was excused, and stepped back to become mate of a much smaller ship—but only for a few months. The proffered mate's berth went to another Friesian Islander: within a month or two, Miethe was given his first command, the bark *Prompt*—not a big ship but no sluggard either.

"She was not a lazy ship," he said. "I was able to get her out to Chile in seventy-six days on my first passage in command, and home again from Iquique to Hamburg direct in ninety-one. She tried."

There followed rapid promotion to the larger—and lovelier —four-masted bark *Pitlochry,* a Scots-built, near-perfect ship which Laeisz had bought in 1894 from the stocks in the yard of Stephen and Sons at Dundee. A light came in the old man's eyes whenever he spoke of her.

"She listened to the wind better than any ship I ever had," he said, very quietly. I liked that expression, which I had not heard before. I had a vision of a beautiful great ship, well balanced, utterly responsive no matter what the sea and the storms might do to her, faithfully fighting it out off the Horn—she and

Miethe listening there to the gale's scream and the sea's smash while, like a magnificent old race horse weaving through some impossible gap to thunder down the straight, she eased herself that vital extra mile to wind'ard that would get her past the Horn. To wind'ard! To wind'ard! And Miethe, that tireless, indomitable granite man standing there, one skillful hand of wondrous touch at the reins, like some master among the truly great jockeys getting better than the best out of some great thoroughbred of a horse. Miethe's sea horse was magnificent in light winds, too. According to one enthusiast, she would gather steerage way in flat calm from a puff of cigar smoke exhaled in the mains'l. (These old sea dogs recognized no hyperbole when it came to talk of great ships.)

With the *Pitlochry,* he made that great passage of twenty days better than Hein Nissen's in the *Preussen.* Nothing was said publicly at the time, of course, for the *Preussen* was the *Preussen,* a sort of national ship. It was no secret that the Kaiser took a personal interest in her. Indeed, there were some who said that his interest could have been one of the main reasons why she was built. Miethe knew that, whether he'd ever been mate of one of them or not, now he was earmarked for a five-master, sooner or later. He said nothing, either: but the prospect pleased him not at all.

I knew him some time before I found the reasons behind that.

"Cape Horn is the place where the devil made the biggest mess he could," the captain summed it up. "It is no place for any sort of handicapped ship, or men, most certainly not in winter."

Outside, the Chilean sun shone warm and constant in a brilliant blue sky, ripening the huge grape clusters that lined all the paths of the *quinta* at Quilpué. We had done the morning rounds, looked after everything, put the young garage mechanic right about some part in the elderly fresh-water pump he was trying to repair, spoken to the ducks by name and every other living thing except the young rabbits which multiplied too frequently for naming. Every now and again the old man burst into a fragment of sea song, always in English, the sort that used to be sung in limejuice ships years ago when sailors made their own dog-watch recreation. Inside the cool house, in the room with a model of the *Potosi* in a bottle (made by Robert Clauss) and a ship's aneroid barometer on the wall, lined with books—all sorts, especially Dickens, not at all just sea books—we sat down for a yarn. In tripped little five-year-old Veronica, his great-granddaughter, babbling away in German to a German-speaking doll not much smaller than herself, and in Spanish to us.

"Speak in English, too," said the old man. "You have to be tri-lingual."

But the dolly had no English. It had no German either unless Veronica manipulated some device inside it by pulling on a string. The little girl tripped happily away, still trying to get the doll to be tri-lingual. The storms of Cape Horn and the world of great sailing ships seemed utterly remote and gone for ever, as indeed the ships are.

"I was not happy to be appointed to take the *Potosi*," the old man said, rather suddenly, "especially after Frömcke. We all knew he had had her aground. I knew she had a weak spot after that. Hilgendorf had driven the devil out of her for the best part of ten years—her best years. Schlüter had driven her. Nissen had driven her. Then Frömcke; we knew what happened to him. How much more driving could she stand? Sensible, *productive* driving, I mean, not just hanging on to too much sail and the devil take care of who goes over the side. That is stupid. The difficulty was that in a ship like that, a man *had* to do better than his best to get good passages all the time, especially with the *Preussen* lost. She'd gone before I got the *Potosi*. I thought then that the *Pitlochry* was a better sailing ship than either of them, from a master's point of view, and I still think that.

"But Mr. Laeisz wasn't picking yachts for a yacht race. They were all working ships, and they had to sail well as part of the job. I didn't get any chance to talk over technicalities with Frömcke. Nobody could. Or with Schlüter or Nissen. As a Laeisz master you were a lonely ship-driver. You could only meet brother masters of other ships that happened to be in port when you were.

"But I did talk with Hilgendorf. The trouble with him was

that he was somehow different from the rest of us. He really did have that extraordinary sixth sense for the wind. Even the wind seemed to know that. I hadn't.

"I'd talked with him early, when I had no thought of ever being in command of a five-master. I hadn't asked him about technicalities—you know, just what quirks or oddities the *Potosi* might have. We'd all heard that she had some. Some said her center of effort was wrong, that she was hard-mouthed on the wind, and didn't go about too well. I found out."

To design and build a great ship like a 4,000-ton five-masted bark was no simple matter of producing a blown-up hull larger than the biggest four-master and adding an extra square-rigged mast. Ideally she had to *balance,* to sail perfectly close to the wind without dragging weather helm, and run before a gale without yawing wildly from one side to the other or flinging herself violently across the trough of the sea. These were the days before wind-tunnel experiments. Deep-sea sailing ships had evolved very slowly through centuries, almost like natural creations: what was "natural" about these huge sea crushers, these (in a sense) scornful exploiters of the great winds? What, indeed? In his innermost thoughts, it could be that the five-masters could be affronts to the sea gods, structures of blind strength and too great size produced by man unready for them . . . Miethe was an imaginative man—unlike the Friesians, maybe. He felt that he was taking on more than just another ship.

Indeed he was: and late.

But off he went. The *Potosi* had every refinement desired for the defeat of Cape Horn—the wonderful Jarvis brace winches, halyard winches (never adopted in British ships but very useful when properly maintained: one thing they and brace winches made possible was for one good watch to work a ship in anything other than the very hardest weather), the long midships superstructure housing accommodation for everyone, winches and gear to whip 6,000 tons of cargo in or out in six days, life nets permanently below the bowsprit to save hands out there when she dived, and others rigged temporarily above the bulwarks in the waist for all Horn and North Atlantic passages. All these she had, and an excellent crew of forty-four.

When she towed down the Elbe bound out to sea, all stopped work for a moment to watch, for she was a striking ship, towering over everything, yet she sat and moved well in the water too, silently obedient behind her tug.

But sailing by-the-wind, she griped badly. There *was* indeed something wrong about the calculated center-of-effort of all that great cloud of sail. She dragged weather helm, having the rudder blade over to keep her head off the wind properly, offsetting her inclination to bore into it—a serious fault, but not uncommon. She took half an hour to tack or wear. She had to be nursed most carefully when tacking—going round head to wind to the other tack—lest the yards got abox, mixed up together, because there wasn't room for three masts of them all to swing clear at the same time. She was usually tacked without calling out the watch below, the watch on deck and the tradesmen—sailmaker, donkeyman-blacksmith, carpenter and cook (this last with his own special job not far from the galley)—being sufficient hands. The only heavy work was hauling the headyards around, for the others swung. Each mast had its own headman, the bos'n or bos'n's mate, or an elderly A.B. Each brace winch had its regular brakeman whose work was vital, and everyone was given a station to ensure speed and precision in the sometimes awkward maneuver. The mate of the watch took charge for'ard, the master had overall charge from the midships deck.

With everything ready, everyone at stations quietly, a blast of the master's whistle brings instant action. Three men on the poop hauled the spanker to windward as the wheel spun hard down, jibs flapped as their sheets were let go, the driving force came out of the fores'l as the cook eased the foresheet away. (All brace whips were already eased to let the brace winches work efficiently.) Into the wind the huge ship came, swinging so majestically, seemingly so slowly. Head to wind: another blast of the whistle—mains'l haul! Which here meant off brakes on main, middle, and mizzen brace winches, allowing a couple of seconds between each to keep all clear. Around swung the yards, across the wind swung the ship, soon beginning to fill on the other tack.

Let go and haul! Around came the headyards, over with jibs and stays'ls, the maneuver completed, except for—well, in the case of the *Potosi,* except for quite a lot of things. In the first place, there had to be that two-second interval between the swinging of the main, middle and mizzen yards—two seconds between each—as the bark swung across the face of the wind, lest the main and middle yards become entangled. (Miethe had to work this out for himself. Frömcke left no brief for working the five-master: no one had.) Crojack, mains'l, and middle sail were hauled up in their gear as the yards swung—only the fores'l was left set, which meant careful attention to tacks and lazy tack and sheets: all the stays'l sheets had to be shifted in order to have those useful sails set properly, not chafing against the stays. The whole maneuver took twenty-three to twenty-five minutes, at best.

Of course, everything possible was done to make it fool-proof. The brace-winch wires were clearly marked for the various settings from yards close up to the wind on one tack through beam and quartering winds, etc., to close up on the other tack. The drill was common to all big Laeisz ships: the *Potosi* differed only through her extra mast and idiosyncrasies. T'gallant and royal braces tended by hand—for these yards swung with the others—were marked, too. These marks were useful day and night. There never was any lighting. There was no dynamo.

To get the ship to "wear"—go around by running off before the wind on the one tack, swinging the yards *before* the wind until they were around properly to take the wind from the other beam as she came around to it—it was necessary to take a lot of sail first from the mizzenmast and sometimes from the middle as well, or she would scarcely go off at all. (Miethe called the five masts the fore, main, middle, mizzen and jigger, and this was accepted practice for such huge square-riggers as far as there was such a thing.)

When a square-rigged ship is put about by tacking, the yards must swing quickly, except for the fore, where the sails remain aback awhile after she has crossed the wind, the faster to push her bow over to bring the wind properly for'ard of the other beam without letting the ship gather sternway, and so lose ground. But by wearing, which is done in bad weather only, wind is kept behind the sails throughout the maneuver. In the ship *Joseph Conrad,* when tacking, the main and mizzen yardarms could get slightly mixed up unless one were very careful, because these two masts were a shade too close together. With her four square-rigged masts—the aftermost mast didn't matter being fore-and-aft rigged, but in the *Preussen* it did—and her very long yards, I could understand the *Potosi*'s problem: but it had not occurred to me. No one else had mentioned it. I had seen a painting showing the *Potosi* close-hauled on the starboard tack* with less sail set on the two after square-rigged masts than on the two for'ard, but had attached no particular significance to this.

But half an hour to tack! And such infinite care and judgment necessary. All three masts abaft the fore should swing together, like clockwork, to have the bark swing across the wind triumphantly without any loss of way: with this defect, she would lose ground every time she was put around. Not that big square-riggers usually got anywhere by beating there: but the defect added to the strain on a master so much in public notice (if not view), always *expected* to make not just fast passages but the best.

After the *Pitlochry,* she must have been trying at times, for the *Pitlochry* was one of those rather rare big square-riggers which were responsive to the slightest whisper of the wind, the least touch at the helm. (Old seamen who knew her agreed that the *Thermopylae* was another, but not the *Cutty Sark,* which was good but not that good.) Miethe told me of an occasion in 1910 when he beat the *Pitlochry* up the length of the English Channel and lower North Sea during a week of glorious summer. Once he stood in toward the English side until he was a ship's length off the end of Brighton pier, in perfect conditions. The long pier was full of summer visitors. Bands played. Gay throngs were ready for a spectacle. Miethe gave them a memorable one, for he spun the great four-masted bark in her own length right before their eyes, giving them such a demonstration of Cape Horn ship-handling as none had seen before and few would ever see again.

* By Glüsing. It is used in the book *Glanz und Schicksal,* by Captain Hans Blöss (Kiel: Verlag Schmidt und Klaunig). A very useful book about the big "P" ships.

On she came at first with the shoaling green Channel water turned to froth at the lovely bow, this great German ship with the Scots name, silent except for the slight lisp of her own way and the whisper of the afternoon wind. Still she sailed onward, bounding at the rate of many knots.

Suddenly an order! Up flew the mainsail and crojack bunted up in their gear almost like blinds. Spanker to wind'ard, jibs flapping with their restraining sheets let go, into the wind came the beautiful ship, sweeping her bowspirit end into the wind's eye off the end of the pier. Sails thrashed, blocks rattled as the lines sang through them.

Mains'l haul!

Around came main and mizzen yards, as if by clockwork. Around swung the ship, her head pushed swiftly by the backed sails on the fore. Now all sail on main and mizzen filled: the ship stood a moment, then began to gather way.

Let go and haul!

Around came the headyards, lee braces let go and weather braces manned, foretack and sheet tended, jib and stays'l sheets shifted over. The great ship leaned again to the wind. Down came main and crojick tacks and sheets. Under all sail again, off sprang the thoroughbred biting to wind'ard, now on the tack out to sea.

The huge crowd cheered spontaneously to see such perfection so perfectly handled, though indeed unaware of that. But the magnificent spectacle stirred them all.

"A man may know an occasion like that only once in a lifetime," said the old man.

He never attempted any such thing with the *Potosi*. Not even Frömcke would ever have thought of that.

Captain Miethe did well with the big five-master throughout the three and a half voyages he sailed her, despite her awkward idiosyncrasies and the great shades of his predecessors, and the knock on Smith's Knoll that the last of them had given her. Twice the wound there opened again and had to be repaired. The big hull must have broken slightly just at the center of greatest strain when falling tide after grounding put 10,000 tons of steel plates packed with nitrate on uneven ground. That was a real weakness:

she was not the ship that Hilgendorf and Nissen had handled. Three times Miethe took her to wind'ard past the Horn, his longest passage westward from 50° S. in the Alantic to 50° S. in the Pacific being seventeen and a half days and his shortest ten days, one hour. Hilgendorf's best 50°-50° passage with the *Potosi* was eight days, five hours, which he managed twice, and his longest was thirteen days, three hours.

On those first wonderful ten voyages, Hilgendorf's *average* outward passage from letting go the Elbe tug off Cuxhaven to anchorage in Chile (usually Valparaiso) was 69.9 days—call it ten weeks. His shortest was sixty-four days, half were made in sixty-eight days or less, and the longest was seventy-seven days. Homeward, his average was 79.4 days—the longest eighty-six and the shortest seventy-three days, back to the Elbe. This was a truly remarkable and amazingly consistent performance for a 4,000-ton ship carrying some 6,000 tons of cargo.

Ten years later, Miethe did not do so badly. He had the ship for her twenty-fifth, twenty-sixth, twenty-seventh and twenty-eighth voyage, but the 1914–18 war brought the last to a stop. Here is his performance from the company records.

Voyage 25

Hamburg-Valparaiso-Mejillones-Hamburg

Sailed April 1, 1912.

Hamburg to Valparaiso	75 days
From Lizard	67
50° S. to 50° S.	17½
Mejillones to Lizard	80
Mejillones to Hamburg	83

Voyage 26

Hamburg-Valparaiso-Mejillones-Hamburg

Sailed January 5, 1913.

Hamburg to Valparaiso	83 days
(N. of Scotland)	
50° S. to 50° S.	13½
Mejillones to Lizard	84
Mejillones to Hamburg	92

Voyage 27
Hamburg-Valparaiso-Iquique-Hamburg
Sailed October 3, 1913.

Hamburg to Valparaiso	75 days
from Channel	71
50° S. to 50° S.	10 days, 1 hour
Iquique to Channel	77
Iquique to Hamburg	85 days

Voyage 28
Hamburg-Valparaiso (interned)

Hamburg to Valparaiso	81 days
from Lizard	73
50° S. to 50° S.	11 days, 7 hours
Arrived September 23, 1914.	

This last outward passage was lengthened by giving all land a wide berth, especially toward the end, to avoid possible interception by a British cruiser.

For a hard-driven ship past her prime in a hard trade, these were very satisfactory voyages. But Miethe knew he had done better with the *Pitlochry*.

"I never got more than sixteen miles an hour out of the *Potosi,*" he told me, "though she was a fine model of a ship. She did sixteen over the ground once in the Channel outward bound, loaded to her marks. I had a steady northerly, out on the beam, and no sea to speak of at the time. The wind was off the land and the sea couldn't get up. I checked her speed against good fixes, averaging with and against the tide. In similar conditions, the *Pitlochry* did a shade over seventeen—seventeen point two, I made it. One thing I watched with the *Potosi,* too, was not to run her square before the wind with so many square sails, some blanketing others. I always kept the wind a bit out on either quarter, first one then the other. She did two knots better this way."

It was a great satisfaction to him that he had lost no lives in either ship, for great sailing ships when driven smash into the sea and can mangle men.

Toward the end, Frömcke had been losing three and four on every passage. It was a sort of grim joke when the crews signed on, to look around their shipmates, wondering quite openly who would go this time. The *Potosi* gave them fast voyages. They took their chance.

NOTE: CAPTAIN PIENING CONFIRMED THAT THE *Potosi* WAS "NEVER QUITE THE SAME" AFTER CAPTAIN FRÖMCKE HAD PUT HER AGROUND NEAR THE SMITH'S KNOLL LIGHTSHIP, ALTHOUGH NOTHING WAS SAID ABOUT THIS AT THE TIME. WHEN SHE WAS HANDED OVER TO FRANCE AT THE DIVISION OF GERMAN SHIPPING FOLLOWING THE FIRST WORLD WAR, NO BID WAS MADE TO BUY HER BACK BY THE LAEISZ COMPANY. SHE WAS ALSO SIX YEARS OLDER THEN, IN 1920, AND AN EXPENSIVE SHIP TO RECOMMISSION. MIETHE WAS READY TO SAIL HER AGAIN BUT HIS CREW HAD LONG BEEN DISPERSED. SO WERE MOST OF THE EXPERIENCED LAEISZ SEAMEN AT THAT TIME. WITH THE DOCKS AT ST. NAZAIRE AND THE SHIP CANAL TO NANTES LINED WITH ITS OWN BEAUTIFUL BIG CAPE HORNERS, FRANCE HAD NEITHER NEED NOR USE FOR MORE SQUARE-RIGGED SHIPS. SO THE *Potosi* WAS SOLD, GOING BRIEFLY TO A SOUTH AMERICAN FLAG. SHE WAS LOST OFF COMODORO RIVADAVIA ON THE ARGENTINE COAST NOT LONG AFTERWARD. FIRST FIRE, THEN STRANDING PUT AN END TO HER.

THERE WERE NO MORE FIVE-MASTED SQUARE-RIGGERS.

Chapter fifteen

SAFELY IN FROM SEA

A CAPE HORN shipmaster was by no means only beset by immense difficulties in the ordinary pursuit of his profession when he was trying to beat to wind'ard past the southern end of South America. He could suddenly face tremendous problems at almost any time. The trade wind passages of his voyages gave both himself and his crew chance for real recuperation, but he had to be thoroughly alert there, too, to make the best use of the winds as offered, for the trade winds are not turned on and off at defined latitudes. They have pockets, seasonal variations, vagaries, squalls. They can waft the careless into zones of calm, to cause days and sometimes weeks of delay.

Getting away from the land at the voyage beginning and—often much worse, for a man may to some extent choose his conditions for leaving and some were exceedingly wasteful over it—making safe landfall at the end, coming safely in from sea, could be very dangerous. About the worst possible conditions for this were during heavy on-shore gales with poor visibility.

Captain Miethe told me about one such incident, bringing home the *Pitlochry* direct from Tocopilla, a nitrate loading port in northern Chile, towards Hamburg, in late 1909. It had been an exceptional passage for winds, although he had trouble to avoid a large ice field near the Falklands and was forced to alter course nearer in towards the east coast of South America than he liked.

The *Pitlochry* was one of those rare ships which seemed lucky with the wind in her own right, and was a lovely sailing model too. In little more than eight weeks, she was in the English Channel

283

having sailed at an average of over a thousand miles a week the whole way from Chile. She stormed through the Channel on the blustery wings of hard south-west wind—a mere Force 8, greatly helpful and never dangerous, for the ship often ran at 16 knots, dashing along with a loud song in her rigging, a louder in the roll of foam at her graceful bow. Sixty-two days out from Tocopilla she was off Terschelling.

But there the wind died, for the depression was racing by. The barometer had gone down steadily. Now it stopped. The *Pitlochry* was right in the center of the depression: there would be wind enough very soon again.

I had noticed as we came through the lower North Sea off the coast of Holland how extraordinarily clear the air was, with exceptional visibility [the captain told me]. The coast is sandy, low and plain, but it looked as if it had been raised and, somehow, though so unusually clear, further away. I knew this was a bad sign. It could mean that a heavy storm would follow. We lay becalmed. The glass stayed down—steady down. You know the old sailors' little verses—folklore, they call it now, simple stuff about the sky and the clouds and the sea and gulls, like:

> Seagull, seagull, sit on the sand!
> It's never good weather when you're on the land:

and

> Long foretold, long last:
> Short notice, soon past.*

*Other well-remembered and useful weather ditties include:

> At sea with falling glass,
> Soundly sleeps the stupid ass,
>   Only when it's high and rising,
> Safely rests the careful wise 'un.

> When the rain's before the wind,
>   Tops'l halliards you must mind.
> When the wind's before the rain,
>   Soon you may make sail again.

They're not folklore. They're sense, in my experience. We weren't close enough to see the seagulls ashore, but they weren't at sea. I noticed that. And the very low barometer was giving us excessive long notice of something nasty coming up. What I wanted to do, of course, was to get safely into the Elbe with the first of it—anchored and safe. I didn't want to be coming in with a stinker, and I was afraid we were going to get something really unusual out of this, most likely from somewhere in the northwest.

What we got at first was a few hours of almost doldrums conditions, cat's-paws from all round the compass—nothing steady. The ship jumped about in an unnatural swell, the sails banging back against the masts and the chain sheets rattling, and everybody getting a little on edge, just outside our home port more or less and not just getting nowhere, but with this queer atmosphere about, almost like the Scots expression "fey." It was eerie. It took real stagnation to stop our *Pitlochry:* she really was one of those ships which seemed able to give herself steerage-way with the flap of her sails.

But for much of that day she didn't steer. What was very odd about it all was that we saw no other ships. Where were they all? This was one of the busiest sea zones in the world, yet only we were there. I guessed the storm signals must be flying for full storm maybe at every harbor-mouth for a hundred miles around, perhaps more.

We expected to be safely in by the following morning. We'd need *some* wind for this. We were ready to use it fast, ready to come into the Elbe, pick up our pilot. But there was no sign even of an inshore fishing boat, hastily scooping up a harvest in the sea. The North Sea was empty. There were no special signs I could read in the sky—only threat.

It was winter. The day was short. The glass stayed very low, without movement. We slipped into the night with a breath of southerly air—just a breath that only the *Pitlochry* could find over that dull, dead sea. Then a calm spell again, then a little breath of wind out of the north. Aha, I thought, stand from under, Miethe! This can be it.

I shortened her down to fighting canvas—the six tops'ls, the fores'l, the lower, very strong fore-and-afters. The wind freshened from northwest. If the calm was "fey," now the wind was ominous, as if it was just getting together in this place all its tremendous breath, whistling down more from Iceland with blasts to follow right from Greenland. I put her on the port tack, to be safer when the gale came. The crew ran to their work: here was at any rate a bit of wind to bring us in.

It was a bit of wind all right. No sooner were we braced round than a hard squall of hail hit her like a smack with sledge-hammers out of hell! After this hail, the wind leapt to gale force, screaming. The sails were like great black shapes of steel.

All hands were on deck, of course. They were there uncalled.

Clew up the fores'l! Take in the upper tops'ls!

These were my orders immediately I felt that hail—rain before the wind, you know. Hail's the same thing, but worse.

In the sails came. We were well snugged down. There was not much vice in the sea as yet. I was already in the area where we could expect to pick up our pilot for the Elbe. There was no sign of any pilot boat. It was dark then after the short December day. They show special lights so that we can recognize them: but there wasn't any cruising pilot boat, nor the slightest sign of any other ship at all. I burned blue flares, our signal for the pilot. I burned a lot of flares but there was no answer. I realized that we had made so fast a passage—we were just nine weeks from our Chilean loading port then—that the office wouldn't be expecting us. With the thick southwesterly blowing us up-channel, there'd been no chance for me to make our number to the signal stations. We'd driven up by ourselves mid-channel. We'd spoken nobody.

Within an hour or less of that first howl of the hail in the rigging, it was blowing full gale—force ten, gusting to eleven, more and more violent squalls all with hail. I couldn't see anything half the time now, not even the length of the ship. I had no wireless, of course. At that time, only the very largest steamers were fitted with that.

Now I was in a jam—just that very nasty jam I'd hoped to avoid. I couldn't get out from that leeward corner of the North

Sea again towards the open sea. There wasn't room to beat a big ship like the *Pitlochry* in a storm like that right in the Heligoland Bight. There wasn't sea room to turn her at the end of each tack. I'd have to beat by wearing—losing ground unacceptably every time I ran off, for she'd scud 17 knots. *Nobody* could tack in that sort of wind: now I couldn't wear, either. Even the best of big square-riggers sails over a lot of ground to wear ship.

One course only was open, for it was obviously unsafe to anchor out there. It was far too exposed. I had to run into the Elbe, without a pilot if there were none who could come, or even a big tug to lead me in and maybe take my line when we reached quieter water. I knew very well that the only way a pilot could reach us was to come by boat from the *pilotsgaliot,* usually cruising on her grounds taking pilots off outcoming ships and putting them aboard inward bound. No ship was coming out or going in either, except us—if we got in. Nothing else was moving.

All the driving hail and sleety rain whipped through the air with such fury in the increasing squalls that it often obscured the lights. A river mouth like the Elbe is well marked: in the few breaks of good visibility, so many flashing and occulting lights showed that it could be confusing to the seaman outside looking in. There was a line-up of five Elbe lightships then—Elbe 1 to Elbe 5—before you got in the river proper at all, and lit channel buoys as well, and leading lights to bring you through the worst places.

Which light was which? That's what I had to know, as soon as I saw the next, and I had to know the *right* answer immediately. You just can't do that when you see only one of a pair of leading lights. It wouldn't be much use to identify one of them, anyway. It's the two kept in line that hold your ship to the course that she must make.

I was already off Elbe 1. I signaled again for a pilot. None came. The tide was strongly with me now. The northwest wind was at near hurricane strength in the squalls. I had served out life jackets, for if the ship touched anything in those conditions she was gone. All hands were at stations—the mate on the foc's'l-head with the donkeyman (blacksmith) and sailmaker and the carpenter below—those three grand tradesmen, the guts of the crew. They stood by anchors and windlass. I had both anchors over, each at its cathead where a blow with a maul at the proper moment would let it go. Below the carpenter stood to the brakes on the big windlass ready to ease or check as necessary when the time came.

So we came on racing, the ship thundering through the seas, tearing into them and past them like the thoroughbred she was, almost as if she knew she had this night to do better than best and was enjoying it! She knew—or I told myself she did. Maybe I liked to feel that impossibility just could have truth in it. I was a little past thirty years old then. I'd not been forced into a gale-driven dash into a great river like this before. At any rate, the *Pitlochry* was my idea of the perfect ship long before this. She was a beautiful Scot Mr. Laeisz had bought from the stocks in Stephen's yard at Dundee, untried. He'd seen her. He knew her pedigree—her dam the fast *Eudora*, her sire a century of the unrivaled knowhow of Scots shipbuilders and designers. She was an improved version of the *Eudora*, which was almost a carrying "clipper," though I hate to use that overworked word. A "clipper" if it was a type at all was a ship in which all was sacrificed to one thing—speed. You just couldn't have the perfect ship sacrificed to anything. If she was built too slight in order to rush through light winds, then like as not she couldn't take the storms. She'd better leave Cape Horn alone. If she was heavy to run before the gales, then she'd have a touch or more of ships like the *Pamir* about her—turn bitchy at dangerous moments, or stand still in light winds when other ships would be sailing. Maybe she wouldn't maneuver too well.

No, the *Pitlochry* was my idea of the perfect ship, or I'd not have been there that wild night, sixty-two days from Chile. She steered with a few spokes of the wheel, in the worst weather. She'd tack in a doldrums air that wouldn't blow a candle out. She'd wear round fast, too, if she got half a chance. She was a race horse, perfect of line if perfection can be found, with the grace and harmony that go with that. But she wasn't a hell-rusher. I never heard of her sailing up on more powerful ships, like the

Preussen or the *Potosi,* and sailing *past* them. Power counts, too—
size, tremendous rig, great waterline length. If the *Pitlochry* made
outstanding passages at times better than the larger ships, it was
because here and there along the way she'd had better winds—
or made better use of them.

She had a disadvantage or two, especially for this headlong
gallop I had to put her to then. She was a three-island ship, but
she was not built to Laeisz specification. She was a three-island
Scot like those other Dundee four-masters, the *Lawhill* and the
Juteopolis. The center of control was aft, in the poop—old-style.
Here were the officers' accommodation, the charthouse, the
wheel. Only the crew lived in the midships house. The standard
compass—the most reliable you use to set the course from—
stood on a solidly built-up platform between the poop and the
midships house, reached by fore-and-aft catwalk. You conned
her from that platform or from the poop, near the wheel. This
meant you looked along the whole ship before you could see
where she was going, and this could be a real disadvantage in
narrow waters. Our "P" ships had the conning position—the
point of control, the master's place—on the midships superstructure, and everything was there—charthouse, steering wheels,
compasses, *and* good visibility for'ard and aft. A master felt that
he was *in* his ship, not following along behind. From the poop,
it was often impossible to see under the three great sails, the
courses.

This was of little account at sea but that night it mattered,
even though I had no courses set. I had to look past or through
a lot of rigging in those blinding squalls. Of course, I was prepared for this. Everybody was at his proper post—mate on the
foc's'l head keeping sharp lookout and ready to use *both* anchors
the instant they were called for, second mate by the helmsman,
third on the midships house handy for the braces and sail-handling, if and when possible.

I stood by the standard compass. Here I had the "feel" of all
the ship. The second and third mates could hear my orders: the
mate would hear at the proper time. His job was those anchors.
We couldn't hope to stop the ship without using both of them,

down the same instant, cable paid out together, so that she swung to them when they bit the ground and the cables ran evenly—no jerks, or they'd break! But checked in time—at the proper time when it was necessary and feasible. I knew those cables could jump right off the windlass, take violent charge—and that could kill us. I knew that, above all else, our survival depended on those anchors and cables: and on me to get them away at the right moment in the right place.

I had hope only of finding one spot in the river that night where we could anchor at all. This was in the immediate neighborhood of the *Mittelrüg,* a low bank of sand near the fifth lightship, Elbe 5—not *on* the bank for that was awash at low water and would be fatal long before then, but clear of it, with room to lie to a full scope of both cables without grounding. So long as they held, of course.

I had to go this far to find a reasonable anchorage. I knew that all the shipping in Hamburg that had been stopped by the storm either from sailing or docking would be at anchor in the river, chockablock. I couldn't anchor until I got among them for the anchors wouldn't hold—there was too much sea running further to seaward, and too much wind. When I got among them, I'd have to anchor fast, in the right spot the first time! There wasn't going to be a second.

How could I find it? The *Pitlochry* took a lot of room up, lying with the whole of her two cables out. It was not possible to rush on in with a pretty display of precise pilotage, knowing exactly where she was all the time. Half the time I couldn't see properly at all. I thanked the Lord the storm was behind me—we ran with squared yards—and the hail was not smashing into my face. I saw ahead when I could: what was astern no longer mattered. I thanked God, too, that in early youth I'd learned something of this river. Not that one could learn the pilotage, remember the characteristics of the major lights. No, no. Great rivers are never like that. They change. Banks and shoals change naturally or can be changed by the endeavors of men, intentional or otherwise. I'd passed this way outward bound, with a tug, six months earlier. Then I had general cargo and was not deep-laden. Now I was deep-loaded, right down to the Plimsoll marks with solid nitrate. A short, high sea ran: it would be far worse with the ebb, with wind against tide.

I knew the characteristics of the important lights. We flew past Elbe 1, and headed up river at fantastic speed—far more than enough! But I could not ease her. The main lower tops'l blew right out of its boltropes in a terrific squall. Away blew the great sail—it was Double-O strongest canvas—in a solid piece toward Cuxhaven to let them know we were coming. A few rags flapped for a moment or two: then the yard was bare as if no sail had ever been there.

She did not notice it. Her speed did not slacken. The fore and mizzen lower tops'ls were still set. She was well balanced. She steered beautifully, as always. The winking lights of the channel marking buoys marked the sides of the navigable passage: often I could see only one at a time. Light-vessels Elbe 2, Elbe 3, flashed by. Then everything was blotted out in one great mad shrieking of the wind. Now not just hail struck me. Sand was flying through the air. As I turned my head to peer this way, then that, it struck my face. It felt as if I was being sandpapered. In the tumult of spray and hail and sand and tremendous ear-assaulting noise, I noticed the higher sound of the wind's scream at the rigging screws, the deeper roar of that mighty orchestra in the powerful shrouds and backstays, the power of those tops'ls hauling 3,000 tons of ship and 4,000 tons of nitrate bodily along. Too fast! Too fast! With the strong flood tide also helping, she must have been making something like 18 knots over the ground.

I had all the charts for the Elbe entrance in the ship. I'd studied them. But they'd been seven months aboard. There could be changes in navigation-light characteristics, or in the ranges of the leading lights that bring you clear of shoals. The *Mittelrüg* bank lay right in the river. Lightship Elbe 5 marked the place for course alteration to clear it. Deeper-draught vessels must leave Elbe 5 to starboard: smaller craft could go the other side.

The squall passed, for the moment. Elbe 4 came up, very close. I took in the fore lower-tops'l. My splendid sailors were right on the mark. The mate was there for'ard with them. The wind was shrieking so that one would prefer to leave the sail alone, or let it blow out. But that was not our way. I took off the fore first because the main and mizzen gave it a little lee. We had a drill for such storms that we'd learned from Cape Horn, long before. Quickly, quickly, ship racing before the wind, the fore tops'l yards were braced up sharp—as sharp as possible, so that much of the wind now roared *past* the set sail not at it. Up with the lee side now, lads, lively! Buntlines and clewlines together! Sand in the eyes, hail in the teeth, jet-blast of gale in the face, they hauled, hauled, hauled! Up it came!

Aloft and furl, lee side first. Up the weather shrouds they galloped, out along the frozen footropes. With the worst of the wind's sting taken out of it, the lee side was made fast. Then the fore yards were swung again, bringing the former weather side into the lee—such as there was of it—of main and mizzen. Out on this side of the yard the oilskinned figures streamed: and so —in time—the sail was defeated, rolled up somehow on the yard, double-secured with lengths of extra gasket.

Elbe 5 was in sight. Another violent squall screamed warning. As it passed, I saw the black river come alive with anchor lights. They seemed to jam the available space quite hopelessly. Of course, a lot of lights seen suddenly on a black night was bound to look like a city to us. I *had* to find anchorage here, and no doubt about it. Further up the river would be even more crowded, with decreasingly less room. And I knew the anchorage just could not be as crowded as it looked. Any anchorage looks crowded when you come straight in from lonely months of sea.

The ship rushed on. No time for dithering! This was it. I looked searchingly for the most open spot—the least congested. These were big steamships at anchor, mostly: they burned two anchor lights, one for'ard on the forestay, high, the other aft and low. So at first glance it was hard to see which pair of lights was on which ship.

Elbe 5 was abeam. Time for action!

"Stand by to let go!" I roared to the mate, and the wind took my roar.

"Hard a-starboard!" I shouted aft.

The second mate repeated.

Down spun the wheel.

In a flash from the great light of Elbe 5, I saw the mate and sailmaker at the ready. Aft the second was trying to haul out the lower-spanker, the swifter to slam her round to stem tide and wind. It wouldn't go: it would not set. But she spun on her heel like a flash of lightning, and stood upon her wake an instant, her own way off but the tide still rushing her.

Let go anchors!

Now the wind brought me the mate's acknowledging hail loud and clear—both black beauties down together. Out roared the cable. Now head to wind, I braced sharp up, yards abox to ease the windage. Seas driven by the near-hurricane broke at the bow: heavy sprays washed right along the decks bringing more of the river sand with them.

Meanwhile the ship drove rapidly astern. Carpenter and donkeyman tended the compressors and the brakes—big, screw-down clamps, Scots-built like everything else in that good ship. But they could not—dared not—hold her. (A sailing ship's windlass, a hand-operated steel giant of a contrivance, stood solidly built into the ship below the deck of the fo'c's'l-head. It was operated usually by the heavy double-geared capstan on the deck above, or in many of the larger ships by steam from the donkey-boiler through a deck-winch and primitive chain drive.) As fast as they tried to check them, both cables jumped right out of their grooved drums with a violence of sparks and noise, and rushed out through the hause pipes. Sailing ships have—or should have —a sufficiency of cable: 150 fathoms on each anchor—300 yards of it, roughly three times the length of the ship.

Carefully both men checked a little, applying slightly greater force each time: for at full scope the *Pitlochry*'s stern would be very close to those sands. If she dragged? No hope! To touch on such a spot that night was fatal, for the *Mittelrüg* is like the dreaded Goodwins off southeast England, a ship-eater, sucking down its victims. In the morning no one would know what ship had been there.

The cables stood out like twisted violin strings, taut, whipping into and out of the tormented face of the Elbe waters. At the bitter end they stood. Thank God, they stood. With perfection of workmanship the long line of flawless links flogging in the sea stood, held by great shackles to the kelson, and the giant Bower anchors held, and the ship did not drag though she threw her whole cutwater almost under, and the seas flung sand and mud upon her as if she were a dredger. And the wind screamed as if thwarted: and all hands stood through the rest of the night to their sea watches, tending her.

Soundings showed the least depth at low water to give a fathom or so under the *Pitlochry*'s keel—not much, but enough. Even so far in, the water ran foam-streaked, turbulent, ugly, and the gale and the hail shrieked endlessly in the good rigging. There was no dry place on deck anywhere: but the cook had the galley fire going. There was plenty of good coffee.

It took the rest of the night to get the mizzen lower tops'l properly secured, for it was frozen. All the sails were doubly lashed lest the myriad hands of the insane wind found a chink somewhere and tore them to pieces.

In the morning, the squalls no longer howling with such impatience each to replace its predecessor and shriek the louder, the glass hesitant but no longer falling, the timid light of frightened day showed the buoy marking *Mittelrüg* Sand 50 yards astern. All round the steamships lay cheek by heavy jowl, many with their propellers turning.

The *Pitlochry* under God had found the *only* spot left with room to anchor in. She found it. I only recognized it.

So there she was, my good and faithful ship, come safely in from sea.

"Good God, Captain, how did you get here? Where did you come from?" shouted the pilot as he stepped aboard a day later, from the big tug *Roland*.

"From Tocopilla," answered Captain Miethe. "Sixty-three days."

The pilot stared.

"I know you *sailed* from Tocopilla," he said. "But how did you drop in here? How could you find the only safe hole there was, *that* night? Another ship's length and you'd have been in collision—many collisions. The river's choked with powerful ships that wouldn't—couldn't—get out. And along you come and anchor in the middle of 'em! I couldn't even see across the street ashore."

There was no answer—rather, the answer was obvious.

The pilot continued to stare, amazed.

And then, as if he'd thought of something almost equally astonishing, suddenly he asked, "Have you seen the *Preussen*?"

"*Preussen*? I have seen no outward-bounders."

"Not outward bound, man, *homewards*! She's not come in."

Now it was Miethe's turn to be astonished.

"She left Tocopilla nine days before we did. I've not seen her," he said.

"Anything to bother?"

"There was ice near the Falklands—looked like a big field. Perhaps she got in it. We were lucky; it was daylight when I saw it. I stayed to the west'ard of it, making up nearer to the Argentine coast. I figured the winds would break better for me that way, too. Maybe they did. Anyway, we've had a very good passage, though it ended with a bit of an unwanted rush into the Elbe."

It was another eleven days before the giant full-rigger came in. Nothing was said in public of the *Pitlochry*'s better passage, of course, for the *Preussen* was senior ship, and the Kaiser took an interest in her performance.

Comparison of the track-charts, done quietly later with the marine superintendent in the Laeisz office, showed that delay in ice was not the whole story, though it was part of it. The *Pitlochry* had picked up nine days on the big ship before she reached the Horn. This sort of thing could happen at any time: the later-leaving ship sails up on the earlier, bringing her own wind with her. It was not much use to leave early and then get poor wind: but each ship left when she was loaded and ready. The *Preussen* was some 50 miles east of the *Pitlochry* when she first met ice, and this hindered her both because of the need for extreme caution in the ice area and the poorer winds there. Miethe was right: he "smelled" a depression coming out of the Plate moving slowly eastwards, and he used this, and it brought him earlier to the southeast trades. He so placed his ship that the *Pitlochry* was in the favorable semicircle of the depression, with good winds, while the big ship—forced out by the ice field—was so far to the eastwards that she got no use out of it at all. She had northerly winds when the *Pitlochry* had east, southeast, south, then west, right to the southeast trade.

This advantage in turn—and in time—brought her to the chops of the Channel just in good time to pick up the depression that hustled her through with fine southwest wind. The *Preussen* reached the Channel some days later, just in time to have to beat against fresh easterlies. Then Miethe was going slowly through the North Sea and then, with a mad rush in the end, into the Elbe.

Here the big ship lost eleven more days. Her total passage was twenty days longer than the *Pitlochry*'s.

"So it goes," said old Captain Miethe. "A lot of luck, a little skill—and don't ride the luck too hard."

Aye, nothing was said at all, publicly. But the waterfront knew. Hein Nissen had the *Preussen* then. He knew, very well. The company seemed not to notice the incident. But when next he checked his bank statement, Captain Miethe found that an extra bonus of 2,000 marks had been quietly paid to his credit.

Not long afterward, he got command of a five-master himself, though he would have preferred infinitely to stay with the *Pitlochry.*

For those big five-masters were hard to handle: there hadn't really been enough experience in designing and sailing them. The Scot was a thoroughbred with the experience of many such ships built into her.

Ocean-going square-riggers often sailed right into harbour. Here a shapely British full-rigged ship runs before a fresh wind into port. The foresail and the main top gallantsail are being taken in while she runs on under the fore and main upper tops'ls, and few fore-and-afters.

End of voyage—ready to pay-off.

The Port Watch, HERZOGIN CECILIE *1927-28—Finns, Swedes, Germans, Australians.*

The ship CELTIC MONARCH *looked big berthed at San Francisco in 1905, but she was very small off Cape Horn. Procter Collection of San Francisco Maritime Museum, permission of the Director.*

e **POTOSI** *alongside. Published by permission of the Trustees of the National Maritime useum.*

Square-rigged sailing school-ships carry on part of the Cape Horner tradition. A world fleet of 30 still exists. Two Danes at Svendborg.

ARCHIBALD RUSSEL, *last big lime-juice square-rigger built. (In 1905)*

Valparaiso, 1970. No sign that a sailing-ship had ever been there.

Chapter sixteen

THAT OTHER CAPE HORN

ONE OF Captain Miethe's outstanding qualities was his thoroughness. Once when the *Potosi* took a great sea—one of those murderous, nasty "niners" which old-time Horn battlers reckoned snarled along at the rate of one in every nine big seas—right over the midships deck, the captain made a leap for the weather shrouds to get firm grip and not be washed away. But his hands found bights of running rigging, which gave. He did not let go, but the sea and the ship's tremendous roll to leeward spun him over end for end—pitched him a somersault, still clinging to the lines. His head struck the steel bar at the foot of the shrouds inboard where lead blocks were secured to get more purchase at the gear, and cleft it open about a foot. A kneecap was knocked adrift, and he had other injuries. There he was, a dreadful sight, flung on his beam ends, blood gushing from his wounded head (it looked far worse than it was), a collarbone broken, unable to stand because of the leg injury, loss of breath, and a bellyful of sea water. But he still had his grip. The mate helped him up. The ship was all right: the sea had done no particular damage. So Captain Miethe allowed himself to be helped to the little hospital down below.

Here he took command. The collarbone was no problem. The mate knew how to strap his shoulder up so that would mend.

"Knock it back," he gave instructions for the shifted kneecap to be given a suitable tap with a wooden belaying pin. As for the broken head, it was only skin and such: there was no fracture of that hard headpiece.

297

"Sew it up," he said, selecting the best type of needles and so forth.

The mate looked dubious. Though he could cope with ordinary wound stitches, a foot-long gash across his captain's head was something else. "Pinch the sides together and sew like a sailmaker!" he was told. This he did, the captain watching closely in a mirror. It took some time and twenty-four stitches, but it was a very good job. Today the scar is still plain across the captain's head, but the stitches had done their work and their marks had worn away.

"That was the way I'd learned," said the captain. "From the end of 1908 until early 1909, I was laid up several months in the Hamburg docks in the *Pitlochry,* because nitrate freights and all others were very poor. The ship was used as a warehouse: I looked after her, but I had plenty of time off. So I signed (with owner's approval) for a surgical dresser's course at the big general hospital that took in casualties from the docks and ships. So did several other young captains and mates, because we all knew there was to be an official requirement that ships with big crews would have to carry a qualified surgical dresser aboard; good idea anyway. Now we had a little time to qualify. It might as well be us.

"But we found ourselves after a while spending a lot of time in a sort of balcony over an operating theater, to get a close look at the real work. Sometimes it was gruesome, but the trouble was the ether fumes coming up. They made us sick. The others quit, but when I was alone the commodore-surgeon let me come down on the floor. Then when he was short-handed he let me help, especially with straightforward stitching and so on—big jobs often, but simple.

" 'Stitch like a sailmaker!' he said, watching me very closely on the first job. A stevedore had his whole forearm laid open— quite a piece of seaming. There were clips to bring the wound together. I seamed away, and I must have done all right."

I looked at those great practical fingers on the big hams of hands, and was perfectly certain that he had earned his certificate.

"Never waste time," he said. "There is always something useful to do and to learn."

He said the Laeisz Line had learned that lesson long before, and applied it whenever possible. They had learned how to run warehouses, for which there was always need in the Hamburg docks, depression or no depression. So their *Pitlochry,* with just watchmen aboard, was employed temporarily as a warehouse, covered by their own insurance, for five months there and made a little money in spite of everything. And then away to sea again complete with fully qualified medical dresser, and no delay at all.

The captain had time enough to apply his philosophy as the years of the so-called Great War dragged by, while the *Potosi* and a score other big German sailing ships remained at their heavy moorings in Valparaiso Bay. He already could use working Spanish, of course. Now he took up the study of that interesting language properly. That mastered, he enrolled in Chilean navigation school and qualified in due course as a master mariner, *capitán de Alta Mar*—in the merchant service of Chile—a useful qualification which found him ready employment in South America after the breakdown of Germany. When it was required (by a law of 1925) that all seamen qualified as Chilean *capitáns* should be Chilean citizens, too, he complied with that. During the First World War, he also learned all he could about engines, read a great deal, began to write a little, and helped to keep up morale and efficiency among the German seamen. Valparaiso was no safe and placid bay where big ships could lie secure year after year. Captain Miethe learned about salvage, too, after heavy storms called northers cast ships ashore including the big Laeisz four-masted bark *Petschili,* a 3,087-ton Blohm and Voss job of 1903. She was wrecked, but Miethe learned. Later he ran a lighterage company, was port captain of the Chilean whaling fleet, became a surveyor and insurance expert and was busily employed at this until he was sixty.

"The government took away my driving license when I was seventy," he said with regret. "It was the law—no automobile pilots over seventy. But I needed my car to get about that very long coastline."

He managed. His abiding principle for the defeat of Cape Horn, "Make use of the situation offered," worked ashore, too.

"I did not leave sailing ships. They left me," he said. "When they did, I was ready to turn to something else—ready and qualified."

A seaman learns above all to exercise his foresight in square-rigged ships, to be one jump ahead of the shift in any wind. Therein lay so much of the value of their training, for they were a wonderful means of making boys into men.

Aware that he was both one of the last and best qualified men on earth in the business, I asked the old captain to sum up the wisdom he had acquired about getting past the Horn.

"The main point is to use every chance of the weather, day or night. It is all summed up in that old golden rule for sailing-ship masters: Make best use of the situation offered," he said. "I know that is too trite a summary of course: there are qualifications about this rule. I would put them in this order:

"First—*Understand* the situation.

"Second—Have your ship fit to exploit it: at any rate not to be beaten by it.

"Third—Same for the crew. Good morale, well looked after *all the voyage.*

"Fourth—Have understanding owners.

"The first depends on a combination of met. knowledge (which we had to study at mate's and master's school), and personal knowhow acquired by observation and experience. The second and third are your duty. As for the fourth, that could be more difficult. We were very fortunate to sail for experienced and enterprising owners like F. Laeisz, who kept up good ships—they had some bad ships too, but they knew this as well as we did. All the ships made comparatively short voyages, usually: they were never sent off on two- or three-years' wanderings. They came back to home port to be checked.

"So did the crews, of course: each time they signed for a further voyage they got a bonus and the mates got a rise. The mates understudied the captains because they knew they would get command. The captains got bonuses for good voyages with no more than the usual loss of sails, and for good dispatch, good turnout of cargo, and absence of claims. The owners set up organizations in the turn-around ports, too. They knew their business and they cared, and we all knew they did. So there was good morale. They believed in paying masters and officers enough, too, so they could have a home ashore: there was no problem caused by having a captain's wife aboard.

"Getting to windward past the Horn meant constant effort. When sails blow out, change them the very first chance—at once if possible. The captain who spares himself and acts not as head-man of the crew will never lead his crew on a good, fast Cape Horn rounding. Take sail in, yes, and in good time; but don't keep it fast because you know it could be very difficult to get it in again. Set it again the moment you can safely do so. Our halyard winches were very useful for this. Often as the wind increased, I would take the mizzen upper topsail in, maybe, but I would lower the others a little to ease the strain on them, with favoring winds, and ease the sheets a little, too. They'd pull better bellied out like that, with much less strain. As the wind eased, the watch could stretch them again very easily with those winches. Yet I noticed that in some fine ships of other countries, no one seemed to learn anything. It is not sea sense to be old-fash-ioned."

The captain briefly described one of his westward roundings in the *Potosi,* which was then by no means just a great big powerful ship that could slog on through anything. (There never was such a ship.)

"We came through the Strait of Le Maire by night," he said, "with the wind strong northwest and the glass going down, all sails set except the lightest. Beyond the strait and away from the shelter of the land, we came into a storm and shortened down, keeping the upper topsails on her. We passed through abrupt gradients of the storm, and knew its center must be west of us. We pushed through this girdle with a steady glass and reached the storm's center. Here the winds moderated. I again set all sail to the upper topgallants while we had the chance. Push her along! The glass stayed steady. The wind went northwest and north-northwest, allowing us to make good progress toward the west with some southing in the course. So it went all day.

"While we were bounding along, we came upon a bark lying to the wind under two goose-winged lower tops'ls—you know, just a couple of lee corners of sails—and two or three stays'ls. Of course, he was ready for the storm to come, but the storm wasn't there then. The weather was cold and gloomy, but he could have sailed. He must have thought the *Flying Dutchman* rushed past him when he saw us. Later that day we came to the steep gradients of the storm again and had to shorten down quickly. The glass began to rise slowly but steadily: I kept the upper tops'ls all set and pushed on. So we came to the further side of the storm where the winds were moderate from the north, belonging to the next depression. We used that in much the same way, and got well to the southwest'ard of the Diego Ramirez.

"We were past the Horn: there wasn't much difficulty in working out with that northerly to longitude 80° W., where it was safe to make toward the north. We wondered where the bark was. We never saw her again."

How many of Robert Miethe's "rules" for the defeat of Cape Horn were observed aboard the hove-to, waiting bark there is no means of knowing, but the most likely score was none, judging —perhaps harshly—by the state of affairs revealed aboard so many ships by the surviving official logs. Few ships were sailed or kept up to the standards of the Laeisz fleet. Masters there who did not maintain good discipline by their own examples did not last long. These ships were in no sense subsidized, as the French were. They had to make their voyages and their living strictly on their merits. "P" Line discipline was built on competence, the reward of merit, and mutual respect—a respect for ship and shipmates instilled in youth from their first going to sea, fostered by fair pay, decent food and living conditions, and a reasonable assurance of a future with the company, if wanted.

"Losing even one man by desertion from a Laeisz ship anywhere was almost unknown," said Captain Miethe. "I am speaking of the good years, up to 1914."

Even that inveterate wanderer, the well-known Hamburg bos'n Charlie Müller who in his time had "run" from ships at Santa Rosalia, Sydney, and a dozen other places and would take on anything if the wanderlust moved him, agreed with this.

"We knew when we were well off," he said. "The only trouble with those 'P' ships was you never got in much of a payday. They were home again too soon."

Charlie was with Hilgendorf in the *Potosi* in 1901. In 1970, the cheerful old man, now ninety-four, is to be found in Hamburg Seefahrers' Altenheim, on the Karpfangerstrasse, still turning rope strands into beautiful fancywork in the old Cape Horn seamen's style.

Charlie was an extraordinary character. He was well known in the inter-Colonial barks of my youthful days in the southwest Pacific where he became such an accepted fixture that somehow, when the First World War came along, he was not interned though a German citizen. Perhaps no one thought of regarding him as an "enemy." He was just Charlie Müller, bos'n of the *Manurewa* or the *Senorita,* the *Ysabel* or the *White Pine.* But by 1917 things were harder. Charlie thought it prudent to move ashore and lose himself in the big circus managed by Wirth Brothers. Here were many foreigners: he would not be noticed. But one day there was trouble with the elephants. These were such friends of his that he was forbidden to be anywhere near the ring while they performed, for they broke off and came to him. Now he was sent for to calm them. It seemed that the elephants understood only the language they were trained in, which was German. So Charlie spoke to them all in Bavarian German. They quietened at once, but some snooper heard and reported him for investigation. Off went Charlie to internment at last—not that he was too greatly bothered by that. He soon set himself up in the camp in the business of making fancy sea-chest handles, decorative ditty bags, and sailors' sennit belts, and did very well.

When Captain Miethe was given command of the *Potosi,* the *Preussen* (and others) had already been lost through unnecessary collisions with careless steamships. If he foresaw when outward bound that he could have to beat down-Channel, he at once chose the other way—the tough way around that other Cape Horn, the north of Scotland and its Isles. He told me of some touch-and-go incidents during one such passage, begun from Hamburg in January, 1913—a cold and savage month to be heading up toward Iceland. All went well at first, but the only real advantage of that northern route was that there was far less traffic up there, and it had no cross-Channel steamers. There also was more hope of easterly winds, if a high set in conveniently over North Russia. It looked from the data available as if this were probable, and the big ship pounded along at first with a fine fair wind.

But not for long. Instead of romping with favoring winds straight into the Atlantic between the Shetland Islands and the Orkneys, thence in a wide swing far to the west of Ireland, soon she was fighting for her life against a most savage southwesterly gale in such a sea that even that great ship, for the moment— many moments—was next to helpless. For the gale gusted to force eleven and twelve with a short, high, *dangerous* sea that the *Potosi* could not be safely put round in (lest she be swamped) and she was caught on the wrong tack! There was no sailing ship so great and strong that the sea could not kill her, if it really tried. Now it tried.

"There was nothing for it but to heave to, if only for a while," Captain Miethe said afterward. "I had not hove to before, not even off the Horn. I'd had most of the upper tops'ls set. Now they had to come in, and the fores'l too. The tops'l yards were already one-third lowered. Now I braced them sharp up to the wind to lessen its force against the canvas, lowered them the whole way down on the lifts, steadied everything, got all possible in on the buntlines; then, one tops'l at a time, it was lay aloft! It was gloomy and the wind was screaming as if it dared us to get our breath. The night came with the thunder of all chaos, and heavy seas swept the decks while spray and spume flew above the tops. But so far, we'd had no damage.

"We got those sails fast, then tried the fores'l too. Here was trouble. My men were getting beaten by the endless yammer and shriek of the wind, so soon so terrible, for we had only just been a day or two at sea. So I'd thrown off my oilskin and sea boots and rushed aloft, making speed when she rolled to leeward and I could almost walk along the wind'ard ratlines, stopped and hanging on when she rolled the other way. They had the lee side fast: the weather side was far worse. One buntline broke; the canvas began to thrash and thunder. When we were all spaced out along the yard, with the lifeline behind us and one arm through a becket so's not to be flung off, the fight started. All together, boys! Get a grip on this son of a bitch! Go for him! And so forth. All did their best to get hold of the kicking, roaring sail, but it was fighting mad at us, kicking back over the yard, hard as frozen leather.

"When you take that on you have to win. I don't know how long it took. There are lulls. Up on the yard the wet heap of the great sail finally came, like a circus tent on a flooded field in a hurricane. The *Potosi* had short gaskets you could throw over a sail quickly to smother it, once it was in. Now we had the fores'l in we put plenty of extra gaskets on it. Sweat was pouring off us, blood spurted from our finger ends, the nails torn out. But the work was done, the sail saved. Down and aloft again to the next sail!

"I still had to get the ship turned round. The wind had outflanked me. Now it was southwest. The easterly had blown too hard too quickly, and killed itself young. We were already far enough to the west'ard up there on the top of the world, not far from Greenland. But how to get out of it now the gale was southwest? And it still *was* a gale: its terrific efforts of the past days hadn't worn it out."

The situation as construed by the captain (from the data he could see and all his past experience) was that a new depression was upon him from the west: but he was on the port tack—with the gale blowing from his left side—and as it worked round to west and nor'west, it would drive him to the nor'ard. He had to go about, get the wind on the other side. Then the ship could use it splendidly as it eased. But, like as not, the wind wouldn't just slowly work round from southwest or west-southwest to the northwest: it would jump, with little warning in the murk, with all too good a chance of catching the sails from ahead of them— taking the ship aback, sailors say. This could cause dismasting.

She had to get around, to be swung off before wind and sea

somehow and brought up again on the other track—with the wind on the other side.

She wouldn't go. Bucking and leaping, rolling, plunging, flinging herself desperately this way and that as the tumult and the sea increased, she wouldn't go.

She *had* to go.

The southwest wind had brought up a dangerous cross-sea. She threw her whole bow under. Men sheltered where they could, on the midships house, and thanked God and Herr Laeisz that she'd been built with such a useful construction, a high island haven out of most of the worst of the sea. Now she was under her lower tops'ls only, and the minimum storm stays'ls, low-set and super-strong, to hold her head up, keep her straight, not to fall off and broach in the terrible sea.

For the time being, even putting out oil, it was not possible to try to bring the ship round before wind and sea. The decks would be swamped, the men swept from or into the brace and halyard winches—drowned or mangled.

Throughout the whole night the hurricane winds continued. It was clear, and the Aurora Borealis flared fitfully throwing a weird, unearthly light upon the ship. Sails broke adrift from the best of gaskets: up went the men and secured them again.

Hove to like this, the ship drove to leeward. She had no headway. The wheel was lashed. She did not steer. In this way her loss over the ground was minimized. But it was a state of affairs to be brought to an end as quickly as possible, for the ship began to suffer damage. The middle lower tops'l—that set on the middle mast—blew out and flapped itself to pieces in an instant. One of the lifts of the middle yard parted then: the yard at once cockbilled, and the lower yardarm began to smash at the ship's sides. This emergency was dealt with at once, but not before the odd stresses thrown on the yard had caused a brace also to part. Oilskinned mariners lassooed the yardarm with heavy rope, catching turns instantly to take the vice out of its banging about, in peril of being struck by the yard themselves.

The ship had a four-berth hospital in the midships superstructure. Here Miethe set broken limbs, stitched broken heads.

. . . The sea stove in a skylight and broke into the quarters, but never seriously. The galley was a watery mess but the cook did not miss a hot meal and there was always hot coffee, lashed twice a watch with kümmel.

For two wind-screaming, spume-filled, ghastly long days and nights these conditions continued. Watch below fell asleep in their oilskins, sprawled in the sail locker ready for a call. Watch on deck huddled behind a weather cloth of double-nought canvas or in the lee of the big charthouse. In the galley pots played leapfrog over the stove-top fiddles and pannikins danced on the floor. In the little hospital, the carpenter nailed extra planks fore and aft in the bunks to keep the splinted, lashed-up wounded in them.

Still the sea snarled and the gale roared, and the ship plunged and rolled and flung herself in endless anguish as mountainous crest after curling, breaking crest roared at her and broke upon her—but never with too great a strength, for the slight oil slick and the grace of her hull curbed them. As if chagrined, they snarled with their frothy heads and licked at the ship's black sides.

None but the injured missed the musters at the changes of the watch, though throughout that time the musters served little purpose other than to check that all were still aboard, and for the more skillful to get a cup of hot coffee down.

"This we all appreciated," the captain recalled. "To hang on with one hand, the storm shouting and the sea pouring over the decks, to hold a hot cup of coffee between stiff, almost frozen fingers and sip it up before it all got too salted in the spume— you know, in such conditions this could be a little taste of heaven. Folk ashore have many pleasures, but this is one they can't have."

Or miss, probably.

At last even the wind up there began to quieten. From force twelve it became a mere eleven: at nine, it seemed almost a summer air. St. Elmo's lights danced upon the reeling yardarms. . . . At last the glass fell no longer. The center of the low soon now must come, to be followed by the shift toward the north.

All hands wear ship!

Wear ship! Wear ship! Welcome news as never before—all hands to stations. Up helm! Run her off! Hoist the inner jib to give her better way. Watch it at the brace winches, boys! No need to give these orders—except for the first voyage *jungmen,* all knew their work. Though seas still swamped the decks despite the oil bags trailing overside, steadily she fell from the wind, turning her left side from it and swinging still as the yards all swung until she brought her right beam slowly, slowly right up to it.

Heading south! Let her go!

With murmured thanks to the shade of the ingenious Captain Jarvis, Scots inventor of the brace winches, the long, slow complicated maneuver was completed. Troubles were not wholly over—they never are—for the wind soon shrieked out of the northwest every bit as strongly as it had for so long howled out of the southwest. Now it was fair: if the ship merely leant before it she rushed along, and *in the right direction.* The cracked-lipped, muscle-wrenched, overtired little boys and the big tough men smiled though it hurt. They had at once to shift the blown-out sails, for many had been damaged, some flapping in their bolt ropes, and make a thorough job of that damaged middle yard.

Soon the full fores'l could be set for the first time in days. The sky cleared. The sea lost much of its viciousness when the ship ran before it. The cook got the galley straight: and soon the *Potosi* was bounding southward like the great race horse she was, licking the last of her wounds.

After that fight round the north of Scotland the Horn that voyage could do nothing to her, for she would race down to there in the southern summer. Compared with northern winter, this could be almost like a Mediterranean cruise.

The *Potosi* reached Valparaiso that voyage only to become one of the eighty-two large German sailing ships held in west coast of South America ports to rot through the 1914–18 war and at least a couple of years afterward.

When sufficient was known about the problems of these big five-masters, might such giant barks have become the real ultimate in European man's development of deepwater, working sail? One says barks, not ships, for the *Preussen* could no nothing the *Potosi* could not do (except carry more cargo), and was a more expensive and much more awkward rig. There is no data on her particular problems: nobody assembled any. While Boye Petersen and Nissen were about, nobody asked them. Miethe had been left to discover the *Potosi*'s snags for himself, though he was the last of her masters. The center of effort and boxing yards problems of the five-masted bark could have been solved and an improved version built: but the so-called Great War destroyed more than the fabric of ships. That war was great in its destructive powers alone. Afterward the essentials for the successful assault on and defeat of Cape Horn, though the memory lingered awhile with the men of the big four-masters, were gone.

The opportunity to continue to the final victory of the great wind ship over wind and sea was not so much lost as no longer noticed. There was a little experimenting—rotor ships so called, and five-masted auxiliary "bastards" of mixed fore and aft and a little square-rig as in a few Vinnen vessels: smart-Alec stuff, off the true line of development and useless. Man had the chance. There was work for greater *Potosi*s still to do while the ocean winds blew. The unknown Scots designer who produced the *Pitlochry* at Dundee could, very likely, have solved the *Potosi*'s problems and produced a masterpiece. The British, as Miethe said, had the most experience in building good sailing ships. They had the flair. Some glorious combination of the *Potosi*'s strength and power and the *Pitlochry*'s grace and wonderful sea sensitivity would have been a truly effective Cape Horn warrior! Such a ship was never built. The traditions of designing them and sailing them were broken and flung aside.

Man discovered how to ride winds of his own making in the sky: he became power-mad, at sea and in the air.

He has lost a good deal, for the gain of what? A chain of "super" hotels around the world, forever becoming bigger, fuller, more inhuman, more expensive? The ability to roar at great height around the earth whenever he feels like it and has the money, in a state of stress and fantastic ignorance, a docile, sleepy, fare-paying sheep, shuffling in and out of airports when not airborne, learning nothing? Not even enough to cope with the assault on his bodily functions.

"The deep-sea sailing-ship master led a hard and solitary life," said Captain Miethe. "To us the ship was a sort of living thing, and master and crew were with her to serve her, to help her fight the sea and live through the fighting, no matter how hard on her and him, and them. But he mustn't ever let her get in a handicapped position. She can kill herself and him if he does: many did. It was a demanding life: but the demands were reasonable.

"Up to 1915, there were many captains who rarely thought of their job as a means of making a living. To us it was living, a profession of tremendous satisfactions comparable to none."

In Valparaiso where Miethe saw eighty-seven large sailing ships on his first visit in 1894, now in 1970 there was no sign that one such ship had ever been there . . . nor at Iquique, where he had counted over a hundred. From Santiago's airport of Pudahuel, I flew high above the coast north-bound via Lima in Peru toward Europe. Below me the old nitrate ports of Chile had shrunk to names upon the bare, long map, and the arid yellow blobs of the guano islands off Peru were left again to the sea birds, undisturbed by ships. I "flew," I say, using the word loosely. I did not fly. I sat in a comfortable aircraft hurling itself expensively at high altitude through the sky, rushing from one large airport to the next, guided by unseen radio waves or something of that kind, balanced and kept on course by instruments watched by two or three men. I was there because that aircraft could be reasonably relied upon—disregarding a real possibility of the bandits called hijackers and the remote chance of an insanely planted bomb—to get me back to England in twenty-four hours or so. And there were no ships.

I thought of Miethe, Nissen, Piening, Jarvis, Nelson, Learmont, Williams of St. Dogmaels, Hilgendorf, Fearon, and the others of that never-oversized band of magnificent wind-ship masters who had been outstanding in the list of the sea warriors sent against Cape Horn . . . who at last had defeated every force and twist of stormy treachery that headland could bring against them and, in the long battle, had enriched the quiet nobility of working man.

APPENDICES

SOURCES

THE PRINCIPAL sources for material upon which I have based much of this book have been, for the British ships, some personal experience, some of the masters themselves, the official logs and so-called Crew Lists found in the Repository at Hayes, Middlesex, and the files of *Lloyd's List, Lloyd's Weekly Shipping Index,* and the *Shipping Gazette* and *Lloyd's List Weekly Summary,* covering variously the years from 1869 to 1933 (with a few gaps) which are on file in the National Maritime Museum at Greenwich, London, S.E. 10. The Lloyd's journals list shipping movements and casualties, report casualty and other inquiries, and give a wide range of general coverage on matters connected with merchant shipping from all angles, particularly regarding personnel, management, and other business matters. Since it was circulated primarily for the benefit of underwriters, owners, and others directly concerned with shipping, the highest practicable standards of accuracy were set and maintained, and the items reported sought to cover international deep-sea shipping of all nations and types.

As for the official logs, the existence of a considerable store of these came to my notice first through the trustees of the National Maritime Museum at a meeting at Greenwich, though I had heard something about a large store of logs held somewhere around London which was under threat of dispersal or destruction for the alleged greater need of the space they occupied. I heard about this first from Mr. David MacGregor, a well-known member of the Society for Nautical Research and a student of the real clipper-ship era. Efforts to prevent the destruction of these records began, to my knowledge, in 1966, at least seriously. Representatives of the Public Records Office, the National Maritime Museum, the Society for Nautical Research, the Registrar General of Shipping and Seamen, the Royal Historical Society, the Society of Archivists, and three well-known historians in the maritime field—Professor John Bromley, Professor W. E. Minchinton, and Mr. Robin Craig—met at Greenwich. There was a suggestion that owing to the bulk of the

313

records, a ten percent sample might be taken of the crew lists, and the matter left at that. The argument was put forward that this might be sufficient academically, because of new techniques developed for historians in the use of statistics and other data in the economics field. Because it looked as if this (to my view) foolish notion might carry the day, I got busy. A ten percent sample from the crew lists among all these miles of the *only* authentic records remaining in the United Kingdom from the latter days of the deep-sea sailing ship struck me as throughly inadequate, despite whatever new techniques there might be—using sample data as computer fodder, I expect—and, as far as I could make out, there had been little if any examination of the official logs at all. *Each* was a historic document.

The only thing to do was to go and look. I did that, as soon as I could, and kept on looking. Nobody wanted to throw the material away: there was a serious stowage problem, for ships' logs and Articles of Agreement keep flooding in, and where could they all be stowed? I didn't much care what happened to the documentation of steamships and motor ships for there was time to cope with that sort of thing: but the sailing ship was gone and nothing of her that was destroyed could be replaced. I did not care at all for the idea that the dull logs—by comparison—of powered vessels should push out the last documentation of the far more interesting sailers. While I got on with studying the logs, and crew lists, etc., others carried the torch, particularly the director of the National Maritime Museum, Mr. Basil Greenhill, C.M.G., backed by the Society for Nautical Research and many maritime historians, including Professor Ralph Davis and Mr. Robin Craig. At the time of writing, in mid-1970, it looks as if these efforts are heading toward success and the documents will be saved.

In a few cases, I was able to find further evidence from diaries kept personally by former apprentices in British sailing ships and, in even fewer, from the papers of masters. But I found that matter published even in the better of the maritime magazines was suspect unless backed from other sources, and popular magazine stories even in journals which hopefully (and possibly, they imagined, truthfully) alleged that what they published was true, were useless—so much so that unless there were some real reason for paying attention to them they were best left unread. The same went for a great many books, particularly those in the writing of which the person who had been in the ship or ships was "assisted" by some ignorant optimist doing his writing for him, long afterward. These books follow a fairly general pattern—the older are written by former apprentices who at least served four or five years in deep-sea limejuice sail and, being grounded in it, know their business: the newer are from the typewriters of passengers and one-voyage cadets in the big Finnish Cape Horners. These are ninety percent useless, as far as gaining any real knowledge of or insight into the sailing-ship era may be concerned, for the writers have neither. There are however, some excellent works from this era, particularly W. L. A. Derby's *The Tall Ships Pass* (for Derby made a real study of the subject and, as a member of Lloyd's, was in an excellent position to do so: he sailed a voyage in the *Herzogin Cecilie*) and some of the works by Alec Hurst who was in several of the Finnish ships. In the same category are Elis Karlsson's *Mother Sea* and *Pulley-Haul,* for Karlsson is that most unusual of men, an articulate Åland Island professional sailing-ship seaman.

The best picture of the life of the limejuice apprentice is Captain David W. Bone's *The Brassbounder,* published more than fifty years ago: the most useful picture of the tramp sailing-ship master's life is Captain James S. Learmont's *Master in Sail:* and there is valuable source material in all the works by Captain A. G. Course (including his *Wheel's Kick and Wind's Song,* and *Deep Sea Tramp*) and in a privately published work called *The Last of the Cape Horners,* edited (and part written) by Commander Claude Woollard, R.N., and published privately by Arthur H. Stockwell at Ilfracombe in Devon. This is unique documentation on early twentieth-century British Cape Horn ships, as it consists in the main of the unadorned reminiscences of a number of members of the British section of the International Association of Cape Horners, *real* old boys drawing on real experiences unaided by hope of large sales or other efforts of imagination. Because it is this sort of book, the work did not find a general publisher: the Ilfracombe firm publishes at author's expense, which means few if any reviews and little distribution. Maritime historians of the future will be grateful to Claude Woollard, his collaborators, and Arthur Stockwell. Captain Learmont is unique. He was that rarity, the competent Cape Horn shipmaster who, having proved his authority, wrote about his sea life in clear, uninhibited prose, without interference from ghost or other obstruction. He was good: he knew he was good: he says what he did and he says, too, what some other shipmasters didn't do. This did not make for popularity: but it gives us evidence without artifice, and evidence from a most competent witness. There are also the works of Sir James Bissett, one of several who rose from sailing-ship apprentice to become commodore of the Cunard Line: this is the best of the books written by the later famous shipmaster looking back to his beginnings.

From the general historical point of view, there are the Basil Lubbock books, kept in print by the well-known nautical publishers Messrs. Brown, Son and Ferguson in Glasgow, notably the two volumes he called *The Last of the Windjammers,* and the technical works of Mr. Harold Underhill from the same house. Mr. Lubbock was rather the old Etonian gone to sea briefly, but, because he was an old Etonian and became interested, many doors opened for him at a time when companies still existed surrounded by their records. If he had not worked indefatigably and enthusiastically with them, the chances are that no one would; for they did not last beyond the First World War. Like the good Victorian-era Englishman he was, it took a long time for Basil Lubbock to realize that there had been others who developed excellent Cape Horn ships besides the English, Scots, and Americans. Almost his last book was a slim volume on the nitrate "clippers"—how he loved that word!—in which both Germans and French were dealt with in 153 large-type pages. But, according to his lights, he did an excellent job for the Britishers. Since then, Captain Louis Lacroix has produced his useful *Les Derniers Cap-Horniers Français* and *Derniers Grande Voiliers,* unfortunately never translated. The former, *The Last of the French Cape Horners,* was published in 1940, at Luçon, when other events were imminent.

In recent years, one has noticed with regret that some appalling works, allegedly about big sailing ships, have come out of France. It is possible that bad translation is in part to blame for this, for unless the translator has some specialized knowledge or access to it, his task is hopeless. It is wise to be skeptical of the lot no matter what the publisher —and European critics—may say, particularly of the large sleek tomes overfilled with "art work." For the sailing ship lends herself to this to the satisfaction of a few publishers who do not care what their letter-press may say.

In the United States, the standard works are well known not only to scholars—Samuel Eliot Morison's *Maritime History of Massachusetts,* Felix Risenberg's *Cape Horn,* Professor Albion's and Carl Cutler's books, and the publications of the American Marine Research Society of Salem, Mass. Of late years there has been trash offered to the public here, too, originating in America, but there are experts like Captain Harold H. Huycke, Jr. and Director Karl Kortum of the San Francisco Maritime Museum waiting to pounce on these. A notable piece of documentation published by the South Street Seaport in Manhattan in 1969 deals with limejuice, not American ships, but it covers aspects of both. This is *The Wavertree: An Ocean Wanderer,* by Captain George Spiers, an uninhibited account of a voyage in the ship *Wavertree* (which South Street Seaport has acquired from Buenos Aires) which bears out so much that becomes evident from a study of the British official logs. A former apprentice who deserted his first ship, Captain Spiers acted as steward in the *Wavertree* on passage back to England from Puget Sound. In this capacity he had a very revealing view of the master.

But really, when it comes to books, one thanks the Lord for Captain Joseph Conrad, and John Masefield's *Dauber:* for Conrad in his few books of the sea and Masefield in that epic poem distill the very essence of the sailing-ship life and the men who served it. Time and again, I return to these, for the better appraisal of all others.

In Germany, real public interest in the big sailing ship is something new, and there is a dearth of documentation from masters. They did their best at sea and are silent: there were no apprentices in the ordinary commercial ships. There is almost a superfluity of works dealing with the great ship *Preussen* now, useful as they are: books such as Dr. Jurgen Meyer's *150 Jahre Blankeneser Schiffahrt, 1785–1935* give a more useful picture of aspects of German shipping. The best work about the Laeisz Line in English is the Hans Dulk *F.L.* translated by Captain J. Ferrell Colton, the well-known student in this field, and published by himself at Flagstaff, Arizona, in 1957. Official publications of Deutsche Seewarte are referred to in the text, but particularly valuable have been those two classics, the *Segelhandbuchs* for the Atlantic (Hamburg, L. Friederichsen and Co., 1910) and for the Pacific (same publisher, 1897). I browsed through these for months on end in the four-masted bark *Parma,* where they were part of the navigational library.

All these sources would amount to little in the way of red-blooded worth if it were not for the men—Captains Robert Miethe, Hermann Piening, Fred Krage, Robert Clauss, Adolf Hauth, Richard Sietas, and Hans Rohwer; olds bos'ns Charlie Müller (with Hilgendorf in the *Potosi*) and Albert Loose (in all the German five-masters), and former able seaman Herman Theilig of the *Parma.* It has been my good fortune to know most of these men for many years. Charlie was as well known in Australia during the first twenty years of this century as he was in Germany. There has been for years a small group of earnest students in the field of the Cape Horn ship centered on California, among them Karl Kortum, Harold Huycke (a steamship master), Robert Weinstein (of Los Angeles: a fine-books man by profession, and an inveterate collector of rare sailing-ship photographs), J. Ferrell Colton, formerly of Phoenix and lately of Guaymas in Mexico (who was in several ships and, if he thought a specialized book in the sailing-ship field was worth publishing though not as a general work, he published it himself), others in Seattle, Valparaiso and elsewhere in Chile, Denmark, Finland, Norway, and Germany.

This group circulated information in the form mainly of personal letters and, over the years, has built up several very worthwhile files which have been available, and valuable, to me. Captain Huycke in particular has been indefatigable over at least the past quarter century in assembling information mainly from German and American sources, and must rank as one of the outstanding practical students in this field. What he discovers he shares. I am grateful to him, and to all the members of this well-informed small group. Their contacts in the deepwater square-rigged-ship field are far-ranging and almost encyclopedic. They have access to the knowledge of masters like Captains P. A. MacDonald (the *Moshulu, Dunsyre,* others), Fred Klebingat (master in his time of many American and some German ships), both of whom are still fit and well in Southern California in the middle of 1970, and Ken Reynard of the bark *Star of India.* They know what went on in Iquique, Valparaiso, Talcahuano, and Santa Rosalia in the sailing-ship world between 1900 and 1924: and they retain the information.

In Hamburg, Captain Fred Krage and in Chile, Captain Robert Miethe remain invaluable sources. So do the small publications of the Cape Horners' Society—the quarterly *Cape Horner,* edited by Captain Alfred G. Course in England, and the *Albatros,* produced by the German section. For big sailing ships under the Italian flag, the book *Ultima Vela (The Last Sail)* by Professor Tomaso Gropallo of Bobliasco, Italy (a well-known member of the Society for Nautical Research) is the standard work.

SHIPS

As for real sailing ships still in existence, Herr Otmar Schauffelen's *Great Sailing Ships* is an exhaustive work, though it contains many vessels which by no means qualify as "great" sailing ships. There are few left of these, among them the four-masted barks *Padua* and *Kommodore Johnsen,* now training ships—with auxiliary power—for the U.S.S.R.; the *Passat* at Travemunde in Germany, and *Peking* (practically rigged down) near Chatham not far from London, England, the *Viking* at Gothenburg and the *Pommern* at Mariehamn in Åland; the ships *G. D. Kennedy* at Stockholm, *Balclutha* at San Francisco, *Cutty Sark* at London, *Joseph Conrad* at Mystic, Connecticut; the barks *Star of India* at San Diego, California, and *Rickmer Rickmers* (later the Portuguese naval school-ship *Sagres*) in the naval base near Lisbon.

There also are the rigged-down hulls of the four-masted ship *Falls of Clyde* at Honolulu, now being rerigged, and the ship *Wavertree,* shortly to be towed from Buenos Aires to New York to be rerigged as part of Mr. Peter Stanford's scheme for the restoration of Manhattan's South Street Seaport, near Fulton Street. There is one last whaler left, the *Charles W. Morgan,* berthed permanently at Mystic Seaport, Mystic, Connecticut, and in 1970 undergoing major refit. The American bark *Kaiulani* is somewhere still in existence, to the best of my belief, but her condition in 1970 is not known to me. There has been an organization concerned with her restoration for a number of years.

Disguised as the Italian barkentine *Giorgio Cini* and operating as a school-ship for lads in the northern Adriatic, the old French bark *Belem,* built in Nantes in 1897, still leads a useful life. Of little over 500 tons, she was not built as a Cape Horner and was converted into an auxiliary yacht for the Duke of Westminster in 1913, but until then she was a working square-rigged ship in the normal manner. Smaller vessels of this sort found plenty of employment until steamships forced them out of it in the short-haul Atlantic trades from northwestern Europe to the Gulf of Mexico, Caribbean, and eastern seaports of South America. In later years, between the two World Wars, some ended their days in the so-called "onker" trade from Baltic ports mainly to London. This was odds and ends of sawn timber not of standard sizes, and sailing ships could afford the time necessary to lie at mills in small Swedish and Finnish ports hand-loading the stuff, and hand-discharging it later in London. Two former Laeisz barks, the *Plus* and the *Prompt,* finished their days here, and so did the old *Loch Linnhe.*

There are a few old Cape Horn sailer hulks aground in a sort of breakwater at Punta Arenas in the Strait of Magellan, one of them—by the look of her—a former four-masted ship of the *County* class. Until 1970 at least, the large French four-masted bark *Ville de Mulhouse* swung at anchor off this port, her four lower masts still standing with topmasts built on to them, and the course yards crossed. She belonged then to the Chilean Navy.

STRANGE LOSSES OF CARGO-CARRYING SCHOOL-SHIPS

Reading through the files of *Lloyd's List and Shipping Gazette Weekly Summary* for 1906, I came upon the extraordinary case of the loss of the Belgian ship *Comte de Smet de Naeyer,* an almost new full-rigged ship of well over 2,000 tons which had, apparently, just sunk for no good reason, and taken more than half her people with her in fine, settled weather about three hundred miles out in the North Atlantic to the west of Ushant. What on earth sort of casualty was this? There had been, I read, "uproar in the Belgian Parliament" about it, for the *Comte de Smet de Naeyer* was a school-ship. The shipping paper in its issue for May 4, 1906, gave some idea of what surely must be one of the oddest casualties of the whole sailing-ship era. There were nine feet of water in the hold (but no damage): the pumps had broken down: only one boat got away, although the ship had been slowly sinking at least throughout the previous night and her for'ard well deck—she was a long-poop ship, like the *Herzogin Cecilie*—had been awash for hours. Commander Fourcault, I read with amazement, was "bidding an affecting farewell to the survivors before he went down with his ship." Why in heaven's name wasn't he adding to their number?

Two of his officers, another two of his instructors, his surgeon, and nine of his seamen and twelve cadets were in the boat which got away and was still standing by. He'd had five other boats, and none was damaged until the last moment. There had been sixty persons aboard. The upshot of a preliminary inquiry was apparently that the ship went down "from excess of sea inboard," the cause and manner of its ingress unknown. The ship was undamaged, held Lloyd's highest class and had been in no casualty. As she sank, her people were swept from her decks by the seas eddying over her. It was then, apparently, that some of the boats capsized.

The twenty-six survivors were picked up by the French four-masted bark *Dunkerque* inward bound toward Cuxhaven that same afternoon, which was as well for there was neither water nor food in their boat.

I knew of a Belgian school-ship, another full-rigged ship also named the *Comte de Smet de Naeyer,* as she was a well-known feature of the Antwerp waterfront for many years: she did not go to sea though she was in fact the old Scots Cape Horner *Linlithgowshire,* a fine ship. I could understand now why she had not gone to sea: the Belgians had also followed their tragedy by almost immediately ordering a replacement, a large four-masted bark which they named *L'Avenir,* built at Bremer-haven in Germany in 1908. The *L'Avenir* was a long-poop four-masted bark which sailed for many years, finally as the German *Admiral Karpfanger.* But she came to an even worse end than the first *Comte de Smet de Naeyer,* for she went missing homeward bound from Australia with a grain cargo in 1938, drowning her full complement which included many Hamburg-America Line cadets. She had wireless by that time, and had reported herself all well three weeks out from South Australia toward the Horn: since then there has been silence, but a marked lifebuoy from her and a little wreckage also identifiable from her—some small German metal plates put on doors as replacements for the Belgian, and some new wiring were found on an islet near the Horn.

It was rather obvious what her fate had been. She had been coming round the Horn inside the Diego Ramirez islets—between them and False Cape Horn on the Ile de Fonso islets somewhere, a notorious place for indraughts and sets—and she'd somehow got herself up on one of the ugly clumps of rocks which wait for ships down there. In bad weather by night no one would have a chance: the peril and the end would come upon them at the same moment.

But the *Comte de Smet de Naeyer*—here there seems mystery quite unsolvable. She had been built to Lloyd's highest class by the Grange-mouth and Greenock Dockyard Company in 1904 for the Association Maritime Belge, an organization set up largely for the purpose of organizing and running a cargo-carrying sailing school-ship. She had accommodation for eighty cadets (for the Belgian Merchant Service), sixteen seamen including a carpenter, sailmaker, blacksmith-donkey-man and bos'n, galley and steward staff of six, four deck officers including her master, a surgeon, and three instructor-schoolmasters. The Belgians had wisely decided to build up the cadet force gradually, not to have her filled with green boys on her early voyages, and she was carrying nothing like her full complement when lost. She had already made a long Cape Horn voyage lasting almost a year. Any "bugs" built into her would have been found, or any possible defects. She was large for a full-rigged ship at over 2,000 tons, and would have been handier as a four-masted bark: but her size and rig had nothing to do with her sinking. She just sank. Why?

One is left with human act or human error. The usual sailing ship had no hull openings, no water intakes, no sea cocks to be left wrongly open, and no need of any. But the Belgian training ship was built to carry water ballast and had some large steel tanks built in the lower hold amidships for this purpose. These were meant to take their water from the sea, and give it back to the sea again when not required. For this, there were seacocks and a simple valve system. Could someone have interfered with these? But the ship was laden, requiring no ballast. The drill was that the master, mate, and donkeyman dealt with these few vital fittings, the master delegating, the valves kept padlocked. She had a steam pump. If there were something wrong—obviously *some*thing was not as it should have been—it could be coped with.

But she just sank, and was allowed to sink, the master taking his affecting farewells, the chaplain (according to some accounts) conducting a last service as the sea quietly sucked her and her people down— all but that one boat, with the two mates, two instructors, the surgeon, the nine seamen, and the twelve cadets. They were "forced to look on as their comrades drowned, for the boat was full to capacity," the preliminary inquiry was told. Hadn't the ship a few rafts, some spare spars, wooden hatches? She was in the shipping lanes. Even crates and chicken coops would have floated people.

There is more than a touch of H.M.S. *Birkenhead* bravery in all this —the quiet courage of the commander, the chaplain, and the many others left aboard. But it was a courage which would have served them all, and the Belgian Merchant Service, far better had it been organized for their survival.

There were many of these large cargo-carrying sailing school-ships —British, Swedish, German, Danish, Russian—some built for the purpose, others converted. Britishers such as the well-known Devitt and Moore ships *MacQuarie, Illawarra, Hesperus, Harbinger* and others, the *Medway, Port Jackson;* Russians like the *Grand Duchess Maria Nikolaevna* and the first *Tovarisch;* Swedes like the *Beatrice, C. B. Pedersen,* and *Abraham Rydberg,* and the Danish *Viking* did good work for years. So did Germans like the *Herzogin Cecilie* and *Herzogin Sophie Charlotte.* After the First World War, most of the surviving Laeisz ships began to carry thirty-six cadets, but not all. France used another "P" ship, the *Richelieu* ex-*Pola,* for the same purpose, but she was lost by fire in port after a brief career.

(These ships are not to be confused with the considerable fleet of smaller, noncargo-carrying square-rigged school-ships, some of which, like Germany's bark *Gorch Fock,* America's *Eagle,* Romania's *Mircea,* Denmark's *Danmark,* Argentina's *Libertad,* Norway's *Sörlandet,* and Japan's two four-masted barks, are still with us. These do not touch cargo but cruise with large, disciplined crews of boys and young men, some naval, some coast guard officer cadets, others intended for the merchant service. Some such vessels are still being built, like Colombia's auxiliary bark *Gloria* commissioned in 1970: but the real old sea dog looks upon a few of these with increasing bewilderment.)

All these earlier Cape Horn cargo-carrying school-ships did excellent work for many years, although some company ships proved expensive to operate and were given up, until the period following the end of the First World War. The only such ship lost at sea pre-war, to the best of my knowledge, was the *Comte de Smet de Naeyer*. Before the end of the war, Britain had given them up: after the war, the German shipowners tried to get a few going again but, until a workable scheme was established in Mr. Laeisz's surviving (and new) "P" ships, they did not do so well. There were losses, but not tragedies.

These came later, particularly with the new *København*, another five-masted bark. She had been missing since early in 1929 and no light has been thrown on her loss at all. She was a large, very strongly built and heavily rigged vessel, built in Scotland, with auxiliary power, water-ballast tanks, and—an unusual feature in a sailing ship—four watertight bulkheads extending her full depth, as well as several others to the 'tween-deck level. She had a double bottom. If there were an "unsinkable" sailing ship going to sea, it was surely this *København:* nor was she at all outsize. She was some 125 tons smaller than the Laeisz *Potosi* (which had no power) and over 700 tons smaller than the second *France.* She was well commanded, officered, and manned. In 1921, Denmark still operated quite a number of deep-sea sailing ships as well as a fleet of t'gallant-yard schooners of the Svendborg-Marstal type—excellent little ships—and had been giving good lads their *ab initio* training in the small iron ship *Georg Stage* since 1882. So there were excellent pools of sailing-ship tradesmen and seamen to draw upon.

But the big five-master was less than six years old when she left Buenos Aires in mid-December 1928, and sailed off the face of the earth with forty-five cadets as the principal part of her sixty-strong crew, and Captain H. F. Anderson in command. She was bound for Australia to load grain, a simple Roaring Forties east-bound passage. She had plenty of ballast. She had power. She had radio. She was 100 percent A1, had plenty of strong boats sufficient for all aboard and to spare. With all those W/T bulkheads, no sailing ship should have been a slower victim to ice collision, or any other collision: for her reserve buoyancy was immense. It is true that nobody (except Hilgendorf) had much experience of sailing five-masted barks, and Captain Anderson was on only his second voyage in command: but he had been mate. He knew the ship.

The ship was searched for most painstakingly both along her probable route and among the sub-Antarctic islands. There were reports that she had been seen "in trouble" off Tristan da Cunha, but in fact a four-masted bark in no trouble at all had been seen there. There were rumors of a lifeboat of tow-headed skeletons found somewhere half-buried in a beach somewhere near Luderitz Bay. There were inquiries and searching investigations: nothing was found, no tenable theory put forward.

There could have been ice along her track that southern summer: many such ships hit icebergs and staggered away again, though they had only the standard single collision bulkhead abaft the cutwater. She had a lot of heavy rigging though no more than she could stand—but there were seamen one met who knew the ship and said she could be tender. On the face of it (no messages having been sent) it would seem that she had not got very far on her road, and whatever killed her was sudden. A pampero, plus simultaneous ice collision? Flung on her beam ends, ballast shifting, bows stove in, roar of the terrible wind pressing her over, over and down—rudder almost out of the water, all the boats (and everything else) lashed down, hatches stove in, ship for the time being quite unmanageable, and never recovering to be manageable again . . . All this *could* have happened, and fast: for the great strength and bulk of the fine big ship would only sink her faster.

Perhaps. All is speculation. Many ships with three and four masts went missing. Because she was a school-ship, greater attention was focused on her.

Then there was the *Pamir*—that same *Pamir* which had been German, Italian, Finnish, New Zealand, Finnish again, then German again, until she was lost. She, too, was a strong ship, very well rigged. She, too, had been given power—a large fixed-pitch propeller, a diesel powerful enough to give her a speed of 7½ knots—and accommodation for a large number of cadets. Her more or less sister ship *Passat* was similarly treated, and both were put in the trade between the Elbe and the Plate. They had also been given powerful radio, deep tanks for water ballast, and a considerable quantity of additional cargo-working gear. All this was expensive, but the two big four-masted barks managed to keep going until 1957, financed to some extent by the state of Schleswig-Holstein.

In 1957, homeward bound to Germany from the River Plate with a cargo of barley much of which was loaded loose, the *Pamir* was caught in a hurricane, went over on her beam ends, and foundered, taking down all on board with the exception of six junior crew members who survived somewhat miraculously in a waterlogged lifeboat. Of the eighty-six persons on board under Captain Johannes Diebitsch, fifty-four were merchant service cadets. At the time, the *Passat,* similarly manned under the command of Captain Helmut Grubbe, was at sea in the same trade.

If she were not fitted with a W/T station the *Pamir* would be another missing school-ship. She got messages away giving her position, and powerful steamships fought to reach her. But the hurricane—code-named Carrie—recurved on her, stability was gone: the sea came in and down she went. She was about four hundred miles roughly west-south-west of the Azores. She had sufficient boats and rafts for all on board, but in weather which destroyed the ship boats were useless. The water-logged boat chanced to survive because it *was* waterlogged: it lay like a half-full barrel in the sea, and the six lads lay in it.

There was an outcry in Germany at the loss of another school-ship. (The naval school-ship *Niobe,* which was an auxiliary jackass bark, had been knocked down by a white squall in the Baltic and sank with the loss of sixty-nine in 1932, while on a summer cruise.) There was no comparison between the *Niobe* and the *Pamir,* but the public makes no distinction. The *Niobe* indeed had gone over twenty-five years earlier, and the German navy had at once replaced her with not one but a fleet of five steel barks, three of which still sail in 1970, as Russian, American, and Portuguese school-ships, while the tradition is still maintained in Germany by the splendid new bark *Gorch Fock.*

There can be considerable differences between full-powered naval school-ship square-riggers and the cargo-carrying type such as the *Pamir.* In the first place, she was fifty-two years old. In the second place, there were reports, only too well founded, that she had been loaded with her barley in such a way as to cause danger of shifting, for it was loose (to save bagging), covered with a few tiers of sacks. While the furor was going on, the four-masted bark *Passat,* similarly laden, staggered into Lisbon in distress. Her cargo had shifted too. Her deep tanks were loaded full, as the *Pamir*'s were. An ordinary Atlantic storm had struck her. Aware of the *Pamir*'s fate, her master—Captain Helmut Grubbe, a fine man and experienced Cape Horn seaman—took no chances.

When the *Passat*'s cargo had been properly restowed, Captain

Grubbe took her on to Germany, but she has not gone to sea again. Except for the two Russians (the former *Padua* and *Kommodore Johnsen*) she was the last of the big cargo-carrying school-ships. To what extent the two Russians continue to make ordinary cargo voyages I do not know, but in 1970 both are still in commission. The *Passat* lies at Travemunde in Western Germany, rigged and well looked after.

Taking a dispassionate look at the record, knowing the ships, one may think that if the *Pamir* had not been badly laden, if she had not a vulnerable engine room for her unnecessary power, if she were officered and manned from that reservoir of the bred and trained Cape Horn men which used to exist in Germany, then she never would have been overwhelmed by a hurricane in the North Atlantic no matter how vicious or oddly behaved. Those ships were built and rigged to *use* storms. Germans, Finns, New Zealanders had all sailed the *Pamir* for years in Cape Horn trades—but without power, without cluttered decks, without eighty people aboard, and with masters, watchkeepers, tradesmen and the essential nucleus of able seamen, dyed-in-the-wool cargo-carrying square-rigger men.

On that last voyage, the *Pamir* had the best officers that could be found for her. There was some reluctance on the part of many experienced, former Cape Horn masters to join the ship. They had their reasons. Poor Captain Diebitsch had been in as much sail as he could find. Beginning in the ship *Riegel* as boy in 1911, he was A.B. in the *Pamir* during the First World War when she was laid up at the Canary Islands, and he was third mate of a four-masted bark during 1920–22. First mate of the school-ship *Deutschland* gave him no cargo experience for she carried none: neither did war service in the aux. cruiser *Kormoran*, a long spell as P.O.W. in Australia from 1941, nor the three-masted auxiliary schooner *Xarifa* on a deep-sea-diving voyage afterward.

Comte de Smet de Naeyer, Admiral Karpfanger, København, Pamir—that is four too many sailing school-ships gone in the sea full of boys. They were all at additional risk because they were cargo-carriers—the Belgian lost because the responsible officer, perhaps, did not understand the ballast-tanks valve drill: the *Karpfanger* cutting the corner round the Horn, perhaps, eager to do well in the so-called "Grain Race": the *København*, heavy aloft, tender perhaps below, overwhelmed somehow in the Roaring Forties hurrying empty to Australia to load grain: the *Pamir* badly loaded. The idea behind all these was splendid and still operates, though no longer with cargo carriers. A fleet of between thirty and forty sailing ships of one sort and another from tops'l schooners to four-masted barks—British, Indonesian, Colombian, Chilean, Japanese, French, German West and East, Scandinavian, Yugoslav, Greek, Portuguese, Canadian—still exists solely for the proper indoctrination of the seafaring young. But they are all strong auxiliaries (except one low-powered Norwegian ship, the *Sörlandet*): they mostly operate with or from training establishments ashore, fitting into planned curricula on carefully worked-out cruises usually by summer: they do a splendid job which costs a lot of money and still is thought worthwhile.

But the cargo carriers? It is odd that they did so splendidly while part of a living sailing world, and there were men like Dai Williams and Maitland of the *Port Jackson* to handle them, and officers and trades men in plenty to back them up—also in unbroken line of true tradition. When these were gone it was too late for cargo-carrying school-ships. No committee no matter how splendidly led or widely based can be substitute for competent professional management. No hopeful but handicapped optimist, no matter how well-meaning, should enter the war with Cape Horn—unless, as a few have, he takes it on alone.

Then they had better go by summer, as indeed they do. Even then, may the Lord be with them.

Index

329